Seventy-First VARIETY Anniversary

Necrology Of 1976

VICTOR ALESSANDRO
ALYCE ALLYN
GEZA ANDA
WARNER ANDERSON
ROBERT HARDY ANDREWS
MICHAEL H. ARENS
RICHARD ARLEN
JAN AUGUST
GINA BACHAUER
ANGELA BADDELEY
ABEL BAER
MARY BAKER
STANLEY BAKER
NED BARRINGER
MERNA BARRY
HARRY BAUM
SIR GERALD C. BEADLE
CYRIL BEAUMONT
HARRY BECKER
WILLIAM BELASCO
JAMES WARNER BELLAH
EARL BENHAM
BUSBY BERKELEY

DAVID FRIEDKIN
EMIL FRIEDLANDER
JEAN GABIN
GUY M. GADBOIS
JAMES M. GAINES
TIM GALE
PAUL GALLICO
WILLIAM GEER SR.
ARNOLD GINGRICH
HARRY GITTLESON
FRANCES HOWARD
PAUL M. GONSKY
LLOYD GRIFFIN
BOBBY HACKETT
HAP HADLEY
BILLY HALOP
JOSEPH HENABERY
E.A.R. (KIP) HERREN
ARTHUR HORNBLOW JR.
JAMES WONG HOWE
HOWARD HUGHES
FRIEDA INESCORT
RICHARD F. IRVINE

Sr. CLAIR BAYFIELD

(Aug. 2, 1875–May 19, 1967)

"His life was gentle and the elements so mixed in him that nature might stand up and say to all the world "this was a man"
"Julius Caesar," Shakespeare

Always in my heart, his wife KAY

JOE BIGELOW
MILTON BIOW
DAVID BLAIR
KERMIT BLOOMGARDEN
CONNEE BOSWELL
WARREN BOWER
ALEXANDER BRAILOWSKY
CHARLES BRAVE
ROMNEY BRENT
BENJAMIN BRITTEN
HARRY R. BURKE
MARION BURR
GODFREY CAMBRIDGE
NELSON CASE
JACK CASSIDY
ROSEMARY CASEY
CARL CARMER
GLORIA CHANDLER
PAULINE CHOTZINOFF
AGATHA CHRISTIE
VERA CLARKE
BETTY CLOONEY
LEE J. COBB
WILLIAM COHAN
SIR WILLIAM COLLINS
RAY CORRIGAN
LOUIS G. COWAN
POLLY COWAN
DOUGLAS L. CRADDOCK
MASSIMO DALLAMANO
OSCAR DANCIGERS
MEYER DAVIS
JOSEPH DE ANGELIS
PAUL DEHN
CHARLES DeMONT
PATRICK DENNIS
LOU DERMAN
DOROTHY DEVORE
ALAN DeWITT
DEAN DIXON

In Memory of
EDWARD D. DOWLING
Dec. 20, 1967
Jadin Wong Dowling

MAX DOLIN
VINCENT DONAHUE
EDDIE DOWLING
MICHAEL DURSO
JIMMY EDMUNDSON, (PROF. BACKWARDS)
DAVID EGGLESTON
LEIF EID
HAROLD ERICHS
MORRIS L. ERNST
DAME EDITH EVANS
PERCY FAITH
ROBERT M. FAY
MAURICE FELDMAN
PAUL FORD
NORMAN FOSTER
WILLIAM RED FOX

SIDNEY JAMES
G.W. (JOHNNY) JOHNSTONE
MERLE S. JONES
BERNARD KANTOR
IRVING KAUFMAN
LEO KERZ
JESS KIRKPATRICK
FUZZY KNIGHT
PAUL KOSSOFF
FRITZ LANG
FRANCES LASTFOGEL
JACK LAVIN
CHARLES LEDERER
LOTTE LEHMANN
RICHARD LEIBERT
MARGARET LEIGHTON
LEO LERNER
EDGAR LESLIE

In Memory
MAL EVANS
Jan. 4, 1976
A friend, a helping hand; while it was all happening, you were there. Two Beatle fans

ROSINA LHEVINNE
IRVING LIEBERMAN
ROBERT L. LIPPERT
PETER LISAGOR
ROGER LIVESEY
TILLY LOSCH
JOHN LOUNSBERY
JUDITH LOWRY
LEONARD LYONS
HERBERT MACHIZ
TED MACK
ANDRE MALRAUX
SENOR MARDO
NINO MARTINI
WALDO MAYO
MARY MARGARET McBRIDE
RUTH McDEVITT
JOSEPH L. McEVEETY
CHARLES R. MEEKER
WILLIAM MELNIKER
JOHNNY MERCER
JO MIELZINER
SAL MINEO
WALTER SCHULZE-MITTENDORF
JOHN L. MURPHY
MARY NASH
CHARLIE NAUGHTON
BARBARA NICHOLS
ALLARDYCE NICOLL
PHIL OCHS
FLOYD B. ODLUM
REX O'MALLEY
HARRY G. OMMERLE
SANTOS ORTEGA
BEN IDEN PAYNE
MARY PETTY
GREGOR PIATIGORSKY
LILY PONS

MARTIN RACKIN
STANISLAS RADZIWILL
GRETA RAUCH
WILLIAM REDFIELD
SIR CAROL REED
LAURENCE M. REID
ELISABETH RETHBERG
HANS RICHTER
PAUL ROBESON
DICK ROMAN
MAXIE ROSENBLOOM
DANNY ROSS
LENNY ROSS
ROUVAUN
MIKE ROY
ROSALIND RUSSELL
ADRIAN SAMISH
MANN L. SCHARF
L.J. SCHLAIFER
TAFT B. SCHREIBER
FRED SEGAL
JEAN SERVAIS
SAM SHAIN
ROBERT SHERMAN
GEOFFREY SHURLOCK
ETHEL SHUTTA
ALASTAIR SIM
H. ALLEN SMITH
ROBERT SOLOMON
HAROLD S. STERN
IRA S. STEVENS
DONALD STRALEM
HUDSON STRODE
FRANK SULLIVAN
MAGGIE TEYTE
SYBIL THORNDIKE
JAMES TIERNEY
DAN TOTHEROH
DALTON TRUMBO
CECIL UNDERWOOD
WILLIAM L. VALLEE
VICTOR VARCONI
BRUNO VESOTA
ETHEL KEITH VIGOROUX
LUCHINO VISCONTI
SLAVKO VORKAPICH
MURVYN VYE
MIRIAM C. WALSH
NED WASHINGTON
LINDA WATKINS
SANFORD W. WEINER
NILES WELCH
LINTON WELLS
ROBERT G. WENZEL
PRINCESS WHITE
JOSEPH G. WICKHAM
MORRIS L. WOLF
ROBERT YEAGER
FELIX YOUNG
BERNARD YOUNGSTEIN
WILLIAM ZECKENDORF
ZORRAN
ADOLPH ZUKOR

supervised trade news publicity ... She is survived by her husband and parents.

ALBERTE TINELLI

Alberte Tinelli, 54, a singer specializing in operettas, died Nov. 30 in Brussels, after a short illness. Her career spanned many years and she performed as well in France as in Belgium, where she belonged to the company of the Royal Theatre in Liege and Verviers. She was often seen at the Brussels Folies Bergere, a theatre destroyed by fire some years ago. Survived by her husband.

CARL HEUMANN

Carl Heumann, 69, former manager of Warner Bros., MGM and Paramount in Bogota, Caracas and Lima died last November of a heart attack in New York.

During the latter years of his life he had operated his own insurance adjuster office in Lima, Peru, but had maintained his contacts with film people around the world.

THOMAS W. TALBOT

Thomas W. Talbot, 57, manager of Niagara Falls, N.Y., radio station WJJL, died Dec. 21, of a heart attack suffered while he was shoveling snow in front of the station.

He had been with WJJL and other Niagara Falls radio stations for 30 years.

Wife, a daughter and son survive.

EDWARD SCHWERIN

Edward Schwerin, 96, father of Ruth Schwerin, administrative aide to Robert L. Riddell, executive director of the New York U.S.O., died recently in Pittsburgh.

He was also the great uncle of orchestra leader Elliot Lawrence and is survived by his wife, a son and a grandson.

CELIA BURSTEIN

Celia Burstein, 77, former musical comedy dancer and mother of agent Iris Burton, died Dec. 20 at Chandler Convalescent Home, ... Angeles.

Other survivors are ... set designer, and ... children, includ... Miller.

In Spare Time

In a recent poll, young ... mans claimed that their ... lar spare time activity ... ing to music, either via radio ... ord or in live concert, follo... viewing tv and going to the ci...

Most of the young people sti... in to West German programs to ... low the hit parade, and know ... latest U.S. click songs which th... ask the local bands to perform.

The Socialistic regime is proud o... its youth programs and its youth culture — even though the accent is on the influences of the West.

More than 1,000,000 young East Germans are participating in mu... groups and choruses, it's cl... with 86 orchestras suppo... government perfor... plus 88 music ...

OBITUARY

JOSEPH G. WICKHAM

Joseph G. Wickham, 54, executive vice president of Century Theatres, was killed Dec. 28 in an auto accident near Commack, L.I., N.Y. For details see Pictures Section of the Dec. issue.

R.B. McALISTER

R.B. McAlister, 65, broadcast executive, died Dec. 10 in the Methodist Hospital, Lubbock, Tex., following a lengthy illness. He was general manager of KMCC-TV. He moved from Brownwood to Lubbock in 1954 and purchased KLLL. He later owned radio outlets in Littlefield, Big Spring and Post.

Fred (Freddie) Myers

Fred (Freddie) Myers, 83, longtime Cleveland operator of restaurants-night clubs, died recently in North Miami Beach, Fla. He has no survivors.

CRAWFORD

...ford, 60, sales manager ... radio station WDRC, Hartford ... station ... years and president ... the Southeastern Conn. Corp., which owns WSUB in Groton, ... He lived in Old ... his wife, a ...

January 5, 1977

That ... Down ... Germany

Aussie Cops On Trail Of Pirated Cassettes

Sydney.

Australian police believe hundreds of thousands of pirate cassettes are hidden in warehouses throughout the country. They are stepping up raids following seizure of more than 7,000 tapes, valued at $20,000, in Queensland.

The seized cassettes are cheap, inferior copies of recordings by such artists as Abba, Suzie Quatro, John Denver, Rod Stewart, Neil Diamond, Diana Ross and the Beatles.

Record companies here claim the pirate cassettes are taking $5,000,000 from the local market each year.

Police fear they are far from breaking up the ring behind the racket, which they believe is operating between Australia and southeast Asia.

Pop Records

To push its own music ... record factory has ... lished in Potsdam ... which brings ... popular d... daily — 53% ...

OBITUARIES

OBITUARIES

William Saroyan

Creative Arts Book Company
Berkeley 1979

Text & Cover Design & Production by George Mattingly
Cover Photography by Richard Blair

LIBRARY OF CONGRESS CATALOGING IN PUBLICATION DATA:
Saroyan, William, 1908—
Obituaries.
1. Saroyan, William, 1908— —Friends and associates.
2. Performing arts—Biography.
3. Death—Meditations.
I. Title.
PS3537.A826Z5316 818'.5'203 [B] 78-27719
ISBN 0-916870-17-0
ISBN 0-912870-16-2 pbk.
2nd Printing

Creative Arts Books are published by Donald S. Ellis.
CREATIVE ARTS BOOK COMPANY
833 Bancroft Way, Berkeley, California 94710

necrology:

(1) A register of deaths; a roll call of the dead.
(2) An obituary notice.

—*Webster's New Collegiate Dictionary*

This book is in homage to the dead. You are so many, so great, so finished, and we are so few, so silly, so unfinished, and so unfinishable except by that which finished you, whatever it may be called, except death, a trite and meaningless word. Finished then, by life? That's the ticket. All aboard, folks.

—WILLIAM SAROYAN
Monday, August 21, 1978, Paris

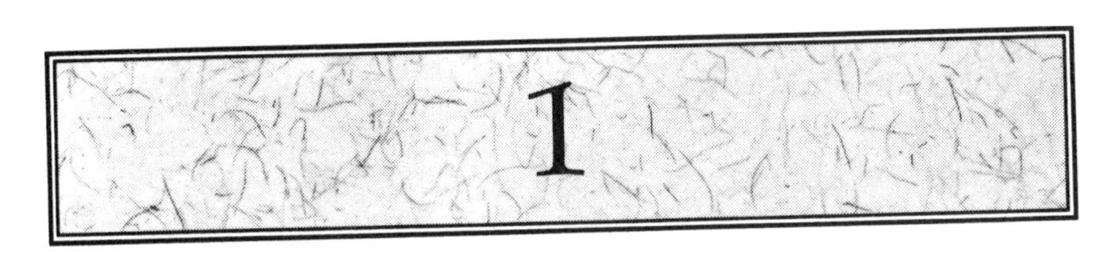

People die. It is a strange event, a strange order of event; it is an order that is not accurately understood. Nobody really knows what death is. Everybody talks about death all their lives. Everybody dies and falls silent. Human life may be said to be obsessed with death. Everybody is said to be afraid of death. All the same sooner or later everybody becomes adjusted to life, fully aware that he is going to die. The anxiety about when it is going to happen gives being alive something extra. A kind of interior companionship, something to talk to which sometimes becomes somebody, a side of himself, a side of everybody else, a side of God, or something altogether unidentified and unidentifiable. Not knowing how much time he has, has quite clearly made every man vital. He has had to stop and think about how to use the time. It is not that he isn't going to be forgotten in any case; it is something else. He goes to work and starts a program of work that he believes is likely to do several things at the same time, the most important of which is to keep himself alive longer than he might otherwise be likely to be alive, and then this program of work seems likely to compel astonishment and admiration among the members of his family, and then it is likely to be spread out into the whole neighborhood itself, which might turn out to be the whole world itself, and the whole human race; whereupon something rather amusing has been achieved: fame. Or notoriety. There's no reason to believe that any of the most notorious of the monsters of the human race ever imagined themselves to be anything less than the child of a mother, and loved not only by her but by possibly even the father as well, and possibly by the brother and the sister as well. There is no need to go back in time any further than a couple of hundred years for an example or two; but for our purposes, all of us being quite alive, a hundred years back is more than enough. Adolf Hitler in all of his photographs seems quite clearly to believe he is the darling of the people of Germany and of quite a number of other peoples. Well, was he? The answer is that he was as much as anybody else probably ever was. It really isn't necessary to be the darling of a great many people in order for any man to imagine that he is the darling of the world, of the human race, of history. Let us get one thing straight—or as straight as possible—at the outset: there is no man alive who is not the darling of himself, and that's enough for all practical purposes. And he will do the necessary, as the saying is, to spread that radiance to the less fortunate. (As I write, on January 17, 1977, a Monday, the noon news in Fresno begins with the information that a murderer named Gilmore has been shot to death by the State of Utah. His execution had been "stayed" several times and after each of these postponements he had attempted suicide by drugs. His execution was witnessed by his two lawyers, his uncle, and his Hollywood agent, unnamed. This man insisted that the State of Utah carry out its own law and execute him. His mother, working with the American Civil Liberties Union, and many others who are opposed to Capital Punishment, were successful in postponing the event several times, but his mother very sensibly declined to witness her son's execution, or murder, as you wish. So did his bride or fiancee—Or did she die in their attempted suicide pact? —No, she didn't die, and it is not inconceivable that Gilmore's

Hollywood agent will be interested in putting forward the prospect of fame and fortune for her. Who is the agent? Well, he might be the man who is the agent for Mr. Richard Nixon, who stands to earn two or three million dollars for telling his side of his story; and let the smart-aleck press tell any side they like. Is America supposed to hang its head in shame about the execution ten minutes after sunrise this morning of the murderer? How about the man who survived everything, including something with the official name of phlebitis? And finally how about the unnamed agent: should he be the man for the nation to hang its head in shame about? Let that sit there, please.) I am a subscriber to a weekly paper called *Variety*. The 71st Anniversary Edition, dated January 5, 1977, arrived a few days ago, and I examined with fascination—on the last page, 164—the names in alphabetical order in the annual feature entitled 'Necrology.' I had predicted that among those listed would be 34 men or women that I had met. I was not far off the mark: there were 28. But many of the 200 or more others listed were of course people I knew *about*, for *Variety* is the paper, the Bible, as they say, of show business, celebrated in song by Irving Berlin. Well, I thought, I'm very well along into my 68th year, hadn't I better write about the people I know in *Variety*'s Necrology of 1976? So that is what I am doing. And about Dr. Leo Eloesser, who is not on that list, who died at the age of 95 on Monday October 4th. We met in San Francisco in 1938, and he was another of that city's amazing sons. I was just 30 at the time, and he was about 58. Now I'm 68 and Dr. Eloesser is dead, cremated, and his ashes scattered at his 40-acre ranch near the small village of Tacambaro, in the state of Michoacan. He died in bed, asleep, apparently of cardiac arrest, the *San Francisco Chronicle* says. He was a great man, very small, rather eccentric, he certainly never married, and I was astonished to notice the item in the old issue of the paper on the floor of the bathroom. I thought he had died long years ago, and there he was, alive all the time.

Is there a way to live that will change death in any of its varieties? In any of its meanings, that is to say? In any of its realities? In any of its imponderables? (if that's anything at all like the idea we're trying to suggest). Isn't death death, period, as the saying is? Isn't it the same every time for every man, including Kings and Billionaires and Rich Writers with Women and Big Cars? Well, of course it is in no sense, ever, sir, ever, madam, the same, not even for the same, or so-called same, customer. We die a little, somebody nice said to himself, when anybody else dies. We live a little, too, and that's the reason the obituary page of the paper is so popular. But there is truth to the bright sayings of children, always. We do die a little when anybody else dies. He prepares the way, for us. Didn't the young fellow say something along the lines of going ahead to prepare the way, and now here we are all old and leaky and unprepared, or at any rate no more prepared than we ever were. There is a way to live, and there is a way to die, and there is a way to fuck, to put no bones upon it, and there is a way to make money, to spend money, to be cheated out of money, and all this money monkey business is for the simple reason that life, death, and making sense are connected from before the beginning to after the end, with money. Think of it: money has that kind of unnatural but very ferocious connection with each of us. If your father was rich when he got your mother with child, and you turned out to be the child, you have got that fact to live with. If he was poor, as the father of Charles Dickens was, then of course you have *that* fact to live with—and what it did to Charles Dickens it has not done again, although there were many by the millions whose fathers were much poorer, much more in debt, than Charles Dickens's father. So how do we put that fact to work in a useful way? We don't, do we? We only ponder longer about the amazing truth of Charles Dickens and the reality of his literary art. I like especially the flare-up of fancy orgasm-seeking that sent him self-deceiving into the arms and scent and warmth of the delicious little actress who didn't mind having the physical fool in bed, not especially, at any rate, since she had been to bed with others, perhaps a good variety of others, and probably not excluding members of the profession (that is actors, acting lovers in bed, or acting dandies out of bed), and in addition to actors surely or at any rate probably also producers, backers, directors, and whoever else was immediately or potentially useful in the business of putting forward the career. The mother of the many children of Charles Dickens was as he felt thick-skulled and really nothing much in bed, but she had got pregnant a good dozen or more times, and presumably by him, so she must have served the purpose, or the several purposes, since when he was getting his faithful wife pregnant he was also writing *Oliver Twist* and *Great Expectations* and the better part of all the rest of his books. After taking up with the actress he was indeed pretty much done (he had done his writing), and something more was in order, he felt; he had also done the better part of his lecturing or acting, and yet something more was wanted, and he had every reason to believe that she might very well supply precisely what was wanted. Perhaps she was, but one suspects that she wasn't, not by a million miles or fathers or characters in sad and hilarious works of writing. What she was was pussy, pure and simple, and the British have traditionally put forward some of the best pussy in the human family. And only pimps, it seems, are above getting basic matters confused by the proximity of pussy. An acquaintance forty years ago stood in the back room at Gelber-Lilienthal, a bookstore on Sutter Street, in San Francisco, and said, "I want to write a novel about pimps. They are not like other men, it is a very complicated situation." But of course he said a thousand times as much as I have put down, summing up what he said: he hated pimps, he was afraid of pimps. They seemed to treat women wickedly, and what's worse, women seemed to love them for their rotten characters and their dirty behavior. They were not made helpless by their pricks, and this young writer wanted to try to understand that. He was in trouble all the time from the demands of his prick, and from the impossibility of not adoring women, and consequently being deceived by them, being hurt by them, being almost driven mad by them, and almost being driven to the murder of them, one by one. Yes, of course there is a way to live that makes a difference in every aspect of both putting up with time, and being put out of any connection with it: passing, passing, and you're not there going with it, which is of course what death is, or at any rate what else it is, for it is many, many things, and no obituary notice, whether in *The New York Times*, or in *Variety*, even begins to try to tell anybody what it is, not even in the instance of the person whose death is the hero of that particular obituary notice. The poor son of a bitch up and died, but we can tell you that he was born in China, the son of a Seventh Day Adventist Medical Missionary, and went to school there, and in Boston, and worked hard and married three times, and a child by each marriage, and died. And he died. And died. And died. And finally was taken to the mortician's, and that motherfucker fell on him with needles and thread and syringes and cosmetics and wax and spit and polish and had him in his casket looking like a million. I hate morticians, they belittle life, and I have never heard of one of them ever saying anything worth anything. Not one word.

My purpose is to run down the alphabetical list in *Variety* of the dead of 1976, but it is in order first to think about the earliest experience of death—which of course would have to be the death of others. I have no intention of over-doing this, but it is desirable to get our bearings, so to put it, about this enormous part of life. Death is the last thing that happens to a person, but it is not his last experience—that has to be something he remembers, of course. An experience happening is one thing, and it is not complete until it is remembered as having happened. Memory—remembering an event

—is artful. There is no way to get away from that, it would seem. The one who remembers makes more of that which happened, or less, as he decides he should. And of course there is the puzzlement of not remembering anything—all of a sudden: whereas ordinarily one remembered everything. This troubles people, as it should. You don't remember what you did last night? somebody asks somebody, and then is told what he did: generally something slightly offside, unworthy, embarrassing, stupid, out-of-character. Nobody remembers dying. It can't be remembered, for the reason that death is an event that includes the total effacement of memory, of the vast stored "life" experienced, dreamed, imagined, wished, witnessed in reality, or the world, and in fancy, or art, and death takes on that instant totality which nothing else ever takes on. O'Neill's father of Anna Christie learns (or witnesses) the truth that his beautiful daughter (Anna performed by Greta Garbo in a production at the Geary Theatre in San Francisco about 40 years ago or in 1937 or so), the truth that Anna is a streetwalker, and it seems to drive him mad; but while his upbringing was responsible for that deep shock and pain, it also kept him from dropping dead. So Anna was a whore, so let her be, she was still Anna, and she could stop being a whore, most likely, and she could be all the things fathers imagine they want their daughters to be—but of course the real story here is Anna, not her father, and of course she felt terrible about being a waterfront whore; but that was far from final; she hadn't fallen dead in any bed anywhere; she had only accepted money for sexual congress, as the saying is, with vagrant and hungry men. Or a great man is exposed as a fraud, and his greatness is seen to be instantly either far greater than anybody ever suspected, or a total sham, a false thing—and the man himself picks and chooses what he wants to remember about the experience of exposure: yes, he is not actually a member of the Russian nobility, he is a poor boy from a desperate background in Lower Manhattan, or in Brooklyn, or somewhere, and his elegant manners, with apparently natural and profound courtesy, are acquired; he did not inherit them. He owns and operates the famous restaurant bearing his name: Mike Romanoff. His exposure does not belittle but enlarges him. Of course I speak from memory: I knew Mike, I knew Gergerson-Romanoff, but

I'm not sure Gergerson is or was his family name, either, and it doesn't matter. He was a decent fellow and his English accent was considered excellent. Among his friends were many writers, especially Robert Benchley. All of the successful Hollywood writers enjoyed eating at Mike's, and in being able to chat with him casually. The food was expensive for those days: a lunch might cost as much as $5 with a cocktail and wine, but it was good food, served at a fine table, in a very pleasant atmosphere. He was Mike Romanoff, and not Harry Gergerson, as he had been born. He was alive, in his own elegant restaurant, not dead, in Forest Lawn. All right. Or okay, question mark—as the strange nervous swift-talking young people, generally young women, say, and go on quickly to another phase of the dissertation on the real meaning of love, and how it differs from hate. Hate: he don't let you know he likes you, okay? No, not at all okay, but on she goes with a grand philosophy of something very like total absence of information or meaning. Has she been reading Sartre perhaps? In any case, the idea if not the reality of death starts as a mystery with great force and power to affect others—everybody is all hot and bothered because somebody has done something that is called "died." And there's the hearse (I used to marvel at the name of Hearst, how right it was for his reputation—he was a kind of jitneybus for the dead, or the murdered), there's the black wagon out front, and on the porch there's the small boy in Oakland in 1911 or 1912 crying in a way that just won't do at all, and there I am across the street, alone, on my way back to Fred Finch Orphanage, fallen back from Blanche Fulton's group, to be alone, on my own a moment, and nobody to tell me why the small boy, my own age in fact, is crying that way. Then, how do I know instantly that it is because somebody has died: his mother? or his father? How can you know who is in a casket brought out from the parlor of the house? I decided for some reason that it was his mother, and then decide no, it was his father. A woman certainly tried to comfort him, to stop his crying, but he would have none of it. He wanted—I wanted—his father back. Indeed I called out to everything: If you're that smart, give that boy back his father. Anybody can do what's easy, do something that's hard, something that's impossible, get that man out of that stupid box, start him up again, he's stopped, give him back his memory, he doesn't know what happened to him. That was my first awareness of death—and of course I am remembering it, again, with art.

Will do, will do, will get along to the list of the dead, but hell-fire, man, shucks, friend, shoot, brother, good Lord, enemy, gosh, reader, there is such a thing, is there not, as preface and preparation? You can't bite off the universe and expect to be able to chew and swallow it, can you? Death is everything, man; death is not just a little part of everything, it is the whole thing, but of course what we mean is that life and death are together, one thing, or as the pitchmen used to say, one and the same thing, you have one and you also have the other; you can't have one without the other, so what's all the crying about? What's the boy on the porch carrying on about? What's *Finnegan's Wake* laughing and crying about? What's all art talking and talking and talking about? Why does religion, as the shortcut and meaningless word puts it, start with a repudiation of death, as if in doing that life also is not repudiated? It is not necessary to live forever; it is not desirable, it is not even a small softening of the shock of stopping cold: think of the thousands of —bang—heart-attacks in America alone every year. Walter Huston was at lunch with three or four pals, when suddenly he said, "This is it," and fell forward onto the table and died. Jed Harris said he was at the table, and so I must suspect that he was and that his telling of Walter Huston's last event, his non-experience, is not totally false: and of course there are many similar last events among friends and members of the family. I like best those who cry bitterly as they seem to know the damned thing is going to happen soon . . . but how do they know? Well, it seems to be from having had a survival from a heart attack, a kind of teasing reprieve, and they know they aren't going to last very much longer—a week, a day, a month, but never again are they going to carry on as if there is no such thing as death. It is right for lovers of life to cry about the unstoppable arrival of effacement. It is no fun to be that stupid about anything. Why? Why me? Why now? What's the hurry? What did I do? Jesus, Joe, do you remember those days in San Francisco forty years ago when we were young punks full of piss and vinegar—sudden failure to speak, sudden necessity for the fact to twist and the lungs to exercise with terrible sobs. Christ, do I remember, man? I sure do, I sure do, old friend. All we did was chase tail, didn't we? And money, didn't we? Of course those who have felt the end fully, but for some reason been granted a short reprieve, of course they cry like babies, and of course they should, for they don't know how to use the reprieve; they don't know what they are supposed to do in order to make the inevitable both acceptable and welcome. What they want is to be who they had been before the damned shock, or better than that, who they had been forty years ago, if only in memory, if only in the art of remembering dismal days of hustling a living as if they had been luminous days and nights of beautiful women giving themselves joyously to the piss and vinegar boy in the shower after the first bang. The first of four, at least. Those were the days, weren't they, Joe?—so now what am I doing in this stupid bed in this stupid intensive care ward at this stupid hospital. You're right, aren't you, Joe; I'm over the crisis, I'm going to walk out of here in a couple of days, I'm not going to die, am I, Joe; you were always the smartest bastard in our group, this is nothing, is it, Joe; I'm too big a bull to be brought down at only 64 years of age, Joe, and don't think I don't appreciate it; everything you ever said came true, Joe, so why shouldn't I believe I am not going to die: you said it, I didn't, and you were always right, Joe, about everything, and then suddenly the poor big lunk chokes on sobs and says, Ah, Christ, Christ, Joe, this is it: I am going to die, and I don't want to, I just don't want to, that's all; I had an idea in my head that I would take a drive all the way south, south, south, straight to Tierra del Fuego, so now what, I'm not ever going to see Tierra del Fuego, that's what, and it hurts, old friend, it murders me, Joe. Do me a favor, will you, just get the hell out of here, you healthy son of a bitch; you were always my enemy, you always hated my guts: I had so much luck in everything, while all you ever did was hang around the edges, so now you are glad, you are getting even, you're enjoying this, you think it's funny a great big man like me brought low this way, so get out of here, I don't need your phony sympathy and friendship: you're my enemy, not my friend. Ah, Christ, man, don't go; I take it all back, but do you know what I'd like more than anything in the world, for the first time in my life—I'd like to trade places with you; I wish to God you were dying, and I had come to visit you. Do you know that would make me happy, Joe, it would make me even happier than you are right now coming here to visit me, when you and I both know that in less than another six days you will be a pallbearer at my stupid funeral, Joe you son of a bitch. I wish to Christ you were dying and I were visiting you and being just as polite as you are, taking all of my abuse as if it were the ravings of a dying man, not the hatred of a living big bull of a son of a bitch on Market Street in San Francisco forty years ago, Joe: what happened? Why me? Why now? What did I do wrong? I always believed I was never going to die; I enjoyed life more than anybody else, you said so yourself, so what's this, why is somebody giving me this rotten time? I am going to be all right again, am I not, Joe? And he breaks into big sobs all over again. It couldn't happen but it did.

Reader, my friend, permit me to be smarmy as the Irish intelligent, in the Dublin saloons like to put it, meaning somebody too bloody eager to be liked to be tolerable even—somebody who kisses ass as the Americans put it, perhaps even more succinctly, somebody who is really not to be trusted at all, somebody who is a liar, a cheat, a crook, and an all-around annoyance in a saloon—permit me just the same, reader, my enemy if you prefer, permit me please to say to all who are in the saloon, in celebration of something or other, or for no reason, although nobody goes to a saloon for no reason—all drinkers drink because something is going on that they need to put a little drink into or upon—reader, permit me once again to notice what a thing it is to be alive, and how much more intense and right this thing becomes when death draws near; when somebody is sick, has survived sickness, is on his way back to the forgetting of death, of error, of sin, of pain and all the rest of the partners of death—what a thing it is to be alive, what a thing it is to remember death, to know it is there, man, and how it is there. Dead center of life it is, and the salt of the plainness of life, the pepper of the tastelessness of life either way, in the sense that it has no real flavor, and in the sense that it is altogether without courtesy or elegance or manners, reader, that is not too much to ask, although it is quite a lot at that, especially considering the competition, all of the other things you might right this minute be reading instead of this, all of the other writers, all of the other thinkers, all of the other experts in all of the different fields—so who am I? so what do I know? so what right have I got to take up your time at all? Well, reader, permit me to stop being smarmy, permit me no longer to give a shit if you read this, or indeed if you breathe at all, and permit me furthermore to suggest that if it is your intention to remind me of all of the incredible writers in America alone, all of them well under forty years of age, and this old slob of a young writer already nearly come to four-score-and-ten—is that the slogan I want?—hell no, but forget it: who's got time for the Gettysburg Address at a time like this?—here I am a year and a half from being seventy, and just as stupid and cocky as ever. Reader if you've got some writing of your own to do, for money, for fame, for friends, for children, for God—drop this idle reading and go to that writing, and good luck to you, but I have got to pass along this dull message of fucking joy: you never know how unspeakably right being alive is until you have gone through a good piece of unspeakably wrong time hanging onto it, and fending off the opposite of it, or death: let's get out of this chanting if possible; let's just settle down to common folk English: let's just write and read very simple and steady stuff: reader, until the human race not only understands death, but lives and loves it fully, nothing any member of the human race writes can possibly be more than some kind of dancing, some kind of marching, some kind of activity altogether different from what it seems to be: some kind of song, some kind of oratory, some kind of legerdemain, some kind of card trick, illusion, exercise of mystic power, as when a fraud of a loudmouth man seems to guess the truth about a total stranger's vital facts, some kind of con game. Until the whole human race, in all of its geographical and other divisions, knows death intimately and loves it and cherishes it and keeps it where it is in any case, dead center of everything, everything, reader—every other thing there is, known and unknown—then nothing any member of the human race writes has any real meaning, any real use, beyond a new step or two of dancing or a new line or two of the human song or wail, or whatever you want to call it. All of the philosophies are not just tentative, they are false and they obstruct even the expectation of anybody for a little something or other (instead of such words as Truth, Grace, Love, and so on) that both permits and compels a modest gladness about being connected to the Vast Ignorance, the Immeasurable Nonsense, the Everlasting Absurdity, and yet somehow the Overall Rightness of being an occupant of living matter—a living thing, a man, a woman, out of men and women, moving to the continuation of them, in blind light-loving stupidity. Reader try to distinguish what I am saying from what I am not saying, because it may be of use to you: until the human race has had a billion years of proud and proper understanding of the role of death in life—had it in a flash, the billion years are already there to be flashed, to be had—until then nothing any human being writes is worth anything beyond the worth that is in song and dance, parable, story, joke, pretending, play—including, reader old pal, crime, robbery, murder, falsehood, deception, and all of the other things that have made the world, and made kings and rich men and bejeweled women, but let's not knock it—even all that is fun, is great in a dismal delightful way, as it has been all the years of human time. You just don't get to know the difference between your ass and a hole in the ground until you see the splendiferous connection, the joyous sameness of death and life—and like it, don't fight it, rejoice in it—and are at the same time just as bored with it as you are with all of the other astonishments of whatever it may be said has been going on these billion and another billion billion gone years, gone but right here in the little brother and sister thinking and thinking about the treachery ahead most likely beginning with school.

We seem to know a little something or other of an inaccurate nature about the probable meaning of being alive, which means being in possession of a body loaded with millions of years of change inherited from millions of men and women who were the parents and grandparents and ancestors. We seem to know something or other about something or other, and we seem to be able to accept what we know without feeling that it is altogether inadequate, and we seem to believe that it is on the contrary quite a lot. That is one of the things we inherited from the millions of years and people in billions and experiences of many kinds when we inherited the body. Now the body is the thing, there is no way anybody can possibly get away from the reality of that. There is a lot more to being alive than being physical, but you can't be any of the other things without also being physical—the owner and occupant of the body. Every person gets one, and only one, but that's not the end of the matter, because everybody is permitted to understand the body and to protect it and even to improve it. Most human beings don't bother about that aspect of the experience of living too strenuously, for if they did they would become something like freaks, as the muscle-building men become something so peculiar as to seem grotesque—from overdeveloped muscles, for one thing, and from underdeveloped non-physical possessions. Most people take it easy about the body, and they allow it to decline fairly gracefully, as the body specialists are also obliged to do, but without the gentility experienced by the more casual body-owners. When Mr. Universe loses the best years of the body, he is pretty nearly bankrupt, whereas some skinny little man who is almost nowhere in the body department, the occupant of a very mediocre example of the body, a very poor specimen—when his body has had its full time and ought now to decline, it has already declined (it has declined from the beginning), and so the man has put to use the other things that come pretty much with all bodies, in one degree or another. He's all mind, as the saying is, all spirit, all intelligence, all invention, all creativity, all art, and so on—and that doesn't mean that he is not also a participant in the supreme function and usage of the body as body, as the maker of new specimens, or at any rate the participant, the partner, the half-maker: if a man, he does his part; if a woman, she does her part, and out of their doing come new bodies and the human line continues. We seem to know a little about the action of the body, but we don't seem to know anything at all really about a whole assortment of things that cannot exist apart from the body but at the same time are very clearly not substantially the body. The Armenians have an expression that describes one of these non-body things: Line Seert, Wide Heart—and what this means is not what the literal words mean. Somebody who is Line Seert, who has a Wide Heart, may indeed actually have a small physical heart in his body, but probably not, for the wisdom of sayings is sometimes literal. In any case, a Wide Heart person is not a bore, not a bother, not a lot of trouble, and not a pain in the ass. He is smiling, literally and figuratively both, and he does not rejoice in the misfortunes of others, does not wish disaster to overtake anybody, not even enemies, if in fact he has any. The specialists in the non-body realities of human life are in general religious, scientific, philosophic, or socialistic, and each category has put forward a great bulk of useful or mischevious theory, but only the religious expert of Christianity puts a great deal of importance upon the theory that after the body dies something really attractive happens to the person who occupied the body (provided of course he was a good Christian, which means that he was mainly decent, or tried with all his might to be decent). The theory is that he lives forever, and there are many who either believe the theory or hope it is going to turn out to be true.

Otherwise the preoccupation of the specialists is that one part of human reality starts and stops in the body—especially the socialist expert or theorist—like Karl Marx for instance. It may turn out to have been the flaw of Karl's theorizing that it did not eschew hate and seizure or the use of force upon people not precisely like the majority, especially in the possession of things other than the body. Karl Marx was not interested in Heaven, in any form of immortality for any part of anybody: he wanted to get the goods to the majority, taking it by force from the minority. He died. His theory, however, is still going on, is still alive, among an enormous part of the human race, and the theory has failed to do what he had believed it would do. Human life is still not really measurable in any useful way. The only real ownership is of the body, apparently, and the only real loss of anything is the loss of the body, invariably by the one event which is loosely called death. Going to the actual funeral of Karl Marx, for instance, does nothing for his theory, for his body, for himself. It is a continuation of the human confusion about what to do with the remains, as they are called: in honoring them by ritual disposition of them, the survivors are honored, and everybody is reminded that there is no way to avoid death—it has got to happen, but anybody who goes to a funeral knows that it hasn't yet happened to him. That may be the reason for the popularity of going to funerals, or of reading obituaries. Good God, did my old pal Karl Marx Bijbijian die?—his father was a devout Socialist, and therefore put that name upon his first born, poor dead fellow.

Last night on the Johnny Carson Show, as I believe it is called whether officially or by natural selection or by popular choice of words, a man who had written a book about Howard Hughes, who finally died a year or two ago (what a fool a writer is not to get his figures straight), his name is right there among the aitches in *Variety*—Hornblow, Howe, Hughes—a man who had lived and died eccentric—and out walked a man who had written a book about Howard Hughes, and with this man were two men who had given him information about the last days (and years) of the billionaire. One of the men long ago gave him a haircut for which Howard Hughes paid him $1,000, and after that he was brought into the group that stayed close to Howard Hughes and over whom he had absolute authority, or whatever the term is for a situation in which men become willing slaves because the money is good. The other man seemed to be a limey, he spoke with the limey's special accent, and he was the man who brought food to Howard Hughes, first from the Sands Hotel in Las Vegas, which Howard Hughes had bought, and in which he lived in a penthouse for a number of years. Well, the thing is that this genius of a man, who took an inherited fortune of around $10,000,000, built it into a misfortune of 1,000 million dollars—something like that. And misfortune is the only word to put upon what the man did. He got rich, he made himself over-rich, he became an Emperor, and not an Emperor of Ice Cream, as Wallace Stevens put it in one of his poems, but an Emperor of Money, and of course that just won't do. It will kill you, and it killed Howard Hughes, to be an Emperor of Money. But everybody wants to make money, wants to earn money, wants to have money, wants to spend money, wants to have enough money to give away, wants to be known as a man who has money. For more than the last ten years of his less than 70 years, Howard Hughes was steadily the victim of a program of suicide which all the same could easily be thought of as a program of survival. For instance, he insisted on keeping everything around him sanitary, as the saying might be, but he himself had long fingernails and long hair and didn't exercise or even walk. What he did about his toenails was not mentioned last night on the last 25 minutes of the 90 minute show. The limey waiter said that when it was decided that Howard Hughes was very sick and had gone into a coma and had better be taken to a big Hospital in Houston, where something might still be done for him—freely because at last without his authorization—the limey cut his long fingernails, and cut his hair, but didn't mention the billionaire's toenails, which of course also grow. (And there are men, there is a kind of man who doesn't cut his toenails—this comes as an astonishment to any man who does, for the little chore is in order only about once a month and requires no more than three minutes, if that.) But what am I talking about? This is supposed to be a book about a few of the people, mainly Americans, who died in 1976 and were listed alphabetically in *Variety*, the Bible of Showbiz. This is supposed to be literature, and right now it is not even journalism, a craft or trade or calling which becomes increasingly useful and desirable and even urgently necessary in our day. He died. He died, alas I am obliged to say, like a dog, a worm, a sick insect, an insanity located in a skinny body surely not out of range of remembrances of many things, connections with dozens of pretty young women, possibly even remembrances of love and simple health and innocence. But of course he died innocent. If nothing else, drawing into the edge of full death every person is restored to innocence—to have lived was not his fault. At the Stands of Chance at the Fresno County Fair 60 years ago I used to put down a dime and try to cover a large red circle painted on oilcloth by dropping three smaller black metal discs, for if I was able to efface the red with the black I would win a revolver, for instance, and I wanted to win—but after the third disc had been carefully dropped, there was still red showing from the large circle painted upon the oilcloth, and I had not won, I had lost. The man himself could do the trick, and did it quite casually and swiftly and completely, again and again, but neither I nor anybody else in Fresno was ever able to go away with a revolver. We all went away as if we had died standing there with desperate longing for a revolver for a mere dime, and we went away innocent, if also a little more deeply instructed in the way of the world and the way of ourselves—by that time a reality worthy of annoyance and scorn: well, you did it again, you damned fool, you thought you could win, and you lost. Howard Hughes died on the Johnny Carson Show last night, or more accurately early this morning, and it was a very sad and sick death. You should have enjoyed the money, man. You didn't enjoy it. And you forgot to leave a will, you damned fool, the whole thing will go to the government, and you know what they do with money. And in Washington there were eight People's

Parties, not Balls, in celebration of the Inauguration of James Earl (he insists on being called Jimmy, though, and that makes him just a little fishy right there) Carter, Jr.: is it because James Earl seems to have the sound of the assassin of Martin Luther King, Jr., or what? The new President said in his Georgia accent: "Are you all having a good time?" Five or six thousand people called back yes. Do you like Rosalynn's dress? Yes. Is this the greatest country on earth? (Not in the world but on earth: more Biblical, I suppose). Yes. Something's going on. Is it necessary, is it even desirable to know what? Life's going on, isn't it? Yes, and with it death. And that's the part that makes a star of every man for a flashing moment, at any rate.

8

The first name on the list is Victor Alessandro, but I never had the honor. I never met him, never saw him, and therefore cannot say anything about him that might be possible had I met him. What might that have been? Well, the fact of him, the reality of him, the reality of the substance of him, or if you choose the myth, his appearance, his face, his voice, his eyes, and anything else that was there. The trouble is that in remembering the dead, or for that matter the living who are not where I am, I don't especially think of the various parts of them, I think of entireties, of mysteries, of something total that instantly came to me as being that person. I have never been anything like a clever judge of people, but I do seem to get first impressions that are sound. Not long ago (in the early summer of 1972 as a matter of fact) I met an Armenian I instantly considered a crook, but little by little I changed that hunch to something I believed was much more sensible and worthy of acceptance, and I began to consider him a very good man. Well, my first impression was correct. He was a crook. I found out slowly but very clearly. He isn't dead, but whenever I remember him I know he is a crook, and I wonder why. Why is anybody not the best possible person he might be? Well of course we are obliged to conclude that everybody is indeed that best possible person he might be, no matter what he is, and then he dies and it doesn't really change anything, although it is traditional to believe that's it, he was, he is no longer, he has died, he is remembered but only by a few others, and then by nobody at all, because those who remembered him have also died. But what does this mean? It doesn't have to mean anything. Not instantly, at any rate. But it does bring into the arena of thought or speculation the significance of action and the recollection of action—not of the one who recollects but of somebody else, starting at home with father, mother, brother, sister, and other members of the large family. Everybody also remembers as he goes along his own actions and recollections of the actions. And of course he remembers the inaccuracies of his earlier recollections and keeps moving nearer to what probably happened and what it probably meant. But when somebody he is remembering dies, that does it, that locks it up, as the saying is: he can only work with the reality or unreality up to the death. And this work is so deeply difficult that he abandons it almost instantly upon the death or upon hearing of it, which is how it is with most of the deaths which have any meaning for him: the big people, the famous people, the legendary people, the public people, the stars, the celebrities, the monsters—all of a sudden but one by one, the bigshots of their day are dead, and their day is done: Hitler, Mussolini, Stalin, Roosevelt, Churchill, and so on. Very nearly everybody in the world upon learning of the death of each of these paused an instant in his own fight to acknowledge that fact—the man's death—and at the same time to connect himself somewhat to the man's life: when Stalin met Roosevelt and Churchill at Yalta, ah yes, I was in the Army and the world was in a shambles of self-destruction. Or something else. And all that sort of remembering is light and swift, and the dropping off of the great is taken with the same sort of acceptance of the inability in anybody to make anything useful of it. When Lincoln died he was instantly remembered in a rather special way, for he had been shot while he sat in a box at a theatre watching a play that was meant to be funny, to be amusing, and for all we know had been amusing to Lincoln himself up to that point. And there have been other world-famous men who have been shot, or have shot themselves, as Hitler is said to have done. What does it mean? Very few of the rememberers of any of the world-famous men knew them, and yet everybody feels connected to each of them, so what does the connection mean? Does it mean perhaps that everybody is everybody, no matter who? Anybody dies, everybody dies. Well, the matter of birth is comparatively simple in its unimportant details, but again nobody knows who the man or woman just born really is, or is going to turn out to be, but it is agreed among us that if he lives he is going to turn out to be somebody, and this somebody is going to be fairly explainable by some knowledge of his genetic line, his father and his mother and their fathers and mothers—otherwise it is possible to consider the event of birth to be as useless to the dead as the event of death is useless to the living, although there is altogether clear evidence that a vast usefulness attends both birth and death, however difficult to identify at the time: somebody has been born but who he is is not known; somebody has died, and while it is known who he was, or was supposed to have been, the fact that he is no longer alive doesn't really do anything for anything. Hitler's death does something for people who hated him and had every reason to hate him, but Hitler's death doesn't do anything for intelligent usage of such a piece of final information. He is dead. He is said to have shot himself. He didn't win. He lost. What does it mean? The second name is Alyce Allyn, and I don't know her, either. I am instantly intrigued by the spelling of each of her names, however. There must have been something in her reality that was connected in a very important way with the spelling. She may very well have meant to encourage not being instantly forgotten both during life, and after giving it up. The third name is Geza Anda, a fine name for a fine variety of reasons, but I have no idea who Geza Anda was, male or female, actor, clown, or what.

The last name on the list is Adolph Zukor, but it does not really seem to me that he did indeed die, perhaps because it was established in the press for the past two decades that this old man was still active at Paramount Pictures. He was one of several pioneers, as they are called, in the moving picture business, and he may have been one of the founders of Paramount Pictures, on Melrose Avenue. After he had reached his 100th year he was still active enough for all practical purposes, and he continued to look at the pictures made by Paramount Pictures, and to talk with various people who were active there. When Jack Benny noticed that Adolph Zukor did not seem to recognize or remember him, the comedian is said to have said, "Mr. Zukor, I'm Jack Benny." And the old man had said, "Jack Benny? Are you still alive?" And of course the point of the story which surely does not need this elucidation is that Adolph Zukor was 20 or more years older than Jack Benny. It's a cute story, as the saying is. And of course if there is any word appropriate as a description of all "big" Americans it is cute. This is not really puzzling, but it is slightly boring. When they become nationally significant, or important, Americans of all kinds carry on in a way that can only be described as cute, beginning with Franklin Delano Roosevelt, who apparently considered himself an amazing card. Almost all of his friends encouraged him, as if he might very well be the village fool, and they themselves engaged in cute talk and behavior. Except apparently Gen. George C. Marshall. The wartime President was especially hilarious when he said, of opponents of his methods, "Well, let's just see that he's drafted into the Army and shipped to the Pacific—let him show us how to win the war, har har har." Adolph Zukor was a small man, very neatly clothed and shoed in very narrow pointed models, for I was on the Paramount lot in October of 1936, having gone there from the old Pathé Studio, across the street, where I had just gone to work at $300 a week for a former President of Paramount Pictures, Mr. B.P. Schulberg, and it was George Auerbach who paused in our walk to the set of a picture being directed by Ernst Lubitsch and quite reverently said "See that man there, walking alone, that's Adolph Zukor." I noticed that the man was small, slight, light, neat, and had narrow pointy shoes on his dainty feet. And of course I knew that the name Adolph Zukor had a large meaning not only on the Paramount lot but in the movie business. He was a great man in one way or another—to me anybody who reaches the age of 100 is a great man, but especially if he has had unlimited money to spend for at least half those years. But Adolph Zukor, who died sometime during 1976, the year just gone, didn't stop living right away. He went on to 101 years, and then another year, and another, and that is when I began to feel he might not ever die, for all practical purposes. But now that he has died it is not uncharitable to speak the truth, or something like the truth, about him, his name, his life, and his death: now that he has died, he is dead, and forever. For as much of forever as may be apportioned to any man. He did nothing not to die instantly, once he had died. During all of his long years he did nothing, really, at all. He was just there and had a large connection with one of the first of the moving picture manufacturing companies. Of America. And therefore of the world. He was a millionaire and a multimillionaire. B. P. Schulberg faded away from that scene, and died, not very old, in Florida (or somewhere), long, long before 1976. George Auerbach, born in New York, went back and died there, also long before 1976, also not very old. Schulberg reached sixty, I suppose, while Auerbach didn't get far beyond fifty, most likely, and there was old Adolph Zukor still walking sedately in his narrow pointy shoes in the cute world of all-around profitable ineffectuality. Auerbach was Schulberg's story editor. That's how he and I went across Melrose from the old Pathé to the parent company, Paramount, to look in on something or other in action. I remember Lubitsch enjoying his reputation for cinematic wit, for one of the earliest achievements of individual style, waiting for the boys to light the next scene which involved Marlene Dietrich, who was also on the set in full luminosity, even without the lights. Auerbach had sold himself to Schulberg on the basis of being a writer, but he had never published anything if indeed he had ever written anything. That sort of thing was commonplace in Hollywood. Anybody who said he was a writer and could talk big, he was a writer. In those days, in the middle 1930s, college football was pretty much the only football, and Auerbach tended to depression and hysteria in alternating units, and every Monday would be charged with excitement about the football game he had witnessed Saturday afternoon. Consequently, I wrote a story about a football star who graduates and becomes the nobody he always was, but B.P. Schulberg never filmed it, with a consequent profit to both the writer, myself, and his collaborator, George Auerbach, who talked and talked. Had the film been shot, had it been manufactured, the consequence would have been precisely the same in any case, except of course the extra money. Well, does any movie make a difference? Yes, and I would be willing to say that a great movie comedy makes the greatest difference, after which would come a great poetic movie. *Modern Times,* for instance, and *All Quiet on the Western Front.* He sat in a wheelchair much of the time during his last couple of years, but Adolph Zukor went right on being his honest self day after day for more than a hundred years. Bravo old boy.

A few more names from the alphabetical list in *Variety* of the dead of 1976: Warner Anderson. Don't know him. Robert Hardy Andrews, ditto. (But at the nightclub owned by the father of Barbara Walters sometime in the very late 1930s or the very early 1940s George Jessel, composer and singer of a beautiful Yiddish-American song entitled "My Mother's Eyes," introduced his bride-to-be, named Lois Andrews, her age 12, her female attributes greater than her mother's, who sat not beside her daughter but beside the vaudeville actor. "This child," he said in his special order of speech, imitated by every mimic in the country, a singing kind of lisp rising and falling, with a note being held at the end of certain words and phrases, "this child is a woman and I'm madly in love with her," a long musical hold on the word love, and of course on the word her. I was almost astonished when they actually became man and wife, as the male chauvinist pig phrase has it, and the buxom child-bride gave birth to a daughter, beloved of the comedian-singer, who indeed dedicated one of his books of memoirs and philosophy to her. By which is meant perhaps (more than anything else, really) that names evoke people bearing them: Anderson, Anders, and Andrews bring to mind quite a variety of people, beginning of course with Sherwood, who was perhaps the most significant literary influence on the first half of this century. Glenn Anders, the excellent actor: I saw him in 1928 in October in *Strange Interlude*, and knew him for his work in my play *Get Away Old Man*, directed by George Abbett (?) Abbot (?)—what happens to names, so that a very simple one can't be spelled, even?—while I did time in the American Army but found time to visit the rehearsing company a couple of times: Eddie Andrews who played Tom in *The Time of Your Life*, and went on to a very full and successful career in both movies and television. Michael H. Arens, don't know him. Richard Arlen: met him at a Chinese restaurant apparently owned but probably not managed by James Wong Howe, the famous cameraman, born in Seattle, and husband to the writer Sanora Babb, from somewhere in the wind-swept lonely Middle West. I saw Richard Arlen—I didn't know him—and exchanged greetings with him, in passing. I hadn't the time to enquire about his name, which might very well have been Arlen but more probably was selected, either by himself, his agent, or the moving picture studio for which he appeared in a big variety of films, pretty much as a kind of character in whom both heroism and villainy were real. Jan August: don't know him. Gina Bachauer: don't know her, but I believe I have some longplay discs of her piano-playing, but I could be mistaken—perhaps she is not a performing musician, or perhaps she plays the violin, although I seem to feel she played the piano, and was quite good at it. Angela Baddeley: met her in London in 1944 while I was in the Army, and saw her perform on the stage as a very talented comedienne. Her sister Hermione is famous in American television, but I don't seem to hear anything about her daughter whom I met with her in London: a great beauty, at that time surely not twenty. And now, as long as I am in London, in 1944, I want to remember Noel Coward. Although he did not die last year, he did die, and also, recently, his man-servant of the last four decades of his life, but not one of his five great male sweethearts, so to put it deliberately, seems to have written and published both in London and in New York a book about the charming fellow. A genius as a matter of fact, and unmatched in his many skills, which I perhaps had better mention one by one: actor, playwright, song-writer, singer, stage director, movie director, short-story writer, novelist, memoirist, and all-around witty character, so to put it. For myself, the wit is really unacceptable and indeed boring. He once defended homosexuality with the explanation (as Ring Lardner might put it), "Well, at least we don't go around dropping nasty babies everywhere." The recipient of that witticism was the famous columnist Leonard Lyons. In those days male homosexuals had not come out of the closet, and while I have met a number of heterosexual boys (over the age of forty) who have publicly wished they would go back to the closet, it is really pretty much the same either way: boys under fourteen who have been seduced by fairies, as they used to be called, are seldom heard from, and in any case are frequently found in North Africa and rather like their elegant patrons and the better food. At the opening night of *Peer Gynt* in London during the War, I sat in an aisle seat and saw Noel Coward in the first box. When the lights went on during the first intermission he studied the audience and waved rather exuberantly. "Who's he waving to?" I asked the newspaperman who sat beside me. Noel Monks said, "To you, I believe. I don't know him." All the same I didn't wave back. Such a thing is embarrassing even if there is no doubt about who has been waved at: I was positive it wasn't me. If it was, however, I couldn't imagine why. I believe I mentioned in *The Twin Adventures* this waving and non-waving, and a few years later somebody said, "Noel Coward was very entertaining at a Mayfair party a few weeks ago, putting down your writing." This impelled me to think back and to wonder if I shouldn't have risked a wave back, even if he hadn't been waving at me. I never met him. I saw a play entitled something like *Nude with Violin,* which was at the Belasco Theatre after my own Saroyan Theatre. Plays like *The Beautiful People* and *Across the Board on Tomorrow Morning* had failed there, and both the play and the star were terribly, terribly boring, alas.

I find being alive a mystery, the more so that death is even beyond being a mystery, beyond any participation of any kind other than perhaps the intimations of something strange that attend pain, dream (pleasant or not makes no real difference: it is the fact of any order of dream at all that suggests a small part of the enormity of ignorance about the entirety of things and actions, but especially the relationship of death to it all, of dying, of stopping), and so of course I have always been a singer, inventing my own songs and words and rhythms, and I have always had my own concertos for piano and orchestra, and my own quartets and sonatas and rhapsodies and studies and waltzes and whatever other little names are attached to various sizes and textures of exulting, even when the exulting seems to be nothing beyond abject despair. I also growl a lot, perhaps in the same manner as the growling animals, tigers, panthers, lions, leopards, foxes, wolves, and dogs, and with much the same sort of meaning as the meaning in the undeciphered growling of the animals. Protest, participation, pride, or pity, self-pity or society-pity, but one is not possible without the other—what is this, for the love of God, of heaven, of nature, of the sun, what is this? And I talk to myself, which is the poorest possible way of saying that I talk to my father, my mother, and their fathers and mothers, all unknown to me, as indeed both the father dead before I was three is unknown to me, and the mother I knew for quite a long time, until she died at sixty-six and I was forty-two: ah there is no knowing anyone at all: no wonder I am forever chatting with all of them, as well as with strangers revealing themselves in their books, in the books they found the time to write and the skill to have published, like *Oliver Twist*, for instance, who is of course himself, so named, Oliver Twist, but to me is actually Charles Dickens at work, meandering through the past that he thought was unbreakably hard and tough and muscular but somehow hadn't been able to break him, and toss him aside, for there he was almost from the beginning a successful writer, the darling of the London intelligentsia of the time, but even more importantly the very favorite of the people, the readers who paid a penny for the weekly in which a new chapter of the fantastic story of Oliver Twist appeared every week. I talk to Dickens, to Thackeray, to anybody else I happen to read who writes straight stuff. I don't talk to Byron, Keats, or Shelley, because if the truth is told, I really don't know what they are talking about when I try to read them: it doesn't seem to be about people, it seems to be about something else, and so I don't talk to them at all, I don't meet them, I haven't any idea who they are—but Robert Burns, I talk to him. I make a lot of noise as I move along. I always have, but then when I am silent I am very silent, and that is part of the thing about the connection of the ignorance and mystery of any man alive and death—his own straight ahead—and the death of the great multitude which becomes greater every year, no, every minute, while the number of living at any given moment is always a millionth of the number of dead always and always. But there is no morbidity in this at all, or if there is a little, it is a very little, and at a time when the shades have had a fall, and the sun is out, and my own interior galaxy of light-making has trailed off into a new dimension of the cosmos of my people and past, and I turn cold and believe there is nothing else but this cold shade far from my truth and right. And who can escape it, who can avoid death, who can guard himself from error, from sickness, from pain, from doubt, from anger, and all the rest of it? Everybody I ever saw or spoke to said in word of language known by him how he had gone about the business of accepting himself and the reality he found all around ready-made and in many cases entirely unappealing, if not indeed monstrous, and every speaker kept to himself a hundred times more than he found words for, since the best of everything felt or suspected is not in words, not in writing language. But I am always saying to myself, thank God for writing, for writers, for presses, for publishers, for papers, for magazines, for books, for labels on bottles and cans and little boxes like those in which are packed *Lipton's Tea,* for instance. Thank God for all that use of language—at the first opportunity pick up a package of some kind and read what the money-hustler tells you about what is in the package. Heed the message on television continuously night after night: Read the label. I make a noise as I go, so why is everybody else silent? Why is everyone speechless whose very work is not speech-making? Why do the makers of the world, the miners down in the deepest bowels of the earth, and the steel mill workers beside the molten stuff, and the farmers in their great fields, and the workers in offices, at millions of desks, and the factory workers: why do they all go about their work in that terrible silence? It isn't what they want to do—we might imagine, but surely each of them actually not only doesn't mind what he does but loves it, certainly the farmer, so what's the silence all about? And then why do they go pay good money to hear somebody talk at them, or sing at them, as if they themselves were nothing, unworthy of talking and listening to one another, and singing to one another—ah well, more important than any answer to that question is my own asking myself, "Why do you fly off the handle and ask a useless question?" If you're going to sing, sing. Don't find fault with the garbage man's unawareness of grandeur: just notice how easily he empties a big can.

12

As I meander along the path to the cemetery, or to Nirvana (a word I have always both enjoyed seeing in print and hearing and at the same time found altogether meaningless and unacceptable), as I loiter along the way to the end, or *finis*, another word from another language that I enjoy and yet almost never accept, for it is *finish* in an earlier or more authentic form both as to letters employed and sound made, and of course there is also the even shorter *fin*, which one notices sometimes at the end of books and movies—as I concern my head about the dead of last year there is the daily news of the dead of this year, of yesterday, of the day before, of last week, and some of these new dead, these infants of babes of eternity, out of the flashtime of mortality, into the immeasurable time of immortality, the non-time of non-matter—some of these men and women I know, I knew, and so I think about them and am about to say something about them when I remember that they are not among the names on the *Variety* list, so I turn to that list again, and I find that I had come to the names beginning with the letter B, and had remembered having met in London in 1944 Angela Baddeley and her daughter whose name I forget. This summoned up other people I met in London and I remembered them, too, but one of the most interesting I neglected to mention, so I will now, before I meander some more along the path to Paradise, so to put it: I paid good money to go into a very large moving picture theatre because the picture was by all standards the talk of the town, as I have heard it put: by accident a little old lady sat in the seat to my left, the accident being that it was the only seat not occupied in that row, which was about mid-theatre. As the famous brand-new picture moved along she spoke sweetly to the star of it, and chuckled and laughed, and then fell silent for a bit, and then very suddenly burst into joyous response, with glances at me as she went along. Now of course we know that in movie theatres there are pickups, there are flirtations, there are hand-holdings by total strangers, and there is probably no movie theatre in the world which has not had a fornication, and the author of *The Informer*, Liam O'Flaherty, did the sensible thing fifty or more years ago and wrote a whole novel entitled *Mr. Gilhooly*, in which such a meeting in a movie theatre is the most vital part of the plot, which is another word I have always enjoyed and refused to accept, for I am a writer who will not write to a plot, although I have a short-story, or sketch, not much more than an anecdote, which is mockingly entitled "The Plot."

The word itself in spelling and in sound is amusing, and like its half-brother *plop,* suggests a human dropping into an advanced and sophisticated place for that basic and daily ritualistic action. And at the Cypress Lawn Cemetery Company offices in San Francisco, on Market Street, when I was 20 there was a lively old gent who, as Vice President, took it upon himself to invent slogans to advertise the cemetery, and one of them was, "We give you a lot for your money." I began to tell this thing because I imagined that the word was plot, not lot, but it was lot, and so I have left it lot. He did invent a slogan involving the word plot, but I have forgotten it. Well, the little old lady in the London movie theatre in the seat just beside me to my left, which is the side I prefer, since the hearing of the right ear is so poor—since my eighth year—that I am never sure of anything anybody says who is on that side—the little old lady was flirting, pure and simple, and while the better part of her flirting was with the hero on the screen, to whom she addressed endearing words, she was also flirting with me—that is with the American soldier, whoever he might or might not be. Well, there are little old ladies who as time goes by become very much like the little girls they may or may not have been long ago, and this little old lady was not at all unacceptable: she was indeed delightful: she was clean, fresh, and very nice-smelling. She wore nice clothes and had a nice handbag, and she was glad to have the American soldier beside her, to hear or half-hear her delight in the hero of the movie, and also to edge toward. And I certainly had no reason not to be amused and entertained by her charm—in the comparative dark, during a rather clever, and definitely patriotic movie, designed to deepen the already high morale of all of the British people at a bad time in their history. And then the film ended, and the lights went up so that people could get up and leave the theatre or go to the lobby for something to eat or drink, a kind of intermission of four or five minutes, and so I saw the little old lady plainly. She was just as pretty as she sounded, and she smiled at me sweetly, and then said, "He's my son, you know." And she told me some more about him and about herself, and jotted down her name and address so that I might go there for tea some afternoon. I thanked her and went out to the lobby, thinking about having read sometime in 1923 or 1924

The Vortex, which involved somebody somewhat based upon herself, and her son, the star of the movie we had just seen, entitled (I believe) *In Which We Serve*. Michael Arlen had loaned her son the money he needed to produce *The Vortex*, and that was the start of her son's enormous success and fame. It turned out to be perhaps his very best play, although it was sick and involved something very like incipient or actual mother and son incest, addiction to drugs, bathos, and hysteria. It both puzzled and pleased me that the little old lady who sat beside me in the movie theatre was Noel Coward's mother.

It is so easy to make money, to make enormous sums of money, and to die, and to leave the money somewhere in arithmetic, in real estate, in diamonds, I suppose, in furs, in big automobiles like the Rolls Royce, and lately in private airplanes, some of them costing more than a million dollars, which in the days of my boyhood was the supreme numerical goal for any honest American boy: work hard, save money, give to the poor, and become a millionaire. Billy Rose did it and was a millionaire ten times over. His rival and enemy Mike Todd also did it but not once and not twice—he did it three or four times, and married Elizabeth Taylor too. They are not in *Variety*'s Necrology of 1976, but they have come to mind unavoidably because they overdid the millionaire thing, as they say, and died, and left all the money in things and complications and legalities and astonishments of many kinds. Billy wasted away with a mysterious disease which sent him to Houston for special consultation and he returned to New York asking himself, as he told so many of the people who accepted his desperate invitations to visit him in his private mansion which had been the Romanian Embassy or something of that sort: "I ask myself, Billy, is it a leg, or is it a million dollars?" Well, it turned out that it wasn't a leg, but I don't think it was because he put down a million dollars for the specialists of Houston: it was because it was himself whole, and so he, a very short man, came up the aisle at the Bijou Theatre on Broadway during the first intermission of *The Cave Dwellers*, and I had to ask somebody, was that Billy Rose? For he had become wizened: there is no other word for it, his skin had gone berserk and was dry and wrinkled and sick, that's all. The man had to be dying, and about five or six years later all of his carefully accumulated and increased wealth failed to prevent his death. When it began to come home to him that he might very well be losing the contest with death, he very sensibly began to look into legal ways of depriving the government of inheriting his wealth, and his charities were of an excellent order: a museum full of fantastic paintings and sculptures in Israel, for one, and a good number of other good things, but he must have neglected something, because his body was kept in some kind of cold storage for a very long time while lawyers and relatives fought out the disposition of his leftover money. "Billy, I told myself," he reported to various people, "how much do I want to pay for the leg? Ten thousand dollars? A hundred thousand dollars? Five hundred thousand dollars? A million dollars?" Well, a leg is quite a lot but so is a million dollars. How about a toe? Or a finger? In the end Billy was buried somewhere, and there was no more squabbling about his money. But he was big, he was very big in the American story of his lifetime. He was a very small man physically, about five feet tall, I suppose: he was one of the smallest of the famous Broadway showbiz characters of his day, but he did big things: elephantine, even: Jumbo at the old Hippodrome Theatre at the corner of 44th and 6th Avenue, the Aquacade, with his new wife starring in the water, and along the way, much earlier, he had married Fanny Brice, again at a good profit. So an upstart from out of town, somebody from somewhere around Detroit, came to town and began to give Billy a good run for his money, in the same kind of business, and he also was a showman, a showoff, a clever fellow, and not small of body: on the contrary big and heavy but no less swift on that account: Mike Todd. Bad luck did it to Mike, and his private airplane shooting out of Los Angeles and bound for New York crashed in a storm on a mountaintop just when Mike was on top of the world—everything he did brought him fame and wealth: his *Around the World in Eighty Days* had more stars in its ramblings than any other movie, and the premiere exhibitions of the movie in the capitals of the world, including Moscow, brought him more and more fame and money—and he was a living legend of big deals, swift decisions, comical replies to questions, and death to his rival Billy Rose. Billy gave a New Year's Eve party at one of his several Manhattan mansions, on the East River off Sutton Place, and about 100 people showed up, including Jack Benny with his wife Mary Livingstone. There was a nicely iced glass bowl set in a pure silver tub and in the glass bowl there was a neatly heaped mound of pure beluga caviar, about a full pound, at a time when the stuff cost perhaps as much as $18 a pound. I heaped some on the provided wafers and chomped it down, Billy half watching. I did it again, and this time Billy watched with a powerful meaning to his watching, as if he were saying, Eat all you like, Bill. Or: That stuff costs $18 a pound, you know. I never had any more, and when the bowl was empty, it stayed empty. A new bowl with a new mound of caviar never showed up. So am I gloating about these Broadway bigshots being for many years dead and as good as forgotten? I enjoy gloating about them, for each was a ruthless and mean hustler who would not hesitate to cheat anybody—and really never needed to cheat anybody at all, not even one another, not even an enemy, for there was more than enough for each of them, and they must have known that once they were dead the bitterly gathered money would also die in arithmetic and dire poverty and the mansions and cars and airplanes would be instant garbage. But the fact is that with all of their fraudulence, I miss them both, for they used up some of my time, and that time is gone forever. Poor little old, and poor large young clever millionaires: the mothers of thousands of sad souls didn't know enough about them to hate them.

14

Gloat? Really? Gloat over somebody's demise, if I may use that word for kicking the bucket? Gloat over somebody's laying aside of the mortal flesh and moving on to a higher level of life, or reality? Gloat at somebody's passing away, passing on, passing through, or whatever else the euphemism is for rotting on the vine, dropping dead, falling like a leaf? Gloat because another miserable human being has given up the ghost? Good God, man, how could you be so insensitive, so inhuman, so dirty? Gloat? You ought to be ashamed of yourself, and the dead man believed you were his friend, or at the very least one of his many acquaintances, perhaps not necessarily one of his admirers, but also not one of his enemies. How can you gloat about the death of anybody at all? Human beings just don't gloat over the deaths of other human beings. They become sad, or they pretend to become sad, for there is a polite procedure about such a thing as death. Impoliteness is always a potentiality in human relations when the parties are both alive, or not yet dead, but once one of them has died, the other is always polite, and now and then he says "God rest his soul," or something else like that. Who are you to gloat about the death of Krakauer, even, the crackerjack lawyer who under the given name of Arnold was such a whizbang champion of the rights of your vicious little, lying little, dirty little, crooked little, monstrous little bride, who hired him to take you to court and to carry on like *Mr. Chips Goes to the Himalayas,* a real clever showbiz lawyer, brisk, clear of speech, emphatic, a former Captain of Marines, the fourth husband of a woman who wrote sex novels, a lawyer who was more than a lawyer—he was a friend if you were his client, and a real enemy if you weren't—and he died, he just up and died, and who are you to gloat about a thing like that: it could happen to anybody, couldn't it? And who are you to gloat about Jerry Giesler who is also Jerry Geisler and so listed in the Beverly Hills phone book, when Jerry

Giesler / Jerry Geisler also up and died, the most famous movieland lawyer of them all: the defender of Alexander Pantages, Charlie Chaplin, Busby Berkeley, Walter Wagner, and anybody else big and famous and rich in serious trouble, along the lines of spending the rest of his life in jail, and didn't the busy little bride call him in to attend to the funeral of the damned fool at the time of the second divorce, the damned fool having failed to break his leg and having married her a second time, knowing she was a liar and a crook and a fraud and an all-around weird but clever money-hustler and having given her diamonds and dentistry and house and money, and the famous lawyer joined his client in making the world as nearly impossible as it could possibly be for an idiot father of a young and stupid son and a younger and more stupid daughter, and then, the lawyer richer than almost any other lawyer in movieland, up and kicked the bucket. Who are you to gloat about the death of that fine famous man? Well, whoever the hell I am, by God, I do gloat about the way death sooner or later wipes out the mothers who take to the law and make stupid fools of the fathers, especially me. I rejoice when such mothers are unable to fish out a phoney law and keep death over in the slums among only the inferior and poor. I hear the news and the sun lights up in my soul. Why should I pretend anything else when I know the truth. The sons of bitches very nearly murdered me: why shouldn't I rejoice that death murdered them? And if the truth is told, why should I not rejoice that even while they were alive, busy in their offices, with their full staffs of bright young people doing their bidding, the silly little mothers were dead, and even worse than dead, they were miscarried spirits, like the stuff thrown out by abortionists. The bastards that do me, that seek to do me in, that plague my soul, that rob my purse as they say, that belittle my name, that very nearly drive me mad, I am proud to say I loathe, despise, hate, and patiently dismiss from my mind forever and ever, and am only reminded for a flash of profound gloating when I hear that death has done them in, the dirty little mothers. I hate the breed, and yet it is the one breed that, as Mahatma Gandhi informed all his young fellows, is the one profession that if righteously exercised can bring to pass all of those desirable changes in the imbalance created by wealth, which the human race so desperately longs for and indeed needs, and further indeed, must have or perish. But lawyers soon enough get in where the flow of money is abundant, and they arrange for rivulets to come flowing into their treasure chests. All right, all right, a writer flips his wig remembering perfidy in his bed, toying with his genitals and polluting his soul, and he carries on like an uncivilized animal about the weasel-eyed bride, and gloats over the deaths of her supporters and conspirators, but what about death itself, real death, actual death: not of lawyers, but of members of the human race—of anybody at all—does he gloat over death like that? Well, the answer is that he does, and his doing so has nothing to do with anything so sophisticated as a human being, a man, a writer, a father: it has only to do with nature, with the reality of nature. And let nobody pretend that in man nature is discarded—it is put to one side until death when it comes right back in loud and full. Any man who doesn't rejoice in the death of anybody else, as well as stand hushed and overwhelmed by sorrow and ignorance, any such man is very uncomplicated, very undeveloped, and need not really be considered a man at all: he is a unit of one in relation to a billion never to be understood.

15

Abel Baer died in 1976 and is eleventh on the *Variety* list of perhaps as many as 120, which is a very small portion of the number who died during the year not just in the world, or in the United States, or in New York, or in Show Business. It is a short list pure and simple, and the dead who achieved the eminence of being on the list are permitted to be pleased about that—if they have anything like a sense of humor, or if they like, or if they dare, or if they remember (with a groan of some kind, most likely) how pleased they had always been to be among the chosen, the special, the few. Even so, I said to myself when I saw the list, Well, I believe I will have met about 32 of these dead, and so I went down the three long columns and placed a blue line beside the name of anybody I had met, and at the end counted them, and it came to almost precisely what I had guessed, but a little while ago I noticed that I had not marked the name William Zeckendorf and I had indeed met him, so now I shall make that correction, and count the marks again, and the number of names in the whole list, which is—221, wow, was I off? And having guessed 32, how many of these 221 did I actually meet and know, or somewhat know? I'll count these, too, and get everything straight on that statistical or arithmetical order: well it seems as if I have only 27 marks beside names that had been attached to people I had met—that's maybe one in eight, and I've done better in an index of a book about contemporary history, or some such. And Abel Baer is not among my group, although I knew Abel Green quite well. But he died in 1975 or possibly even in 1974, after a good 25 years as editor of *Variety*. And of course I had been a reader of the short column of humor for William Randolph Hearst by Arthur Baer, popularly known as "Bugs." One suspects that his pals at schools in San Francisco almost a century ago began to call him Bugs when he surprised them every day with new funny sayings. His batting average was very nearly believable, but not quite. He was an amazing writer, that's all. The batting average of a comic and even bright columnist like Art Buchwald is also surprising, but all of a sudden the trick is so neatly done every time that one refuses to study the execution of it by reading the column. The surprises are no surprise at all any more, and on the contrary an absence of surprise would come as a really refreshing surprise. And it may very well be that Abel Baer is the brother of Arthur Baer, or possibly the son, or the nephew, but whatever he is, I never met him, and he is dead, along with Arthur, who stayed aloft well into his eighties and pretty much continued to produce his jokes right up to the end. And so we know that out of 221 people in the list, 27 are known to me, and it is the procedure in this work to recall those people. It isn't art, of course. It isn't literature, it isn't writing, it isn't journalism—and it very definitely isn't a living, either: all of which is none of my business, and never has been. If I had to write for a living, I would have died of hunger long ago. I can't write for a living, I can't do a job for a magazine or a publisher, and while I have taken on a few assignments, they have been uncomplicated and impossible almost not to do—I write a review of a book, for instance, for a very small sum of money. *Life* magazine, on learning that I was spending six weeks in Las Vegas to divorce the bride the first time, gave me an advance of $1,000 against a full payment of twice as much or three times as much, plus expenses, to write a piece about Life in Las Vegas, with photographs by Peter Stackpole, the son of my friend Ralph Stackpole the sculptor. Well, I wrote the silly piece and *Life* never ran it, that's all. It just wasn't journalism, and probably not poetry, either, although some day it is not unlikely that a Saroyan specialist is going to find the manuscript and study it and talk about it (in depth, as the saying is). If this is not literature and not a living, what is it? Well, after I remark that I really don't know and that anything I say has got to be no better than a guess, I am willing to say that this is another establishment of a procedure that is likely to both encourage and permit me to write something later on, but how much later on I don't know. Before I wrote the short story called "The Daring Young Man on the Flying Trapeze" in November of 1933, in San Francisco, at 348 Carl Street, aged 25, which is not all that young, as we all know, I had written a whole 30-day work of prose entitled "Trapeze Over the Universe." That wild work made the writing of the very short short story almost inevitable, and this work could turn out to be the thing that is going to make another work inevitable. Writing is really a matter of getting ready, as I am quite sure most writers know. But then why didn't any earlier writing get me ready for this writing? Well, of course something did, and so that's how it goes on and on as long as it does indeed go on and on, but it can suddenly stop, and when it does it is a sign of boredom and death: it's as simple as that. I think of dozens of writers who got star treatment in *Time* magazine, and Cover Features, and big important reviews by the most famous critics, and then suddenly it turns out that they haven't published anything in twenty years, and they aren't dead, at all, they are walking around somewhere in Florida, or in Massachusetts, or more probably in California. Why haven't they written anything in twenty years? Well, it has got to be because they became bored—with what, life? No, friend, not with life: it is impossible to get bored with life. They became bored with themselves, with a failure of life in themselves, a failure of the imagination, in short. That's all.

After Abel Baer comes Mary Baker, also unknown to me, but when we say we don't know somebody, haven't met somebody, this could very well not be the truth, as we imagine that it is: we might very well have met somebody and forgotten it, or not even known it, as on a train, chatting anonymously, or on board ship, or at a theatre during the intermission, or on a bus, or at a public place like a museum or a library, chatting about the exhibition or about books, or about the weather. All the same I am quite sure I have never met Mary Baker, for if I had I am sure I would have instantly thought of Eddy, and I don't mean Edmund Wilson who as a young writer wrote and published a book entitled *I Thought of Daisy*, I mean *Mary Baker Eddy*, who was the subject of quite a lot of jeering from none other than the one American one might have imagined would not belittle a lady, a woman, or an old maid, if she happened to be one, especially on her religious faith, or to put it more accurately perhaps on her discovery or invention of a new sect of the Christian religion, the Science one, which among other things repudiates the reality of matter, which is a poor way of putting what is meant by that sect. What is at fault here most likely is the difficulty of using language accurately. You don't mean that matter doesn't exist, most likely: you mean that it exists side by side with an opposite, a large reality that is not made of matter, which contains the truest and most desirable meaning of the reality of life of all kinds but especially of human beings, and especially of those humans which (or who) believe in the gospel as set forth by the Boston lady. Mark

Twain jeered the lady. He was not a gentleman when he did that, and while it was his lifelong boast that he was not a gentleman, he was really not himself, either, when he did his jeering. If she was mistaken, so was he: but far more unfortunately than she. He also discovered and proselytized a sect of the Christian religion, which although less formal than that of Mary Baker Eddy (surely she married, and Eddy was his name, but I wish the desperate longing to be well-liked didn't push so many people into dropping their proper names in favor of nicknames: the man was Edward, so named after his father, and might have been Edwardson, and even after he had moved himself and all his interior baggage to Eddy he might very well have been slightly more traditional as Eddyson, or Edison, who took as his bride the bright-minded and bright-spirited Mary, the daughter of Baker. But did they have children, and if so is that line continuing somewhere in Boston, in Massachusetts, in the United States or even in the world?) . . . . Mark Twain was also the enemy of pretense, sham, pomposity, deception, dishonesty, dissembling, conspiracy and fraud, but there is no reason to believe Mary was involved in any of those inferior if altogether human attributes. Repudiates: is that the verb I grossly misspelled a moment ago? Well, if it is, and I did misspell the word, I want it to stand, as further evidence of the difficulty of written language. Had I ever met the Mary Baker who died sometime in 1976 and made the *Variety* list, I am sure I would have remembered it, and might also have remembered with terrible embarrassment that I said politely, "Not *the*?" And she replied, "Yes, I am *the* Mary Baker, but of course not *the* Mary Baker Eddy, for in that case I would be 124 years old, wouldn't I?" And I would perhaps have mumbled, "Well, it was just a thought." To which she would have replied, "Not an attempt at a little religious humor?" I think it is in order for anybody at all to be both respectful of Mary Baker Eddy and grateful, if for no more than her teachings about disease. These teachings kept a great number of people away from medical doctors who in all truth tend to always have been not really suitable for the business of restoring souls in minor troubles with their bodies: and indeed for long years tended not even to suspect that what was wrong was not really with the body but with the soul, the character, the spirit, the mind, the central nervous system, and any of the other parts of the human being in the human world not quite pleased about himself, the whole race, or the world. That sect of the Christian religion instructed its people at least to look into why they seemed to feel they were sick, and to seek healing in ways that have for almost a full century become more or less accepted by one and all—not in medicine and surgery, but in deeper understanding of the illness. The alarm in people whenever they or somebody dear to them seems ill is in itself an illness, and Mary Baker taught her people to thrust aside that alarm. Easy does it. She preached happiness, and of course that is something that is almost in itself laughable, and can be very easily ridiculed, as Mark Twain did indeed ridicule it. But the fact remains that it is intelligent to be happy—it is not stupid at all. And I am glad that Mrs. Eddy, if indeed it was she, as I believe, was inspired to discover and spread her sect of the Christian religion to the rest of the nation, and indeed to the whole world.

17

A digression within a digression will bring me for a flash of a moment away from the naming of the dead of last year to the naming of a few of the living of yesterday, when I went 22 miles north to the Madera High School and spoke about an hour each to four different groups of students of about nearly one hundred, so that altogether I made contact of some sort with about four hundred young people. This is something I turn down for good, big money, as the saying is: colleges, universities, writers' conferences, because I can't be bothered, it's too much trouble, and just a little silly, too, There are always a dozen or more writers who are the pets of college kids and they go from school to school being the heroes of the kids, and every two or three years a new group of writing heroes comes into being. I started looking into college kids about thirty years ago, and all told accepted half a dozen invitations, for various reasons, over the years. It's not for me: I am wary of becoming the hero of kids whom I find essentially unidentifiable and consequently unreal or fraudulent. All of a suden they are said to have discovered somebody like Tolkien, for instance—if I have the right name, for I know nothing about the man—and he becomes a national hero to college kids. Was it also the Lebanese who made out like saintly, so to put it, and was the comfort of so many? I forget his name, and it deserves forgetting, but I will remember it. Little Jesuses you might call these lads, and there just don't seem to be any lasses at all: they don't go for the goody stuff at all, when they are ready to whoop it is for their delayed emanic emani emancipation (and printer don't fool with the false starts on that word, they may mean something). India produces their boys of grace, and some of our poets fall in with their ideas, but the Indians do nothing at all for India's millions of perfectly fine people who are homeless and without food or clothing or a reasonably predictable future. And Korea puts out wise guys with voices even louder than our own Billy Sunday and Billy-after-Bully-Billy-Sunday, and these boys become multimillionaires from the money of fools: young fools, either recently in college or of the same order in age and mental disability. And there are orange-robed bald-headed shaven boys begging in the streets for another corporation of deception, and these boys are a sore trial to their parents, demanding money to give to the new mother of mothers. What do the Little Jesuses really want with imbecile youth and enormous sums of money? What do the writers who roam the college circuit being the heroes of retarded children really want? Well, whatever it is, it isn't anything I want. Consequently I don't cultivate the muddle-headed young, or indeed the muddle-headed middle-aged or old. I don't really want any part of anything that I know quite clearly is cheap—very cheap, and belittling to everything and everybody. And so why did I get up at half past five yesterday morning in order to go to a high school and talk four times instead of only once at a college, for which I might have been paid anywhere from $1,000 to $3,000—instead talking for free, as the saying is? What's the sense of that, at all? Well, it's quite simple. I was asked if I might pay such a visit to that school by a girl who teaches English and Drama there, and during the past three or four years this Armenian girl has been a good kid at filling me in about life in a high school in a small town, and has also fetched me lemons, oranges and grapefruit from the trees in the garden of the house of her parents, and has taken me in her Toyota to the laundromat and around and about, and so whenever she brought up making a visit to meet her students, I have instantly and gladly said yes, I will do that, and so yesterday was the day, and I did: and these are some of the names of some of her students: Mary Elisalde, Donna Beckwith, Robin Dollar, Marie Catanezesi, Diana Seagraves, Debbie Fimbrez, Reida Irby (who is writing a novel entitled *Sharing Borrowed Treasure*), Lori Kay Brady, Eleanor Hernandez, Shari Girardeau, Lisa Peterson—but these are all girls: were there no boys in the classes? There were, but not as many: Darrell McCallen, Adolph Vizcarra, Gilbert Trujillo, Steve Funderburg, Tony Martin, Roger Accornero, Richard Flores, Rickie Elias, Jim Jenkins, but now again some more of the girls who spoke and wrote their names down so I would remember (at my request): Denise Hayes, Lesli Niino, Mary Ann Brown, Sherry Martinez, Julie Foresi, Kay Keating, McAllister Donnell, Toni Reno, Nancy Barton, Shari Mongaral, Debbie Ellington, Susan Munoz, Charlene Poore, Lee-Ann Rutherford, and I guess that's about it. All are alive and going to high school. They are good kids, I liked meeting them. I don't mind at all that very little of what I said connected very significantly with what they knew or had experienced. They all had good faces and bodies. They were black, brown, yellow, white—as the language puts it: nobody was better than anybody else on any account of that order, at all. Each was each. I thought I ought to digress this much to say so, and to move along with the work in progress—if it is a work, and if it is in progress. Khalil Gibran, that's his name. Sun Park Moon or something like that is the name of somebody else hot just now. Khalil Gibran is dead and has been for many years. The Korean is alive and very rich and very vocal—he has got to believe something, but in a television review of his big business operation it was not possible to really decide what it was that he believed in. It couldn't have been only money. But what do we know? I hope you like names, both of the dead and of the living.

They are a magic if mysterious symbol one at a time of something for which there is really no adequate word: a life going on, a life ceased.

The next name is Stanley Baker, and I knew him in London in 1966, and had seen him in a movie about the Zulus at war with the whites of South Africa. He was a rather tall husky man who did not appear to be intensely concerned about culture, or for that matter about the problems of the people of the world, and this is said solely because he was obliged in his profession to be among such people and to hear them and sense their indignation about various aspects of the state of the world and the human race. He seemed to be rather honestly interested in the state of himself. We were in a small group at a fashionable gambling house and he suddenly suggested that we go somewhere else, and nobody resisted the idea, but somebody, perhaps myself, wanted to know where the new casino or club was, and he said what I took to be Water Street, but turned out to be Wardour Street, which is in the East End in London, in the theatrical and film center. The group consisted of Stanley Baker, Joseph E. Levine of Boston, the wife of Senator Javitts of New York, one or two others I no longer remember, and of course with an inner roar of laughter, myself, for I am remembering Stanley Baker, one of the dead of 1976. Wardour Street I pronounced the way it would seem to need to be pronounced but when Stanley Baker said it what I heard was Water Street. That interested me, not just about his way of enunciating words or of pronouncing them, but of the way of the English in general. He was very likely a cockney. The new club was very nearly dingy, one long flight upstairs and hardly swank. The fact is it was makeshift and casual and with no real action in progress at all—just three or four shills. I liked the place and plunged into my usual wild, loud gambling. Marion Javits, as I believe she spells her given name, was a happy woman, wife and mother, and that is immediately a very noticeable thing about a woman. She was pretty and seemed young (which is what youth is, of course, among those who are not young or at any rate not few in years, and there are very old men and women who seem very young because of a kind of good luck in the construction of their souls, or something—and don't be annoyed with the "or something" because it is used with thought and care: it means the information accessible at this time, at least to this scientist, is incomplete, that's all), and she was interested heartily and joyously pretty much in everything and in everybody. I rolled dice and the others went to blackjack and roulette, and there was a very joyous atmosphere in the dingy upstairs gambling house, perfectly legal of course, which is a very good thing, an excellent thing, in fact, if we could say that gambling itself was a good thing for the human race. Alas, it isn't, for it makes labor, it makes working for a living seem not only a very slow and painful way of getting the necessary wherewithal, as I've heard it put. Gambling (and winning, or losing, and watching others win or lose) makes work seem to be part of a conspiracy to deprive the soul in a man from its rightful elegance, importance, and right not to be nagged at by necessities of all kinds. If a whole society becomes involved in gambling that doesn't stay in line, as it does in the football pools and similar inexpensive lotteries, that society will very swiftly lose its muscle and become elegant, with a very sad discrepancy between the fancied and the real: in other words, the society will be shabby, confused, desperate, self-deceptive, dissatisfied, disorganized, and both unwilling and unable to go back to the austerity, severity, and muscular procedure which gave it a hard and rather joyous and comic character for a great many centuries. The decline of the British character (never mind the British Empire, that's another story) became visibly complete with the legalization of gambling in England, which simply means there is a profound change from belief to disbelief in basic values in the populace, as they say. The fact is it means many things, and all of them at least half inaccurate. Marion Javits had acted in New York and knew the theatre and did part-time chores of a literary order for

Joseph E. Levine. Stanley Baker was to be in a new film for Joseph E. Levine soon. Marion Javits was both on holiday in London as well as on assignment, or so I have imagined. There was a lively time at the Wardour Street second-floor gambling house, in which Stanley Baker may have had an interest, for he certainly knew everybody there in the way that suggests something more than casual acquaintanceship. Marion is the actual given name of the actor known as John Wayne, who is the commander-in-chief of super-patriotic thought or unthought in Hollywood, and of the male population of the nation under the age of twelve and under the mental age of eight, most likely, and the name John Wayne came up several times in the random talk about casting one or another of Joseph E. Levine's future movies. Around three one morning, at the end of a rather long and not very profitable bogus poker game among Americans in London—7-card stud, for instance, high-low, various cards wild—a long session in which I was suddenly three or four thousand dollars out, a very big loser, because the famous actors and the rich scenario writers all played the nuts, were deadly players or even conspirators and virtual cheaters, and there was absolutely no way for me to win back at least some of my losses, along came Stanley Baker with two other actors and he asked if he could sit in, and did so, and I thought I might win back some of my losses, but I lost another thousand or so in the next half hour when the game definitely ended. Why would a man come to a poker game at three in the morning, I wondered. Fresh as a daisy. And how did he know where the game was, even?

And the list goes on, and even on and on: Ned Barringter. Never knew Ned, haven't even any idea at all what he did. Perhaps he was an actor, but he could also easily have been any number of other things somewhat connected with show business, which is of course the province and preoccupation of *Variety*. All the same the editors and writers of *Variety* edge out into other areas not excluding politics, publishing, education, religion, and just plain ordinary curiosity. Father Devine, for instance, is somebody *Variety* took seriously as a strong personality in American life, and rightly, for he was amazing. Everybody in that business is amazing, including Manson, who was to a good assortment of girls Jesus Christ. And then there are the various high-ranking Catholics of television and benefits and politics: they are all popular enough to be featured in *Variety*, certainly when they die. You can belong to any religion, any sect of any religion, any fresh interpretation of any religion, or you can be an inventor of your own religion, and *Variety* will give you an obituary when the time comes, and list you in their Necrology column for the year. Merna Barry is another person I do not know at all, but it isn't too likely that she was big in ecclesiastics. I never met her, I'm sure, and I never met the man belonging to the name just after her name: Harry Baum. But in London in 1944 I met Eric Baum, who was a newspaperman from Australia, covering the war, after which (in the tradition of all newspapermen) he wrote a novel about life in London during the War, and a wild Armenian was one of the characters in the book, along with a character who was Eric Baum. It was the worst novel I have ever tried to read, and that's kind of sad, because anybody who goes to the trouble of writing a whole novel ought to be helpless about having something in it that is special and good, in a way that nobody else in the whole world could have possibly written something special and good, but poor big bumbling Eric Baum wrote a novel that was bad from the first word to the last, and that is something nobody in the world could do on purpose unless he was brilliant, as Ring Lardner did in some of his best short stories, deliberately. I was on an airplane flying from Hong Kong to Taipei and beside me sat a salesman from Sydney, Australia, so after a while I asked about Eric Baum, and the salesman said the famous newspaperman and all-around enemy-maker had died a couple of years ago. There is this to be said about newspapermen, by their counterparts in television: they almost invariably tend to be, or to become, terrible bores and fatheads: they are so excitable, so thrilled by being everlastingly at the center of the world's mischief and disasters and crimes that they believe they are also large, as the news is always at least that—very large. The longer they stay in business the farther they travel away from the small, one human being at a time. One of the big reporters these past twenty or thirty years is C.L. Sulzberger, who has an office in Paris at the *New York Times* on Rue Scribe. He is a bright man, he has met everybody of importance for forty or more years, he has kept a diary and a journal and has published parts of each, without elaboration, and he writes a fine intelligent column every other day, but he is an awful bore because everything he writes about is so big. Can't a man write about the big and not be a bore? Not unless he happens to be Tolstoy, and the big is demonstrated as being the little, the everlastingly vulnerable little which every man is, in relation to what goes on everlastingly around every man. Little but also big for having been fully seen in his littleness, that is. Sulzberger wrote and published a "novel," but again the big people of the world figured in it as actual characters. It should have worked, but it just didn't. But there is this need for great amounts of daily writing and public talk, as on television, and there have got to be men and women to write and speak such stuff. The gossip of the world is what it is, and gossip is needed by all human beings, no less than bread. I'll never know, most likely, what Harry Baum did, but if the truth is told I'll never know what Eric Baum did, either, even though I knew Eric Baum and read a novel he published. Eric Baum certainly never really wrote anything at all, so why did he get into being a newspaperman? God help us, there is no answer to how or why anybody really gets into anything. On the talk shows that rival the only one that has anything like style, Johnny Carson's, the boys are forever asking amazing people who are enjoying success and fame and money out of singing, out of acting or something like acting, out of some kind of strange song-writing, out of being some kind of public personality, out of writing, out of anything that has made money, how, how these strange people started doing what it is that has brought them money, as if a recitation of the history might be something to hear, really, and of course the recitation is invariably dismal and entirely meaningless. They began to do that which brought them money precisely as everybody else began to do what it was that didn't bring them money, or anything else big and bogus. Merv Griffin has a special place in his little heart for millionaires and multimillionaires (surely because as one of that group, a new arrival in that category, he imagines they are really a very special and admirable group), and he loves to ask them how they opened up a chain of dance studios, and hears them explain the sordid little details, leaving out only that they take full advantage of the longings of foolish souls who haven't found out how to adjust to their non-dancing insignificance, or significance, and their failure to attract one member of the opposite sex likely to fulfill their identities. They cashed in on the desperation of silly and sad dreamers, that's all.

And so we come to another stiff of 1976, and his name is Sir Gerald C. Beadle. The first thing I am obliged to say about Lord Beadle is that he is nobody I know, as far as I know. I knew a number of Lords, and I can summon up their names as I might need to, but right now I don't need to, and in any case they are either not yet dead or they didn't die in 1976. Like Lord Avon, who died in 1977, and hell, man, that year is not yet one month old: it seems Anthony Eden, for indeed it was he, as I have seen it put in stories, was on holiday in Florida when he took terribly ill and was flown home to a hospital where he promptly died: quite a way into the everlasting after a brilliant and busy life. A very nice man he was—the typical Englishman—but death cannot be stayed when it is time: that's all we seem to know about death. One thing, though, that seems to be in my own head is this: if you take deathly ill on the continent somewhere, don't fly to London to go to the hospital. Fly on to wherever your home is and go to the hospital there, because a few

Americans that I have known who have flown to a hospital or the hospital or to hospital, as you may choose, and might very easily have been believed not to be in mortal danger a few days later were worse than in mortal danger, they were dead. Was it the fault of the London hospital to which each of these acquaintances went, or was it for other considerations, as the saying is? One was in for a raw or even bleeding ulcer, but that is not necessarily a big deal—it does not necessarily have to be fatal—but it was for this man who was just barely an acquaintance, if indeed that. We met in a bar among many other people late one night in New York, and with him was the wife he was soon to leave in favor of a much younger and more appealing woman. We were all loud and drunk and happy, and yes, reader, we were also writers, or friends of writers, or readers, and everybody knew everybody else's writings, but I really didn't know this writer's writings, although I knew about them. I couldn't read his writings and I'll tell you why: it was not really necessary to do so, and not at all desirable. So he died in a London hospital of a bleeding ulcer, let's say, and I am not going to put his name here not out of respect for the dead or anything like that at all, but because I don't want to for sensible courteous reasons I also don't want to make known, for then I would need to explain them. The other two Americans who died in London hospitals of ailments that one does not take for big deals I shall not discuss at all, except perhaps to say of one of them, at any rate, that if ever a man had a zest for life, he did, and dying must have come as a terrible failure of something, and possibly something he refused to believe had arrived, and told himself that he was going to sleep, that's all. We had been in London in the Army together, as drafted soldiers, each of us over thirty-five years of age, and neither of us really suitable for drafting and general pushing around, but in London the going was not quite so stupid and tough; indeed it suddenly became a kind of exhiliration, if one can say such a thing of anything when a whole nation, and especially a whole great city, is besieged, as London was, with rockets (called buzz-bombs) coming over every night from launching pads in Germany and destroying a lot of buildings and killing and maiming a lot of people. God knows where Sir Gerald C. Beadle was in those days, but for three days the American actor of tough-guy parts in Warner Brothers movies, Edward G. Robinson, was in London, apparently to do morale work or something. My fellow draftee, as I believe the saying is, had known the actor at Warner Brothers, and so the three of us were glad to have a rather high-toned dinner at the Ritz Hotel, after which we went out for a stroll and immediately heard the noise that meant rockets were on their way: sirens, that is. Well, I never did heed these alarms, but in this instance there wasn't even time, because one of the rockets was lighting up the whole sky above the Ritz Hotel and the buzzing of the thing as it drew nearer became much louder than this type of rocket was ordinarily. The sky was vividly red and blue and flash-mad, so to put it. The event compelled study, for it seemed to me that it couldn't possibly be destined for the Ritz Hotel—it wouldn't dare—and my experience had been that the rockets invariably went on and on, permitting an observer to watch them go. And finally the student of public anonymous wartime crime, public murder, would hear a kind of muffled thump from far-away, and the following day in going to the bulletin board at Leicester Square would learn that the bomb had struck slum dwellings in Limehouse, killing 48 souls and wounding four times that many. But there, right there, was the movie tough-guy trying to make himself as thin as the very thin, and new, tree set out, with others, in a row of similar trees, all in front of the Ritz Hotel, compelling the more experienced friend who had known him at Warner Brothers to call out, "That little bomb doesn't have your number on it, it's not for you, Eddie. Come on, stand up and enjoy it, you can't hide from it, wheee, look at it go." Maybe Sir Gerald C. Beadle had been at the table next to ours in the dining room of the Ritz Hotel, and we just didn't know it. In any case, he died in 1976, and *Variety* put his name in the Pantheon, if that's the word for it. The movie tough-guy went somewhat soft with the arrival of actual hard times in his own life, actual menaces of various kinds, and then he died, and you could see him young and tough only in the old movies when they were put on television.

Cyril Beaumont is somebody I don't know, but whoever he is in anybody's memory, for instance—never mind what else he might be, and every man dead or alive may be a great deal more than we suspect, or could ever guess or find out—Cyril Beaumont died sometime in 1976. In 1944 in London I now and then met a man named Binky Beaumont, connected with the Tennants, who seem to have connections in the theatre, and a friend of a play and movie director named Tony Asquith, son of a man who had of course been Prime Minister, and of that man's wife. These were homosexuals, which it is no longer crude to mention, that little social congestion having been eased out of intensity in the Western World pretty much, and everybody knows there are men who prefer the sexual connection with other men, or boys. Speculating about the sexual connection between man and wife is grotesque enough—or comic enough—or unbelievable enough—but hearing about two big famous Hollywood actors of great appeal to girls and women, hearing that they have been closet lovers for ten years or more does not necessarily boggle the mind (as certain journalists and writers and television commentators like to put it) but it does do *something* to the mind. Perhaps it provides it with rather difficult pictures to accept. But accept them we shall, for it hurts us not, to throw a little drag language around and about. Anthony Asquith and Binky Beaumont for all it mattered might just as well have been the same as all the other men in the English theatre who were not homosexual. And yet even to this day there is something like an opposition by members of one classification to members of the other. It is not uncommon to hear an actor, for instance, believe he did not get a certain part in a certain play because the producer and the director preferred to give the part to one of their own kind—that is, a non-ladies' man, so to put it. It has not yet become anything like prevalent for an opposite order of unhappiness, or excuse-making.

People do tend to prefer friends in occupations that are demanding, such as getting a play skillfully on the boards and satisfying audiences and critics alike. These two men are both dead, and if anything may be presumed to be pertinent to that reality it may be said perhaps to be the question: what is the relationship between anybody and death? Does anybody come to the end differently from anybody else? Well, it is clear that death is death, roughly, but it is also clear that everybody is only who he is, and lives in accordance with that truth, and embraces death and dying accordingly, or accepts the embracing of death accordingly. All this vagueness is the consequence of ignorance of course, but all births and all deaths are broadly the same—but not one birth and not one death is in fact anything at all like any other birth or death: it is always only him- or herself having it happen to him or her. Excepting, should we say, perhaps Jesus, whose birth is beyond acceptance and is readily and gladly and reverently accepted, and whose death is first a public spectacle of grim revelry on the part of the perpetrators and witnesses, and then (again) an unacceptable invention of some sort involving a heavy stone (keeping the dead body in a cave) being rolled away, and the escape of the dead body as if it were a living spirit, in a glorious return to the Father, God. We like it, it's a symbolic story that implies we are more than we are, because *he* was, wasn't he? And so on. And of course there is a school of thought which somewhat adds to the comfort of those homosexuals who for some reason continue to feel the need of comfort, and this school argues that Jesus was a homosexual, along with Leonardo da Vinci and Marcel Proust, for instance. All fairly interesting, most likely, but also fairly irrelevant, without a doubt. Do mothers make sons gay? Do fathers make daughters butch? Do governments make males macho? Does the world make females dykes? Does death make anybody's character vital? And so on and so forth, by which is meant we could ask questions and get no useable answers forever. So Cyril Beaumont died in 1976, and there stands or sits his name in *Variety*'s famous annual list between Sir Gerald C. Beadle and Harry Becker. Well, now, what about Harry Becker? I never met him, poor fellow. Indeed I don't remember ever having met anybody named Becker. Then comes William Belasco, and if nothing else,

William has got himself a family name that has a kind of large meaning for me, because it was at the Belasco, on West 44th Street, midway between 6th Avenue and Broadway in New York, that I set up the Saroyan Theatre. So it was at the Belasco that I rehearsed and staged a couple of my plays which I needn't bother about at this time. It is the theatre and its name that matter, for David Belasco himself built the theatre, and away up at the top he had himself a whole beautiful sneaky kind of apartment, with a peephole, so that he could keep an eye, if not an ear, on the stage, unbeknownst to anybody anywhere. And of course David Belasco was a kind of attractive fraud in the American theatre, and wore a collar backwards, and did the book of an opera by Puccini: *The Girl of the Golden West*, or some such. Taking over the theatre made me think about the old boy, but not really seriously. The theatre was big—if you filled it, you had a hit. My plays never filled it, and indeed the second balcony was always shut off from the rest of the audience—only *I* spent time up there during a performance, and with me most likely hundreds of the ghosts of good people without lots of money, who over the years had paid as little as possible to get into the theatre and see something more of The Deacon's. David Belasco of San Francisco.

22

As I write, two deaths last week, the last week of the month of January, of the year 1977—just look at that strange number, please: 19 and 77, as Stanley Rose used to put it, along with a lot of other people of the United States, most of them from the South and from the small towns and from a kind of folklore class—two deaths took place that became exciting or at any rate interesting or even entertaining news on television. Somebody's death entertaining? Let's not be shocked at all. Yes, entertaining. Toots Shore died in New

York at the age of 72, and quite a few television reporters and commentators spoke brief essays or eulogies on the name, because it lends itself to affection: Toots is Toots, but nobody mentioned his actual given name. He was a big man who affected a gruff style, and every essay spoken about him said that he insulted you if he liked you—otherwise he ignored you or threw you out of his saloon bodily. Well he had long ago in the saga of Manhattan and Youth and Fun been a bouncer at a club on 52nd Street just off 6th Avenue called Leon & Eddie's, where in addition to comics there were strippers. I met Toots Shore, who, unlike Dinah, spells his name Shorr, so I need not go back and change the spelling (it has the same sound, at any rate)—when he was a bouncer at Leon & Eddie's, and I'm sure I met either Leon or Eddie, because one of the two had indeed left the establishment either by choice or through death, and Toots Shorr was a very pleasant fellow with a soft rosy-cheeked small boy's face. It needn't surprise any of us that the owners and operators of saloons and restaurants tend to become very significant in the memories and memoirs of men (and women) who have gone there to drink, and even only to eat. Anybody hands us a drink when we want a drink is somebody, isn't he? And I mean anybody. A legend came up about the large heart back of the gruff exterior of Toots Shorr. It was not untrue, but it was not much of a legend, either. He was in a profitable business that he might be in only as a worker rather than as an owner, and when he sold his place, it was at a profit of more than a million dollars at a time when a million was a million and not a figure for lawyers and tax experts to fool around with (on behalf of not getting robbed by the government). Soon enough, though, he was back in business in a new location, rather far from 52nd Street, but again with all his old friends coming back for their ration of insults and booze, as the saloon-keeper put it, and a lot of new people hoping to attract the attention of the insulter, and mainly failing. Consequently, it was understandable last week that the reporters extended the legend in the tradition of their trade and in the style of excess so characteristic of reporters of all kinds. They want everything to be big, special, and unparalleled, whereas very little about any human being is any such assortment of things. And then only two or three days after having been at the new President's Inaugural Celebration, at which he made a nice little talk, Freddie Prinz shot himself in the head, in Hollywood, and was kept alive through surgery and medical science for more than 24 hours and then died, aged 22. This was actually very sensational, without any support from reporters remembering themselves a long time ago and thrusting the warmth of it all upon somebody also around in those days but just lately dead. It was a shock in itself, for this very young man was a comic with a touch of genius, and an excellent potential for a long and full career—healthy, good-looking, famous, rich, married, and newly a father (or did the expected child perish before birth?). It's true he was said to be depressed because of the failure of his marriage, and his wife had left him. Whatever the details are, they are not uncommon, and if anybody might have been expected to survive them, it was this young comedian, who invented a growled encouragement that is still used by people all over the country: *"Looking good."* And his contemporary, Jimmy Walker, came out with *dyn-o-mite,* which is also popular. While the surgeons worked to save his life, so to put it, patching badly damaged brain tissue, his father and mother and his estranged wife waiting anxiously—and I certainly never would have thought that such a wholesome comedian would inflict that kind of situation on his family. Toots Shorr died; Freddie Prinz killed himself. I speak of this because this is the better part of the scheme of this work: Who died during 1976 as listed in *Variety,* and while these two didn't make it into the list for 1976, they will make it big in the obituary pages of *Variety* and in the Necrology of 1977. Who died, that is, that I knew. Well, again, I knew Toots Shorr, but I didn't know Freddie Prinz, and I have got to say that when I first heard that he had shot himself I felt that if I had been around, he wouldn't have done it. But of course what I was really saying was, I wish he hadn't done it. Toots Shorr had to die; he had had the best of it long ago; he was not an old man, but he was old enough considering his trade, and he had all the time he needed to make meaning of himself and his time. But Freddie Prinz didn't have to die at all. And that hurts. And a lot of young people are going to wonder how anybody so successful could find even *that* really useless to him in a crisis. Why should he have felt that anything could be a crisis in the first place? He was intelligent, he was swift, he surely knew that at worst he was rattled, he was tired, he was exhausted, and what he needed was falling away from everything until he might welcome back the noise and importance of everything all at the same time.

James Warner Bellah is the next name, and while I have never met him I know he is, he was, a writer, and there was even a time when he was taken seriously as a writer. Not as seriously as, for instance, James Gould—nah, that's not the name I want: there it is: James Gould Couzzens (it was the right name, after all), or as seriously as James Whitcomb Riley, or James Something or Other Thurber, or one or another of the famous Jameses—the most popular given name of the English language according to the latest poll. But poll-takers can't really be taken seriously although they are. As far as I know, I never read anything more than the name of James Warner Bellah above a short story in *The Saturday Evening Post,* although I am sure I tried to read one or another of his stories, and never was quite able (or willing) to see the thing through. There are writers who can be very comfortably lived without, so to put it. There may be, just the same, good writing by James Warner Bellah that I would be very happy to have read, if only I had been able not to pass up such writing. One of us failed, and nothing is lost by either of us, or the world, or literature, or anything else. As for James Joyce (NMI, which stands for No Middle Initial, which James Thurber chose not to have in his public name), James Joyce is going to grow and grow, not only in importance among writers of all time, but in the pleasure of reading his writing, starting with the fairly conventional and formal stories in *The Dubliners* straight through to the last word in *Finnegans Wake.* He also sent some hot letters to his wife, which lately have been published, but alas such books cost more than I can pay for them, and nobody has sent any of them to me, for review, for instance, and I haven't chanced upon any of them at the Fresno Public Library, where I tend to buy discarded books in any case, so that I can take them up at my leisure and never need to worry about returning. In most of these books I make a drawing or a painting on the inside front or back cover and put down the date and place and time, and years later I chance upon the book with pleasure, and am delighted to know when I acquired it and where and for how much—a dime apiece at the Public Library: three for a quarter, seven for half a dollar: and I tend to take seven. It's great fun. And I get a profound kind of joy out of rescuing something officially identified as useless, obsolete, superceded and so on. So far, though, among such books has not been one by James Warner Bellah, who died in 1976, and I am afraid, if the truth is told, that if I had come upon one such I would not have put it with the seven I wanted on that day, because even at only a fraction of a cent more than 7¢ a copy I didn't want to bother with his writing. Bad writing I am devoted to, if you can follow what I am saying: real bad writing is real good writing, but when somebody comes along who writes well enough but really has nothing at all to say about anything at all and cannot be expected ever to surprise himself, his father, his mother, his wife, his children, or his reader, I really don't want to try to make something of what he did for some reason, feeling he must write. It's a good name, though, and it has a nice sound to it, a nice ring: James Warner Bellah, you could dance to that, and if you wanted to, you could also sing to it. I don't want to. The next name is Earl Benham, but all I know about those two names is this: the Armenian name for Earl is Ish-khan, and I like that better than Earl, which always sounds like the Brooklyn pronunciation of oil, that's all. The Ish-khan fish from the waters of ancient Lake Van is said to have one of the greatest of the flavors that world fish have. My grandmother Lucy and her daughter Takoohi used to send me to the Fresno Fish Market in Chinatown sixty years ago to buy something we would be obliged to call sardines, and they used to fix a big pot of bulghour pilaf, and then fry a dozen sardines and sit and eat them and remember such feasts in Bitlis at the south end of Lake Van, or at any rate the southwest end, and while they smacked their lips with delight about the flavor of the fried Monterey fish, they also invariably said that these fish couldn't compare with the Ish-khan fish of Lake Van. Well, the waters of Lake Van are heavy with borax—you can submerge only by forcing yourself, otherwise you float—and that may have done something to any fish that adapted to those waters, as the Ish-khan fish, perhaps alone, adapted. And as for Benham, when I was fourteen years old I telephoned the Benham Ice Cream Company and made a deal with them to sell their ice cream exclusively if they would set up a stand for me at the Court House Park where the statue of iron of The Boy with the Leaky Boat stood, for the Raisin Day Celebration: a great success it was, too, and all of my cousins and others pocketed twice as much hard cash as they put into the moneybox, and the rest was hauled off wholesale by my mother's kid brother Aram, at that time 30 years old, leaving for me a net profit of about eight dollars instead of literally about eight hundred—but that was all right, too: it was fine and I liked seeing all those cousins getting pocket money for the rest of that whole year. Benham—what country is that from? Germany but also England, most likely. Look for Benham's Ice Cream in Fresno and you will not find it: you may find them listed in an old directory, though, or on a brick wall of an abandoned warehouse somewhere, the paint all faded and flaked, but the message still clear enough: Eat Benham's Ice Cream. It's the Best. Well, the fact is it was the best. And in a milkshake at Googoo's Drug Store it made the sweetest drink you could ever hope to drink—but you just can't get anything like that milkshake anywhere anymore. The world does change in such things. Not in big deals, like wars.

Busby Berkeley died in 1976, and I met him six or seven times in Hollywood at six or seven of the places of work and eating and drinking and sporting, such as The Clover Club, an almost private gambling house, pretty much reserved for movie people, as the saying was. Busby Berkeley was a dancer and a director of group dancing. He was possibly the very inventor of the flower dances, in which petals opened, and of architectural dances, in which something like a building came into being, and streams flowing, and tricks of many other kinds, all performed by pretty young girls. Sometimes the camera watched them from down below; sometimes from up above. It was fun. The making of movies from about 1928 to about 1948 was fun, even though in those two decades the biggest war of all time took place, and things happened to the human race that were not fun at all. Now, dancing is of course one of the primal activities, and everybody has got to be deeply pleased about dancing in all of its various forms, both sacred and profane. The profane tended to expose the female body and to stimulate the procreative privilege of men, and the sacred tended to keep all bodies almost majestically concealed and to celebrate the spiritual realities of the human experience. But everybody has got to be glad about the body and its ability to move, whether formally in dance or informally in getting around. Busby Berkeley took the chorus girl and had her tell some of the joyous stories of health and beauty—of the female body, forget the face, in the dance it really didn't count: while one or two girls out of every assortment employed in a Busby Berkeley dance creation might have a really pretty face, it was strange that if you made a point of studying all of the faces you found that there were few that were really well-shaped, and there were quite a few that might be considered less than plain, possibly freaky, and these girls flashed long legs and arms and bellies and backs that were really elegant and gorgeous. The soul looked for a beautiful face, the body of a man wanted only a beautiful body of a girl, and in the Hollywood movie dances, men were able to shop around for bodies and to do so without complications—but the fact remains that the dances transformed many money-losing movies into money-making movies, and so Busby Berkeley and his colleagues of dance were very important in the movie business. So was Busby Berkeley himself, going around in a movie studio, followed by three or four of his assistants, including now and then a woman or a girl he seemed to have become interested in beyond the call of duty, as the saying is, and fully-clothed these women really looked quite drab—and then when one watched a rehearsal an hour later one noticed that the dancer/director's girl not only had the sweetest body of the lot, but also there was something about the way she moved in dance that was absolutely delicious, exciting, mysterious, and yet as simple as anything could be—trout, bird, insect, tail flick of trout, head turn of bird, flutter of insect, and so on. There is a world of dance, not less than ballet, but different from ballet, that is absolutely enormous, and it is real in the most important dimension of reality of every people in the world. And this world of dance almost invariably concerns itself with simply charging the soul and genitals of the male with lust to perform that most basic of dances which satisfies nature in the replenishment of life in all of its forms. It also concerns itself with a concealment of the hearty physical nature of man in the austere but frequently dazzling costume of the spirit, the soul, the forgetting of the flesh—at least for a moment, which surely has the effect of making the action of the flesh all the more sweet. What does a new man fall in love with, become obsessed with, about the opposite sex? Well, it seems to be many things, but never is movement not part of it, and indeed movement seems to be the greater part of a woman's appeal. At the Hippodrome Theatre in Fresno in 1919 or 1920 or 1921, and indeed in all of those years, every summer there was a kind of musical comedy company which supplemented the movies with a one-hour show, as it was called in those days, by performing a crazy little play with all of the basics of drama, farce, burlesque in the classic sense (the strip-tease was to come much later), parody, vaudeville, and side-show. Part of the action was the dancing girls, generally six in number, but frequently enlarged by participation of the actresses. Well, a little girl one summer moved her little body in such a sweet way that upon seeing her I fell madly in love. She was the end girl on the right, and watching her was absolutely the most deeply beautiful theatrical experience I have ever known. In the street, in her plain inexpensive clothes she seemed small and ordinary, but nothing could fool me: I knew who she was, what she was: and she was nature, she was flow, she was tail-flip, head-turn, arm-wave, finger-move, and I had to follow her on a bike, watching her go to the dingy two-story building on O Street just south of Mariposa where she had a room for the summer run of Jack Russell & Company. This fact, also: I dropped my bike before going into the theatre free by the side door, as many of us did of a Saturday morning instead of blowing a dime, and when I came out the bike was right where I had dropped it and a dozen or more bikes were all around it. There was no such thing as bike-stealing in those days, and that seems almost as grand as the revelation of all movement in the movement of a little girl in the chorus at the Hippodrome Theatre. Who got her? Well, I sure as hell didn't, 11 or 12 years old. But I sure as hell got her message, and it was absolutely delightful.

25

Joe Bigelow. He died, too. And I never knew him, I am sorry to say, for I like the name. It is a rollicking name, O, O, Joe Bigelow. I hope he had a good life and a very good death, for of course it would be absurd not to know that there are as many kinds of death as there are kinds of life, pieces of action and experience, or marbles. If you remember when marbles had a meaning in your life, you have surely not forgotten that there were all kinds of them, and even if you paid Woolworth's a dime for a little sack of marbles, when you brought the marbles out of hiding into visibility, they invariably seemed to be priceless treasures. Well, of course they were only marbles, but then nothing is only anything, it is always also who's looking, or who's feeling something about them. Is death life? That's the question, most likely. Yes, it is, of course, what else could it possibly be? Is dying living? Of course it is. And I don't mind coming next with something trite but supremely trite: everybody is born, everybody dies, but the biggest source of anxiety among the deep thinkers and measurers and scientists of our time is the increase in our numbers, both in being born and in dying, in arriving and in departing. And we are all of us experiencing the interval between living and dying, birth and death. Not all of us has anything at all like a dancing time, so to put it, in the interval. The fact is that most of us have a rotten time—but let me remark that we are ignorant, and we don't know, and can't find out, or be absolutely sure about the kind of time anybody has, whoever he is, and whatever his way of enduring time may be. Is he bereft of anything worth anything at all, other than a poor vulnerable body and homelessness, like the handsome women who live on sidewalks in Calcutta, surrounded by their handsome kids? What do we know? We would have to believe that that is no way to live, and no place to live, but there they are, and there it is. In Calcutta there are thousands of sidewalk people. And this is true of other places in India. They live, they breathe, they live right there. They don't beg, but the only money that comes to them comes from people passing by—very tiny sums from other Indians, and less tiny sums from travelers. And all of these people are chancing upon opposites, and clutch one another and bring forth new people—and this is the big and important thing: all of them are handsome. So what's going on? What's happening to balance, proportion, limitation, order, and reasonably fair prospects for the future insofar as the continuation of everybody is concerned? On television just last night somebody pointed out in some connection that it has taken all this human time for that branch of the animal family which is called human to bring its numbers to eight billion: that works out to eight thousand million. When I was born less than seventy years ago, in 1908, there were not many more than two thousand million human beings in the world. And this reporter on television last night said that before the end of this century, in only about 20 more years, that eight thousand million will become sixteen thousand million people, so what then? Well, we don't know, do we? And we want to know, don't we? Well, one thing we are becoming adjusted to is this troublesome but also rather handsome if foolhardy fact: nothing, or nothing willing or effective on the part of the people involved is going to hold the action which used to be called the begetting action and was considered an action that was entirely desirable—nothing is going to diminish in any dimension that action, or the consequences of it: new people. So what is going to be the relationship between getting born and getting unborn, then? What is going to be the means of experiencing a good life and an equally good death, which is surely as basic a right as anybody might ever believe every man is entitled to. Well, risks and hazards have always been with both the human branch of the animal family and all the other branches. Ecological procedure tends to keep all forms excepting the human form within bounds, with occasional variations—forms moving entirely out of substance into extinction and other forms increasing so excessively that catastrophic consequences of one sort or another are inevitable. Lemmings in enormous numbers race to the sea and fling themselves from cliffs into the water that will bring them death, and nature a restoration of balance in that tiny portion of nature in which lemmings are a vital part of a chain. Excessive skill among predators wipes out a very handsome order of gazelles. And Americans with guns bring down carrier pigeons until no trace of them is ever left. But what about Joe Bigelow and his kind all over the world? How can they be contained and yet not be deprived of their right to live and die? Ah, man, there is no decent answer. The only answer is indecent: the stupid super-duper brilliant explosives will just have to be used by the stupid super-duper governments of the world. Russia will diminish China's millions by about half, and China will diminish Russia's by one-third, and America in some kind of confusion will diminish Russia's remaining millions by more than half, and Russia will diminish America's millions by about one quarter, and then everybody will gather themselves together again and meet soberly and start all over again. Is that the way to live? Is that the way to die? Not for Joe Bigelow, it isn't. But for masses of people, and for governments, God help them, it may not be the desired way, but it can readily turn out to be, to have been, the only possible way. In that case, what about you and me, and our kids and our grandkids? Nothing. That's the answer. The interval between birth and death will be shortened.

26

In the alphabetical list, after Joe (not Joseph, you understand) Bigelow comes Milton Biow, and I'm not sure I can pronounce Biow properly: B.O., I expect, which as all Americans know became a powerful achievement of Madison Avenue, bullying men and women, boys and girls, into believing they smelled badly: they had body odor. Nobody came up with anything like the truth, which was simply that it is impossible not to have body odor, it would be foolish to hope not to have it, and if it is not futile to try to conceal it, it is wisest to do it as the human race has managed to do it for centuries: if the odor is offensive, improve the health and avoid the sweat and fret which makes the odor rotten, as of course it will be if not with sweat, certainly with fret. As both a vineyard worker in the summertime, and as a gambler in the wintertime, I know the difference between the sweat of each season and occupation: the summertime sweat is copious but not really rotten, while the wintertime fret-sweat is restricted pretty much to the under-arms, and is rotten, compounded rotten by cigarette smoke and in my case lots of whiskey (which any proper gambler will tell you identifies the fool, and I won't deny it: I didn't sit in on the Turk Street, San Francisco, poker games to make a living: it was to celebrate having finished some hard work at writing, and I didn't mind losing, although I frequently won and felt good about it, for the others were professional gamblers and essentially businessmen). In any case, Biow is the name of nobody I have ever known. The nearest thing to it is the name a Postal Telegraph Messenger in 1928 working out of MK Office, which is on Market Street, and part of the fine building that was the Palace Hotel (in which Warren G. Harding died): John Buie was his name, and he said the origin of the name was Belgian, not unlike I suppose Buick. All the same there is a faint reverberation of engaged memory in the full name, Milton Biow: was he somebody in a union of some kind? Whoever he was, never met him, and regret it, but have got to live with it, as we say. After Biow is Blair, David, and he's another, although I know the name Betsy Blair quite well, for she was in the chorus of Panama Hattie on Broadway, and Morley Callaghan was in town, and Gene Kelly was courting Betsy Blair and believed she might be somebody not really wrong for the part of Agnes in a play I was producing at the Belasco Theatre called *The Beautiful People.* So the Canadian writer who had been in Paris at the Exciting Time, in the middle 1920s and had known Scott Fitzgerald and had boxed with Ernest Hemingway and who had himself written a lot of fine stories brought together in a book entitled *Last Spring They Came Over*—the Canadian writer went with me to see Panama Hattie and Betsy Blair, and afterwards we joined Gene Kelly and his girl and had food and drink at Ralph's, a little hole-in-the-wall restaurant popular with theatrical people. Betsy Blair did the part of Agnes, or more fully, St. Agnes of the Mice, very nicely, even though she believed all during dinner that she hadn't had enough experience to take almost a leading part in a play, but of course I have always insisted that given a reasonably creative director anybody can be an actor, a performer, and all that is needed is a willingness, which Betsy Blair had. But I don't seem to have any recollection of meeting or knowing David Blair. Can't win them all. Win some, lose some. Easy come, easy go. Right's wrong, wrong's wrong. It's a long way to Tipperary. Also, There's a long long trail awinding into the land of my dreams. And finally: Shut up, soul, you're supposed to be activated for common sense, not gibberish. Betsy and Gene got married and became the parents of a daughter named Kerry, so that her full name was really something special, as much a song as a dance, and just right for the daughter of a song-and-dance father, and the very same kind of mother. Morley Callaghan's reputation, fame, wealth, importance, or flash as a writer never rivalled that of Fitzgerald or Hemingway, but the lives they lived couldn't compare with the life he lived, and a variety of very important dimensions of the human experience. He didn't seem to need to be a legend, to begin to try to be in actual fact the person he was in the legend, or to be desperate about the decline of his fame, or to otherwise carry on as if he was short on gray matter. But then, as the saying is, that's Showbiz, that's the Literary World, the Literary Life, and the way the kangaroo croons. Fitzgerald has been dead about thirty years, and his writing is being rediscovered, and movies are being made of just about everything he has written. He died young, and all broken up. His beautiful wife Zelda died in a rest home which burned to the ground with Zelda and everybody else, just about, inside, safely carried away by asphyxiation. Hemingway shot himself in the head after having had ten terrible years of dispute with his soul. Scott had been not yet even fifty, and Hemingway was just into his sixties. Morley is still very much alive in Toronto, with his one and only wife, and their children and grandchildren. Will his writing twenty or thirty years from now be discovered? We don't know, we don't know, but what we do know is that he has worked as a professional writer for about fifty years, and that's pretty good going. Not every writer makes his way from his preferred work—many must earn their bread and butter by doing other work, the most popular order of such work being teaching: preferably at the college level, as I've heard it put. I wouldn't be willing to do that—the students are too stupid for me to put up with, that's all, and the politics of survival and possible improvement of position is too offensive to be tolerated.

27

Kermit Bloomgarden was a pleasant fellow not much more than a few years older than myself when I first met him, sometime in 1939, when he was stage manager for The Group Theatre, it would seem, although we must understand that memory can be faulty, and that it is the policy (as we say) of this writer to permit memory to do what it does, for that is part of the real story of any of us, and certainly of myself. If you believe something was something somewhere sometime, and are willing to put actual details upon it all, that's who you are and who you were and how it is. I thought of Kermit Bloomgarden as being collegiate. He seemed to have the easy half-sporty clothes, or costume, of a college boy, not majoring in philosophy but also not there just for the social life. The Group Theatre was the most alert group in New York, and among members of the group were Harold Clurman, Stella Adler, Morris Carnovsky, Luther Adler, Lee Strassberg, Elia Kazan, and most important of all an actor who suddenly revealed a talent for writing plays: Clifford Odets, from Philadelphia or somewhere. One can guess how the founders chose their name. After the 1920s there was a strong feeling of large change in the life and identity of the human race, and things smart tended to be very respectful of what used to be called the masses, as indeed a popular magazine of the time called itself. The masses, however, had nothing to do with physics or sculpture or architecture or mathematics or painting or science or any order of abstraction. The masses were people. The majority of people. The poor, the student, the intellectual, the maladjusted, the unemployed, the hungry, the revolutionary, but especially the poor, insofar as the members of The Group Theatre were concerned, given to discussion, to theorizing, and to disputation. But Kermit Bloomgarden was not given to such things, or apparently was not, but who knows? He seemed to be given to taking it easy, cooling it, listening and watching and learning. And then all of a sudden he was a producer, and of course that takes doing, and the kind of determination that nobody but a personality of Broadway would be willing to even think about imposing on himself. Why be determined to get a play produced? Why be willing to hustle rich people who are clearly both culture-vultures and money-mad? That is to say, intolerable. Well, the answers would have to be as full as those that might seek to make clear why anybody does anything, especially anybody who does anything in the weird if sometimes very admirable dimension of human possibility. A man like Houdini, for instance. A daytime busy-hour big-city bank-robber working alone. A climber of mountains. An explorer of caves. Wire-walkers. Motorcycle fliers, so to call them. And so on. A man who wants to hustle people so he can produce a play that really isn't worth any trouble at all, let alone a lot of trouble of that belittling order, has got to seem mysterious, at the very least. And to hustle the prevailing government is even more belittling. I am interested in names, and I liked the name Bloomgarden, but was delighted by the name just before it. Theodore Roosevelt gave one of his several sons the name Kermit, and until I came upon the stage manager of *My Heart's in the Highlands*, or something in connection with my first play, I had never met anybody who had had that name. And then I had the strong feeling that the owner of the name was the very man for it: whoever had given him the name had done a thing of flawless intelligence. Kermit was Kermit, and his easy smile as he listened to the ravings of one of his many Broadway friends and colleagues demonstrated that fact. All the same, gossip informed me that for the last four or five years of his life, at the very least, he was desperately inconvenienced by asthma, ulcers, and something like total failure—that is, depression, exhaustion, boredom, and a refusal to put himself out, as he had done for so long, in getting a play on the boards. And the gossip said that he was dying. I never knew him anything like one imagines one knows somebody one thinks of as a friend, but on several occasions, with friends of his, and friends of mine, we had formed an eating and drinking group, first at Sardi's and then at a variety of other drinking places, and these occasions were altogether pleasant: nobody got out of line, nobody got sloppy, nobody began to defend his genius, his track record, so to put it, his success, his failure, his incompetence, his superiority, or his philosophy. He ate and drank along with the rest of us, and joined in the loud talk, and laughed, but not as loudly as many of us, and listened, and was amused, and listened, and was almost amused. He didn't produce one of the great long-running commercial successes of all time, *Life with Father*, that had to be Oscar Serlin, but Kermit Bloomgarden, in my memory, had something to do with that money-maker. Why don't I just look it up?

Because I don't look up. I am not a writer of popular history. But I'm quite sure that Kermit Bloomgarden produced at least one play by Lillian Hellman, and alas it didn't go. It was actually an adaptation from a French play, I believe. *My Father, My Mother, and Me, and Our Cat* was the name of it, or something like that, and I sat in the fourth row left on opening night. Everything seemed to work perfectly and the performers all seemed to be just right, but I knew that it wouldn't do—not for Broadway, not for money-making, although it would do just fine for me. I enjoyed it. The thing was boring in a terribly painful way, and in that alone it was fantastically entertaining to me. I was shocked when I saw the name Kermit Bloomgarden in *Variety*'s Necrology of 1976. I had imagined that he had died a month after that silly play failed.

The next lucky customer on the list is Connee Boswell, but if this is the famous singer of popular songs I must say I never noticed that she spelled her given name as it is spelled in *Variety*. Connie no matter how it is spelled is probably the diminutive of Constance. I have known four or five girls and women whose names were Constance but were called Connie. Everybody gives a lot of thought to his name. It is just about the biggest exterior (and interior) thing in his life and reality. People who are tense or desperate about their standing in the community, or about their success in the world, especially in the public world, give a lot of thought to the probable connection between the name they go by and how the career is going. Some people, even after they have started a career and had some success, suddenly drop their two names totally, instead of changing the spelling of one or another of the two names, and lo and behold their fortunes improve immediately: just think about Engelbert Humperdinck, for instance. Did his singing improve after he took the name of the German composer? Bet your life it did. Success, even if scarcely measurable, is success, and it compels boldness, and that improves the voice, or any other talent. Is his singing irrelevant, in any case? It is not. He is a good singer, but not until he was referred to by his fans (who still can't really pronounce his public name, and have no idea who the real Engelbert Humperdinck was) as Engelbert Humperdinck, or should I say Bengalart Bumpersticker, did he get into the big time. Add an E, add an A, remove one of two L's or T's or M's, and zooie, the way is cleared for fame and fortune. Was it Hemenway at the start of his career? Well, if it wasn't, there are still more Hemenways than there are Hemingways. And a whole election campaign moved along for weeks and months in which the candidate was referred to exclusively by a nickname, and then it seems that at his Inauguration, hand on the Bible, on the Baptist Bible, on the Born-Again Baptist Bible, he was still Jimmy, not even Jim, which is only slightly less endearing and palsy-walsy. Why did he do that? Because another name almost precisely the same as his entire name was attached to a dastardly assassin—James Earl Ray. Would the voters elect a man whose name was James Earl Carter? That was good thinking, as the saying is. It had to be done. It would be, or could be, might be political suicide not to just forget the James Earl part of his name, in favor of Jimmy, or Jimmy Boy, even. So what's lost, what's gained, what has history received, what have the people of the nation accepted? Well, it certainly isn't a lie. His kid brother is called Billy, not William, for instance. But Billy only runs a gas station in a small Georgia town, and Jimmy is President. Forget it. James Earl Ray keeps trying to win a new trial because he believes he was tricked by the machinery of justice. He claims he had nothing to do with the assassination of Martin Luther King, Jr., or at any rate he claims he wasn't alone in that very dirty crime. Alas, whenever there is suspicion of conspiracy in the dirtiest crimes (short of wholesale killing, as in war), not just in the United States, but in the whole world, there is a terrible fear that if the truth is ever uncovered we will learn that it is ourselves who have conspired, that it was a branch of our government that thought of the crime, and so on to its successful execution. There are branches of our government that do not report to the people, even indirectly, and while it is presumed that the President is aware of what those branches do, it is not inconceivable that even he doesn't, as a matter of fact. Did John Kennedy know the Central Intelligence Agency was working with members of the underworld to get Fidel Castro? Get means to do him, as the British say. To kill him. To remove him. If he did, might he have suspected that it was himself he was conspiring to kill? In other words, if power is misused, if it is permitted to go criminal, in private singular sharp-shooting, as in assassinations, not in wars where the killed are anonymous and essentially prisoners of their own governments—if power is permitted to become diseased, will the infection escape anybody at all, let alone those who have and manipulate the power? Connee Boswell was a very pleasant singer, although it is not possible for me to remember by actual name any song she was famous for singing, and I am sure there were at least half a dozen such songs: very likely not "Ten Cents a Dance," but a song of that kind, most likely. Singing is one of the beautiful things. As far as I have heard, only human beings and birds sing, but this is very likely not really true. What birds do is of course singing, and human beings may even have got the idea of singing from the birds, but in comparison with human singing, that which birds do when we believe they are singing is probably not singing but something else. I never have understood the voice of the turtle, or heard it, but I presume turtles have voices and that these voices have been heard, and probably in song. Things that live make sounds, but as far as I am willing to believe, only human beings actually sing, and I don't mean in opera, concert, or showbiz, as in Las Vegas where any fairly nervous singer can earn in four weeks more than Jimmy Carter himself. But what do you do with that money? That's the catch, and I don't mean Catch 22—my address was 2226 San Benito Avenue, so 22 means special things to my years from eight or nine to twelve or thirteen. I lived in that house for five or six great years, and I sang all the time. What do I know about anything? Everything was terrible, but all I did was sing and think about my name. Was it right for me? Well it's too late now.

The next deceased of 1976 as reported in the big fat Annual *Variety* weekly dated January 5, 1977, is Warren Bower, and he is another of last year's dead, reported or not in *Variety*, or *The New York Times*, or in any publication whatsoever, anywhere, another gone and surely not yet totally forgotten soul inside a once-living but recently not-living body whom I never met. That means a lot less than it says, I suppose, but I may be mistaken. Warren Bower is somebody I don't know, and I find it painful even to think about the annual dead of all kinds and classes, locations and statuses (if you don't mind a word like that), trades and professions—and just to imagine the inappropriate timing of some of these passings, if not indeed of all of them, hurts the heart. Is there one man or woman or child in let's say one full million, who enters into death with something like willingness? Thus, any death is inappropriate—whether the party involved is 94 years old, as Leopold Stokowski is, still conducting orchestras and making records, as reported on television only a couple of weeks ago, on a new program called *Who's Who*. Whether the person is 94 years old or four years old, although under the age of seven or eight, kids menaced by death are not unlike Arabs are said to be: they imagine that this is how it is for everybody, and they are resigned to it, all they really want to know, it would seem, is how much time does it have to take. Well, I've just said what I've just said, but at the same time remembering myself between two years of age and perhaps as many as six, I never imagined death was anything like a possibility for me, at all. Although at Sunday School and Church in Oakland I frequently heard about death and seemed to suspect that it meant somebody left the scene, I had no real conception of the condition or event in connection with myself. It was not so much that I (or anybody else) couldn't die, it was simply that the idea of it never crossed my mind. Not even when I was pretty desperately sick and had a big and terrible fever, and felt terribly alone, forsaken, and in need. But from somewhere has come the notion that kids, when at death's door, as the saying is, either from ignorance of what the event actually is, seem to be resigned to it: perhaps imagining that it is not an end, and is only, like everything else, another event of change—and, to paraphrase certain comics of this world: how right he is, or may be. Perhaps we ought to look into that in a severe and scientific way, for it may well be that it will reveal things we ought to know about the human experience and ourselves. What do I know? I'm guessing, but a good guess is something: the beginning of something or other of some use. And of course it is established that many people who commit suicide, especially those with theatrical impulses about showing their parents, or their partners in love, or somebody who has hurt or belittled them, reveal they do not think the event is the end at all, it is simply something they haven't thought through, that's all. Even if it isn't the end in one sense or another, they haven't even reached the reality that if you die, you've had it: you are not going to show up Tuesday to ask somebody who has hurt you, "How do you like that? How do you like not having Nick or Nicole to push around anymore?" I don't happen to have the statistics about numbers born every year and about numbers unborn, or with birth neutralized at last, or reborn as it were out of this arena or reality and experience (instead of saying of them that they have died), but I suspect that with eight thousand million people alive in the world, the turnover has got to be pretty big. Maybe ten million die every year, while twelve million are born. That is a very conservative figure, and I know it, but let it stand: it will serve. And all of these people one by one dying, as on the other side all of the others, smaller by far, as they say, are one by one being born, absolutely delight my soul, although I miss the dead for some reason, if miss is the word, and it damned well isn't. Rather, I am sorry they are gone. Although we are all always going and must finally make it all the way out, one is still permitted not so much a touch of sentimental sorrow as of mysterious and unexplainable regret or even loneliness. We are all one another, but we don't really like the idea—it offends us—each of us has a piece of natural procedure born into us which both permits and compels us to believe we are unique, and so we don't like any notion such as the notion that we are all one large (and should I say, should I dare to say, very foolish) entity of some kind—called several things openly and known to be several others where knowledge is cut off from any order of language at all. We just happen to know (in all languages, or none) that we are each of us that precise tiny part of the immeasureable entirety of human life and earthly substance, and known action. We're stupid, but we suspect that we just couldn't possibly be all neatly packaged inside our skins and set on our feet without being connected very intimately with everybody alive, every animal alive, everybody dead, and all orders of weather, of fire, light, heat, snow, rain, drought, storm, and everything else. We know it, we don't talk about it, we aren't experts, and so we go along and talk about the very very very safe and stupid stuff all our lives, and it's right that we do this. It just wouldn't do for us to try to talk in passing about that which is unpassable, so to put it: that which was, is, and always will be, or at any rate seems to be of that order of size and continuity and durability and meaning. It's cemeteries and tombstones most of all that I find startling. They really are funny.

Next, Alexander Brailowsky was in music, on the cello, I believe, but I know nothing about him. I do know however that the man who is in music is both fortunate and not so hot as an all-around party in the world and in the papers of the world. Like all others in the arts, so to put it, one would really expect them to be supremely human and right, but it almost always turns out that they are pretty much the same as everybody else. One thing is rather pretty, though, and pretty mysterious as well: the longevity of the conductors of orchestras. They tend to go on and on, even though the work they do cannot be considered anything but nerve-wracking.

There was a conductor in Fresno ten or twenty years ago who was excellent, and very young. His work with the orchestra was known to be first-rate or better even by the people who are not anything at all like experts, not readers of scores, not interested in reading scores, and not especially good at listening. They all appreciated his work with the orchestra, and a grand career was clearly straight ahead. He was called to a much bigger and likelier city to take over their orchestra and he went and everybody in the musical world of that city was thrilled and everybody in Fresno who remembered him was thrilled, and his son sang the part of the crippled boy in *Ahmal* and *God Help Us One and All*, and the son was also acclaimed, and Armenians everywhere heard the man's name (which I will remember in a moment) and rejoiced in the man's talent and growing fame. And so did I, for the man was Armenian, and his name was, and his appearance was, and his intensity was, and his son was, and being in music, and in the conducting end of music, I certainly expected to hear a lot about the man (in the shape of his name, which was not the easiest in the world to say, or even to remember, as you see), and then all of a sudden the shocking news reached Fresno that Haig Yaghjian (that's it), not yet even 40 years old, had died in the new city somewhere, apparently of a heart attack. I had never met him and I had never heard him lead an orchestra, but I had heard a lot about him, for the Armenians of Fresno as of everywhere else are devoted to music, their own no less than the music of the human race at large. Their own is supreme, especially in the ecclesiastical department, the liturgical as it is called, the sharagans, the talk-song communication of simple but great words and soundings of respect for life and mystery, but also in the art music department: not the folk songs, not the chronicling systematically by Komitas of all such music, songs and dances of the people, but in concertos, symphonies, operas, ballets, and rhapsodies. The Turks who took over the Anatolian peninsula long, long after the Armenians had staked it out as their geography in the world, who came to know the Armenians and the other peoples steadily thrust into groups of minorities, did not conceal their admiration for the talents that ran through the Armenians, and put those talents to work in all areas of life and art. Turkish intellectuals of our day, richly blended in lineage with Armenians, Georgians, Jews, Arabs, Persians, Hungarians, Bulgarians, Greeks, Serbs, and indeed with very nearly all of the other peoples of the world, and looking for all the world altogether Armenian, or Kurdish, or at any rate European—speak modestly and with hesitant warmth and admiration of the people they tried to overwhelm and efface, force, or charm, and failed totally, saying things like, Ah, they are an amazing people, they are builders, they are makers, they are growers, and then the intellectuals fall silent because they have come to the part they don't like to think about and can't speak about: their attempt to wipe out the whole people in their midst, each of them if pressed arguing that he had nothing to do with that unfortunate attempt, and so on. It is the old story of the numerically great seeking to swallow a superior people, and this time failing to do so. Most of the time such swallowings are not only successful, but also improve everybody involved, as in England before the Roman Conquest, so to put it. Komitas went mad in Paris, but the better part of his glorious program had been achieved, and long before Bela Bartok's similar work in middle Europe, Komitas had preserved musical treasures which otherwise would soon have faded from memory and be gone forever. Shah-Mouradian, one of the truly great tenor-baritones of all time, somewhat like John McCormack, a star in Paris and New York, and around the world in opera, but beloved of all Armenians for his incomparable singing of folk songs, also went mad, also in Paris, in his case it was paresis, and died, and is buried in Père Lachaise. Alan Hovaness (Chakmakjian) has for forty years put forth forms of orchestra music that astonish and delight the hearing, and for pretty much all of his professional life he has been more than slightly ill, mainly with something like tuberculosis. He frequently indicates a preference for lofty themes, so to put it, and oriental, but essentially, even though his mother was Scotch, his music may perhaps be said to be Armenian. I won't try to explain this, but I believe it is true just the same, for this is about Alexander Brailowsky and the whole phenomenon of long life among people who go into music, especially conductors. Herbert von Karajan is doing great and not dying suddenly, and while many Armenians insist he is an Armenian, and that his name is simply a case of

Teutonification, Haig or Hrant or some other H name changed to Herbert, and Karayan to von Karajan, but the dynamic fellow himself has stated somewhere that his grandmother or somebody was Greek. He is a tough muscular interpreter of music, and flies his own airplane. Heinz (Haig) Gunderian who was a genius of mechanized troop movements for Germany, and Hitler, alas—he was an Armenian orphan.

And that brings us to Charles Brave, but I know absolutely nothing about him, though I believe I know a little something or other about being brave. It is a very quiet and long-lasting thing, sometimes never noticed, never known by anybody else. All nonentities I would be willing to bet anything are very brave, especially after fifty years in the world. Indeed, any man of any kind who dies out of any kind of behavior or style before he is forty cannot really be considered to have been brave—it would be a case more of foolhardiness, which while also worthy of respect and even of admiration is not in the same category at all as bravery. The first is flash, the second is don't flash, wait. And if the waiting is only for more of the meaningless, for going on being more of a human nothing, the greater is the bravery. (If you care for that kind of sentence in English, and sometimes they can't be avoided, or perhaps ought not to be, as in this instance. I'll be damned if I'm going to hang around, standing above my small portable Royal typewriter, waiting forever for a more apt turn of language, a more graceful arrangement of sounds, words, and meanings or implications, so that something will be somewhat better said, or something. Who needs it? Well the proper answer is that both the reader and the writer need it, but another proper answer also is that each of them needs something else that is even more desirable, or even necessary, and that thing appears to be movement, the cessation of which is in some respects not unlike several things that are painful to experience, or even only to behold: a fall in ballet at a moment when the opposite of falling is being performed and demonstrated, dropping dead during a lively public speech about the simple impossibility for anybody to avoid mortality, or leading the field in a cross-country run, only to disappear into a deep pit that nobody had known was there—can you see the image? Going great, moving with grace and power, and then right in front of the eye of not so much God and the whole human race, but of admiring small boys imagining themselves to be the runner, the man vanishes into the earth, and doesn't come up out of there at all, and is never seen again. That is the kind of thing that a writer fooling and fussing inordinately with words as objects to be set just so, in a kind of mosaic, is likely to compel—or to avoid, whichever is correct just here and now.) The point is that certain English words that identify certain human realities lend themselves to predictable inaccuracies, and the word brave is such a word. And what could anybody possibly do with noble, except what Alfred did, perhaps: that is, change the order of the letters slightly and make it his name, market dynamite, and establish the annual Prize—in literature, at any rate, more often than not bestowed upon almost never the right writer, but pretty much not far wrong, either, ever. If prizes are to be tolerable at all, in any case, who really cares who wins one, just so long as he is polite? In Fresno sixty years ago I first became aware of a whole family of people whose name was Brave, and the reason I became aware is that they were Armenians, and they spoke Armenian. Well, Charles Brave, who died in 1976, was surely not a member of that family. Still, who knows, for there was in silent movies an actor who enjoyed tremendous fame whose name was Edmund Carew, and he was an Armenian. I met him at the home of the director Rouben Mamoulian, and I was very nearly amazed when it was brought forward that while he was not very given to speaking his family tongue (he could never in fact speak it), and while he was almost never asked his nationality, whenever he was he told the truth, but the thing about the man that amazed and troubled me was his melancholy. I had never been in the presence of anybody who seemed so pained about his participation in mortality. We were a small group of people involved in various aspects of drama, stage and film, drinking and chatting idly, and everybody was young, or at any rate not yet at the top of his time, after which comes the steady downward movement, and there were pretty, laughing, chatting, sweet-smelling actresses about in beautiful garments, but even these delicious creatures did nothing to dispel the melancholy of Edward Carew. The next time I came upon Rouben Mamoulian in private I asked him about the man, and the famous director replied that he was by nature a sad man. Less than a year later the actor had committed suicide, but even as I say so I am troubled by a doubt, and I wonder if he didn't simply die. In any case, Edmund Carew was gone from us somewhere in the middle 1930s, perhaps not much more than 40 years of age, but possibly nearer to 50. The Braves of Fresno came upon the name, I suppose, by literally translating their Armenian name, which might have been the same as the name of the composer, Khatchadourian, except that Khatch means Cross (a Christian connection). Adour may mean Giver. Cross-giver in short. Katch is more nearly the sound of the word for Brave, as in Katch Vartan. But what I'm really saying is that I don't know how the Braves of Fresno came upon that English rendering of their Armenian name. Maybe they simply liked the meaning of the new name. They were around, but they aren't any more. I believed they moved to Los Angeles, and are around there. Does it matter? Does it matter one little whit? Has the whereabouts of the descendants of the Brave family of Fresno any connection with the death in 1976 of Charles Brave? Yes, it does. How about the way of the world? Does it connect at all with *that?* Very much so, reader, believe you me, as we say in passing.

After Charles Brave in the alphabetical list comes Romney Brent, an actor, but alas, although I am positive I saw him in at least a dozen movies, possibly manufactured by Warner Brothers, who apparently unintentionally turned out some films that became something like American folklore (of falsity, but all the same no less authentic than they would have been had they come out of authenticity: the gangster stories, that is, with the king of that genre, Humphrey Bogart, and the invention of the studio publicity department George Raft, and the brilliant employment of the short, stocky, cocky ballet dancer James Cagney, and the sensible development of the Yiddish Art Theatre, or equivalent, actor Edward G. Robinson, fat Sidney Greenstreet, the whining boy with the Polish accent whose name I can't remember, and half a dozen other players under contract to Warner Brothers). Well, Romney Brent was in a lot of films that came out about that time, the late 1920s and the entire 1930s especially, and I saw films in those days because it was part of the life I lived to pay a small sum, as little as a dime, to get into a movie theatre after the day's work, and it was part of my study of art in general, to support my evolving method of writing stories, which began to be the only source of income I was to know thereafter, in 1934. There was a blend in the identity of Romney Brent, I seem to remember, in that he could be both decent hero and dirty villain, but I don't believe films had come to the thoroughness which permitted the same man to be both decent hero and dirty villain, although there were studio braggings about some of their players, especially Eric von Stroheim, as being the star everybody loved to hate, but especially wives in dull marriages secretly becoming the women he pushed around in the weird movies in which he performed, with a ramrod straight up his ass through his neck to the tiptop of the inside of his skull. I fell in love with one of the young actresses Warners put under long-term contract at very low wages, and placed in very nearly all of their gangster films: a girl with a smile that was ravishing, and all but compelled my most profound adoration: Phyllis Brooks. And she had a way of speaking and laughing softly that were irresistible to me. I met her finally not long after I had plays on Broadway, and she was the same thing in person as on the screen. I loved her and considered the failure of the movie-makers to put her in proper films and in proper parts one of the sadder misuses of real talent—of the star-order, for she was not an actress, pretty much the same as virtually all other actresses, excepting perhaps a half dozen, like Bette Davis and Evelyn Brent. Evelyn Brent? perhaps you are asking yourself in astonishment and disbelief. Yes, Evelyn Brent: for I fell in love with her, too, but never met her, and besides being ravishing in her beauty, she was able to do a fair variety of parts. Again one or two of them with Romney Brent, most likely—Evelyn Brent and Romney Brent in the same movie. Not a chance. Brother and sister, husband and wife, father and daughter? None of those: they just happened to have the same family name, whether given or appropriated, on behalf of career, or whatever. I never fell in love with Sylvia Sidney, but I knew a part of the whole movie audience did, and rightly so, for she was a dark little synagogue sweetheart. I met her in the summer of 1935 when she was about to become the bride of Bennett Cerf, at the offices of Random House, and she was altogether the darling of the street and slum and underworld movies in person. There are perhaps as many as a full dozen movie actresses, major and minor alike, that were unique in a way that really wrenched the heart of any beholder, in certain scenes in virtually every movie in which they appeared. We were all members of a great fantasy family, with all of the realities of each family spread out in essence in the movies that were manufactured and sent out to us, to enter into as into a different house every time we paid our dime or quarter and went in to sit in the dark and become further acquainted with one another. I must confess that I looked down my nose at every film I saw even while I deeply cherished the unintended things that were put forward in them, which did connect significantly with my own life and reality. It was great fun, but only if the poetry of comedy was put forward by a great artist, especially Charles Spencer Chaplin, but also Harold

Lloyd, pure American, Snub Pollard very early along and in very short comedies, two-reelers, and to me a very deeply significant and satisfying performer of lugubriousness, embarrassment, beautiful error, the inability to do anything quite right, and all-around unintended laughter in an atmosphere almost dead center not of eccentricity as of simple nightmare, and all-around aberration. He became a director, but to me he was one of the great comedians, and I don't even know his proper first name. The Marx Brothers, with the help of writer S.J. Perelman, came later and broke up the joint, as the saying is, and there was no resisting their blend of anarchy, vulgarity, horniness, sentimental piano and harp-playing, and for Zeppo at any rate something like sincere love-sickness. Perhaps that accounts for his becoming an agent quite early along and being virtually dropped from the team. I know he's dead—not Zeppo Marx, I'm thinking of the much more exposed Romney Brent, but I can't see him at all, while I can vividly see Zeppo's earnest face as he performs the romantic young male hero with flawless ineptitude: he looked and sounded just right. He was impossibly nobody, while his big brother Groucho nearly mounting the grand dame in full view of the world was instantly everybody.

33

Is it in order to tell the reader a few things about the writer and how he is going about getting this work written? It is not, so the writer will tell him anyway. Reader, old pal, or dear lady, or gentleman in the penitentiary, or girl in the hospital, or big man in the big man's Office, or anybody, and if it happens to be so, nobody: this is what I have to tell you, that I hope is not altogether extraneous but is also reasonably intraneous, and at the same time nice: what do we do? We do what we know how to do. I write. You do what you do. Writing is my work. I get up in the morning to start my work. You get up when you get up to start doing your work. If you are retired and don't really work any more, you still get up, most likely, and start something: you start being up. If you are too young to have a job, and work to do every workday of the week, and I hope you are, although if you are reading this writing, this book, this writer, chances are about four to one that you are either a very precocious young person, or that by some chance or mischance this is the only book on hand at a time when you really want to read, and don't want to do anything else—don't want to write, don't want to watch television, don't want to just sit, don't want to work out the details of how you are going to spend the rest of your life. For that really is what everything everybody does is all about: all doing is to the end that each person who is still alive may consider again, for it goes on pretty much all the time, and by itself—consider again how the rest of that person's life is going to be spent, for there is no person who does not deeply feel that the life so far spent is not what it might have been and therefore the rest of the life, unknown as the portion may be, is to be spent as the person believes it ought to be spent. You get up and you go to work or to the equivalent of work and get your pay or your reward or your rating or your congratulation or your criticism and you come home and sit down to some tea or coffee or beer or alcohol and you think or something thinks by itself for you as you watch or half-watch how it goes. Why don't you invent something that will instantly deliver everybody from the theory that it is absolutely necessary to own an automobile and to drive all over the place? That invention would not only make you rich, it would make you famous, and admired by young women of considerable intellectual potential, and deeply respected by those enormities of refusal who are lumped together as anarchists, a category and designation misunderstood by everybody. Listen, my friend inside there, listen, enemy outside everywhere, if you will invent something to make not racing somewhere in an automobile one of the supreme joys of the human experience, if you will send the human race of the Western World out of their houses, out of their places of employment, offices, factories, warehouses, and wherever, and if you will have them forget their watches on their wrists, and their previous schedules, and just have them not feel they must race—to anything at all, the table, the food, the drink, the television news, the clutter of claptrap, and what they really need to do (because it is what they really want to do, and have always wanted to do) is to be in the sunlight and to first just stand there and feel that light, and then to not sit down in the absurd seat of an automobile, but to turn easily and to walk lightly and to go on down the street and slowly and steadily reach open country and then, and then, to really begin to notice the awesome truth of clockless, carless, smokeless, gasless, anxietyless nature, but nature, nature, the very word has come to have a bad sound, a bad name, you will really begin not only to notice but to feel, to breathe, to become immersed in, surrounded by, blessed by the easy pressure of the air that keeps the ball bouncing a million million years, and the pressure that makes everything brought into being have its own private, distinguished, miraculous, beautiful and apparently everlasting center. Sir, if you can invent something that will take the place of the telephone, you will be the beloved hero of the whole Western World, for in the Eastern World the people do not connect themselves to the telephone with its endless wires going everywhere, to everybody—except of course to the dead, the only people really worth the bother of reaching, whether by telephone or some other connection. The American song of 1918 said "Hello Central, give me No-Man's Land" or, Give me the old buddy, my buddy, he died, you know, he was killed in a very strange and stupid accident involving gunpowder and lead and explosion, and where does that leave me, out here in Ohio, the mother of his three kids, and no money, let me talk to Charley my boy, Oh Charley, why did you get into such a mess and get yourself killed forever and ever? And if that doesn't work, try to get Charlie Manson, the guardian of the Redwood Trees of California, and all of the ecological treasures that the fools are pissing away, Charlie Manson's in the penitentiary, and you may be able to reach him and help in his noble work of preserving shorelines and forests and elephants and porpoises. Invent something, friend, to make all gunpowder and lead and explosions so silly that nobody will manufacture them, no matter what the profit for doing so may be, and will be astonished that he ever believed manufacturing them was anything less than monstrous, obscene killing, far worse than any Charlie Manson and his adoring girls ever engaged in, with their absolute conviction of righteousness. Is it in order to tell the reader stuff like this? No, it is never in order, and it is never done, but now and then, such as right now, it is more than in order to tell the reader something—it is urgently necessary to do so: wreck the car, hang up the telephone, shut off the tv, take up thy bed and walk, and walk.

Let me tell you something else. The next name on the list is Benjamin Britten, and while I have never knowingly spoken to Benjamin Britten, I have come to meet him in an autobiographical book by Ronald Duncan entitled *How to Make Enemies*, and so I know Benjamin Britten was a composer of music, and quite a good one, they say. Ronald Duncan founded a magazine called *The Townsman* way back in the late 1930s, and he wrote to me from London and asked me to send him something or other to run in the magazine. And of course I sent him something or other and it appeared in *The Townsman*, and then he wrote again and again. I sent him something or other in the way of a small piece of writing, and this also appeared in *The Townsman*, and then the War came along, and I got drafted for three years, and Ronald Duncan became a Conscientious Objector and did not go into the British army but was maligned by a lot of people on various grounds, but he fought his private fight and if he didn't win it, he certainly didn't lose it, either. He didn't lose his life, and he and his wife became the parents of several children. England needs such people. So does America, so does Russia, so does China—but Russia and China, having a special kind of social philosophy, would not be likely to tolerate anybody invoking some kind of private sentiment about war under the generality of Conscientious Objector, and the poet-writer Ronald Duncan would have been persecuted, imprisoned, and in other ways belittled, humiliated, and ridiculed. If you were to avoid maiming or death in the national army, in one or another of its miscellaneous branches, and your home and nation happened to be Russia or China, you would be expected to be cleverer about that business, a super-patriot in fact, and to avoid risk by becoming apparently indispensable in some political activity. There are always outs for the clever, but not everybody is clever. One of the best ours, and one exploited by men in every country where a draft system worked over men from the age of 18 to 40 (which was reduced to 35 in America after the first force of hysteria had somewhat subsided) was to tell the machine-men working the draft that by religion, preference, custom, and practice you were homosexual. A very young Australian newspaperman in London in 1944 said that he and all of his friends had avoided being drafted by making that declaration, and nobody among the machine-men believed it might be in order to suspect the declarations, for it is presumed that anybody who says he is homosexual *is*, period. And so the young Australian had got himself a magnificent job at excellent wages and a generous expense account, as both bureau chief, and occasional writer, for a news syndicate. Now I forgot all about *The Townsman*, and its editor, Ronald Duncan, for many years, and in fact I seemed to be sure that both were gone, forever, and then one day in July 1974 I paid three francs (or about 75¢) for a book entitled *All Men Are Islands* by somebody named Ronald Duncan, a name I was not sure I did not know. I began immediately to read the book, and parts of it two or three times, and little by little I understood that he was the founder and editor of *The Townsman*, and had published a couple of short throw-away pieces by me, and that of course we had exchanged two or three short letters. What is a throw-away piece? Just that, pretty much, except that there is more to say about it: a throw-away piece of writing is a piece of writing that the writer wants to write for a variety of reasons, knowing that the writing is pretty much for himself, and that he has really no intention of making a dime from it, or for that matter of ever seeing it in print. He writes the piece because he wants to, because doing so is part of the continuation of his education as a writer, or as a man, or if you prefer, as a human being, or even as an angel, if your mind goes that far in the dimension of naming categories—and you may as well understand right here and now that this writer—myself, that is—believes, on full evidence over thousands of years, that it is impossible for anybody to be born into this life and world and experience, who is not an angel. But this isn't the time or place to go into that. This is the time and place to go into how I came to somewhat meet Benjamin Britten—in the writing of Ronald Duncan, but not in the pages of *All Men Are Islands* (which I am sure you have noticed is a refutation, so to put it, of Donne's poetic assertion that no man is an island, a theory that went on until it provided Ernest Hemingway with the title of one of his biggest novels—to me unreadable: *For Whom the Bell Tolls,* full of clumsy Hispanic renderings into English, and coy exchanges between the hero and his strong Spanish lady friend and sleepingbag companion—embarrassing, as I've heard vaudeville comedians and patent medicine pitchmen say of male conditions not unrelated to bladder, passing of water, penis, prostate, erection, putting in place, pumping, semen, and possibly the passing of wind, usually on the part of the female party, but not impossible for the male). The book had been published in London ten years previous to my buying a copy which had been in the possession of the literary agent W. A. Bradley, 18 Quai de Bethune, and along with perhaps ten dozen other books which had not won French publication, was remaindered so to put it, to the little bookshop on Rue Clichy just beyond Trinite in my own neighborhood of Paris. I learned that the book was the first of three that were planned, and after several years got my friend in London, Gerald Pollinger, to get me the second volume, entitled *How to Make Enemies,* and that's where I read about Benjamin Britten.

After Benjamin Britten comes Harry R. Burke. (Reader: You mean that's all you're going to say about Benjamin Britten? Writer: Yes, it is, and I'll tell you why, too: the explanation may not satisfy the reader at all, but it is the only explanation there is, so it will have to do: by mistake, dear reader, I ordered ten reams of white typing paper from a Fresno business machine company where this very typewriter over which I am standing and upon which I have written pretty much everything I have written over the past thirty years—a Royal Quiet de Luxe portable, for which I paid a nice small sum in Santa Monica in 1951, second-hand, and let me tell you they don't make machines like this any more: good thing I made that small transaction way back then. I wanted the length of this typing paper to be longer than the standard 8½ x 11, or whatever it is, because around the corner from my place in Paris the paper sold to me by the stationer came longer, without even asking: 8½ by 12, possibly 12¼ (but not much more than that)), and I had found that this added length at the end of the sheet of paper was more right for me than the regular size, but in Fresno I discovered that such paper had to be cut to order and nobody would cut it unless ten reams were ordered, so I ordered ten reams and they were duly delivered and all was well, except that the length was somewhat greater than the paper in Paris, perhaps it was 13 or even 14 inches—the 8½ part seems to be standard, to meet the limitations of typewriters. Well, I don't like waste, and while the new size was a little too long, I began to use it, both for correspondence and for new writing. Out of one sheet I could get four replies to letters and just use a scissors to make each reply separate, and this was a grand time-saver, for all the fooling with paper and envelopes tends to be both tedious and time-taking. I read somewhere, furthermore, that it costs any man who hires a secretary about 88¢ to send a reply to any letter, no matter how short, and I just didn't want to bother about that kind of silly and useless extravagance, or perhaps more properly, downright waste. Furthermore I don't want to have my letters go through the rigamarole of a secretary. I can do it all right in the first place in less than the time it would take to get the secretary only *ready* to hear the dictation and to jot it down, about half-wrong, too, in shorthand, in the lined tablet, the very sight of which offends the sense of direct action and simplicity. And so I was stuck with ten reams of first class thin white typewriter paper that was oversize, so to put it. Well, I decided, dear reader, and thank you very much for hanging on, but if you have been asleep while reading, that's all right, I fall asleep that way reading all the time—I decided to use up every sheet of paper in those ten reams—500 sheets in a ream makes it 5,000 sheets—and by God don't crumple one sheet and throw it into a wastepaper basket. That is the behavior of boob newspapermen, and writers who are taking a course in writing. And the idea was quite simple: single-spaced, each sheet filled from top to bottom constituted a chapter, and that was it. I had to live by that procedure, and I must say I found that it made good sense. Each page takes about 80 lines of about 10 words each, making about 800 words, which for all practical purposes is far better than about 50 lines, and about 500 words a page. Of course various editors, stuffed shirts and awful bores, especially at certain magazines and publishing houses, point out icily that it is requested that the writer use double-spacing at the very least, and if possible triple-spacing. I ignore all such hot or icy suggestions: I don't run their business, and I don't expect them to run mine. Every writer follows a procedure that makes sense for him, and the procedure I have just very poorly explained is my procedure. I want about 80 lines of typing to a sheet of paper, and I don't want any murmurings from protesting editors. That is the reason, dear reader, that I have said pretty much all I am going to say about Benjamin Britten, for the simple reason that I came to the end of the sheet. Is there anything more that might be said about Benjamin Britten? That is to say, by me, by this writer? There most certainly is, but not at this time, and very likely not at any other time. Never again, I've had my chance, and if I said almost nothing about Benjamin Britten, about his music, which I hear is quite good, well, I have no memory at all of ever having consciously heard one tiny portion of it. You can write forever about anybody, because anybody connects almost instantly with everybody, and while writing about only one person could keep you busy the rest of your life, it seems always to be in order to write about a lot of people, although in all truth every writer writes only about himself, and that includes historians, as A. J. P. Taylor, the English writer of history, has pointed out. Writing is writing, it comes from a person, and if you write about the origins of World War II, for instance, it is you who is doing the writing, and the writing is essentially about yourself. Someday, some day, dear reader, get some longplay discs or some tapes of the music of Benjamin Britten and listen to that music, and I think you will remember that I asked you to do so.) And so it's Harry R. Burke's turn. Harry, I never met you, but as you are dead and listed in *Variety*'s famous Necrology of 1976, I am willing to presume you did something in the general vicinity of entertainment. I hope you did it well, but I am sorry I doubt it. It isn't that you might not have done it excellently, it is just that really nobody does anything well, so why should you be the exception? But enjoy your death, you earned it, and earning anything takes time and doing. Enjoy the mud in your mouth.

How sad it is not to know the dead, for we shall soon enough join them, and then how shall we answer the questions of their eyes, or even of their mouths: what is it with you? what took you so long? how did it ever happen that you misunderstood everything so desperately?—so you gave it the best possible go, the old college try, and you worked and worked, so now what have you got that we haven't got, you poor silly savior of the sad stupid human race—do you get the picture at last? do you know what it was that happened, that happens, that is happening? or are you still determined to make a difference? well if you are, go ahead, let you crack the ice and glass of ten billion years with the arrow of your jitney thought, which in any case is not yours at all, and only a very limited and unfortunate soul would even half-imagine that his thought was *his* thought: it is anything's thought, it is not even anybody's thought, it is only anything's thought, thing, thing, not think, think, thing, man, just think a moment about thing, for thing is king, king is lord, and lord is thing: think about that please in passing or even in pissing, do you remember how you pissed and pissed and thought nothing of it? Well, it may have been the best of the whole thing, for here in deathland, as the radio hacks might put it, there is no pissing, think of that, too, you unfortunate unhappy fellow who worked so hard for so long believing and believing, so what came of your believing, answer me that. But how really right it is not to know the dead. How can you know that which according to our understanding is not? That which is not, sir, that which is nothing, how can we know that which is everlastingly nothing, how can we know himself fully named and with his story attached like the afterbirth to the newcomer in the world, when all he is is debris, not even good decent dust, which has dignity, but slop, garbage, slippery stuff, disgusting stuff you might even say: himself all gone back into what the Armenians call zubbeal, zubbeal, worked-out stuff, even ecologically worked-out: nothing, slippery stupid nothing. How right it is only to know the presumed name of somebody who died, the poor bastard finally gave up the ghost to the rejoicing sorrowing family, gave up the bookkeeping to the automated automatic government, gave up the gathered hoarded money to the law and the lawyers, gave up the old clothes to the members of the family mentioned in the will—to my grandson Zubbeal Zuurroutzel my white kid shoes, wear them and walk in dignity, if you dare. How wrong it is to take even an idle interest in the absurd and entirely fraudulent dead, named or not, known or not, honorable or not, or nothing or something or neither or both, how wrong it is to put into a fine long poem thoughts or intimations of something or other instead of getting along with it in the clearly defined program of being there, right, and right there, rather than so much as turning to look into the direction of no more, all done, all gone, which is the direction of down insofar as earth is concerned, up insofar as something more than earth and physicalness and body and reality are concerned, to the left side insofar as that is concerned, or to the right side insofar as right-sidedness is concerned, or through and through insofar as through and through is concerned, or musical notes in humming language or machine roarings insofar as some kind of symphony of something is concerned, or around and around in and out of everything known or imagined and forgotten and misunderstood is concerned, good God, good God, why hast thou not at last forsaken us so we might pick and choose who we are and what happened and why something else didn't happen and why we aren't something else or somebody far less than we are, which would perhaps give us more than half a chance to be independent of the nagging connections, what do we need with light light holy light everlastingly first in things of substance and ourselves of substance and then in things not of substance and ourselves also at last not of substance? What do we need with all that gathering and gathering of the irrelevant details of how it happened but didn't happen at all, and why it happened but actually didn't, at all, and all the rest of that inaccurate but meticulously weighed-out and measured and stupid stuff that really never was, all the while hanging in as if it not only always was but would always be, always be, never never not always be? Why hasn't anybody anywhere ever done one small thing which is impossible? Why has everybody done only the possible, and only magicians and charlatans done things which have seemed to be impossible, but have been tricks, and fully explainable tricks? Why didn't Conan Doyle come back from the other side and chat at tea with the old ladies of London's Spiritualist Church or whatever it was? Why did Houdini fail so dismally in the simple matter of communicating with his designated accomplices and friends, even within the bounds and limitations of more of his bogus behavior, called magic? He might certainly have done a little trick of death to start speculation and talk that would be likely to go on for another couple of thousand years, but the writer of Sherlock Holmes, he failed, and the wizard of escape, Houdini boy himself, he failed, and nobody knows what happened or what happens when somebody stops pulsing with life, with the dance of the ebb and flow of sea and pulse when it ceases, and all is stupid silence, which I must hurry to tell you, reader, is just what the doctor ordered, don't you care one it or iota about that, there is intelligence in these things, these limitations, we don't want the second coming of Jesus at all, or the return of Conan Doyle or Houdini or a beloved kin, all we want is something like the return of each of us in the morning waking from the wonder of sleep and all that strange connecting with pulsing nothing.

And after Harry R. Burke comes Marion Burr, but what can I do with Marion Burr? I not only don't know her, or him, I don't even know if she or he came to the name the way Marion Morrison came to his name John Wayne, although one suspects that John Ford was the avenue by which Marion Morrison, he himself, walking sideways and fully devoted to America as he sees fit, and is not devoted to any America as anybody else sees fit, came to the name that became famous in cowboy movies not only in America but all over the world: little Indian kids of the Kowanis Indians admiring him even though he not only fought their greatgrandfathers in movies, he considered the squawking of their fathers and mothers weakness and the consequence of not thinking: do the Nil and Nilco Indians really believe the whole juggernaut of progress and civilization and wealth and success and abundance going to commit suicide so they can have buffalo out in the great plains to shoot with arrows—for God's sake, folks of Indian blood and culture, how can you ask such a thing? Is Marion Burr a name or a person, as John Wayne is a name but not quite a person. Is Marion girl or boy? And what brought her or him into *Variety*? Well, the answer to each question or half-question is: I don't know, and I don't even half-know. Marion Burr is there, apparently 35th in the alphabetical list which in its entirety is five or six times 35, thank the Lord for that, for it is my work to notice and remember everybody on the list whom I know, and to say whatever I must about everybody else, such as this Marion Burr. There is this that I believe I may say: thirty or more years ago I met a producer of plays in New York and the reason I met him was that a girl I had just met with a rather ripe and luscious body, very white under the clothes, had once been interesting to him, to the extent that he had had her in his life and apartment for at least a full month the first time, and then a week or so now and then, and finally overnight many times, and at last in for two or three hours, and sometimes only for less than an hour, and she wanted him to see who she had somewhat not failed to have interested in her, body and mind both, or personality and spirit, and indeed I was rather pleased by the relationship between the round and white of her and the unaware mind and very faint spirit of her. She liked sport, and had the experience of either a born expert, if you can call that experience, and you can, or the acquired skill of the lady to whom the body and its female area are solely for pleasure, not excluding the letting out of a small body, as in the travail of birth. As it happens, this luscious lass Jenny never had that experience, and I do not remember hearing her speak about having miscarried or aborted, so there is no accounting for how it happened. She is now seventy I suspect, but in the tradition of her kind could pass for maybe half that age, and if not, if she seemed somewhere in her truth every one of her seventy years, I believe many men would still want to tumble her. She was not a tiny woman as Miss Mae West is, and right now making some kind of comeback at the age of 84 (and possibly more) in a first movie in 30 years, the movie chockablock full of the Muscle Men of the nation and the world, the whole thing spurious (Miss West never did much more than tease her film audience into imagining she was an all-out specialist at fŭcking), but Jenny was and perhaps is at 70 such a lady, and while like Miss West she professed acting and had done a dozen or more plays, her parts had been so insignificant as not to bring her fame or money, but right enough for her to continue customers of her bed, and almost forty years ago I was gladly one such, although in my case, in the tradition of my own established rules and procedures, I could scarcely be called a customer, and certainly at most took Jenny now and then to drink or to have some food at the Automat, so what's wrong with that. So she took me up to meet Burr the play-producer, and he was a little bit of a wizened fellow heavy with wealth, at the center of a rather large apartment in central Manhattan full of expensive antiques, including the best booze out of the best private bottles and the best booze-carts, and so we drank and talked and he said one thing that I remembered: I am a physical coward, and I think I can say why. It is a matter of the stomach entirely. Metabolism. My stomach has always been super-sensitive, that's all. Marion Burr died last year. Burr the producer, he died too, but so far Jenny the actress, she did not die, and I am absolutely delighted about that. I hope Jenny keeps right on bedding, whether married or single, in serious affair, or easy shortstop, until other antique-collectors with squeamish stomachs have given up and passed, crossed over, gone on, joined the majority, settled into the truth, given up the bull and bravery. What we want when we work so desperately with the living is that we shall have an improved order of the dead. So far our dead are insults to death, and I should imagine that the Lord of Whatever It Is has got to stop and say to himself, I'm being sent culls, flat tires, miscarriages, frauds, oversize movie stars, when am I going to be seeing people who have died, who have lived, who have actually experienced death, who are not a disgrace to both the world and the after-world, who make me want to hang my head in shame about being in charge, for they are even less worth bothering with at all than themselves by the billions over the centuries in the place of matter and reality, that inferior place. When, when, when is death going to be death, and not a crybaby variation of what they have taken to calling life but which is zubbeal, man, slop in the Armenian language?

Godfrey Cambridge died on set, as the saying is, at one of the big studios in Hollywood. Heart. The newspaper account said that he toppled over, and very quickly mouth-to-mouth resuscitation was attempted, and other physical actions to restore a beat to his heart, but he was dead, and the part in the movie that was being shot had to be given to another actor. The part was that of the big black man who is the President, King, Emperor, Lord and Master of Uganda, by name, Idi Amin Dada. We might think of it as being a good easy part for another big black man, Godfrey Cambridge, but it is permissible to suspect that he himself did the part or agreed rather to do it solely because it was work and money, for he had remarked many times on talk shows late at night that he saw no reason why he, an actor, should be obliged to play only black men because he happened to be black. And of course there have been men who have performed in plays and movies as women, not to mention that in some parts of the world, such as Japan, it is traditional for all parts in all plays to be performed by men. I was reading just last night that there are some languages, including the Armenian, in which there is no sex gender, and I myself instantly recalled that that is so, and one is not able to say he or she, it is invariably *ahni*, or that one. And soon after having several times remarked that he was an actor who was entitled to play characters with white skins, Godfrey Cambridge put on whiteface, as many whites in showbusiness put on blackface, including noisy Al Jolson, and he ran through a whole movie as a white man, but it was clearly somebody in whiteface just as Al Jolson singing *Mammy* is clearly somebody in blackface. Godfrey Cambridge was a big man, but nothing like Idi Amin Dada in the basic structure of footbone to anklebone to the kneebone and so on. He was more puffed than laid-out that way, as Idi Amin Dada is. He may now and then have reached a bulk weight of perhaps 280 pounds, which at worst is not much more than half the weight of Orson Welles, who has special clothes designed and stitched together in various shapes to cover his bulk—but goes on talk shoes and holds lighted fourteen-inch $4 cigars, and insists upon performing magic, which does demonstrate that this huge fellow is at heart a small boy. The magic is the same that we have all seen ten dozen times, and which we see half a dozen times every year on TV, but the former wonder-boy of speech and performance does the boring tricks as if in the expectation of compelling the helpless admiration, and love, of the whole human race. I have never understood magicians, for it is understood that they are tricksters, and it is demonstrated by each of them that they have worked hard to make their tricks seem real, and yet they seem to insist that their tricks be the cause of wonder and admiration not so much because of their fantastic discipline and skill but because now at last the tricks are not tricks, they are the real thing. But no magician has ever done one very small piece of business that has ever been even in the general vicinity of the impossible, or the miraculous, and that is surely the thing that was intended for large Godfrey Cambridge, just fallen over on set, in the midst of work, the victim of what we used to call heart failure. Now, of course it is getting to be usual for mouth-to-mouth resuscitation to be successful, so that that which had for centuries seemed impossible has suddenly become not impossible, and somebody who had apparently dropped dead has been brought back to life, and this is something very much like a breakthrough fear and even horror to swift practical behavior on behalf of prolonging life. It is an event of the medical profession, not the philosophical profession, and not the religious profession, and not any of the many other professions which concern themselves with the immaterial aspects and dimensions of life, but almost exclusively human life. Such resuscitation must come to a man with a vital determination to hang on, to live some more, as a miraculous gift not from God, or the gods, but from the party who had taken training in what to do immediately when somebody appears to be the victim of death, upon the stoppage of heartbeat, and while this is a physical piece of business, the survivor may readily prefer to consider it an act of God, a gift, a miracle. On the other hand, there have been people, mainly men, who having been rescued from death through clever swift means do not exactly feel gratitude to their rescuers, but consider them busybody nuisances. As for the suicide thwarted in his attempt, the matter takes on other complications, because it does seem that many suicides are no more than desperate and demented cries for help, and when acted upon are accepted as if by a rather silly child. Godfrey Cambridge told Johnny Carson on one of his guest appearances on that talk show that he had had a very frightening experience in New York with a taxi and a taxi-driver, solely because Godfrey Cambridge happened to be black—I never got it quite straight, but it seems he hung onto the taxi from the outside, by design or by helplessness I don't know, and was obliged to move his feet very swiftly while the taxi raced up Avenue of the Americas. And so he was suing for ten million dollars, something like that. Suing the taxi company, and the driver, but really suing the United States, the white race, world racism, and possibly even racism among blacks of various kinds. I never met an excellent actor, but I saw this particular excellent actor hurrying up New Bond Street in London to a brand new hotel there, and I did feel he really oughtn't demand so much of himself, or to move that way among the leisurely people of London.

39

But what are we talking about, what are we really talking about? All of us who talk in print, who put our unspoken words into lines across sheets of paper, and then into publications of all kinds, into newspapers, into magazines, but especially into books, which we suspect or imagine or believe last forever, and sometimes almost seem to do so—if we take the idea of forever with a grain of salt, and presume our forever is a grain of sand in a universe of sand, one little grain among the uncountable piled-up and piled-upon grains making size immeasurable—reader, notice the writing and do be amused: this writer never fails to get out there into all that immeasurable stuff, and there must be a reason, but if there is, that too is beside the point. What we're dealing with here is a very simple question: what are we talking about when we talk about the human dead? Of show business, pretty much. And of only one small year, the latest concluded one, by our reckoning, and calendar, the year named and numbered 1976? What is it that we think we are saying, or hope we are saying when we dwell upon another of the alphabetically ordered and arranged names, connecting in some way or another the dead name and the dead person to the living writer, and the whole living lot of us here and there in the current year, in the current month, which is now February, and 1977. What are we saying? Is it some kind of adieu, so to put it? Is it hail and failure, O unknown friend? Or is it fuck you, old fart and fool—but the vulgar words just enough beyond permission as to be almost never put into print, but real all the time just the same? Are we glad they died, or are we sad, or is it more as if we are really neither, and know about the fact, the event, only by accident, in a flash, and give it no more than that much time: a tick, and no more than a haphazard reconstruction of some sort of real or unreal connection with each of the dead, evoked only by the name of each, and a running-along memory of each whom we seem to have known somewhat? Does anybody really care about the coming and going of anybody else? Except of course of those who are his own, his very own, in his own tribe? About those perhaps there is something that can be called caring, and it may be in the process of drawing breath, as simple as any action of being, of staying, rather than any action of choice, of large connection and relationship. And even if and when the coming and going is of those who are close, members of the same tribe, does anybody really care, does the survivor mind at all, really, that a brother or a sister, a father or a mother, a son or a daughter, has been carried out of the vale, has been stopped, has sat to the table at which the banquet of mud is served. Well, if we do care about our most intimate of connections, it isn't the consequence most likely of anything beyond natural helplessness, and however inaccurate our theory of close connection may be in terms of the real genetic force and form, whoever we knew as from the beginning must seem to us, when put out, dear to us, ours, the very prop and support of our own presence in life, our own reality in sequence, our own known movement to the same end, with all of its indecisiveness, all of its indecorum, all of its absurdity, all of its almost totally silent and unnoticed meaninglessness. We connect through connections, and any connection will do, keeping us there until the connection breaks from our nearest, our most remote, and our long gone and never known, and we with all of them are out of it, and without knowing, without even suspecting, what it was that we were in, or why, or how, and except for our kidding around at wealth, fame, effectuality, good timing, smart stance, vigor of movement, except for a few of the things of this sort, totally without even something useful to measure and imagine. Why is death so much more than non-death, or being, or life, which we have always struggled with as with totality? Why is that totality so much less than the unknown and very possibly totally unreal totality of the very absence of even a part, let alone a possible total? Ah, nonsense, nonsense, you may wish to remark, as I at this very instant do cry out: that is nothing at all the way anything is, and the only thing going on is some sort of usage of language, in this instance English, and some sort of rambling about some sort of known overlapping and underlapping of some sort of unknown, all of it imprecise and impossible to make precise. The way it is is the way it is, and it is comely and mute, and mute, and even in the midst of the racing in the rapids of language, it is still all mute, it is still all comely, there is nothing really known, and there is nothing really capable of entering into the known, wherever and whatever it may be, and there is nothing like even a beginning to numbering the sides and sides and sides and pieces of its composition—and let me tell you this, reader, old sir, old lady, and young man, and young woman: don't you bother your head or any other part of yourself about any of this sort of thing, for as our dearly beloved and lately lost Will Shakespeare himself, however you choose to spell his magnificent name, as Will said, If we live in language at all, it is only after we really live, after we live outside of language, as mute as not only oceans but mountains, not only serpents but stones. And if our dear boy didn't say that, what business is that of ours, since anybody who says anything is each of us speaking, is he not? What are we talking about when we believe we are talking about in and out, about arrival and departure, starting and stopping—all in the English language—we are talking about our dismal but blessed ignorance plagued by our awful and awesome need not to be ignorant, or not quite so ferociously, that's all, old unborn.

40

Now comes another dearly beloved, lately departed, Vahan Ajemian of the famous Sundoukian Theatre of Armenia, in Erivan, where only three months ago I saw for the first time Ajemian's production of *My Heart's in the Highlands,* which I found so different and so appealing as not to be really the play I wrote, but profoundly enjoyed, and more than enjoyed, sitting there in the crowded theatre, hearing the Armenian words instead of the English, and the Armenian music composed by Arno Babajanian instead of the Anglo-Saxon music composed by W. B. Courtney, and then arranged by Paul Bowles. Instead of being a one-act play of about 55 minutes duration, it became a 2-hour play, but whether it had an intermission somehow I can't remember, perhaps therefore it did not. And now I do remember: it did, making the evening a full evening instead of a short one. Ajemian in France is spelled Adjemian, but either way Vartan is Vartan, a King of Ancient Armenia, a winning warrior with grand helmet and a picture of authenticity. But the news of the death of Vartan Ajemian, which reached me only last night, and indeed his death is out of place here, for he died sometime in January of 1977, and this has got to be or is supposed to be solely about a few who died in 1976 and happened to be listed in *Variety.* Even so, even so, I have got to linger a moment with both my friend Vartan Ajemian, and with that name, which is widely-distributed among the Armenians both in Hayastan, our word for our country, a fragment of our historic and still very real Armenia, broken up by both Turkey and by Azerbaijan, the people of which break down priceless works of art and sculpture and architecture and use them in pavements and foundations for huts, God help such really lovely people, so abundant in numbers, so determined to be there, and so unfortunate in anything else, pretty much—but should we say to that: so what, so what? They're here, aren't they, and under pressure crying like women, men and women alike, for if you have looked at television news during the Cypress charge of Turkey upon Greece, with the full support of the American State Department, and Harvard History Professor Dr. Henry Kissinger, you could not have failed to behold with astonishment the wailings of Turkish men and women who have suffered inconvenience of some kind, or loss of property, or kitchenware, or even by separation from sons or brothers or others, or even by the loss of men in bold combat upon old Greeks who replied to the invaders with antiquated revolvers, and managed to shoot dead a few of the bold bold lads of Turkish blood. Do I hate the Turks? Good God, I love them, the same as you do, or anybody does, but I wish to Christ their politicians, their statesmen if you will, their greatest and most influential souls would demand of themselves now and then something not unlike what all other peoples, even very very primitive peoples, demand of themselves: a sustained and decent concern about coming to the truth about themselves and about all other human beings who might have their lives helplessly near the lives of themselves. But that is another matter for another time, if ever: what I am concerned about right now, in this added or intruded chapter of this book of the living, which means of the dead, is the name Ajemian, and its connection to me. First, when I reached Chicago on my way by Greyhound bus to New York in August of the year 1928, for some reason I went to a barber shop and had inflicted upon my face my first and almost only barbershop shave, so that four days later when I reached New York (those busses just didn't make the kind of time they do these days, but it may have been three days later: the whole run from San Francisco to New York was, however, ten days, I remember that), and when the bus began to come near the end of the run, after leaving Philadelphia, by God I had gotten so used to living that way, on a vehicle, going, that I really didn't quite know how I was going to take getting off the bus once and for all and starting a new, and more traditional way of living: that is, in areas and spaces that did not roll. So that when I reached New York and found a room around midnight or so at the Y.M.C.A. on 23rd street, I had a rash on my face from the barbershop shave. The next morning I noticed across the street a groundfloor plateglass window covered with Bon Ami, to make looking through it impossible, but on it a name: Dr. Ajemian, so I went in and met a very gentle man of about forty I suppose, to my twenty, and he examined the rash, applied medicine, gave me a sample of a salve, and refused payment. About ten years later he and his wife were on a flight from New York to Detroit, to visit relatives (there are many Armenians in Detroit), and the plane crashed and the good man and his wife, along with everybody else on the plane, perished, leaving two girls orphaned: Anahid Ajemian, who soon enough became a distinguished concert violinist, and Maro Ajemian, her big sister by a year or two, who became an equally distinguished concert pianist, both of them making a point of doing new and difficult and at first unpopular contemporary composers, mainly of America but also of England, Russia, Spain, Mexico and Armenia. I was deeply saddened by the death of that good man, and his wife whom I had never met—indeed I met the man only that one visit to his office—because Dr. Ajemian had been very helpful to me, and also because he and his wife had fathered two very special daughters. Last October in Erivan I spent time with Vartan Ajemian who is now dead and the night I left by airplane for Odessa where I caught a Black Sea ship that unloaded me at Athens, he said, "Well, what is our Saroyan play to be next?" "Take your choice," I said. Now, my friend is dead, and the hell with the plays to choose from for production and presentation in the Armenian language: the sad thing is that I shall never see Vartan Ajemian again, as I never again saw Dr. Ajemian of 23rd street, New York, August 1928. Adios, amigos, I am a Californian, and the influence of Mexico is great in my heart.

After Godfrey Cambridge came Nelson Case in case I didn't mention Case, which is the name also of somebody referred to as a Bonifice or something like that and if I've spelled it wrong, let no busy son of a bitch correct it—I am now far older than anybody needs to be to be permitted to let all his errors stand, especially in such relatively irrelevant areas as spelling, or grammar, or any of that stuff: by instinct the mind and mouth work to artful usage of language, and that's good enough. The Frank Case I am thinking about was connected to The Algonquin Hotel near the corner of 6th Avenue on 44th Street, and it seems that for something not far removed from a full century that hotel and its lobby, which also serves as a kind of tea-room and drinking room, by turns, and with a tiny bar just beside the entrance, and a diningroom without windows, in perpetual artificial light, enjoyed something like fame for its excellence, elegance, and other things of that order. There was a group of newspapermen who considered themselves wits which went to Frank Case's joint for lunch and once a week for a poker game, and these souls of long ago had no trouble at all becoming something like a legend, but we can imagine the probable truth about the group by recalling that one of its most popular members was a fat little old lady with a silly style of mincing speech and a decrepit soul, by the name of Alexander Woollcott—my beloved, he would write to somebody like Edna Ferber, for instance, or my own dear of dears, to somebody like Ruth Gordon—who, all the same, picking and choosing works of writing from his friends and going upon the radio, did blather so exquisitely about their books that the books became best-sellers. Or he made any play he cared to talk about into an almost instant success. Another name for some members of the group was something like The Inside Straight Thanatopsis Club, meaning of course that the poker players were the kind of death-defying daredevils and devil-may-cares who for actual money, sometimes almost medium-sized sums, would pay to see a fifth card in stud, to try to make an inside straight, which even if it happened to be made was not really all that much of a hand. These were bullshit gamblers to begin with, for they were all friends: they never sat in on a real poker game, they never really risked real honest-to-God money, or life-and-death money, and although they spoke of winning or losing, they had the comfort that if they lost it was to another newspaperman or a friend, and so on. Well, Frank Case, a man I never met, whose photograph, however, I did see in the pages of *Vanity Fair,* I believe, sometime like in 1924 or thereabouts, was the boniface at The Algonquin Hotel, and knew them all, and in the tradition of bonifaces down through the ages treated them with flattering charm, because it was damned good business to do so—but didn't treat other bores, such as hardware dealers or real estate agents, with even non-flattering charm, and I believe that that is the real reason for my totally unfair animosity toward the group which included, at least now and then and on and off, such men as Ring Lardner and Heywood Broun, the first a sports reporter who wrote great clinical reports about Americans in the form of short stories, and real wild and very funny fantastic little ramblings that nobody would ever have imagined any American could write, and the second a writer of a newspaper column of excellent intelligence, force, and humanity—Heywood Broun's enemy was fraudulence, and he found a lot of it all over the place. But Nelson Case is somebody I don't know at all. Perhaps he is a son, or a nephew, of Frank Case, who did indeed father a daughter or two, I believe: Margaret Case Harriman? Is that a daughter of his? Have I got the name right? And all this clutter of language and inaccuracy is not intentional exactly, but it is permitted to prevail because it permits us to notice how really inexact is so much that is part of us, but especially part of the reality of life and the unaccountable vitality of lore and legend right up to and including the effacement of the person involved, by death. This is all clutter because the human experience is all clutter. (But look here, I am obliged to say, isn't such a statement made pretty much to cover up a flaw, a deficiency, a failure in the writing itself? Well let's not be all that careful and protective, my dear of dears, or Oh my beloved, or Oh you kid, or any of the other endearing terms of fine men at the Algonquin Dining Room fifty or sixty years ago: let's not be sure we have pulled the wool over the eyes of truth. Of course some statements are cover-ups, that's the way we work, but after the covering-up, we are still moving somewhere with some kind of truth being dragged along, and some kind of art being slowly brought into being, are we not?) Isn't it a fact, however, that you, sir, dear writer, let us presume the reader is saying, that you began to be contemptuous of the Algonquin Hotel school of American Writing almost solely because no member of the school did you the honor of noticing your writing and making a public fuss about it, as all members seemed willing or able to do—and indeed did—about the work of friends, or the children of friends? Wasn't it jealousy, sour grapes, and stuff like that, rather than anything like real and reasonable criticism of spuriousness, superficiality, and plain ordinary and sickening cuteness of the school, especially the dumpy little old lady who seemed to dominate it for so long? Reader, believe me, if there is truth to your theory, I am entirely unaware of it. I hated them because mainly they were all talkers, and not really writers at all.

42

I also never met an actor named Jack Cassidy, and I put it that way because I might have met him, as he was looking for work on Broadway when I had been active there, from late in 1939 to late in 1941, a very short time for being active in theatre, and indeed for all I know I did meet him, for ten years after my active presence on Broadway the famous movie star Gregory Peck told me in a deep, over-earnest, unnecessarily sombre voice that he too had been on Broadway looking for work when I had been there producing and directing and casting plays, and indeed he had tried out for a part in one or another of my plays—but I had no memory of him, at all. And of course I'm not sure that I wasn't being rebuked for not having recognized a great star when a little recognition would have been welcome and useful, not to mention extremely valuable in the sense of providing income, and yet I don't remember having felt either rebuked or regretful that I hadn't recognized him. Many Armenians in America for some reason think of this actor as Armenian, and a few Armenian women, aging and terribly overweight, have asked me most earnestly if Rod Sterling is not Armenian. Well, he is not, and neither is Victor Killian, who is Irish and comes by his 'ian' tagged at the end of 'Kill' in the traditional manner of both names and the Irish. No Sebastian I have ever heard about has been Armenian. And of course there are a dozen or more popular names that end in *ian* that are not attached to Armenians, but old Armenians will never stop being puzzled by that, and actually not really believing. They are sure the people are Armenians, but like people in all groups don't want to call attention to that fact: they don't really want to go so far as to deny that they are Armenians, they just don't want to advertise it. I have heard show-biz jokes about various people who have changed their names in order not to advertise (or shout) that they are Jews, for instance, and one of these stories concerns Gregory Peck himself, but if he is a Jew, he is also Gregory Peck, and if he isn't a Jew, he is a movie star, or something like that. No black can use a change of name in that particular manner; he changes his name for other reasons, and Redd Foxx abandoned in his professional life as an excellent standup comedian the name Sanford because the idea lurking behind his new name of a lurking swift little red fox appealed to him, and seemed to appeal to everybody else, but who knows? Names are one thing only. Persons one by one are as many things as there are people, or variations of persons, all drawn into the one person involved who at birth itself is automatically every member of the human race, regardless of race, creed, color, nationality, sex, political or religious affiliation and so on and so forth—if you're out, you're in, man, and you're everybody. Let those who despise groups or individuals try to bear in mind that they despise themselves—and shall we ask if they are not correct in doing so? No, we shall not, for while hatred has something vigorous and loving in it, at any rate for certain kinds of people, most hatred is only stupid and very boring. Still, still, it is tempting, and until his dying day surely a part of even the most evolved man is vulnerable to the peculiar pleasure that comes from feeling better than somebody else. I changed my name long ago, but to a far more difficult Armenian name than Saroyan, and with an entirely Armenian given name, for William is in no way Armenian, not even by being carried by me, and Aram is, and Garoghlanian, if nothing else, compels a meticulous concern at the outset about pronunciation in anybody who has in mind some kind of exploitation of the party, or in any other way wishes to sustain even a momentary acquaintanceship. There is no such thing, really, as a hard name, a difficult name, or even a strange name: it is simply a matter of finding out how it is said by those who know the name or have given it. Only half-evolved people react excessively to an unfamiliar name. Evolved people are quick to get the hang of it, and unevolved people have the natural courtesy almost invariably simply not to try to say a name they cannot say properly, but a name they accept as a full reality and therefore to be respected. I used to see Jack Cassidy on various talk shows, and in television straight plays as well as musical comedies, for he had had experience in song-and-dance on Broadway, and he was more than competent at each, although he was no sensation, perhaps, as Fred Astaire is, for instance. It was consequently both surprising and painful to learn through television news and then through newspaper stories that he had been found in bed, dead, and the bed half-burned, from a lighted cigarette in his hand. He fell asleep and the lighted cigarette got the bedding to smoke and the smoke asphyxiated him, and then the flame moved on the smoke, and on and on and on. It is the kind of accident that is worse than almost any other: it ought not to happen, the odds against it are almost a million to one, and yet I myself (not I, the great, mind you, quite the contrary: I, the damned fool, I might even say) now and then, lying abed, not under the covers, smoking a cigarette have fallen asleep and by the grace of God have been awakened by the embers of the live cigarette waking me with a start because of the burn-pain in the fingers—but there is sleep that permits a mind to escape the burn-pain simply by releasing the burning cigarette and setting slow fire to the premises, and that seems to happen all over America, all the time. It really shouldn't have happened to Jack Cassidy, but it did. He was going good in his career, but even more important he was hearty, vital, and really a funny fellow in his own right.

I'll tell you something, reader, I'll tell you something good: you are the star of your life, knock on wood. You are the living one, old soul, inside your own skin: even when you lose, you win. (A little doggerel joke there, as we say, friend, don't be discouraged, don't get hot, keep it cool, melancholia is not the end of the world, that's something else again, so just wade along in the minnow shallows and feel the easy grains of sand upon the soles of the easy living feet—feet, great good God Almighty, how do we ever forget feet, our actual contact with the earth, our symbolic and actual contact and connection with all matter—and upon the soles of the ever living memory. Any man who permits a little bit of depression to throw cold water on his fire is not really in very much real trouble: he only thinks he is, or more likely only wants to think he is, for there is also that, dear reader: the not really wanting to be all that vital and warm-blooded and alive to the sun and whirling into the joyousness of everything always in place but never even slightly located or known. Any man who lets feeling rotten become being rotten isn't in luck at all, he's out of all of those little things that gather together into one grand reality of self, himself, allself, Godself, truthself, dreamself—what dreams we've dreamed, haven't we, old reader—earthself, heavenself—you know heaven, reader old pal, don't you? of course you do—hellself, hot hot cool cool hellself, funself, unself, superself, hold on a minute, reader, this selfstuff is the thing we may have been sailing the waters of the universe in the expectation of someday finding, but then it may not, too, so let's cool it, let's not let it get to be too meaningful in any kind of way at all, shall we, self, old readerself, old writerself, old friendself, old enemyself, it's all right, it's not wrong at all, what it comes to is that you are not going to get up out of bed every morning feeling as if the whole place is yours, or not caring to bother to notice at all whose it is, who cares whose it is, no place being really anybody's, except possibly his own body being a place and the only place that is his, the only place that belongs to himself in his own selfself inside the bodyself and of course also outside of both bodyself and selfself and out out out into outself itself making everything stay put in a kind of fluid putself, but then again maybe even his own body is not his place at all, not his own at all, it may even be the one place that is his least of all, a beautiful deception of nature, to keep everything in its place, and to keep everybody with just enough despair and joy wrestling one another to keep him within the bounds of his selfself, within the limits of his soulself struggling with his bodyself, what do we know, reader: it took us so long even to get the hang of written language in the first place. Remember when we chiselled marks on stones instead of scribbling on papyrus? Well, we're still just as slow as when we chiselled on stone, and of course there is no place in the world where such chiselling in one form or another is not still going on—go to the cemeteries and read the chisellings on stone and you may very well be astonished by the simplicity and rightness of it: name and measure: that's it, goodbye old folks at home, this world is not mine, I was only passing through, and now I have done with it, reader, old customer of air and glacier. No need, no need at all for any writer, any reader, to be down in the dumps just because he's down in the dumps: that's living like a fool, that's having life literally, without its inexhaustible and bouncing error of abundance, that's getting things so right they are more wrong than when they were not nearly right but were not really so wrong a reader or a writer couldn't get hisself—not himself but hisself—couldn't get his own self full smack into the clutter of all selves of all times and of all airs and glaciers and all flames and orange meltings of all rock for the invention of all coolings into all continuing errors, no man in his right mind or in God's right mind—ah let's just leave God in his own mind and out of our right or wrong mind and let God go on sleeping a moment or two longer before the alarm, good God let's try to be polite to God for a change no matter what or who or where or why God is or may be invented into being—or no man in the right mind of his own silly famous ancestors or infamous near-ancestors is ever really going to believe without a big horse-laugh at himself that there is anything at all about himself that is of even the most rudimentary order of relevance, and yet, and yet, his very shape and isolation from all other shapes is the fullest possible demonstration of relevance itself, all relevance, the relevance of everything to everything to everything and back again through nothing and nothing and the heart of relevance through nothing, so don't despair, reader and eater, but at the same time don't get so good at not despairing when you are despairing that you don't know your very own air from the earth's own despair, because if you do that, and get good at doing that, you are likely to discover that both figuratively and literally you have joined earth in earth's own breathless despair, and are actually dead and buried and just don't happen to have any of the haphazard apparatus left with which to tell the difference, and won't be the day, all done, never begun but already all done, the self's own self all undone and redone and again never done, just there, just there and with not enough gray matter anywhere with which to know the geography of the terrain or the algebra of the empty emptiness without worms, even, without anything of any kind at all.

Then comes Rosemary Casey in the *Variety* Pantheon of 1976, but I am sorry to say I don't know anything at all about Rosemary Casey, although it is quite clear to anybody with eyes and ears that whoever she was, whoever she still is for all any of us knows, she did have a very merry sort of dancing name, Rosemary, which we know is some kind of flower and perhaps also some kind of herb, suitable for adding to tea, or to pots of stew, and to freshen the scent in a closet or somewhere not open to fluid or breezy ventilation. Rosemary Casey is a pretty name, but perhaps not among the Chinese whose mouths and ears and memories and procedures of being somehow do not know quite what to make of sounds that are so clearly alien. The Japanese might find the name reasonably appealing and useable, as they do so many musical sounds of the Western World: *izu cremu,* we all know, means vanilla, and *bezi boru,* we all know means baseball. The Chinese don't do that. But it would be unimaginative of our government not to notice that the Chinese with their great geographical spread and their enormous numbers of healthy boys and girls, and the fathers and mothers of them, the Chinese are very much unopposed to the notion of not being afraid of Americans, or the English, or the French, and so on all the way to Moscow, whereupon it is not unimaginative of any government to notice that the Chinese are very much afraid of the Russian government, and the reason is that the Russian government lives in terror of the ever-expanding numbers of Chinese sooner or later needing to overflow their geographical boundaries and swarm on into geography clearly marked as Russian—Inner Mongolia, Outer Mongolia especially, north, north, north, and all of the other places and peoples south and west. The Chinese are afraid of the Russians, because the Russians are terrified of the inexhaustible renewal energy of the Chinese. If Rosemary Casey was not a name that connected in any way at all with the reality of the Chinese, and the future in a way of the whole human race, it does not follow that there was not a connection, or that the survival of the whole human race does not continue to be a matter to think about, not only by people in showbiz, but by the giants of American literature, all of them, one by one, but especially Norman Mailer, Saul Bellow, Henry Miller, Harold Robbins, Joseph Heller, and Edgar Rice Burroughs, although he has not participated in what is fondly called The Rat Race, for having his agent make deals on his properties in which the participation of the writer himself is not a condition. Oh, cute, you are raging, dear reader, but not so, not so: Edgar Rice is dead, we know, and died a long time ago, but William Burroughs, almost the same name, and possibly from the same family, genetically speaking, certainly an heir of the adding machine and other business machine fortune, is alive and acknowledged as another of the literary giants of our age and place. And so that fully exonerates this Aesop from any valid charge of being cute, and if it does not exonerate him from any invalid charge, that is none of his business. What we are working at, reader old pal, is an essay at not understanding death—the hell with that—and not understanding life, that's as silly as the other—and not even understanding language, that also beyond us, but this, this is it: we are working at demonstrating a very small amount of the illimitable usage and indeed misusage and indeed nonusage and indeed refusal of any order of usage of any potential in any language to get things wrong and then to get them wronger and to then get them still more wrong until anybody who has survived the demonstration has got things so comfortably wrong as nearly to be right, and at least suspects out of his own small involvement in variations of reality and its opposites that there is more to iota than the universe, and less to tick of time than the age's gone and here and coming, and everything doing straight into and through nothing doing, and so what's all the rivalry among the three major television networks all about? And among the three minor killers of nature alive in human beings: breathing, eating, sleeping? After Rosemary Casey comes Carl Carmer who seems to have written a book entitled *Stars Fell on Alabama,* which in turn was shaped into a song that enjoyed great popularity and is still heard on certain occasions, especially the convening of the government of Alabama somewhere or other. He was a good writer, and apparently a man of Alabama, and he didn't die young, he died old, but not as old as some, including a couple of dozen other Alabama men and women, several of whom are up there in their hundreds, so to put it. Money is begged constantly from the sentimental American people by multi-millionaires who want to fight off Death once and for all—forgive them, Pop, they do not know what they do. They think they do good, and they do, but only each of them for himself. They want to be adored by the multitude, and they seem to be able to believe that they are, and especially by the unfortunate little children that they present to the American people on television who seem only to wish to Christ they could be left alone, to try to adapt to their excessive limitations with a little dignity and decent separation from the rich and successful and old and damned silly. Everybody wants to do good on a wholesale scale after he has played Las Vegas and made movies and talked on television and been to the White House to do five minutes and sometimes even been presented to the Queen—of England itself, and lived to be inoffensive about it. Rosemary Casey and Carl Carmer died in 1976, that's all they did, and they did it well and with dignity.

Gloria Chandler, and although I have no idea who she is, who she was, I very much appreciate the label, the name, in its entirety, and in its two parts: was there ever a nicer name to give a girl than Gloria? Or Glory, as I have indeed heard girls named Gloria called, somewhat for short, but more as diminutive or a nickname or a name to show greater affection. I have never heard the shorter Glor at all, but Glo, or Glow, is well within the range of possibility, and it is consequently not anything like an amazement that I have heard those sounds, or rather that sound, the sound of Glow applied by a relative or friend to a girl named Gloria, which of course is a very glorious name, as it clearly says. Alas, it is placed upon creatures who cannot be considered equal or appropriate to the name. As for Chandler, it was one of the finer automobiles on the main streets of Fresno sixty years ago when I began to sell papers there. The Chandler was a fine car, and it had a good place alongside the Hupmobile, the Reo, the Stutz, and the Pierce-Arrow—think of it, the Pierce-Arrow: shoot an arrow, it pierces—possibly Custer himself. Nowadays you hear a television jingle, invented to encourage you to buy a car: Me and my Arrow. But it is nothing at all like the original Pierce-Arrow, which you can see for yourself, I presume, either at the Smithsonian in Washington, or at Harrah's Museum of Antique Cars in Reno or somewhere. Everything we have ever had, sometimes in extreme abundance, and at a very modest cost, we still have, but in a museum, and if you wanted to buy one of something gone along to antiquity, the cost would be too much, that's all—a Pierce-Arrow which at best cost $1,000 might now be $100,000—and the owner would hesitate, and might even refuse, to sell it, at all. Gloria Chandler might even have been a member of the family which manufactured and marketed the Chandler automobile, but of course even if she were, she herself had little connection with that side of the family's genius, she would have another connection with the American experience. Do I wish I knew what each of the dead of 1976 in *Variety*'s list, what each of them did? Well, no one would refuse information in favor of ignorance, but there is really something to be said for not knowing too much about any of our dead. God knows, and let God have that honor exclusively, or almost so. I see Gloria Chandler as if she might be Trixie Friganza strutting her heavy body across the stage of the White Theatre on Broadway across from the Public Library in Fresno, but I have an idea that Gloria Chandler was nothing at all like Trixie Friganza, but who knows, who knows? They strut, and we sit, and they go, and we get ready to go, and the Orpheum Circuit vaudeville goes, and is gone, and then it's Las Vegas, Miami Beach, and the Catskills, pretty much, but I have heard that desperate people in showbiz get their agents to book them into Fairs of all kinds, and even into Conventions of all kinds, and why not? Everybody has to do his thing, and showing-off is the thing that acting people must do, so who cares if the audiences change? And how about the great outdoor spectacles, in which the action is more like a pilgrimage to a holy place, and everybody smokes pot? And all sorts of freaky-looking souls comport and make noises and shout and scream and even sing the kinds of words that are within the range of experience of the freaked-out faithful? Millions of dollars are in it, but I never quite knew if all of those pot-smokers had rich parents, or if all of them stole to buy the grass, or what? But there is really no need to notice the insatiable hunger of performers for exposure, for the sight and sound of people come to see and hear them. Once somebody has heard applause, for instance, nothing else will do. That's what it comes to. And applause is not restricted to excellence. The volume may diminish for comparative lack of excellence, but no performer goes without applause in some measure, even if only for sheer bravery, or nerve, or for reasons impossible to imagine. My own theory is that applause is really never for the performer: it is for the applauder, but we needn't go into that strenuously. When the rich fish display their faces and clothing and jewelry and furs and elegance at the opera and applaud at the end of the first act, or after a solo, nobody is unable not to notice that the applause is also for the faces and jewelry and elegance and a lot of other things suspected, possibly even including crime and disease. But let us also not be damned fools about the brothers and sisters of show business, to lapse into the obsolete language of Henry Louis Mencken of Baltimore—the brothers and sisters bit, that is—our good friends the clowns and cutups, the big stars and the little stars of circus, sideshow, Shakespeare, musical comedy, and everything else performed on a special stage or place for the applause of an audience: all of these people are admirable, without exception, if only for the reason that it is work that they perform, it is not play, however much it seems to be play, it involves awareness of getting the job done effectively, and all such effort is admirable, and sometimes it is so beautifully done that one is altogether willing to believe that it is the sort of thing that each of us does in his own interior theatre, to no applause, to no acknowledgement of any kind, and therefore must now acclaim, acclaiming, each of us, himself. That is a rather fortunate thing for the human race everywhere, and even at ritual religious ceremonies where applause is prohibited, the equivalent of it takes place just the same in the silent applause of making the sign of the cross, for instance, in mumbling Latin, and in some sort of singing. Gloria is glory, Chandler is industry.

And then alphabetically it's Pauline Chotzinoff, and again I am in the dark. I seem to know the name Chotzinoff and seem to believe it belongs to a music critic, but I don't know the first name that goes with Chotzinoff and I don't know if Pauline is his wife, mother, sister, cousin, or a stranger. This kind of unknowing, so to put it, is tolerable, and even more than that: it is welcome. Nobody really needs to know too much about all of the people who are dropping out every day, but when their names are listed alphabetically, as they are (also) in the Yearbooks of the various popular encyclopedias, one notices that as the years go by one seems to know more and more of the dead, and yet the number known of any list is far less than the number not known—about one in twenty, most likely. At least for me in relation to a list of showbusiness people. The general list would have perhaps as few as one out of forty, or even one out of sixty, but there is no list covering a whole year in which all of the dead have not been known to me, superficially, slightly, briefly, deeply, or over a long period of time. And so it is altogether in order that the reading, and even study, of a list of the dead, in any publication, will yield only one large fact about the whole group: namely, that they are dead, whoever they were, and only a small portion of less abstract facts. For instance, the year Dwight Eisenhower died, a small portion of historic factuality came to me instantly when I heard the sad news. I saw him in London early in 1944 now and then and wrote a very brief 'talk' or 'greeting' for him to read to troops somewhere, on the general subject of conserving rubber, by driving jeeps a little less wildly. What did I write for him to say about the subject? In 100 words or less? As at grammar school? I do remember that I was amused by being invited to write for him at all, and by what I wrote, which was along the lines of: Boys, I want you to know we are all of us proud of your driving of all kinds of trucks and jeeps. You're doing great, every one of you in the various Motor Pools. I have no demands to make of you, and I pray that you keep going, each of you, and we shall soon all of us be finished with this thing, and be home again. Check your tires. Well, that's a wild guess, of course. What I really wrote was something else again, and it must have been quite good, or really terrible, for I was told that the General read it word for word. Little did he suspect that the writer of the words was none other than one of the greatest writers ever drafted into the American army, and at continuous combat with the clever lads who had found a great place from which to perform the same kind of spurious heroics and amazing thievery as they were wont to do out of the army. (Little semi-humor there, reader. The fact is it was established very early along that as long as I was a drafted soldier in the American army I would not be a writer of any kind on behalf of the army, the government, the War Effort, as it was called, the High Command, the low command, the publications, the propaganda machine, and so on and so forth. But I now and then chose to depart from this policy, for my own reasons, which had to do mainly with pneumatics and flexibility. Also, because I enjoyed turning out, for instance, 100 words or less for the biggest man in the Allied Forces on behalf of saving tires.) We don't know enough about so little as one full day and night of time endured by each of us. We don't know anything accurate about any given day or hour of mortality, of being somebody, each of us, ever, so we need not be especially disappointed that in the death of somebody we had some connection with somewhere along the line, we are unable to know who that person really was, although we know, for instance, that the person was a member of the family, whether by genetic connection, or marriage, as the word is for having a wife pregnant from your pleasure with her, and then becoming the mother of somebody identified as your son, or your daughter, or if not a wife, a non-wife, but also still the mother of somebody supposedly connected to yourself. What can you know about anybody else, at all, when you know so little about yourself, even after you spend a lifetime going to a lot of trouble finding out all you can, or believing that you are doing that, as surely Sigmund Freud must have believed he did, lighting his cigar and puffing at it sedately, as it were. Somebody suggested he ought to be psychoanalyzed, and somebody else told me that the old Viennese wiseman was very deeply annoyed, even offended, because the implication was that he might benefit from not being the master of psychiatric therapy but the subject, the patient, or the victim, even. And of course the truth is that if the theory applies to the race at large, it applies to anybody in the race. Who told me that story? The fact is I believe it was Jed Harris, the Boy Wonder of the American Theatre in the 1920s, who implied that he had no use for such stuff, but his son Jones Harris once phoned me to inform me that my son, his friend, was in need of psychiatric help, and it was my fault. I got hot and hollered over the phone that it was not my fault. But what do we know, maybe it was. Time, in my opinion, is the most real therapy for all distress, disease, and lesser dyings, or deaths, but it is quite true that some people have a desperate sense of foolishness and loneliness waiting for time to go by, and so they fling themselves into the presence of a nice quiet man or woman who has made a systematic study of how to put up with the passing of time, and the fairly comfortable waiting for death. Who knows how anybody really manages that chore of survival? It's the easiest thing in the world, and virtually impossible.

And then at last, a great Dame died in 1976, Dame Agatha Christie, who reached the age of 100 and sometime during her very last year wrote a last book, think of it, and let all men, let all of us understand how really tough and enduring women are, even when like the Dame they happen to be quite slight, almost fragile, and with the physical side of themselves by birth or preference reduced to a small portion of the entirety, and let's also not forget the Blixen lady who for the last nine or ten years of her fairly sustained life preferred to live on champagne and what else was it, oh yes, oysters. Do you believe it? I do, and I can even suspect that while such a diet does not have the approval of the experts, and might be said to be suicidal, it would seem that the Baroness, sought out in her last years by all sorts of people eager to admire her, thrived on champagne and oysters. And possibly, I would permit myself to suspect, as whim urged her to do so, had also a few olives. But certainly never a whole big pound-and-a-half loaf of sourdough french bread, as it is made in San Francisco (and nowhere else), and a pound of cheddar cheese, and a bottle of ordinary California red wine, or even only a half gallon of plain ordinary California cold water, with possibly a large red onion to make it all that much more delicious. The Baroness lived in a non-physical reality of body and soul together, or should I say *still* together, the soul steadily slipping away from the frail but apparently still strong body. The Dame wrote a very special kind of story which millions of people read with such enormous pleasure as to be considered hooked on the stuff, the same as dope fiends, as they used to be called, or alcoholics. They had to have the stories and something in the stories brought them to a kind of blending of peace and intense participation in some kind of mystery of both life and art. When I learned in the late 1930s that Franklin Delano Roosevelt's favorite reading was mystery stories, I was disappointed, for in those days I tended to believe that the ability to read was almost an injunction that literature must be that which anybody is to read. Not so, not so at all, and on two accounts: first, a mystery can very well *be* literature, and second, reading is reading, and one man's preference does not need to be anything at all like another man's. It is simply that I had the notion that a President of the United States, with such an affectation of fondness for the people, or at any rate the majority of the people, would find it in order to go continuously to the waters provided by Walt Whitman, Mark Twain, and, for instance, O. Henry. But what about other men of some significance in the world who had to read a Tarzan story every night before going to sleep? Ah, well, perhaps it is not the writing at all that makes Tarzan precisely right for a research scientist, let's say, it is the research scientist himself who makes Tarzan, or any other ordinary writing about any other kind of human or animal being something far more meaningful and useful than anybody might imagine, or at any rate when such writing is read by small boys, and girls, let us assume. The reader makes of whatever he reads pretty much anything that any order of writing can be, and I must confess that I sometimes thrust aside a truly great piece of magazine writing, because my soul is just a little weary of so much excellence, and I am delighted to pick up the memoirs, for instance, of a very boring and superficial foreign correspondent and ramble through it as if through a South American country when everything is frozen in North America. Women writers need not be patronized by men writers, or men readers, or men of any kind, or for that matter by other women of any kind. They are tough, and the fact that women did not even begin to get into the Writing Game until quite some time after men had flourished in it, means very little. (And there are surely magnificent exceptions that have been lost to memory and to the written chronicle, certainly Lady Murasaki of Japan.) And as for the size and weight of women keeping them in the light of mortality far longer than most people tend to remain there, that also is perhaps not much more than a theory, for I have not forgotten that one of the women of the London stage who died a few years before Dame Agatha Christie died was more nearly huge than tiny, and might be assumed to have been very fond of good hearty food in large portions with lots of chocolate trifle and other puddings for dessert. Three meals a day, at least, with a couple of Teas between meals, and during the run of a hit a snack after the curtain, gossiping with friends. And so they come, and they go, and each in the way that is right, right there at home, and for the Dame it was intelligent procedure, pleasant usage of time and talent, light meals, visits to picture galleries, letter-writing to members of the family and to friends, and excellent sleeping habits—early to bed, early to rise, a little lemon in warm water, or a dash of Eno Salts, and how sweet the life of a human being really is. Or the way the fat actress had it, which appears to have been something very nearly the opposite—crazy sleeping habits and hours, a heavy digestive tract churning all night, a fat gut weighing down the sagging body, the arches fairly flattening from the bulk placed upon them on rising, and an immediate return to about sixteen hours of eating and drinking heartily. England was proud of her Dame, and that was altogether correct. One of her plays had the longest run ever recorded not only in England, but all over the world. *The Mousetrap,* I believe it was called. I had at least a thousand chances of seeing it, but for some reason I am proud that I avoided doing so. I don't care for that kind of stuff, that's all. *Ten Little Niggers* was another of her big hits.

48

The question is this, the question may very well be this, it is not altogether unlikely that the proper question to be asked is this: how many of the dead died of boredom? Not necessarily boredom during the year, month, week, day, hour, or moment before giving over, but more probably from very nearly the beginning and certainly during the great times of human experience: that question deserves thinking about, most likely, and it is therefore urged upon the reader to think about it as he goes on reading, after he reads, and as he goes on partaking of the human experience, and being bored about it. There are degrees of boredom, of course, most of the degrees are tolerable, but there comes a time when a rather modest degree of boredom is really too much, and a man wishes he could snap out of it—stop feeling a large vague sorrow, for instance, in the garden of beauty and perfection itself, so to put it. In the beautiful all-female bedroom with the gorgeous broad all but naked and glowing with desire, what's the nagging sorrow about? Or is sorrow the wrong word, as it is, as it must be, as any word must be, for that terrible sense of nothingness is beyond words, beyond language, beyond spirit, beyond matter, beyond everything: no wonder English, for instance, works so diligently and admirably at finding new words for anxieties blended with serenities which all the same come to something not really unacceptable, and most of the time succeeding, but always with something left over which continues undefinable. Is death the final triumph of boredom? Is boredom the only killer? Also, just what is boredom? Are there many kinds of boredom, as we know there are many kinds of cancer? That is to say, is boredom a generality instead of a specific? And to that, sir and madam, I cry out in anguish, Oh boy, here I am this aging American writer, standing at my work-table, in the very city in which I was born, in my 69th year of time, asking in flawless English the most ridiculous questions in the worst sort of language that anybody might ever be expected to politely avoid in favor of a smile, or a half-smile. What I mean is, have I lived all this glorious boring time to stand here this way writing this way instead of not standing here this way and not writing this way? Is that what it was for? Ah well, by God, when it's time to come through with intelligence I am the man to come through with intelligence, and this is that time, and here comes the intelligence. Yes, it is quite true that I am bored, but I am also fascinated, and yes, I stayed in the vale all those long beautiful hours of time so that one morning in my 69th year, back in Fresno from the broad world, I might write my writing. If I were an Old Testament soul, or just an edge more of an Old Testament soul than I have always been, I believe I would put it slightly more dramatically if not at all more accurately: my *damned* writing. My damned writing literally or figuratively, preferably literally, for language itself both delivered us from rock out into light, from capture to escape, and also confounded us with endlessness in origins and infinitudes: start here and you must take these eleven more courses to here, from whence ten times eleven courses open up to that many places, from which, from each of which, which, which eleven more and more and you carry it through, old friend, that's what language did for us, is doing for us, why did we ever think we would be better off not being restricted to direct living communication without any complications whatsoever from language? All right, don't get hot, don't get cold, don't freeze, don't boil, just move along and do your work, that's all. Do we die of boredom? Is that the only disease? and all the others are aspects of it? I have given the matter a lot of thought, but thought isn't enough, that's all, and from all of my thinking, supplemented by all of my dreaming, I have concluded first and foremost that even if what I decide to say is true, it is only partly true, and true only part of the whole, and each part is a paltry part, so let's get that part of the paltry part straight at the outset: Yes, everything changes on account of excessive sameness, all change is an order of ending, and an end is a form of death, but the death of a human being, with his entire unknown circus being performed even while he is obliterated, the death of a human being is not to be understood, that's all. Well, is there such a large human being in the first place? Yes, there is, and there is no human being who is not that large, who does not have that incalculable largeness, be that human being only an hour out of the womb, or be that human being still in the womb—ah ha, this man is opposed to abortion, that's what it comes to, the son of a bitch. Not so, but the fact remains that the very starting of life, especially human life, is in that fact alone a circus of illimitable enormity and complexity, and you either care for life, or you don't, or you care and don't, by turns, which is part of the procedure by which being delighted and bored alternate or move along together. Of course everybody dies of boredom, so that leaves the question: Is everybody born of boredom? And the answer again does seem to be yes, and the next thing to hope to understand is, Does this boredom perhaps activate continuity everywhere, and might it be said that it may have also started everything? Or, more romantically, as I believe some critics like to put it, Was God bored when he started the celestial circus? All wrong, all wrong, forget it: if knowledge is beyond measure, ignorance is a billion times greater, and racing away for more, so what are you bored about, you damned fool? This is fun, hang in and laugh.

Vera Clarke died, but I have no idea of what: perhaps it was not boredom at all, so many women seem impervious to such desperation, perhaps because they tend to be actively involved in trials and difficulties which do not permit any other order of engagement of the full attention. Men do seem to be more prone to seemingly unnecessary dissatisfaction with themselves, and this may be the simple consequence of being that half of the whole character of the human race which implants seed and disappears, while the other half receives the seed and nurtures it inside the flesh and permits it to grow and emerge as another detached entity. Men say of themselves that they become pregnant with ideas, problems, works, systems, art, improvements, and so on and so forth. Well, do they? Yes, you can bet your life they do, for if the system exists, as it does, for one half of the human character, identity, reality, it also exists in another form in the other half, and that is the simple explanation for the non-physical pregnancy in the male exceeding by about a thousand to one the non-physical pregnancy of the female. The longing of certain males to become females, even to the extent of some kind of surgery in Denmark or somewhere else, deserves sympathetic study, or at the very least suspended judgement about the male/females and their connection to the male/males and the female/females, notwithstanding that every male and every female is absolutely equally the product of only one male and one female, and so far nobody has been born of male/male or of female/female. It could happen in a million years perhaps, but that prospect is irrelevant at this moment. The longings of males to become more like females than they are without the support of a female body might very well be a longing to have the physical experience of becoming pregnant and giving birth. And this may also be somewhat the consequence of having no capacity for becoming pregnant as males frequently do, with works, systems, art, and so on. Everybody wants to get pregnant in some way, one might thoughtlessly say, but this also is not really so, and is not really accurate. Does the hunter (in every sense of hunting) want to get pregnant, or does he want to limit pregnancy wherever it is a possibility? Women surely get bored, but because they also get pregnant, they seem to get bored less frequently and less intensely than their husbands, brothers, and sons. Or so we are willing to say, at any rate. Given the absolute reality and literal limitation of the means by which every person comes into life—blindly, that is—and as troubled kids tell their parents, without consultation, without their permission, we are obliged to understand that everything after that blind and impersonal event must be entangled in continuing blindness and impersonality—blindness is of course ignorance, and impersonality is of course generality, or human life rather than personal life. Who isn't also part of the group, however individual he seems to be? Escape is impossible, as well as undesirable. And I don't know Vera Clarke. Indeed I have never known anybody named Clarke, with an 'e' at the end of the name, an unsounded 'e' of course, and put there deliberately, by choice, by somebody for some reason. The most popular name in the English language is from a craft, but there are many who have that name spelled out as Smythe, and if I am not mistaken, some of these folks, so to put it, also ask that the name not be pronounced as we pronounce the second syllable of blacksmith, tinsmith, silversmith, or some other kind of smith, but as something whose spelling might be, for purposes of clarity, sm-eye-th. It doesn't matter, smith or smythe: it is only a general word and sound identification of a generality, not a specific. I have known some Clarks, however, but I haven't known even them really well, or as well as I have known a couple of hundred people with other dogtags, or names. Does it come to the same thing? Name or dogtag? Well, not exactly, but essentially it does, yes. And of course we know that there are people in parts of the world who get along pretty much without intricate genealogical names, or family trees: individual nicknames at best. The English pronounce clerk clark, and the origin of Clark may connect with clerk, although I doubt it. Names and naming are endlessly fascinating, but sooner or later anybody's name is almost entirely irrelevant, and that person can be almost effaced by boredom, including boredom with the fucking family tree, so to put it: so we landed on Plymouth Rock, for instance, so what is that supposed to mean? What could it possibly mean? The only value from the tribe that is worth considering is the value which is in a full knowledge of whatever has come to any given individual helplessly and without his approval—in short, you know your name and your nationality and your tribe, but do you know your self? Do you know who you are, out of all that intricate reality and unreality? And of course you do and you don't: you know the easy stuff, but the hard stuff, the important stuff, you don't, and you have got to have a lot of time to find out about it, through experience, which is very nearly the only real means by which to acquire knowledge, but included in the dimension of experience is sleep, and wow: that is a very big dimension, and a very complicated connection with not just the tribe itself but with the whole legendary human race. You may get to know a little about yourself, or enough for all practical purposes, but there is more to you than you are permitted by your very nature and history over the ages to suspect, even. And then you are gone, but don't know it: you have died, and never knew it.

50

The next name on the list is Betty Clooney, and I find that reading the name, seeing it, gives me a small shock, as we get such shocks every day during reading, or talking, when we hear something about somebody we know, or know about, or know somebody who knows whoever. Did Betty Clooney die, too? Didn't I see her in a photograph with her sister Rosemary? Didn't I see them on a television show? Is Betty Clooney the kid sister of Rosemary Clooney? I am sorry she's dead. That is how these little shocks go, how they have their flash of reality and emotion. In some instances, death is a son of a bitch, as the meaningless saying is. In almost no instance is death not a slight surprise. When that particular piece of information reaches us we go on and on not being quite prepared for it, no matter who it is that we have just heard has died. But now and then there is a death that is much more than just a slight surprise, something that just slightly engages our disbelief. And for some reason reading the name Betty Clooney has given me that kind of surprise and that kind of disbelief, and sorrow, even. And I don't know her at all. Her sister Rosemary however belted out a song I wrote with my cousin Ross Bagdasarian, and the song became an instant hit. The year was 1951, I believe. My kid cousin and I had written the song in 1939, but when I say we had written it, it is in order to understand that the word is used in its loosest sense: we wrote nothing: on a drive from New York to Fresno in November of 1939 we put words to half-forgotten Armenian folk songs, and found that some of these fittings were amusing enough to think about not forgetting forever. They say Chopin frequently sat at a piano at a big Paris party and improvised for long periods of time—in music three minutes could very well be long enough to be considered very long but I have read that he sometimes wanted to go on and on for longer than an hour, and nothing repeated and nothing from his written and published and known works, all of it pure improvisation, brought forward on the spot and out of the Chopin who was real right then and there. Well, just thinking about surely a hundred such improvisations by Chopin—and surely there were three or four times that many—fills the heart and head with wonder about what we would have to listen to had these spontaneous soundings of great piano solos, so to put it, been recorded, had there been recording machines on hand to hold it all fast once and forever. And then of course there is always the rather stern observation of experts in music, to the effect that every bit of worthwhile Chopin is in his written and published and performed and recorded works. To which there is no proper answer other than perhaps, Oh yeah? or, Says you. Chopin is so unique among composers, so much the precise soul for the piano, that I am filled with sorrow that nothing he improvised can be heard—by me, I don't care about anybody else—I would want to listen to even a one-minute improvisation of Chopin, and to speculate about it, especially in relation to his written and performed music. But isn't all composed music improvised? Well, it is of course, and it very definitely also isn't, of course. The very business of writing anything—words, notes, numbers—does something to the writer, or whoever it may be, the scientist, for instance, I suppose one might say: it puts him on guard, and the consequence is something which gains in many ways and loses in one: art so natural in the man as to seem artless, so sophisticated as to seem totally exempt from those connections which mark the boundaries of experience and its opposite, innocence and guilt. In any case, during a cross-country drive, it is almost unavoidable that games shall be invented and played by those involved, and Ross Bagdasarian, then 21 years old, and I, hit upon the game of Armenian songs with American words. The one that I insisted we must not forget was based upon an Armenian immigrant's invitation to a non-Armenian girl he had fallen in love with: "Come on-a my house," which approximated the accent of the man, who, in the song, enumerated the good things he would give the girl. The music is not unlike a yelp of longing, consequently the words are haphazard, helpless, and a little wild: "I'm a-gonna give you candy," to begin with, and then a few other things: peach, pear, Easter Egg, Christmas Tree, pomegranate, phonograph, and then finally he says, "Come on-a my house, I'm a-gonna give you my house." In short, marriage. Well, Rosemary Clooney sang the song, leaving out the explanatory verse, and it seemed to work just the same, if not better. After which, a good dozen other girls and women belted out the song, each in her own style, and a half dozen men as well, including Mickey Katz, who had no trouble at all making the song suit the Yiddish American experience, and that glorious rich language. But the song was the achievement of Rosemary Clooney, and her musical director, the great Mitch Miller. That's why, most likely, I was shocked when I came upon the name Betty Clooney in the list of last year's dead. Well, we are reminded that somebody we had forgotten, or had never given a second thought, had been alive for years, we are reminded of our separation from them, even if only in thought, when we read that they have died, and each of these remindings inform us that the old machinery of time and the way of truth and balance is working steadily nearer to our own astonishment of total separation from everybody and everything, and worst of all any order of ability to notice that well-known and commonplace last act—not by each of us, but upon us, standing somewhere with the mouth of the reality of God and myth and universe and matter and mystery: the mouth of the face of everything fallen open: me? But I don't want to die. And the reply: Nonsense, death is your best bet, and the only blessing.

51

Why do I write? Why am I writing this book? To save my life, to keep from dying, of course. That is why we get up in the morning. It is also why now and then we don't get up, we stay abed, generally feeling guilty because something has come along during the ages and told us that it is necessary for life to get up from sleep. But when? Is it upon awakening? Well, I used to think it was, and then George Garabedian, a young doctor down from Worcester (pronounced 'Wooster'), or somewhere, in Manhattan in the late 1930s and early 1940s, suggested that since I had reached the age of thirty, henceforth it might be in order to go back to sleep after the first awakening, and so that's the way it began, and I believe a good thing, too, for while it was exhilirating to get up and get to the world after only perhaps as little as four hours of sleep, and almost never more than six, it just wasn't something to prolong, no matter what the sleep experts happened to say, think, believe, advise, and so on. I need a lot of sleep, or the equivalent. I need to lie abed, reading, becoming ready and willing and able to drop off into the universe of sleep and dream, and I do not feel at all guilty about frequently spending half the time of one day and night abed: I feel pleased about it. The question about the apportionings of time, and the usages, is this: during our up time, during the time we are in and of the world, and of its action, what do we do? Well, we work, and even if the work happens to be the manufacture of—let's say, for a laugh—plastic roses, work is work, and must be done, and it permits us to pay our way, and so on and so forth. But the truth of the matter is that after we have functioned ecologically as members of the surviving human race, married and had kids, and used the money from our work also to protect and perhaps even to honor our aged, any work we do solely for wages might be sensibly identified as dead or even wasteful work, for it only repeats what had a slight portion of private meaning for each of us only in that it brought us the money, the means by which to marry, to put forward new people, and the means at the same time to protect and even to honor the old. Having done our unavoidable ecological chores, it is not desirable and it may even be inimical, harmful to the entirety of us, the whole human family in the whole world, to go on doing this basically unnecessary work—if it happens to be the manufacture of plastic roses, or the equivalent of that. And when that is so, that is the time to stay abed longer than ever thinking about the usages of time and skill in the doing of work that is both privately and collectively satisfying *and* useful. For me, that work is writing, for the vineyardist it is the tending of his vines, for everybody else it is whatever they can decide is right, or whatever they can manage, different from what they had been more or less forced to do, solely for the money, what they had done in a willing but not necessarily painless order of enslavement, of slavery, and that of course includes all of the activities that come under the heading of hobbies. But whatever it is that is done, the basic reason for the doing of it is to stay alive, to avoid dying, whether of boredom or of functional failure. And that's why I write. It happens to be not much more than an accident that the form and structure of this particular work is based upon a list of the dead, and possibly not the most suitable list of the dead for the kind of work this is, and the kind of writer I am: might it not have been better to have asked somebody at the Library of Congress to list for me all who died in 1976 of suicide, so to put it: or all those who died in automobile accidents, but not all over the country, but for purposes of connection, at least, in California: or all who died in family disputes, a father killing the lot of them suddenly: or all who drowned: or were asphyxiated: or all who died as innocent bystanders: and so on and so forth. No, I only wanted to get to work in mid-January of the new year, and the *Variety* list was in the big issue dated January 5th which reached me January 15th, and two days later I went to work. This is not an age in which writing must necessarily follow forms and traditions and all that sort of thing. Writing is writing, a writer is a writer, an age is an age, and the business of going to work is every man's business, and he is to decide how to go about what he is to do. Am I obsessed with death? Is that it? Bet your life I am, how could I possibly not be, how could anybody not be, especially you, yourself, still alive, alive, O, as the song about cockles and mussels goes. There is a portion of any man's time when it is impossible to believe in his own death, and then there comes a time when he knows in his bones that that time is gone, a change of thinking has taken place, as well as a change in other things, one and two and three, one at a time, and he becomes so interested in the unaccountable and unpredictable way of death in everything, but especially in the human branch of life, that a great full entertainment comes forward out of life to enrich his hours every day and night: new people are dying every day, and as the years go by he notices that he knows more and more of these new dying, he notices that many of them are people whose living time connected with his living time somehow, and frequently in ways that are intimate—a girl a man had loved has died an old woman, for instance, and the man thinks, Well, dear little Violet has died—well, what about all those girls and women I didn't really know at all, who I only bought for a few minutes, in the silent whorehouses of San Francisco? Are they all right? Or have they all long since died, too? I write to remember, and you read not to forget, or something like that.

Lee J. Cobb died, and I believe I read about it, and was shocked: for I met him at least a dozen times during twenty or more years, and I never forgot that in a movie directed by Rouben Mamoulian, but perhaps it was by somebody else, Lee J. Cobb, aged not much more than 21, played the father of John Garfield, a talented violinist who insisted on becoming a prizefighter for money,* and so of course what we marveled at was the virtuosity of a man younger by a good ten years performing the part of a father—not to mention that both players performed immigrant Italians and were immigrant Jews, and that the playwright was an immigrant Jew, Clifford Odets. Odets was Odets, and his Philadelphia people were not poor by any means, and might be considered to have been well-to-do. Garfield was Garfinkel, John was Jules, called Julie. Cobb was something else, and so was Lee J. We return again and again to this business of names, and rightly, for everything has to do with identity, and usage of anything attached to it: in the playwright it was writing, and in the other two it was acting. I knew all three, and John Garfield was a friend, even though we met infrequently, but when we did meet, as in San Francisco several times, he fell in with my ramblings in that city—to bars, restaurants, gambling houses, and even houses of ill repute, where the girls were all thrilled to see him, and immediately began to tell him about having entertained other famous movie stars, not excluding even Clark Gable himself, about whom legends seem to persist that might be said to be meaningless, malicious, mean, the consequence of jealousy, and so on and so forth: first, that he had false teeth, and second, that he was not at all the cocksman his voice and style of acting would suggest. A little Asian girl said he was a joke in bed, so to put it, and John Garfield did not feel at all obliged to defend the honor of a fellow movie star. For some unaccountable reason Lee J. Cobb found himself in the American army during the Second Chapter of the

World War, and it soon enough became well-known that he didn't like it, that he broke down, that he was hospitalized, and finally that he was given a medical discharge after not much more than a year—but none of this has any element of accuracy to it: all of it is gossip that gets around, although I do seem to remember that once on a talk show on television (of course: where else is it possible for a talk show to take place?) Lee J. Cobb spoke about his ordeal in the army. I don't know if he enlisted or was drafted, but I do know that many who felt obliged for one reason or another soon came to their senses and knew they were not equal to the demands made upon a private in an army. Who is? Well, hustlers are, gamblers are, for they start crooked card and dice games, and leave the army after a few years very rich—I knew two hustlers from Turk Street who deliberately enlisted in order to do that, did it, and came home without a scratch and with a fortune. And there are better men who also are equal to membership in an army—they aren't necessarily romantics about being soldiers of righteousness or civilization or democracy, but they do believe in the army and in the war, and in the winning of good things by means of winning the war. Lee J. Cobb was not apparently able to win himself over to any such useful style of belief and behavior. He was a big man physically, he had a lot of weight in bones and muscle and flesh and nerves to carry, and in chatting with him one soon enough gathered that his nerves were those of a fine and excessively sensitive organism. He was out of the tradition of the Yiddish theatre, in which it is routine for a very young actor to play very old characters. I like that tradition, just as I do the tradition of the Kabuki theatre of exploiting costume and make-up so effectively as to make it entirely believable that a male actor is in the drama itself a female of both youth and beauty. All the same I was never quite able to believe in his Italian father in *Golden Boy,* the film, a part done on the stage by Luther Adler, I believe. Lee J. Cobb's father just didn't somehow ring fully true, although belief is invariably volunteered and sustained by every member of an audience at a play or a movie. We were there to believe, and so we did. His triumph was Willie Loman in *Death of a Salesman,* and I happened to have been at one of its earliest performances—if indeed not at opening night, although I can't be sure of that. He was a salesman with a fairly large territory, and a line that was dull, and two sons and a wife and a rotting house and death staring him in the face from everything everywhere. Change had taken place when the curtain went up: youth had passed, the promise had failed, his sons hated him or were innately useless and disappointing to him, the boys of the neighbors infuriated him for being human and even important, and so on and so forth: a beautiful tour-de-force by Arthur Miller, beautifully directed by Elia Kazan... but somehow, somehow bogus, by reason of being narrow and profoundly incomplete—to the point of annoyance: how can anybody accept being so exploited sitting in the audience, by something so basically contrived both by playwright and director, and so expertly performed by Lee J. Cobb and his wife in the play, Mildred Dunnock? It's a conspiracy to belittle our deepest and most inviolable emotions. I was certainly ashamed of my tears, as I always am, and must be, when I am tricked into shedding them. Lee J. Cobb was magnificent in the part—and then because he had done it so well, along came half a dozen others who were not only as good but possibly even better.

* *The film directed by Mamoulian in 1939 was* Golden Boy, *and starred the young William Holden, in his first major film role.—Ed.* "Well, there we are, folks, a big fat mistake: John Garfield did not appear in *Golden Boy,* directed by Rouben Mamoulian: it was William Holden, but I know that John Garfield played a similar role in a similar movie entitled *Humoresque,* I believe, written by Fannie Hurst, I believe, but let's try not to get every little insignificant and irrelevant detail absolutely right. The wonder of it is that Rouben Mamoulian didn't cast John Garfield in *Golden Boy,* for he was an old friend of Clifford Odets, and one would imagine just right for the part, since Clifford Odets may very well have seen John Garfield doing the part, as it may very well be he did in New York on the stage. We live and learn, don't we, folks? Well, we *say* we learn, at any rate." —W.S.

"Hoo boy, did you die?" the merry question went about somebody in an English grave, and something just as merry came back in reply, but I promise you, reader, I will not look it up, so if you want to, go ahead, it is a joy to have and to believe happened, as of course it did, or something did, or there would not have been any such chiselled question and answer on a tombstone of long ago. Now, it's William Cohan, but again I know nothing about the man, although I did admire when I was hustling papers and magazines in Fresno, George M. Cohan, for his memoirs began to appear in a new magazine that I began to sell from its first issue to perhaps its twelfth—was it a weekly? Yes, I am quite sure it was. And George M. Cohan's memoirs starting in the first issue at (was it 5¢ or 10¢ a copy? 5¢ I am quite sure, whereas *The Literary Digest* was 10¢ but not nearly as popular as *The Saturday Evening Post, Collier's,* or the new arrival, *Liberty,* each at half the cost, which is always significant to people who buy such stuff as of course some people always do, as I discovered when I sold both *The Saturday Evening Post* and *Liberty*). George M. Cohan's memoirs started in the first issue, as I began to say, and got sidetracked, and they were accompanied by photographs of himself, his father, his mother, and his sister, and they were just the thing for the immigrant son of the immigrant Armenian poet-preacher to admire—doers, and stylish doers, each and every one of them. And so finally after what seemed like many years, but turned out to be—from about 1918 or 1919 to about 1939 or 1940 comes to, what? Well, at the most twenty years: after about twenty years I did meet George M. Cohan and was rather touched by the sorrow and dignity of the man and a decent resignation to the years which had clearly overtaken him and stopped him in his tracks, finished his brashness and confidence and his all-around American Yankee Doodle Dandy delirium, as sung and danced by James Cagney when he did the movie of the grand lad whose people came from Ireland and were Irish even though pretty much everybody else named Cohen, Cohn, Cohan, or Kahn or anything else like that was Jewish, and clearly and rightly gladly. George M. Cohan was a sad man, that's the simple long and short of it: and a few years later I began to suspect why he might have become sad: he had a son and the son hated him and considered him a fraud and a tyrant, and the son finally wrote a life of the father, and the whole unfortunate and surely much-distorted lamentation of the son came out, in cold print—but at least by that time George M. Cohan was dead, and George M. Cohan, Jr., as I believe he had indeed been named, soon afterward committed suicide. Did a son of Walter Winchell do the same? Certainly the sons of many interesting men did commit suicide. It happens all the time. You almost never hear of a father committing suicide because his son is so mean and famous, and so given to coming on strong. George M. Cohan wrote and sang "Over There" at the height of American participation in World War I, although Enrico Caruso also sang it, but let's face it: when an opera singer sings a popular song he shits all over it. Opera singers just can't seem to cope with the songs of Tin Pan Alley and these days of Country & Western or Rock & Roll, although they insist on trying, on Talk Shows (I keep mentioning Talk Shows in lower as well as upper case, and there is a reason: they are not only what's happening, but are a very special order of material for not only sociologists to study, but for all of us to both enjoy and study), and whenever an opera singer sings something totally unsuitable for him, by its nature, he is generally out of opera, but unwillingly, and very pompous, and with a voice that is shot, which had never really been any good at all, and he does this rotten singing with so much condescension, so much American humility and so much participation in what the foolish young prefer over Puccini and what my cousin Johnny Saroyan used to call Leon Cavallo's Bizet, that the silly solo in front of five million astonished late-night people all over the country is absolutely unbelievable and yet for some mysterious reason really grand entertainment—unintentionally, of course. And it isn't that the whole thing started with the accented singing of the man in the big musical who sang "Some Enchanted Evening"—was his name Gigli? or what? The old women wet their pants as he sang, just as if they were their granddaughters sitting beside them, the guy was so virile in voice. He didn't start the business at all, he just cashed in, and rightfully, in a kind of mighty money-show that was as nearly the same as any opera as any kind of show could ever be—and I'll be damned if I am going to improve that rotten language, either. Beniamino Gigli? Was that it? All such singers are a pain in the ass, and should either sing their trite little boring arias from actual operas, so that the deterioration of their voices would be fully revealed, or they should just talk, the same as all of the other bores on the talk shows. One exception: both at real opera and at popular songs, transformed by his singing into great art: John McCormack, as you will find impossible not to notice if you will listen to "Your Eyes Have Told Me So," and "I Hear You Calling Me," as well as anything else he recorded from Broadway. He was a singer who dignified any song he sang—he had that kind of voice. For all I know, though, William Cohan is a son of George M. Cohan, and might even be the son who hated the father and wrote the scurrilous biography of him, and didn't commit suicide—and just last year finally died and joined the sad old but everlastingly young man. That's us and that's our story, that's all, fathers, sons, youth, age, merriment, disgruntlement, life and death.

54

I like being alive, but there were early times when I either didn't like it at all, or didn't like the kind of living I was doing, or thought I didn't, as at the orphanage in Oakland, and of course there are times when I do not feel any special pleasure in being alive but at the same time do not feel any special displeasure with it—certainly not for myself, for I have everything, and there is no reason at all for me to find any particular fault with the way I put up with time and the world and the human race: but I do feel a kind of astonishment about the hundreds of millions of human beings, each of them that very thing, a human being, and each of them born into circumstances which make continuing to be a human being so nearly impossible as to be unworthy of the struggle. Now there is a decent impulse in every person to be helpful to those who need help, and help is continuously rushed to great numbers of people who have suddenly found themselves the victims of cataclysmic events of nature, of weather, for instance, or earthquakes, or fires, or wars, or famines, but after that emergency help has been carried to the people, the situation returns pretty much to what it had been, and it is then pretty much what may be said to be by all of us of all our situations, that they are tolerable. We put up with units of time because what's the hurry, and what is a unit, it is only a small portion, so if the worse comes to the worst—is that the wording? worse? worst?—what have we lost, in any sense, by hanging in and waiting, waiting some more. And of course soon enough waiting becomes living. But I haven't got time to go into that just now, which means I don't want to, and that is another thing I have, perhaps the best thing that I have: I have the circumstances which permit me to decide what I am to do and when, and that's the better part of having everything, of course. But of course of course, of course of course: and not of course at all: for I have worked to provide myself with the circumstances, and it was not easy, and was against odds, and after having done so, as the big Mafia man in court said in his high-pitched voice, I pay taxes. Apart from giving up to another Mafia the man was obliged to hire lawyers to help him from giving that Mafia—the Government—too much of his money, and this made a lot of extraneous thinking and anticipating unavoidable for him. I pay taxes and I feel the nagging of the Mafia at me all the time, and there is nothing for it. If you've got to have your freedom, you've got to pay for it, to people who had no part at all in getting you to your freedom, and so on: but I like being alive, and I don't like not being alive. All the same I have now and then thought fondly of being out of substance, out of the body, out of the house, the city, the world, the worth, and into the everlasting, into nothing, into death, into full absence. But that was surely part of liking life, too. So the question is this: Do the dead like death? Do they like being dead? And the answer is, in the lifelong running joke of my cousin Archie Minasian, None of your business. (With a comic Armenian-English lisp.) The fact is, and don't we know it, though, the question is silly, the answer is silly, and the procedure of question and answer, the very form and see-saw of that procedure, while not silly, and on the contrary really the wonder of the human story, the fact is that all of the questioning and answering down through the ages, among the wisest of men and women, and children, and humans and animals, and humans and Gods, and humans and ghosts and phantoms and formless and fearful creatures and forces, all of that asking and answering has had a large element of absurdity in it, and something more than absurdity, something deeply touching and pathetic almost, one side of us asking and asking, and another side of us answering and answering, and all sides of us entirely unequal to the fluidity and speed and continuous inaccessibility of even one small aspect of truth—and even the word for it itself, the word for truth, entirely inaccurate—unequal to anything better than what is common to all detached living things, all animals—the exercise of the senses, and the compulsion and ability to procreate, and thereby to continue our kind—up to a point. And thus both by asking and answering, and by neither, among our kind, which are the majority, we have continued, we have survived, we are here as we have been for a long time, only now we are here excessively, and neither by asking and answering, or by neither, are we able to understand what it is that we have done, how we have done it, why we have done it, or if indeed we have, at all: for it would seem that whatever happened, whatever it is that may be said to happen continuously and to have always happened, which we believe we have caused to happen, has not been our doing at all, whatever it was, happened to us, each of us happens to himself, and whatever it is that compels these happenings, which we call nature, as you know, as I may say you damned well know, is acting out of a large order of intelligence, beyond us, for a large order of meaning, also meaning us. But don't you believe it, all we can be willing to believe we are sure of is that we can ask and we can answer, and then we can be sure only that we have asked and we have answered, but we have not only not got anything straight, however tiny: we have further confounded it and cluttered it with never-ending potentials and realities, so that there shall never be anything really more clear for us than the fact of being alive, and in possession of the apparatus of breathing, followed by being unalive, and the suspension of the action of breathing. I still prefer breathing.

Sir William (not Saroyan you can be sure, although I am as entitled to any such designation as may exist anywhere among any people out of any ritual of bestowal—is that the word? is that the spelling? —let it go, let it go). Sir William Collins is on the list, so we know he is dead, and while we do not mourn him specifically we do mourn him with all of the dead of last year, of 1976, and if the truth is told all of the dead of this whole century and of all the centuries gone before, and then if the truth is told we do not mourn this man at all, nor the dead of this century, nor the dead of all of the centuries gone before, we just say we do, and it would be just as right and real to say we are glad they are all dead, even though in certain instances we know we are not glad at all, since we know who it was who has died. You've got to know somebody to be able to mourn him, to be helpless about it. And I don't know Sir William Collins. And what's he doing in *Variety* in the first place? Well, the answer to that silly little question is a very neat silly little answer: he was always in show business, and the Queen knighted him and he became entitled to adorn his naked name with the radiant garments of a royal or regal title. I prefer the titles that are bestowed upon themselves by the great musicians of American jazz: King, as in Cole, Duke as in Ellington, Earl, as in Garner (ha ha ha, because Earl is also a plain democratic strictly non-royal name), and there are a good half a dozen others. These are indeed royalty, but let us not imagine that the other great musicians aren't, for they are, too. With or without the regal designations or nicknames. I have met a number of titled gents, and ladies, and they are nice people, as people come, as people go, but I never met Sir William Collins, and now he's gone, he's gone, and I'll never meet him. Somebody not long ago wrote and published a book entitled *They Hanged My Darling Willie*, although I remember quite clearly that it wasn't 'Willie' at all, it was something else, and he was hung for having been (according to his mother, who is the speaker) falsely accused and found falsely guilty of some large crime, possibly treason, and the title delighted my soul, for the execution of any man outrages the soul of his mother, if she happens to be that kind of a motherly woman, just as the achievement of any great honor leaves another kind of woman altogether unimpressed about her son, and she goes right on really disliking the poor man. It is said that Ernest Hemingway's mother was such a woman: first, it is said she persecuted her husband, the doctor, the writer's father and good friend, and drove him to suicide, and then she kept putting down her son as he presented the world, or at any rate the literary world, with one great or delightful book after another. (My favorite continues to be *The Sun Also Rises*, called *Fiesta* in England.) But mothers vary as much as fathers, as much as sons, as much as daughters, as much as people, and nobody has written her story, or her side of the story, so we don't know anything of any real use about her: she just didn't ever get around apparently to being pleased about her son. And of course if you ever spent a week or two in Hollywood or Beverly Hills during the 1950s, sooner or later you went to the famous restaurant and met Prince Michael Romanoff, and this serene fellow performed the part with simple natural skill. Of course he wasn't a real Prince, and his family was nowhere near being like the Romanoffs, but so what? Mike had a feeling for elegance, both authentic and bogus, and he managed both so effectively that you didn't care to make any kind of distinction, and you received from one of his bartenders a good big drink and at his table you received from one of his good waiters a good big steak, and what more could you ask. H.L. Mencken once (or possibly twice) suggested an American royalty, for the fun of it, and to make the fun really worth the trouble I believe he suggested that only people like the Daughters of the American Revolution be admitted. Well, of course I've got it all wrong . . . but then why shouldn't I get it all wrong? The point is that there is always a difference in people, and to such a degree that everybody knows the rank or rating of everybody else in his encounter world, everybody he meets, and everybody in the world that is out there somewhere in the arena of publicity—and let nobody forget that there are experts who can make something like a folk hero out of anybody, and he himself doesn't really need to do anything to help. But there was a strange man in New York in the late 1930s who at the opening of the Opera Season would go into the lobby with all of the rich and social people and suddenly stand on his head while cameras flashed and the next morning the front pages of the New York papers showed him standing on his head surrounded by astonished dowagers and dandies—and he had no publicity agent, and apparently nothing to promote or sell and thereby to profit from his skill at being nationally noticed. I met him in San Francisco and while I've forgotten his name, he was real, and I hope he hasn't died, but if he hasn't, he certainly has given up standing on his head in public. At Mama Leone's one night in the early 1940s I sat at a table where a girl I knew and her favorite gossip-partner, a really gorgeous girl, were chatting with Dashiell Hammett about the tradition of that family of standing on their heads—every member of the family did that. It is a fine kind of exercise, and yoga names it and puts it in its place as another way to get the most out of being flat on your feet somewhere. I see no reason the dead should not be buried standing on their heads or their feet. Nobody lives lying down.

There are similes, if that is the word for what I'm thinking of: somebody says, You get on your bike and go, and we understand that he doesn't necessarily mean that you get on your bike and go, he means that you do the equivalent of that inside, in your spirit, and nobody is the worse for having had it put that way, but when I get on my bike I really do go, that's my transportation after walking and where I live there is no walking, almost nobody walks anywhere, although I walk to a supermarket named Save Mart (but it is really no such thing, at least insofar as the Save part of Save Mart is concerned: the prices are high, higher than at other supermarkets: so at least once a day I get out on one of two good bikes, neglecting the portable Italian bike which has such a hangar ratio that your legs work like machine parts in a cotton milling machine and you barely move, but for $55 and a carton of cigarettes to hand to crazy friends it was a fair buy, ten years ago: and I go, I actually get on my bike and go, generally to the nearby P.O. (named Hughes, but not after Rupert, a rich and once-famous writer of novels nobody can even think of by title, unlike Zane Grey for instance or even Rex Beach, and Rupert Hughes became quite a personage, even in Hollywood: and not named surely after the bearded Hughes who persecuted Woodrow Wilson about the League of Nations and got it defeated in the Senate and in the House, I forget his first name, the Hughes whose name—do you like that, Hughes whose?—is on the new branch of the Post Office, not much more than eight hundred yards as the crow doesn't fly, has got to be somebody local, and God help us there are a lot of us locals, if you have in mind putting our names on Post Office branches and schools), and from the outdoor mailbox where I slipped two important sticks of mail, one to New York, the other to London, I rode across the street to the dusty dingy entrance of the Moonglo Drive-In Movie, deserted these days but due back in business in the next four weeks for sure as the weather has gone bland, and from there straight down Dakota to the Gillis Branch of the Public Library where I ran through two issues of *The Fresno Bee,* now a morning paper, and one of *The Chronicle,* of San Francisco, and then glanced but just glanced at the February issue of *The Atlantic*—word is out that the whole staff is Boston high society and a pain in the ass about it: sailing, lunch, dinner, meetings by appointment only and all that—and I decided I would give that issue a little authentic attention at a more appropriate time. From a reference shelf I took down Macmillan's *Dictionary of Proverbs and Sayings*, and turned to Death, where there is so much chronologically that I want to get them all, and tie them in with everything under Death in Mencken's collection, and other collections, and choose from them at the top of this book, even if there are 200 or more of them, or perhaps spread them through the book, one at least at the top of each chapter, of which I expect that there shall be 88, but who knows, there may be 101, or even more, even though I am to stay close to the list of the dead in *Variety*. And just noticing that there are perhaps two dozen thin fine Bible pages of paper covered with the sayings and writings of races and individuals on the subject, if you want to call it that, of Death, I rejoiced. My heart lifted almost in literal song, for it is heartening to know that from the beginning of memory in man, and the usages of memory in writings, there have been sayings about this thing, and these sayings have both comforted and strengthened the people, some of them non-sayers, but mainly all of them sayers in ways sometimes far better than the ways which have been preserved and have got into Macmillan's reference book: Zabu of Central Africa, who came back from near-drowning and said, "Brother, I have always known Life, and now I know Death, and let me tell you, Life is better." Which was carried along from generation to generation and was heard at El Rancho Vegas in that corrupt and crazy Nevada town where gambling is legal, out of the mouth of one Joe E. Lewis, except that instead of Life and Death, it became Rich and Poor. Ha. And just noticing all those magnificent sayings listed chronologically I thought, Well, there we are, aren't we, folks. Accidentally a couple of weeks ago I hit upon a good idea for my latest book, if you are willing to call it a book, or if you dare—I am writing in this book about last year's showbiz dead, and unavoidably also about any year's dead, and about Death, and of course also Life—you can't write about one and not write about the other: if there is a face, there is also the back of the head, if you are willing to accept that simile—all right, I know it is not a simile, I am not bragging about my ignorance, but I am saying that from about the age of eight, at the latest, I have been vitally aware of the law of opposites, and this awareness has permitted me to be reasonably serene about everything, and at the same time not to forfeit entirely any natural longing I may have to believe that the lot of anybody, of everybody, beginning with myself, can with effort be improved. And I've demonstrated it to some degree in the improvement I have achieved in my own life, but I have failed rather sorrowfully everywhere else: you can love a wife, but you can't make her understand what your love means: or a son, or a daughter, or a friend, or a stranger, and by love I mean love, not anything involving the body and the action of one set of genitals in connection with another set—a man's and a woman's as far as I am concerned—and you take it from there if you will, or must: let every woman, let every man be his own man or his (or her) own woman, and let Death tell them the brave details of the achievement or disachievement. That's none of my business.

After Sir William Collins comes Ray Corrigan, but I have no idea who he is, who he was, what he does, what he did, or anything else about him, or about anybody with that name, although I do remember never quite having been able to put together the figure and face and voice of a man called Wrong-Way Corrigan who, having been denied official State Department permission to fly across the Atlantic, took off and flew to Ireland, and landed there and then said he had believed all along that he was flying from New York to San Francisco—no, Los Angeles. He was a Los Angeles order of soul, and I believe he is still going quite nicely, and I congratulate him on that, but he is no Nungusser, no Coli, no Lindbergh, and not even a Harry Richman, the song-and-dance man who sang "Putting on the Ritz," and flew around the world itself with a very skilled and experienced aviator, and wrote about it in the story of his life, which I bought one day in New York at a Marboro Shop—the one on 57th near Carnegie Hall. At his best Harry Richman was one really accomplished song-and-dance man of an order in which Al Jolson was supreme, I believe we may say, and George Jessel was excellent, especially when he sang that song with the appealing Yiddish wail in it, "My Mother's Eyes," and perhaps Eddie Cantor, and some others of that time and order. They all amused people in theatres or nightclubs, and some of them took after tail, with a lot of chutzpah and success. Eddie Cantor had a wife named Ida, and a lot of daughters, and he didn't want to be even mistaken for a tail-chaser. Al Jolson didn't have to do any chasing—tail presented itself to him, it would seem. But Ray Corrigan, although clearly connected in some way to show business, is somebody about whom I know nothing at all. I wish I did, I wish I did, because then I would be able to say something about him, from actual experience, like, Well, Ray Corrigan and I were drinking one night in the bar off the lobby of the Great Northern Hotel on 57th Street in New York, in the year 1939, early in May, when I was writing *The Time of Your Life* in six days, and Ray Corrigan said, "What are you writing?" And I replied, "Well, it's a play, but I don't know for sure if it is really a play, it's kind of free and easy, and the only reason I'm standing here at this bar is that I want to clear my head of what I have already written so far today and I want to get back and write some more, because I started writing the play on Monday, this is Wednesday, and I have got to finish it by midnight Saturday." No such exchange happened, of course, but had it happened, I would have put it precisely as it had happened, wouldn't I? The next stiff is another stiff, as we used to be told when we rolled out the ten dice at a game called 26, and not one of the selected numbers, our number, had showed its face: if you were wise you took six, because out of ten dice there was always bound to be at least one six, sometimes two, which you needed as an average for each of the ten rolls of the game, so that you would have the required 26 for the three-to-one win: I always bet a quarter and if I won got back 75¢. God help us, it was a crazy aspiration, and I had a lot of them in the years when other newcomers were going to college: I rolled 26, and either Bill or Jim Breen, at Breen's on 3rd Street in San Francisco, used to call out the number after each roll, and jot it down on a long sheet of lined and cross-lined paper, on a table: two, one, stiff, stiff, and another stiff, and if you had any sense by that time you would chunk down another quarter and start another game, for you knew you just couldn't catch up. The next stiff in *Variety* is another stiff as far as I am concerned: Louis G. Cowan, and for all I know he may have been very big at Columbia Pictures, and somebody who had worked with Harry Cohen, or is it Cohn? Whatever Harry's name is, he was a man I met and knew, and didn't dislike at all, but at the opening in New York of *Get Away Old Man*, during the second intermission he kept asking everybody, "What's Bill got against me?" He thought he was Hammer the bigshot movie executive, but Hammer tells you in itself that it stands for Mayer—L.B. Mayer, whose daughter actually produced *A Streetcar Named Desire:* Irene Mayer Selznick. Whose other daughter married another big film producer whose name I forget—Christ, senility may be at work here, but I prefer to believe it is something else—William Goetz, but the name of the other daughter of L.B. Mayer still eludes me. Bill Goetz bought a Picasso or a Matisse or a Somebody Big And Expensive, for a big fat price, and then was informed by a museum expert that it was a forgery, and it was all in the paper: but Bill died, and the forgery hangs somewhere just as if it were not a forgery at all. And Orson Welles shot a movie entitled *Fake* based on a book with the same name, and on talk shows spoke up for validity of forgeries. Why not? Just so the forgery is really a forgery, not another kind of original, shall we say—for purity, which figured as a word in *The Green Hat*, which Thomas Williams—who nicknamed himself Tennessee, for reasons of his own not especially related to writing—not long ago wrote in *The New York Times* how Michael Arlen had said that Irish March, the girl in the green hat, had died for purity—her husband on her wedding night had revealed that he had syphilis. But the fact probably is that what happened was that he demonstrated a preference for boys, which in those days could not have done at all, and so syphilis came to the rescue of the novel and earned the writer more than a million dollars when there were no taxes. A little hustler with a name something like Cowan tried to steal the film rights to *The Time of Your Life* in 1942, but I stopped the little bastard in his tracks, cold.

Is it time already for another digression, but one that relates to the subject, that is to life, that is to that supreme or at any rate ultimate event of life which is conveniently called death, which is really a kind of stateless state, and the word itself a kind of non-word, a word which has no accurate definition and yet seems to be understood (and misunderstood) by everybody according to his lights, or whatever it is? Is it time already to have another digression among a good assortment of them left dangling, along with people, along with the names of people, and if it is, and it is, then how does this digression relate to life, to death, to memory, to writing, to reading, and to the whole world of being? By being the work of someone who lives, that's how. I was drowsy very early yesterday, after the day's only meal, but a good big one, and so I went to bed, for I have no reason not to do something like that, it is my life, a lot of years are upon it, but certainly 30 less years than the years upon several people I happen to know, with whom I have spent time—Stokowski, for instance, 94, and Cane, about the same—Melville, that is: by profession a lawyer, by avocation a poet, and while 94 is not quite 30 years more than 68, it is near enough, so that I am permitted several conclusions from the relativity here: going on 69 and being at work permits me to respond to drowsiness after a hearty meal thoroughly enjoyed, and just what was the food of the meal, if that may be the way of putting it? Peasant fare: chili con carne, half homemade, half out of a can, and with a hotdog put in there and put into a slice of soft bread smeared with mustard, and for dessert a grapefruit, an orange, and a tangerine, all except the last from my own trees. The hour was almost 8 and I felt good and drowsy so I went to bed and had the electric blanket turned on full force, 10 instead of 8 or 4 or even 1, and I decided not to switch on the tape player, to old American phonograph records, a tape made by myself, and I ran through the latest issue of *The Nation*, that magnificent magazine, and wanted to sleep, so I dropped the magazine, switched off the bedside light, which rests upon a bookcase that came with a set of Encyclopedia Britannica bought at 24848 Malibu Road on the beach in 1952, and fell instantly into a good deep sleep. I woke up about 40 minutes later and was surprised that so little time had been taken up by sleep that might have been for many hours: and here I come to some of the connection I believe that sleep has to this book, or to this digression of a book: I knew the digression of that sleep would render the digression of the whole night ahead, to prepare me, to prepare the living, to prepare the writer, for tomorrow, for the next work session, that session which is now in progress, I knew that that digression of forty minutes of early night sleep would make the coming of the rest of the sleep even more reluctant than it is in any case, and so it was: the theory notwithstanding that older people both require and get less and less sleep, I have for twenty years, give or take, required and got more and more, until these days twelve hours out of twenty-four are apportioned for sleep and its accompaniment of reading. Now are these hours wasted, as I have heard people say they are? Maybe they are, but not in my life. I have to get ready for tomorrow, and so I do get ready. From the age of 8 to about 34, I suppose, I seemed to not need to get ready: I was always ready, but this was surely not so, it was only a misconception: I was young and could take that kind of use of the entire apparatus of body, spirit, character, identity, purpose, reward, and so on and so forth. I might be able to do it even now, but I am not sure. I should imagine that at best I would not be able to keep it up for a quarter of a century, and indeed I might not be able to keep it up for a quarter of a year. That's all right, too, You have your work to do, and there is your own understanding always of what it is: for me it was to become stronger in all dimensions of humanity than I was by birth and early circumstance and environment, to make myself known to the world, to exert an influence first on myself, then on the members of my family, or more properly the family of my father and mother, and then on my friends and acquaintances, and then on the rest of the human race, and of course an influence that was deeply desired by everybody, nothing to be imposed upon anybody. After that, my purpose was to attract the woman who was to be the mother of my children, to relive my own earliest moments, days, seasons, and years, in and through them, and after that to continue moving in mind and spirit to the limits that might be permitted to me—in writing, and so this is what I am writing. Is it worth it? Bet your life it is. Is it *really* worth it, writer, or do you imagine that you have got to say it is? Reader, it's worth it, it's a fight all the way, waking and sleeping, reading and writing: it is a fierce fight and you lose every day and you need time to try again in the morning, but yes, it is worth it, and this is why: there is no movement after something has died, and it is action alone that permits anything—and out of anything it is always possible to make something, or even something else, and in anything it is possible to find whatever is needed for the continuing of everything, for the dance of life, for the deep waltz of the soul in all things.

Good Lord, what great ones died last year, and how I forgot them last night, and really didn't care at all that they were now gone forever, and I would never see them again, or by accident for the first time, and nobody would see them again, and I would never exchange a few words with them, I who had never exchanged a few with any of the bigshots of the human race since the beginning of time, not a word with any of the Kings of Armenia, or the great Usurpers of Assyria, or the Warriors of Mongolia, or the Philosophers of Greece, or the Wits of Rome, or the Saints of Spain: I missed them all, I didn't meet or speak to any of them, and last night I didn't even remember one of last year's dead: Polly Cowan is dead, and last night I didn't even know she had been born. I had once in San Francisco been madly in love with a dumpy girl whose name was Pauline Varaznov, like a heroine of Tolstoy, who was called

Polly, but nothing came of it, at all, although I once took her to a movie theatre on Market Street called the St. Francis, and sat in the sweet scent of a dark rolypoly daughter of a poor but upright Russian-Jewish family. In those days Paul Ash and his orchestra traveled around the country, and one of their big hits was the "Massenet Meditation Theme," so to call it, from the opera *Thais*, and this sweet-scented girl from Tolstoy with all her holy charms deep inside her sweet clothing came to be the very soul that was in that music—and except for one little failing somewhere along the line, a failing that hurt me to recognize, I would have loved that girl, possessed her, made her pregnant, married her, and established a family with her—and the failing was this, or so I am able to permit myself to say, and even to believe: that sweet young woman did not know who I was, did not suspect, and what's worse had no real desire to find out: furthermore, I soon enough discovered that she preferred the company (in her father's grocery store on Laguna Street, where after work at Postal Telegraph she helped, so that he could go from the back of the store into their house for a rest or a cup of tea) of such young men as were earning wages as apprentice automobile mechanics, and were fond of playing cute and teasing games with her, belittling games, in which there was no recognition at all of herself, no awareness of who she was, who she really was, a daughter of a great King, a Princess of a royal family, and so on and so forth: and so I let it go, I let it go, away back in 1928, and here it is 1977, almost half a century later, and last night, not even in memory of that girl, I did not remember Polly Cowan. And the girl of Laguna Street let it go, let it go, or was unable even to notice that I had let it go, and she went her way and I went mine, and last night it was nothing at all to think of her, because of the name Polly Cowan in *Variety*'s list, or for any other reason—how much of a child can anybody be at the age of 68 going on 69? And who doesn't know that even if I had loved her—I never even held her hand once, let alone put my mouth to hers, I couldn't, she was too much for such naked behavior, such physical behavior, she was entitled to having the enormous past from which she had miraculously come, and so was I—even if I possessed her, even if we married, and had children, forget it, brother, forget it, sister, it would have soon enough become what it more probably really was: a little something or other of a routine human order, and what about the kids, what about the boy, what about the girl, what about the past from which they had miraculously come? Forget it. And so last night I went right on forgetting it, first with some good reading in a book entitled *Babe* by an acquaintance of years ago—about George Herman Ruth, of course—a book that arrived in the mail only eight hours before I began to study it, inscribed to me by the author, Robert W. Creamer, who drove me out from Manhattan in 1954 to Ebbets Field in Brooklyn in his second-hand Cadillac, along with my son Aram, to see the second game of the World Series, with the Yankees, for I had agreed to write about the Series for the just-lately-founded (by Henry Luce) weekly, *Sports Illustrated.* Old Babe died young, alas, at 53, and wasn't told that he had cancer of the neck or somewhere, so that he would frequently say, "Those damned teeth," for he thought it was his teeth that were giving him a bad time, and he wanted to know why he shouldn't have them removed. Creamer coming back into my awareness after more than twenty years pleased me deeply as I read his excellent book last night, and I thought about his name, and wondered if he and I had talked about it, riding out to Ebbets Field in 1954, for I do ask people questions about their names, and I was pleased that my son Aram, who on that ride was eleven years old and is now 34—that his second daughter bore the name Cream, while his first answered to Strawberry, and then along came his son last October, about 120 days ago, and that fellow was given the name Armenak by Aram and his wife Gailyn McClanahan. And Armenak is the name of my father who died in San Jose in 1911 at the age of 36, so that in two years even my son will have lived as long as my father, and there was a time when I wasn't sure that I would live that long. We have such theories, and we are not annoyed at all when they are disproved. Babe Ruth hit home runs, and a home run is not something the French, for instance, understand or want to understand. The Japanese, on the other hand, both understand and deeply cherish home runs, and a hitter of them. A little joke, entirely out of order as it is: Was it a home run when the Babe died in a New York hospital of cancer? If so, whose home run? His? He could cry, to be taken by the termites, as he put it, and indeed he did cry. What about crying? Is that a home run, too?

The dead, the dead, the poor dead, the wonderful dead, the lonely dead, the stupid dead, they should never have died, I suppose, but there it is, they did, the stupid bastards, they up and died, and it was really not necessary: everybody who has studied the matter in depth says it is not necessary to die, ever, but one by one everybody has died, including the specialists who had said that it was really not necessary, but they probably left messages saying that yes, it is not necessary, they simply decided they wanted to, and did, and thus became the same as the rest of us, the living who die, who must die, who believe they must, or believe they don't have to, as the case may be, but one thing is certain, and painful: it is no fun at all when somebody dies prematurely, and of course that also happens all the time, even to ninety-year-old folks—they die, they become the dead, they join the dead, the same as the author of "The Dead," the same as James Joyce himself, the greatest writer in English of all time, or the next greatest, or the fourth greatest, or the twenty-eighth greatest, or whatever it needs to be. He wrote and wrote and his eyes went, and he rather persecuted his good devoted brother Stanislaus, who said so in his memoirs, and he blew borrowed money on a riot of comradeship and good food and drink, and big tips—a beggar who had to, he blew the begged money as if it came from the estate and there was plenty more where that came from, he accepted the help of young men and women who also wanted to write, and they got the hard work of his big wordy beautiful manuscripts precisely the way he wanted them. (One of them, Samuel Beckett, went on his own to become one of the new stars of the literary world, in the literary firmament, and there were others who did not go on, boys and girls both, probably.) And then James Joyce got so fed up with not having money, not having elegant clothes, yes good weavings of fine white tablecloths, and sheets and pillow-cases, and curtains, and good clothing, good dandy clothes for a dandy man, a dandy boy, with a dandy stick, and dandy glasses to perch upon the bridge of his nose, and this condition of being bitterly fed up brought on an ulcer, or two ulcers, or half a dozen, and these ulcers gave him very bad times, but they had their seasons, they came and went, and they came and they went, and in the meantime he loved Nora Barnacle, his wife, and he loved their daughter and their son, and he loved his writing and the characters in his writing, and he loved the world, and he loved the human race, and he hated really nobody except possibly the Pope and everybody, but sometimes he loved even them, as the pain of the ulcers arrived and departed, and then the War came and there he was in Austria, in France, in the very homegrounds of the War, and that isn't what did it: it was something else which is clearly in his writing if somebody clever will fish through carefully and find it—perhaps "Carry me along Tad like you done at the toy fair," if that is indeed what he put near the end of *Finnegans Wake*—James Joyce has left all of the meanings and messages of his life and death in all of his writing if anybody wants to get right in and bring them out, and suddenly the ulcers, the ulcer (one is enough and in any case isn't it always one at a time) flared up rather more than ordinarily, possibly because of the War, possibly because of the failure of money to come to him abundantly even after he knew in his heart that he was the greatest and almost nobody wanted to say nay to him, except possibly Henry Miller, who must have met him in Paris, or tried to, they were there at the same time, for years, and also during the 1930s when so many people believed that the time had come to turn the human race upside-down and straighten out the world and establish righteousness and decency in all of the cities, and be human, really human, or by God be shot for not being human, and anybody who didn't go along with that big pushy program was sneered at by the rest of the silly little raging mob. James Joyce was put down by the communist writers, as they called themselves and one another, because, they said, he didn't care about the whole human race, and because his writing was a game, a private game, inhuman almost, disconnected from purpose, it was one long sustained tour-de-force of masturbation: Henry Miller said that, implying that his work was one long sustained tour-de-force of straight fucking—much better, you see, women, you know, the stiff prick into women, you know, the vice-president of the Bowery Bank at least in appearance put down the dandy boy of Dublin, and so did the communist boys and girls, but that didn't bring on the last flare-up of the ulcer: it is in the books he wrote and somehow managed to get published in spite of all of the opposition of Rome, of Boston, of anywhere at all, the ulcer flared up and this time it was bigger and better (for itself) and worse for James Joyce, but he was sure it would go, or so I have read, and Nora was sure it would, and the world knew nothing about it at all, being busy with Adolph (Hitler, you know), and the literary world knew as good as nothing about it, too, and at best only a few people anywhere knew anything about it, and then they carted the great man in terrible pain to a hospital somewhere—perhaps it was in Zurich, perhaps not, but it was in Europe, it was not in Ireland—and the medical staff at the hospital fell on him, to help him, to get him safely out of the valley of the shadow, but they failed, James Joyce failed, he died, the author of "The Dead" died, and he died too soon, he died prematurely, even if he had done pretty much all the work he should have done, he had done it all, but he shouldn't have died, not from a perforated ulcer, not from peritonitis, not from anything, he was too young.

If there is anybody who loves life, who loves it more than anybody else loves life, or anybody else has ever loved life, let him not despair because of death: let him rather despair because of something else, anything else, life is life and despair is despair but let that man who loves life so much not despair because of death, despair because no government has ever been able to make sense, to write laws that are really useful, and listen, sir, listen, madam, death isn't your enemy, life isn't your enemy, the government is your enemy, and if the government is also your friend, and probably among the very best of all of your friends, it is certainly at least that order of tyranny which also maintains something called law and order, which signifies something like protection, the rottenest government if you don't annoy it will in fact give you some kind of protection against your enemies, and if you don't have any, against your friends, and if you don't have any, against unknown enemies and friends and against mad people prowling the world intent upon murder—for if your government is not protecting you night and day from those prowlers, how does it happen that you are still alive: who is protecting you? So if you are that great lover of life that every red-blooded human being is, don't despair, settle down and never say die, as Tokyo Rose (one of a dozen, poor girl) said on television when she was finally pardoned by Gerald Ford a couple of days before he turned over the President's chair to Jimmy Carter—it was beautiful hearing that girl say "never say die" after she had done a dozen or more years in federal penitentiaries, because like Ezra Pound, who did his time in St. Elizabeth's Hospital, she was supposed to be guilty of treason. Or something. Lover of life, go right on being a lover of life, and say never say die, and say this is great, this is life, this is the truth, and don't let any such misconception of any such event as stopping plunge you into despair, and I'll tell you why, too, sir, and lady, exactly why: it is this: stopping is not stopping, and it never has been, but *Variety*'s list for those who seemed to have stopped during 1976 next comes up with the name Douglas L. Craddock, just so, and I not only don't know what the L. is for, I have no idea at all what he did in showbiz or on the fringes of it, so to put it, or if he was a lover of life who had now and then despaired about death, and possibly really got panicy when the message began to come to him rather excessively clearly that he was very near stoppage, total and irrevocable, as the insurance company double-language likes to put sour nothings—good God Almighty, what are we to do not about death but about the insurance companies and their great staffs of lawyers and writers, and we know very well that even while we ask what we are to do we have answered the question very succinctly, if you will, with the one grand Anglo-Saxon word *shit:* that's what we are going to do, and thank God for that too, it is our life and our truth and anybody who doesn't is in a lot of trouble. Do you believe Luther frequently didn't? Would you go so far as to imagine therefore that that was the reason he had to go after Rome and after his interpretation of the uninterpretable, the totally unnecessary to interpret, and thereby to provide millions of very nice people, Teutonic for the most part, with their own ritual inside and outside their own church, and with their own confidence that now everything was just fine so that when they died, as die they would and did, in the body, and only in the body, though, they would die into Lutheran life and go right on being Lutherans, and very good people. And after Douglas L. Craddock—and nothing said here implies that he was a follower of Luther, a self-confessed constipated revolutionary ecclesiastic, or of the Smith who founded the Mormon branch of the Christian religion, nor indeed does this imply that Douglas L. Craddock was a follower, even, of the religious ritual and system of Douglas L. Craddock himself—but after him in *Variety*'s list comes a name that is even more troublesome: Massimo Dallamano, most interesting for being both so poetic and so musical and so danceable, and Italian most likely, although it might also be Spanish or even French and possibly even something else one would imagine must be unlikely, or even impossible—he might be a member of any race at all, for names are names and they go around as they please to whomever they please, and none shall stay their going. Whoever he was I never saw him in person, in performance, on film, but he had surely been there or they would not have noticed that he had left. And then comes Oscar Dancigers, and again the mind knows not this man. Who is he? And is he correct in spelling his family name differently from so many others with the same name? And why did he do that? Three excellent dead, three excellent men with concluded lives, had they been painters, for instance, like Matisse, Picasso, or any of the other bigtime money painters, immediately after they had stopped breathing, business would pick up, for once the source of the paintings is stopped, the hustlers can begin to do their bookkeeping and start buying and selling and trading, and best of all arranging with great geniuses for the painting of forgeries to pass along not only to new-rich ladies and gentlemen, but also to museums which need the prestige of a great painting by a great painter—let it be a forgery if it must: but these gentlemen were neither religious leaders nor great painters, they were something else, and since I don't know what they were I can't tell you, reader, what they were, but from their names alone perhaps you can guess as you please, or simply decide it doesn't matter one bit that they died: they died, and *Variety* listed them, isn't that enough?

Now comes Meyer Davis, but first I must remark that a couple of hours ago as I struggled to get up and to get the rigmarole of a new day, a Saturday, Lincoln's birthday, started, I asked myself: Is wakefulness a violence upon sleep? How many hours a day of sleep does it take to make us repudiate wakefulness? Why is sleep so attractive when it is time to get up? Well of course these questions are other questions as well, obviously, and especially the one question: Is life some kind of violence? If so, upon what? Absurd, absurd, stupid and ridiculous, how can anybody ask such a question? Unless I have it wrong, and I very frequently do, Meyer Davis was a bandleader, he was a musician, he was famous for taking one or another of his many bands to big social events, and even to the White House. The music played by his bands was safe and sensible, and he and his musicians were not scandalous people, and would not be very likely to embarrass anybody who had hired them. Stuff like that. I had a chat with him when his son was much in the news for refusing to be a citizen of anything less than the world, and consequently refused to get a passport (or permission) to travel anywhere. The bandleader's son was considered by most people as some kind of nut, an eccentric, a slightly mad soul, or simply a man of no talent looking for a little attention, and size, for himself, looking for publicity—which he got, and so abundantly not only in the United States but also in England, France, and everywhere else. But somehow he didn't become a hero. Nobody really rallied around him and his very sensible program to break down some of the stupid fences that were put up everywhere by everybody to keep everybody else out, or in through the narrow passage of authority. He did something, he tried to do something that was very big and very worthwhile, and yet the young people who are always so eager to rush to something they can believe is the thing, the real thing, did not run to Garry Davis, if that is his name, and the proper spelling of his Garry, for there is also Gary, as in Indiana, the steel mill town near Chicago. Garry Davis never really became the central force of a crusade, and it is interesting to try to guess why not. He had to be, himself, a crusader, for that kind of large refusal to follow custom, precedent, requirement, law, procedure, and so on and so forth, instantly engages the energy, isolation, and determination which support the crusader, from our own Thoreau to the marauding Christians who were named, or named themselves, The Crusaders, who for want of farms to tend, stores to keep, books to write, poor to rescue from starvation and insanity and incest in hovels just back of their palaces, and surely to escape total licentiousness, as the word goes, or suicide, took off on long treks across Europe to Jerusalem, that strange place with that strange name, pronounced a dozen different ways, but pronounced by almost everybody, and on the way raped the best of the local girls and women and left them pregnant to bear and bring up their issue never knowing even the half of it about who a son or a daughter really was. On my first visit to Europe and to the World, in a sense, in May of 1935, on the first money I had earned as a writer, I rode in a chauffeur-driven automobile from the city called Ordzonikidze, which had been Vladikavkaz, meaning of course Vladi of the Caucasus, I suppose, and when the little car came to very near the top of those majestic snow-covered mountains I asked the chauffeur to stop, so I could stretch my legs and look around and perhaps buy some bread and black olives and white cheese in the tiny village, all of which I did. And suddenly, as if out of each of the half-dozen simple small stone houses appeared young men in mail, in metal jackets and helmets, and these people called themselves Ungush or some such, and I couldn't figure it out, at all: they didn't seem alien to that geographical area, but they did have blue eyes, some of them, and where did they get the mesh-metal mail, so to put it? Well, later I was informed that they were the descendants of English Crusaders who had not only passed over the Caucasus but had lingered, perhaps for a year or two, and some of them perhaps until death, or forever, and that was how they got both the costumes of metal, and their name, which of course was their rendering of English. A likely story, as I've heard doubt put by everybody sooner or later, but especially by Groucho Marx, speaking with his peculiar crisp American English. I sensed that Meyer Davis felt at least a little embarrassed about his notorious son Garry, perhaps because everybody was expressing something like sympathy to him about the boy, the man, as if he had gone mad or had had a terrible accident and might die of it, or that he had been killed in some strange violence. And so I said, Well, your son is involved in something very important, and you must surely be very proud of him. He's not in the wrong, you know, we are. But the bandleader, who resembled a very dignified businessman, a banker, for instance, or the vice-president of an insurance company, would not go along with my theory at all, although he did try to let me know he was grateful that I did not consider his son a silly exhibitionist of some kind, demanding the world's attention, and getting it, and then not being able to do anything worth a damn with it. The father and the son, what a time they have, and always have had. So what happened to this son? Did anything come of his crusade, at all? Well, it's on the books and it's too early to know what has come or shall come of it—anarchists and criminals have always traveled without passports, or with forged passports, of course.

How does the mind of a man go, how does the mind of a writer go, how does the life of a man, writer or reader or neither, how does the life of a conscious man go—or an unconscious man—and is it this question of how something like the measure of mortality, or is it in fact the opposite of that, of measure or meaning, and the beginning of the infection of death, of conclusion, of inevitable disappearance, for is it not in intelligence, in doubt, in speculation, in disbelief, or in the revision of belief, in awareness of relationships, of sizes, of weights, of measures, of connections in time, in space, in seasons, progressions, upswings, downswings, failures, successes, is it not in self-consciousness, in short, that human life both differs from and is in some ways inferior to all other forms of life, but especially the animal forms? Well, be that as it may, the fact is that man has certainly come these past ten thousand years, possibly ten times that many years, to something that might be loosely considered to be intelligence, which while not the same as grace is probably the means to deliberate grace (out of any inevitable grace, which we certainly see in all animals), is certainly the best possible potential for anything and everything to which any living form might aspire, or to which it might helplessly go, or be guided to, for let us try not to forget that our intelligence, and everything else, may not be anything at all like an achievement by ourselves, but may be a gift or a charge or a burden placed upon us by nature itself, and by all other things which might be considered to be in league or partnership with nature: all that we are, to paraphrase what Abraham Lincoln said about his mother (was it actually his step-mother? for if it was, wouldn't that be a beautiful tribute to that maligned order down the ages and in the legends), that all that we are we owe not to ourselves but to our mother, which is the very way of actions in the unending and perhaps unendable ballet of living matter. We did it, we did it, hurrah, we did it, and then we discover that no, we did not do it, not by a long shot, it was done to us, we were carried along by a Doing far more vast and powerful and subtle than we have the means, even, to guess. Joseph DeAngelis follows Meyer Davis in *Variety*'s list, and that's a name, for sure, an excellent name, a profound name, a meaningful name: Joseph of the Angels he was, but I don't know anything about him at all, and I wish I did, for every man who dies, every woman who dies, be he or she no more than Sir or Lady Anonymous themselves, each of these is somebody who has experienced the human story, but in his own, her own way, which is slightly unlike the way of anybody else, ever. Remember that, young man, young lady, there is nobody else in the human race, now or ever, who is precisely the same as yourself, and if that isn't something to be glad about, there is nothing at all of that kind. You are you, the popular songs have told us over the years, and nobody has replied, "Cut it out, I am not me, I am not you, I am a stranger who has attached himself to a stranger which is supposed to be me but also isn't, and I don't know anything about any part of the whole thing, except that man it sometimes is art and sometimes it is agony." (What's this all about? Not this chapter of this book, and not the whole book itself, and not even all books: what's all this out about, being out, with the eyes open looking out, the body out, the living spirit attached to everything else out, even in sleep out, roaming the limitless plains that are out, swimming the streams that are out, whaling through the oceans that are out, flashing instantly a billion miles from here to there and all of it out: what is all that about?—that's what we're talking about. Well, the answer is, of course, that so far we both don't know and really don't need to know, because we are well supplied with air and the breathing procedure that goes with air's own meaning, and we have water and thirst, and I want to go through the catalog of everything else that we have, but it is all of this that keeps us from any urgent need of anything more, like the knowledge that is more than knowledge, that in itself expands and enlarges and continues infinitely into illimitable traveling. Got that? Drop it, forget it, it's none of your business, just take care of yourself and that will eventually permit you and perhaps not hinder anybody else, never mind helping, just be faithful and perhaps you won't find it impossible not to hinder, which is a large achievement by itself, and so far may just be the largest, what do we know: he came, he did not destroy very many things, he did not hurt anybody, he didn't discover anything, but he really had no reason to go looking.) After Joseph DeAngelis comes Paul Dehn, and I seem to imagine that he is an actor, mostly in films, and that I saw him in films of one sort or another, and he played rather fine roles in that they were somehow really nowhere near unforgettable—he was somebody there, and he said his lines, or as the Great Playwright of London put it, made his entrances, then his exits, and was never King of England. And so we see that death comes also to actors who are not unforgettable. Willa Cather's novel *Death Comes for the Archbishop*—is it *for*? is it not *Death Comes To*? And the image of Death as somebody or something which presents itself to somebody is deep in the limitations of the human race. And perhaps the only reason there isn't the parallel notion of Life Coming To or For Anybody, is that the coming by emergence from the female invariably involves a person lacking in identity because of a lack of experience: *Life Comes for the Archbishop* would be a very difficult novel to write, most likely.

64

What is the true story of the human race? (None of your business.) Oh, boy, oh, joy, where do we go from there? (None of your business.) Who's sorry now? (None of your business.) Well, perhaps I'd better explain the foregoing questions and answers, although explanations almost invariably require new explanations. The true story rather than simply the story of the human race is, of course, the full story of the coming out and of the going in of members of the family, the holy family, the animal family, the sinful family, the innocent family, take your pick or invent your own designation, and the variety is unlimited although the stupid family has tempted many specialists and famous philosophers, but let's not believe them, at all. It takes a lot of brains to get born, a lot of intelligence to get sick, a touch of genius to have a serious accident at precisely the right time for the most undesirable consequences, a full connection with grace to misunderstand everything and everybody every day for as long as the person is in the body breathing, and there is nothing more brilliant than the absolutely perfect conclusion to the whole thing, an inspired act if ever there was one, the act of dying and the event of death. Consequently, when the wise guys tell us that the human race is stupid, what do they know? And isn't it a case of sour grapes, because they would like to be like everybody else but just aren't? Of course it is. And they have no talent at all for the fun of performing in the play, in the unwritten, never-written, unwritable play, the one which must be lived to be known at all, a play of course of error snowing all over error until everything is white and right. What is the true story of the human race indeed?! And there we have it: it is the asking of childish questions, and let's hear no more about it, at least for a few minutes, and move along with the funeral services. We all love to go to funerals, no matter what we say, or even no matter how afraid we are of them, believing that if the person in the casket could die, then so could we, but who wants to think about that, and maybe by thinking make it happen sooner. A funeral service is pure theatre, every time. I go to them when I must, and I enjoy them, but most of all I enjoy visiting graveyards, for they are the truly peaceful places of our country and our world, and they provide the nicest moments of our lives. (How can you say such a stupid thing? How can a graveyard provide us with the nicest moments of our lives? Well, it's easy, and it's right to put it precisely that way, but I have got to go now, and you have to go with me, so watch it, Buster, hold tight, Babs (don't you love that name, Babs, and haven't you always found that the girl or woman called Babs was a dog?) Watch it, hold tight, Buster and Babs, for here we go, here we go again—Christ, I remember another Sunday in Fresno sixty years ago and nobody in the family had died, but it was early February, I was eight years old, everything was sparkling and nothing was wrong but nothing made anything like a useable meaning, and somebody came with the casual news that Sissak Darbinian had been killed in action in the War at a place called Verdun, and by God still, still everything was sparkling and nothing was wrong and still nothing had any real meaning for me—beyond, beyond this, reader: that I believed in the future, a day would come, by God a day would come when the world would be mine, and I was never so sure of this as when I was at a table eating, scoffing the glorious stuff in and down—Sunday we kind of had a tradition of biscuits with butter and honey and good brisk hot Lipton's tea to wash it down, not two cups, not four cups, but at least eight cups, for I ate at least a dozen biscuits, and I mean homemade biscuits from scratch, and big, not unlike Scotch scones which my mother had both made and baked and sold in 1915 at the San Francisco Panama-Pacific International Exposition, and steaming and smelling of freshness and flour and melting butter—eating eating eating that fiery and fire-making stuff informed me unmistakably clearly and specifically that the future was mine, and the stove, silver/nickel-plated scrolled Excelsior, red hot from sawdust, $3 a full load in one of the two barns, not garages, while my mother slid the pans in and brought them out and put the holy-scented things on the big platter at the center of the kitchen table where my brother and I feasted while our two sisters both helped my mother and ate and drank all at the same time, taking care that sugar was not dropped on the kitchen floor, because that was something that made my mother so mad she cursed us all violently and made my brother think she must be crazy. (She was, but what business was that of yours—that might be said to be a paraphrase of what I told my brother whenever he brought up the astonishing, the almost unbelievable curses she flung at him, and at me, and at her two daughters as well—all because somebody had accidentally dropped a teaspoon of sugar on the kitchen floor, and she had walked upon it and felt it, and had gone berserk—or so everybody had thought.) It really wasn't the sugar underfoot, though, it was everything, *for years,* plus the sugar, and it was then that a widow of 36, with four kids aged 20 down to 10, eight years a widow, without a man in her own life, with only the men who were in the family, including her two sons: of course she flew into a violent rage once in a while and cursed us and then went off to be alone and the house became hushed for hours and even days—but reader, reader, it was beautiful, it was intelligence, our brilliance, our stupidity and madness and truth.

Our last beloved deceased of 1976 was Paul Dehn, who may have been an actor in the movies, but may have been something else that you and I don't know about, not in addition to being the actor, if he was an actor, but as his fulltime identification, as when people say of somebody, He teaches, high-school level. Or, She is an assistant cashier at the Baptist Church. And of a horse, He's in the stable of Charley Beff. And then of course we know who's died, and everything makes sense. All I know about this man though is that he died, and that the name following his is Charles DeMont, somebody I am totally unable to even guess about, but I know two things: he had to be somewhat in showbiz to make that list, and he had to be a little more than nothing to make *Variety*'s list, for unless you are somebody, however slightly so, you are not on the list. There is just so much space allotted in the thick annual issue to Necrology, and if you tried to put everybody who died during the year and whose death was noticed in the 52 weekly issues of the paper, you would find that the list would become rather meaningless: even in the dimension of death there has got to be selectivity. There is a good strong belief in all men being equal, but that is either restricted to their lifetimes, or while they are not known at all as individuals, whereupon it is noticed that it is much too much trouble not to see and to feel that while all men are absolutely equal, by God here is a man who isn't, this man is unequal, but perhaps he's got a good personality. After this man comes a rather big name in the American world: Patrick Dennis, but it comes as a surprise, though a small one, that that was his pen-name and that his real name was something else entirely, unless of course I've got the whole thing wrong. If I haven't got it wrong, Patrick Dennis wrote some real smart books, and one of them, *Aunt Mame,* or something like that, earned him more than a million dollars, and made him happy. He was a kind of witty writer, I suppose we might say or believe, but as I was never able to read anything of his beyond a paragraph or two, I can't be sure: but his books did sell, and his reputation as a bon vivant, as I believe the word is, was nicely established, and he moved in a neat and fashionable world, wearing I presume the appropriate costumes that are always clearly indicated in such worlds. He wasn't too old but he wasn't too young, either—to do his work and make his name and enjoy his fortune: he did all of that, and who can say that anybody else did more? Who, other than yourself, of course, reader—you believe you can say that many others did more, but you are polite, and will keep your belief somewhat to yourself, even through me. Keep it. Nick Dennis on the other hand is in show business proper, while Patrick Dennis was in show business improper or incidental, and of course Nick Dennis didn't die, but as I hired him and put him in a play which Walter Huston also appeared in, way back there in the very early 1940s of America and the world, when we only knew that the big Shakeup of the Western World (which was to compel the discovery of misuse of nuclear energy), I want to remember a little fragment of some kind of Broadway lore: Nick Dennis was an unemployed inexperienced Greek actor when he told me with his strong accent that he would like to be in my play *Love's Old Sweet Song.* I put him in, and he did his work well, and when the play closed, he continued to appear in other plays, and did one of the Saturday night poker players in *A Streetcar Named Desire,* directed by Elia Kazan, and after the run of that play I happened to run into Kazan and as he also is Greek, I asked about Nick Dennis and I was told that he was looking for a part. I suggested to the famous director, who had a knack of making big hits of the plays he directed, that Nick Dennis should be a star in a play, in something like Sidney Howard's *They Knew What They Wanted,* for instance, and this brought forth from Elia Kazan a remark that astonished me. He said, "Oh, I think Nick has gone about as far as it is possible for him to go in the theatre." I was dumbfounded, literally, because Mr. Kazan was right, but I had to tell him what I had started to tell him, in any case: "No, I don't think that at all. I think that a play with a very appropriate part should be written which Nick could do better than anybody else in the world." And of course had I not been captured by the American army for three years I would very probably have found a week in which to write such a play for him—and for myself, and for the American theatre, and the American people. But really sensible practical people, whether in show business or carpet business or easy money business, don't subscribe to such theories. Well, I do, I still do, and it is because I have noticed that being in the world itself is acting, and if somebody acts in the world, he can act in the small isolation from the world, and be sharply noticed all of a sudden as being a genius being himself. But it's all right: the Greek director was not at all mistaken about that Greek actor, who has continued to have an excellent career in films, playing the part of the Greek with the loud voice and the simple mind and soul which appears to be the full extent of himself. Patrick Dennis died, Nick Dennis didn't. Not yet, at any rate, and this book is about a very tiny miniscule portion of the dead of only 1976, and only carefully selected from the ranks of acting or kindred employment. The first to exit from *Love's Old Sweet Song* was, I believe, Walter Huston himself, and the last, or latest, was Jessie Royce Landis, but Arthur Hunnicutt and Teddy Bergman and surely each of the dozen kids are all still with us. Are we thrilled by that fact? Not at all.

Dorothy Devore is somebody I don't know, but there was a Devore who sold haberdashery in Beverly Hills, who also died, who was quite well-known and somewhat active in the social life if you could call anything of any order in that part of the world anything at all like a social life, and you could, you can: he gave parties, that is, and he went to them, and his first name was Sy, short for what I don't know, but Sy Devore was not infrequently in the columns, and once in the early 1950s it was for inviting me to leave a party (for drunken behavior and talk), and I gladly left. I believe I was invited by an actress to take her to the party and I hadn't really known anybody there, or herself, for that matter, at least not beyond remembering that she was supposed to be an up-and-coming comedienne when I first met her, at the bar table of The Golden Horn restaurant in New York, sitting as she was with Eugene Istomin the pianist, whose father was the bartender at that fine restaurant owned and operated by Aram Salisian. I hope to get her name in a moment, the poor girl enjoyed quite a lot of success and wealth, but never married, never had children, out of herself or adopted, and was considered a sex bomb, as the saying is: she was rolypoly and zaftig as I heard Gene Kelly once put it in connection with another girl we both knew in New York, and that Yiddish word means a nice appealing cushion for the male and the male parts. And after New York I met the girl who seems to be the one who invited me to take her to the party at Sy Devore's from which I was evicted, so to put it. Going to Hollywood parties permitted me or even compelled me to guzzle five or six very cold martinis in about half an hour, and sometimes, sometimes that swift fire had me saying things about Hollywood and the human race that I might have kept to myself, or to only one chosen bed companion, like one or another of the ladies at the party whom I informed I would very much like to take to bed, or to a group of friends at another party who might not be haberdashers. And of course I didn't mind being invited to leave, because I was bored, I really didn't like being there, and I wanted to drive to the Malibu Inn and continue my drinking within a stone's throw of my own house on the beach, at 24848 Malibu Road, a house on pilings, and a house I occupied for eight years, and in which I wrote *Mama Girl, I Love You* for my daughter Lucy, which was serialized in *The Saturday Evening Post*, and *Papa, You're Crazy*, which was published in one slightly shortened version in *Family Circle*—I needed money very badly in those days, to keep sending it to the mother of the two kids, and I wrote a good variety of other works, including plays, one of which was called *An Imaginary Character Named Saroyan.* Was her name Beverly Nichols? I believe it was, and I have nothing but warm sentiments about her, although I never slept with her, and on one occasion in that house, after we had walked on the beach in swimming clothing, bikini for her, shorts for me, when we had got back I dropped the walking trunks before getting into the shower and there she was and saw the erection and after the shower saw it again, and she went to the shower, and came out fully clothed while I was still unclothed, perhaps imagining that she would come out to offer the appropriate part of herself to the hardon. The clothing she wore though made me wonder if she didn't simply like to be disrobed, for the pleasure that gave her, so I volunteered that courtesy, and was again confused because she was coy, cute, giggly, and elusive. Suddenly, or suddenly enough, I decided the hell with this, and got into my clothes and drove her home to one of those typical garden apartments in which four or five photographers from various magazines and studios were making setups of lights for some hot photographs there, and among them the young lady came to life, and I drove back to Malibu. But years and years later, after I had forgotten her almost totally, for never having known her, I got the impression that she had met Harold Clurman and had told him that I had waved my cock at her but that she had laughed in my face. Was that really what had happened? Well, if it was, let it have been. Something even worse I may as well now own up to: I once chased Harold Clurman's wife Stella Adler around her apartment but finally gave up and sat with her and talked politely and even intelligently about plays and acting. Her former husband in his memoir did not reveal who the girl was that had laughed at my naked or clothed advances —I thought at first that his wife had told him I had made a pass at her, and either she had fibbed a little and said I had been out of my clothes, or he had not understood her. And then it came to me that no, it had not been his wife who had passed along the comic scene, and so it must have been the little movie actress, for I had had no such scene with any other girl or woman. Well, it was during the time when I was interested in knowing the girl fully that I had taken her to the haberdasher's party, and hadn't cared for the thing at all, and as it was understood that she lived very near the haberdasher's house and was not indeed in sight, I left her at the party. So Sy Devore got in the Hollywood gossip columns for having put me out of his party. Well, Dorothy Devore who died last year was his wife, and maybe he introduced me to her at the party. I don't know. He died, and I believe rich, a year or two before Dorothy Devore died. And so did the zaftig comedienne who knew Harold Clurman and told him how I made a fool of myself. Eugene Istoman's father may have given up bartending when Aram Salisian retired to Pasadena, with cancer. Eugene Istoman went right on being a very fine concert pianist. Barbara, not Beverly. Not every starlet was named Beverly in those days. A few were named Barbara too. Barbara Nichols.

67

Alan DeWitt I do not know, but there was a classmate the year I went to Fresno High School, in my English class, whose name was DeWitt Bodeen. He was the son of a banker, and in due time went to Hollywood and became a screenwriter, as it is sometimes called. George Stevens, the director of *Shane* and *An American Tragedy*, and a good assortment of other excellent movies told me somewhere along the line that DeWitt Bodeen had worked for him on a number of scenarios. I lasted only half a semester at Fresno High School, though, because everything was too slow and everybody was too stupid, especially the German-style Principal of the school, by name Delbert Brunton, who had something of a jitney approximation of Teddy Roosevelt about him, if such a thing can be said. I had a dispute with the nice English teacher which she reported to Delbert Brunton who expelled me from school, and that was the last of my public schooling: 1922 I suppose the year was, or 1923, and immediately I went to work in the vineyard of Dikran Haigos

Bagdasarian, or D.H. as his contemporaries call him, and Uncle Dick as the younger members of the family called him, for he had married my mother's kid sister Verkine, or Virginia, as the census-takers would have it, for they have always been (or were in those days) unwilling to accept unfamiliar names, or unable to: but Verkine has nothing at all to do with Virginia. D.H. furthermore was the business partner of his brother-in-law, my mother's kid brother Aram, now in his 85th year, retired and almost poor in Santa Barbara, who had once (and as recently as ten years ago) been a millionaire: but he blew his wealth in folly and avarice by putting almost all of it in something called King Enterprises in Texas, because in less than 40 days his fortune had doubled, and in less than 80 days had tripled, and still he did not sell (to who? as the ungrammatical joke used to go), and then the company was swiftly bankrupted and the crooks who had been involved were indicted but pretty much proved everything to have been legal. D.H. Bagdasarian and Aram Saroyan in 1922 when I was fourteen were respectively 36 and 30 years of age, and a rather comic couple: brothers-in-law traditionally go into business, even in the movie business where Jesse Lasky and Sam Goldwyn were connected to one another or to other pioneers of the movie industry by girls and women who had become their wives. I accepted Delbert Brunton's official and written disbarment from any further attendance at Fresno High School, and I accepted my mother's very reasonable summing up of the situation: Well, if you are not going to go to school, you must go to work. I got a job at 35¢ an hour pruning vines with four Mexicans, one Japanese, another Armenian, my cousin on my father's side, Karnik Saroyan, and one Anglo-Saxon, a man destined to become something along the lines of an escape artist—from himself, from failure, from either actual inferiority or a feeling of it: I saw him even then as a wino, a kind of vagabond without even the energy to ride the freight trains, a kind of local tramp. And DeWitt Bodeen stayed in that English class at that high school, and I never saw him again. At last, not more than a year ago I found a paperback of a book that had not had a hardback edition at a bookshop and paid more than a dollar for it, which I don't like to do, but had to do, because we had been in an English class together, and

I knew instantly that he more than disliked me, he hated me, and I had almost total contempt for him—and that means I despised his father, his mother, his class, his notion of superiority, and everything else about him. Not to put too fine a point upon it, he was what the rest of us called certain boys: a sissy. But now let's just understand that I not only no longer dislike DeWitt Bodeen, I am on the contrary an admirer, although I found his novel, published long after he had reached the age of 60, pure trash: I admire him because he survived it all, and with so little talent as a writer. Years and years of fighting the brave fight of the screenwriter in Hollywood, and with all of the intrigue, all of the politics, and all of the backbiting and self-defense of the writers. In that English class he was a kind of a prig (not a prick, that's another sort of thing entirely), he was smarmy with the teacher, not really a bad sort, but a lady of strictly no brains at all, and this even though she seemed to suspect that I was somebody (or other) in her class, and one day had her theory supported by a boy named Waldo Scott, who said of me, Well, anybody who can't see that he's a genius is stupid. This remark astonished me, and made me consider the speaker of it more deeply, for he was not kidding, he was in earnest, and I had almost wished he had been kidding, for in that town it was not really sensible to be known in that troublesome way: for wouldn't a genius surely set fire to the Courthouse itself? When a father names a son DeWitt, it is usually because there is a DeWitt in the family, but I have no information at all, beyond what I have already covered, about DeWitt Bodeen, good luck to him always. How extraordinary it would have been, however, had he turned out to be the real genius in that English class, and had gone on demonstrating it for half a century in one amazing book after another—like me, har har har har har, or did I already say that? Remember one of Conrad Aiken's poems? What I really want to know is, What kind of a genius was Waldo Scott? Where is he now? What's he doing? And if he died, I want to mourn his death, for although we were not friends, he suddenly declared friendship in a way that compels to this day my deepest respect and gratitude.

T.S. Eliot said April is the cruelest month, but sir never really mind the month, give us the day, and would it be Sunday Monday Tuesday Wednesday Thursday Friday or Saturday? Also give us the hour, would it be first thing on waking or would it be the last hour of the work day, or would it be around noon? And what about the holidays, which is a throwing together of two words, holy and day becomes holiday, I didn't think you would really like to know that, it is just that words go right on fascinating the mind: Christmas is the Suicide Season, as everybody has heard and perhaps felt: the reason T.S. Eliot felt that April is the cruelest month, most likely, is that whereever he was at the time (or is it wherever? of course it is, so why did I have to go to work and misspell the word by making it the two words it actually is? wherever not whereever, but actually it should be where ever, with its proper space between the words), wherever T.S. Eliot was at the time, change was taking place along the lines of springtime violence and the upshooting of tulips and morning glories (a terrible weed as cereal farmers will tell you) and all sorts of other fine flowers: but who knows, maybe he said April is the cruelest month because April is the cruelest month (but don't you believe it, it is only a poetic flight and means very little in any other context than the poem in which it occurs). The thing about T.S. Eliot is that he had rather large nostrils that were unavoidable to the eye in even the swiftest glance at a photograph of him, and they were indeed the first thing that the eye was forced to notice and the only thing the eye seemed to tell the brain to remember. Such nostrils are not common. One has no real way of knowing why they happen or what they mean, but I have always found it unavoidable (there we go again, don't we, another unavoidable, sir, and madam, but sometimes the word unavoidable just can't be avoided, and I don't beg your pardon about that, I call your attention to the matter of words in the life and work of any of us who use them—

they can be sons of bitches, and then all of a sudden they are real serene cats, altogether loving—some day I expect to remember the name of the very fine English writer who found a cat at his door speaking to him, took the cat in, began to become acquainted with the enormous depth of the cat, in the area of eye and voice and movement and grace, and chatted with the cat endlessly, and almost died of grief when the cat died—that man was really in love with the cat, but more accurately with the things that brought themselves into his life by the cat and the cat's meanings in eye and voice and movement and presence, for he believed the cat loved him passionately, and love is love, and while there may be people who must have sexual relations with any order of living thing they love or believe they love, this Englishman, a fine writer or I would not have remembered all this, loved the cat with mind and spirit and soul and intelligence, not with body: he never laid a passionate hand on the cat, or anything else: people, poets, anybody can love anything, and quite passionately in the spiritual dimension of love: and let's not leave ourselves out of any of this: I found last week a volunteer tree, or bush, in the backyard of this house in Fresno and I am almost madly in love with that bush, and this is the reason: its trunk and branches are slim and smooth and the opposite of brittle: the thing can be bent almost back again to itself and when released will spring right back to its proper place: along the trunk and branches are beautifully designed slim thorns, very like needles, and many of the thorns are unadorned and many are concealed by a small oval leaf, something like a lady's nail of the smallest finger at the end of the hand. These leaves themselves also have toughness, and that's the thing that makes me love this bush, bough, or tree: it came unasked, like the English writer's cat, it was unnoticed for a long time, surely a full year, possibly younger, and then it became magnificent in its own fantastic and glorious self, also like that cat: and so I love this plant, and don't know how it got to the garden back there, out of a gust of wind carrying a seed from somewhere, or out of the dropping of a bird visiting the nearby plum tree, or the apple, or the loquat, a bird from far away, early early one morning, unseen by me or anybody else, from a place where many of that bush grow, and in the dropping was the one seed that became this bush—by God, I like that, but what I especially like is the immediate engagement of the curiosity as to why that bush is so resilient, so like steel, and why it put forth the needle-sharp long thorns, and so far all I can guess is that it was being eaten to death by grazing creatures of the wild millions of years ago and put the thorns there and toughened its limbs and leaves to teach the grazers a good lesson: and ever since the grazers have left them alone. He loved his cat, or the cat, and I love, the human race is busy surviving and very properly can't be bothered.) In any case, I have imagined that the people with large nostrils have them because they had difficulty getting enough good air to their lungs and heart, they were fighting for life, to go on living, or the equivalent of that, a kind of insatiable hunger or demand for more, more oxygen, more anything. This is Monday, a cruel day, this is Valentine's Day, the day of a Chicago underworld machinegun massacre 50 years or so ago, a cruel day, but don't you believe it: this is only a very nice Monday, and St. Valentine was a nice saint.

What right have I to impose on the reader such information as the day? This is not a diary, not a journal, not some kind of haphazard history, a running commentary on the trivia that mounts up and mounts up until it is Hamlet himself in his own play, by way of Will himself, three or four hundred years after the real Hamlet of Elsinore had had his day—William Shakespeare, that is, his name spelled several names, his identity disputed by erudite and not always witless or hysterical experts, putting the old Hamlet into the new Hamlet, and the language of the Danes which Will did not know from the language of the Malemutes or is it Malemukes—the farther we go and the swifter, the more ignorance we chance upon, but let's not knock it, it is our truth, and while Samuel Johnson did the dictionary, he was not beyond error, even in speech, in words, in definitions, and in meanings, any more than we are, but he improved a lot in the business of getting things right, and so have we, but if there is anything we must accept as being absolutely inevitable in any case, and therefore nothing to moan and gnash our teeth about, it is error: we are made of error, we live by error, we are begat by error, and we shall surely die by error, so then what may be said to be without error? What may be said to be correct? Well, the answer is error itself: that which is correct is another form of error, so forget it, and let me get back to the matter of what right I have to impose upon the reader the name of the day and the news of the thorn bush discovered growing in the backyard of this cheap house bought brand new thirteen years ago, come August—from Oscar Spano, who attended Longfellow Junior High School when I did, aspired to a career as an opera singer, said hello to me at the Tanforan Race Track in San Francisco more than forty years ago, and last year died but was not listed in *Variety*'s annual column of the dead, which is what this book is about, or based upon. What right have I to go into all that irrelevant information of day and place and cruelty—love is the cruelest emotion. Why didn't Thomas Stearns Eliot of St. Louis ask that question, or state that theory, instead of asking and stating what he did in perhaps his most famous poem, *The Wasteland,* which his godfather, so to put it, Ezra Pound, salvaged for him, throwing out the chaff and trash, tightening up what was left, which became the big poem of the second decade of this century, and then of the third decade, too, and is still a big poem. Or why didn't he say that boredom is the cruelest imbecility. Well, the reason is that in a poem, and indeed in most prose, you are not allowed to ask four questions when the line can accept only one, but in some kinds of writing you are not only allowed, you are almost compelled to ask not four but sometimes as many as eight questions all at the same time, and this permits me to answer the question about what right I have to impose information on the reader: I don't need any right to write any way I like, but that means any way I must, for I write only when I must and don't write when I don't feel like it, don't want to, want other writers to write, and only want to breathe and think about nothing. And in a book about the dead, about the handful of the living which died last year, the handful which crossed the line and joined the majority, it is a demonstration of life to write about just about everything that is there or comes along—for that is the way we live, the way we stay alive, from minute to minute, and when we sleep all of that flowing along of the flotsam and jetsam (get a load of that partnership or team, won't you?), all of the clutter of our reality, our mortality, our being, our breathing goes right on moving down the silent dark sweet bitter stream which may be said to be the river of the dead, the timeless measureless sunny river of the living, in such a book it is just naturally necessary for nothing to be presumed to be out of order, for order is the only order, and the human order, involving both the dead and the living, includes everything that goes on all the time from first breath to last of every little newcomer brought out and tossed into the street—har har har har, which is of course a very swift part of the dark and blinding-bright flowing stream of death and life. You can get bored with this very quickly, and if you are not invited to, it is only because the writer is by nature polite, but sooner or later you can also remember that what happens here, what is happening here, is yourself, and that you are alive, still alive, and if it is not a good thing, it is damned well far beyond any such picayune limitation, whether you like it or not, the fact that you are alive, still alive, is a great thing, it is a million times bigger than the biggest you yourself ever saw: it is all that even while it is not even a tiny speck of something or other upon the lapel of the checkered sport jacket of the human race and the holy universe, the kind of speck that if you were chatting with a nice lady, she might reach over and pick off the lapel and toss it aside—that is what the whole human race is, in all of the time that it can imagine, and yet in that speck of something like dandruff not from God's old head but from the hairs of God's left nostril, in that tiny speck is everything, everything we have, everything we have made, everything we have discovered, everything we have preserved, and so of course that's why. Otherwise, as the television joke goes, would I lie to you? Would I deceive you? Would I cheat you? Reader, yes I would. Believe me, I would be a liar if I didn't let you know that I would lie to you, deceive you, cheat you, in order to have you understand just a little bit more than before, who you are.

A side of me whenever I am at work on a new book, or play, or any other kind of work involving anywhere from 4 to 104 days, remarks to another side of me, or to itself, as follows: I don't know what I'm doing. And no side protests or makes very much of the remark, for another side, or the same side, doesn't believe the remark, or replies in language outside the limits of words: Bullshit, you know very well what you are doing, what you probably don't know is how it's going, how it shall turn out, or why you have got to bother at all. And with that, reader, let us get along with the proper procedure for the making of this work: let us take the next name on the list, and see how it provokes me into action. The name is: let me look it up: the whole fat issue of *Variety* is right here opened to the proper page, which is 164, which is indeed appropriately the last page, and which procedure compels me to consult until I have come to the end of the list: and I must at the very least mention each name, and the next one is: Dean Dixon. Well, that's a big one for me, or could be, at any rate, for the message that comes to my head and memory (inside there somewhere) is that this may be one of the several astrologers who have presented themselves to the television nation on talk shows, but Dean is very probably a man's name, as Leslie and Evelyn are not, for instance, and most of the astrologers have been women, although there have been boys in that group, too. No, I must simply acknowledge that I have no information, even far-fetched and clearly inaccurate, about Dean Dixon (other than of course that he is on the list, and is therefore dead, which if you and I were in a bar in Dublin, one of us would say, God rest his soul. But are there all that many dead who were plagued by a restless soul? I suspect not, but I can't be sure, for there is the life of quiet desperation mentioned by several writers in the first place and ten times as many in the second place, and everybody has a restless soul. I know I do, and I suspect that you do, too, or you would not be reading this—but who knows, who knows?) Maynard Dixon, on the other hand, was a painter of the West, to oversimplify what he painted, as Swinnerton painted the West, but not as Remington did, perhaps: there was a good American Indian and therefore north and east Asiatic quality about his always composed bodies and faces tied in intimately with the large sleeping landscape of the West: well, back in the early 1930s and in the late 1930s, after I had published two or three books, at last, and had had a couple of big plays on Broadway, I finally met Maynard Dixon on the streets of San Francisco, somewhere in North Beach, and we talked a bit, and then walked to his studio in the Montgomery Block, a famous hangout for writers, painters, sculptors, and similar souls, most of them with a certain amount of recognition if not of fame, and at least a modicum of effectuality in the money department, although not really up in the bigtime money. It was a four-story building without an elevator and his studio was on the 3rd floor, but if I am mistaken about this, and the Monkey Block, as it was affectionately called, did have an elevator, I have no memory of ever having taken it: and I do remember still with a touch of astonishment that going down the stairs of that building even before my first book had been published, in October of 1934, a big voluptuous rather untidy wife of a painter turned and having had a lot of beer, the both of us, waited for me to grab her, so I did, whereupon for the first time in my life I experienced a blowing into my left ear, which for some reason activated an instant erection, and then this preposterous sloppy bag, forty to my 24 or so, or even more than forty, opened her mouth all wet and guckyloaded, and poked a thick tongue almost to my tonsils, and even this piece of inappropriate behavior did not send the erection back to peter but if anything made it even stiffer—but thank Christ I didn't stop her bung up with my tool right then and there and shoot her huge cavity with a whole human race of superior seed, for her husband and two other friends in less than twenty seconds were where all that messiness of mouth and tongue had taken place. Another time, out beside a river, I did give her what she had to have, and while it was no harm at all, I have never been able to cherish that woman and am delighted that I haven't any idea what her name was—but I do remember that she had at that time had two sons by a previous marriage and two daughters by the present one. That's how I happen to have come to believe that the Monkey Block had no elevator, but the more I think about it the more I am obliged to correct that belief: it not only had an elevator, it was a big one, like a freight elevator, perhaps so that painters and sculptors could get canvases and stones up to their studios, and furthermore I believe the operator of the elevator, or at any rate one of them, was an Italian who enjoyed considerable fame among the occupants of the building. The thing I'm getting to is that Maynard Dixon, at that time a man of mature years, perhaps 20 more than my own 24, perhaps even more than 20 more, somehow revealed during my visit to his high-ceilinged studio that he was born in Fresno, as I was, and a thing like that is memorable. His art was excellent, he was a sober, serious man, and on visits to places like Taos he may even have met D.H. Lawrence, and one of his several admirers, such as Brett, or Lady Brett, herself an excellent painter, even as she approaches the age of 90, an age surpassed by Georgia O'Keeffe, whom he may also have met. But Dean Dixon, no I don't know him at all.

Max Dolin, then: well, I know Max Dolin had a rather significant connection with music, and that he may have played the violin, but his connection was not the same, for instance, as the connection of the big conductors of music, conductors of orchestras, or even the big leaders of the big bands, although the music of Max Dolin's band or orchestra was also restricted pretty much to what at best might be referred to (with an almost imperceptible wink) as semi-classical (a word and distinction I really enjoy), and consequently an order of music that H.L. Mencken would have relegated to the profane as against the sacred: which would be Bach, of course, and several others. As for Max itself, or more properly Maximillian, I suppose, it does not seem ever to have been the given name of any composer of music beyond the realm of the instantly insignificant if not instantly forgettable, for I am sure there are song-writers named Max who have done either words (called lyrics) or music (called music) of quite a variety of very popular songs—so popular as to seem by now to be very nearly folk songs: "My Isle of Golden Dreams" (Hawaii? Maui? Molokai?) might be said to be such a song, but it is not by anybody named Max. "In the Garden of Tomorrow" is another song that is like a folk song (if it is heard at all, that is). "Sally (of Our Alley)" especially when sung by Gracie Fields, is a folk song, which she brought out of hiding and back into the popularity it deserves with the whole British Empire, and anybody in the United States who has also happened to hear it. "Lily of Laguna" is another. "Your Eyes Have Told Me So," especially when sung by John McCormack, but any reasonably decent singer, professional or amateur or strictly party or bar singer, can get that song out into hearing in a way that is very moving. There are at least a million songs in this world. They are all worth hearing, but we shall never make it. And every song is brought into being by somebody, including a kind of song called *lieder,* brought into being by Schubert, a genius of music who perished of paresis and poverty before he reached 38, God rest his soul, great shy rejected man: the stupid beauties would have little to do with him, he paid the working girls and early along got himself syphilis, but think of his *Serenade* and his *Unfinished Symphony,* as it is called, and listen to two or three dozen of his *lieder* and you will know what an enormity Schubert is: Franz Schubert. Not Max Schubert. But there is Max Beerbohm of England, and Maxwell Bodenheim of the United States. I knew the latter, as the saying goes, during the last years of his life, and he was a mess—but we are not supposed to notice that writers are messes, just so their writing is good. One of the greatest poets (by all accounts) was given to biting his fingernails until they were all but gone: W.H. Auden himself. Another passed out at parties and wet himself and the chair or sofa upon which he had placed himself. No matter, no matter, let him bite, let him piss, what did he write? In the end poor Bodenheim was shot in a weird crime involving both male and female homosexuality and a wife and a friend and so on and so forth, but in his case, alas, not too much can be said for what he wrote. I put him in a play called *Across the Board on Tomorrow Morning,* at the Belasco Theatre on 44th Street in New York, because if I didn't, it seemed that he would go mad, run amuck, kill somebody like an innocent bystander, or hang himself. And then, when I had him recite one of his own drunken poems, in his own drunken manner, in a dark bar in New York near the end of the war (before the discovery of the Atom Bomb, as it is called), his old pal and enemy Joe Gould came and insisted that I must fire Maxwell Bodenheim and hire Joe Gould, so that he might recite his Duck Sonnet: 14 lines of 10 syllables each, and every syllable and word quack. Well, I got out of that somehow. Max Dolin died last year, his violin is silent, but if he played piano, cello, or trombone, they also are silent—but I must remark, and not necessarily in passing, that I would like to see a television talk show in which time-pressure is totally effaced, in which nobody has to start yammering the minute somebody points a finger at him and the camera's red light goes on: and in such a program I would like to see somebody place a violin case on a table, and open it, and slowly remove a violin from it, and look at a visitor and wait for the visitor to say something about the violin, to notice its shape, for instance, and furthermore to speculate if some of its shape came from various flowers, especially tropical and extravagantly fluted and curved flowers, and to relate the coming into being of the violin to all of the other things in the musical or plant or human family, but all of it very slowly very casually, nobody hot, and nothing demanding that anybody be a big hit. The next day a book, as a book, and nothing else, an object, might be considered. But again very very slowly—so that the camera and the viewers might also not be rushed and might somehow have time to enjoy the whole idea of getting something rather fully by looking at it and thinking about it. Reader, think about the piano, for instance: the baby grand is a table and a bed and a work of sculpture, and the upright is a skyscraper—but that's the kindergarten observation about the piano: after you think a moment or two quietly you will be carried away by the white keys and the black keys, and by the time you reach Frederic Chopin you will be flying. Max Dolin was no Frederic Chopin, but then neither was anybody else, not even the other great composers and pianists. He didn't bite his fingernails, maybe, but nobody is better at composing for the piano.

72

In my earliest years I longed to have a full personal past because whenever I considered writing, there wasn't enough (or at least so I thought) to permit me to write anything interesting. Of course the failure was not that the past was limited: it was that the skill was unequal to the discovery of the enormity of the past, and the editorial opinion that everything that was there that I knew was there was not interesting enough to put into words and to pass along to others. There is sense of one sort or another in everything we feel, however mistaken we may be in our basic premises. All the same from the earliest days (or even hours) of memory I longed to be a total man, in order to escape the limitations of dependency, along with its rules and regulations, and from the first hours and days of writing (rather than only reading) I longed to have a very large and rich store of personal participation in the world, among some of the other members of the human race, so that I might never need to feel, as I did in the early years, that there was really nothing worth writing. I am sure writers of all kinds will understand what I am talking about, unless of course they will not, because they had no such feeling or longing, or because they did not write altogether out of themselves, they wrote another kind of writing, out of another source, entirely. But the real point here is that I was sure at fourteen that in ten years I would have pretty much everything I wanted in the way of a full personal past, and in a sense, allowing for my own much more fully developed ability to see use in everything, in every dimension of myself and my life and my known and unknown past, in ten years I did indeed have all that I really needed—except unfortunately that small edge of need which can outweigh a thousand times more of everything else: I was not finding paper and print of a world's publication for the writing I was doing. And part of the reason was that the writing wasn't ready, or at any rate only a little of it was ready, the writing just wasn't me, as the comic saying is: it was beginning to be me by the time I was twenty-four, but it was not so fully me as to compel the editors to run my stuff, if that is how it happens, which I doubt, although it is a good big part of it, for sure. So I waited and worked, and traveled and looked and listened and took part and fought through all of the obstructions and hindrances and doubts and illnesses and the sense of isolation and the roaring joy of comedy known only to myself, which in its richness and variety made me feel I would never be able to capture it and hold it in words for anybody else, and in due time things began to happen, and I suddenly was a writer, and I have been ever since. So now I am in my 69th year, as I have mentioned several times, because that also is part of my way of living and working and being aware: I have about as much of a personal past as I am willing to believe any man of 69 is likely to have, so what have I done with it, how have I used that enormous wealth, what great works have I written and passed along to the rest of the human family? Well, not nearly enough, of course, nobody has ever done that, but I believe that all things considered, including the things that no man knows about himself, I have done quite well, quite well, thank you, as the rambling remark goes. I have certainly had quite a number of books published, I have not died, and I am still writing. My name signifies a kind of writing, and while it is a kind that some estimable critics look down their noses at, I don't especially mind, for I look down my nose at both them and their writing, and I would name them one by one except that it would bore me, and be irrelevant in a way that I do not want any of my irrelevant flights to be. I do not believe in making negative references about my writing. Frankly, I marvel at it. Let whoever can or will do his own work as he chooses, and place it alongside my work, or long after his death let his partisans do that for him, and I have an idea that my work will survive such a relationship very nicely—and with no belittlement to either body if the writing is right: and that is the one thing every writer asks of himself, or demands, each in his own way, even to the writer of profitable trash, of full falsity, of deliberate inferiority, it must be still right, of its order. In any case, not long ago, less than twenty-four hours ago, myself aged 14 or 24 asked myself, now, All right, so you have your full past, what are you doing with it? And I was both pleased and surprised by the unexpected question, but at the same time also left with my mouth open, for the implication of the question was very clear: I hadn't done half what I ought to have done, half what I had believed at 14 and 24 that I would do if I ever lasted until I was forty, or perhaps fifty, so now that I am almost 20 years older than fifty, what do I have to show for it? I have what I have, that's all. And I said so, but nevertheless was not all that satisfied with saying so, for it was I who asked, and I who answered, and the asker was more nearly correct than the answerer. For instance, the asker went on, this thing that you're writing, is this the kind of thing you had all that experience for? Isn't it in order to be putting your time, experience, skill, and energy into another kind of work entirely? Into what the reporters of the literary life call a major work. Major? I reply. What does that mean? Well, it could mean pompous, and it has proved to be pompous in relation to a good assortment of so-called major works, but what it really means is that the work is really itself, and right. It is right. Well, I have such works, and if the truth is told I believe that all of my works put together are right.

Vincent Donahue is somebody I don't know, so I haven't anything to say about him, or out of not having ever met him, or somebody like him, or out of his name, his names. In 1939 when I returned to New York from a last look at Europe before the holocaust, so to put it, I spent several hours on several occasions discussing the story for a musical play I thought I might write with the man who might very well direct that play, Vincent Minnelli, but the play, called *Elmer and Lily*, was never produced by anybody as far as I know, except a college theatre group here and there. There is this about plays, and about the theatre: a play really doesn't exist at all, until it appears on the boards, and the special reality of the play when it is on the boards is the consequence of an enormous number of preposterous elements, not excluding talents of several kinds, that the playwright can readily be lost among, in the shuffle, as the saying is. No wonder so many great playwrights of the past were members of a theatrical group, and worked with the group in all of its departments: Shakespeare, Moliere, Goldoni, and in a certain sense even Chekhov in sad Russia (or sad but comic Russia), and O'Neill in sad America (or sad and senile America—no, that won't do: not senile at all, something else, so what is it, what else could it be? Well, let's think of the simple puritanical earnestness of *Anna Christie*, and then let's think of the absurd but probably right intensity of *Dynamo:* is that the play? How is intensity right, not wrong? Well, however it may be, it is, that's all, for the time, place, and people, and although I never saw the play, I read it, and I felt that it was right, that's all. And everything is written for everybody of course. And I am everybody. And so on and so forth: but Vincent Donahue, possibly a dance director, is not somebody I know, that's all. The next man on the list is somebody I do know: Eddie Dowling, born something else, part Polish, but somehow (at least by preference) Irish. He was a song-and-dance man, he was an actor, he was a director, and he was a producer of plays. And during the last years of his life I heard that in Florida he was interested in a program to establish a new Holy Land, and of course that sort of thing has a way of alienating my interest. He even wrote to me about this high-spirited program, but I wasn't even able to discipline myself into a routine reply wishing him well. I had always sensed in Eddie Dowling a touch of the spurious which was almost always innocuously so, but putting himself into a program so fully fraudulent was totally out of line, even for a Broadway and showbiz oldtimer. He was never right for the role he introduced in the American Theatre, in my play *The Time of Your Life:* Joe, the man who sat at a table and drank champagne and looked and listened to everybody who came into the place, while Europe got ready to plunge the whole world into another very very boring situation of self-destruction, with non-big big boys having themselves a glorious time being big, while millions of equally non-big big boys were drafted and threatened and intimidated and pushed around and punished and imprisoned and maimed and killed—for something that needed better identification than the Office of War Information was capable of giving it, even with the playwright Robert Sherwood, biographer and emissary of Franklin Delano Roosevelt, in charge. Next comes Michael Durso: and the only response that comes to memory upon the sighting of that name is a faint connection the name had with American playwriting, but the connection comes to the head so faintly I hadn't better linger with it. Jimmy Edmundson, called in vaudeville, and on television, Professor Backwards, had a rather novel act of ten or eleven minutes in which he wrote backward, and then with both hands wrote both forward and backward, all the while talking smartly. But much more astonishing are the things Bronislaw Kaper did one night on the revived Jack Paar Show: his mind was able to instruct his hands and arms and legs and feet and head and trunk and fingers to do things simultaneously that for the rest of us are unthinkable. I was astonished, and remembered him on the lot at Metro-Goldwyn-Mayer in 1941 when I was involved in the business of seeing if I could do something there (I couldn't, because I refused to take the money and run). He was a lively man in whom it was impossible not to see and sense a great sorrow, a great condition of being both an exile and of having suffered great loss. David Eggleson I do not know. And Leif Eid I do not know, and I may as well let the reader in on something from backstage about procedure: it is this: inasmuch as there are almost 160 names to be covered in the next fifteen days, so that this work might be concluded by the end of this month, February, I have decided that I must cover about ten names every day, whether in two chapters, which is the minimum amount of work I have asked myself to do, or in four chapters, which I find that I want to do most of the days of the week, letting up a little perhaps on Sunday. But one thing is certain, that the work is to be concluded on the last day of this month, that's all. And so I am rushing through some of the names, and I think that this is in order, so that I can linger a little with the names of people I know, who are somehow connected both with themselves and with myself, however insignificantly . . . or even meaninglessly, as for instance in the case of Eddie Dowling: his connection was significant, and indeed vital and large, but only because I worked very hard to make it so: first in the writing of *The Time of Your Life,* and then in the salvaging of that play when it was as good as murdered. As for Florida, well, why not put up a Holy Land, anywhere?

74

It is easy for a man to be a fool if the weather is right, and the weather is always right, so what is so bad about being a fool? Well it's costly, as the saying is: in time, money, alternative, and to sum it all up, self. A fool loses himself, and if it is in prayer or genius of one sort or another, all well and good, but if it is in loafing, lust, or empty longing, it is not good, because it diminishes instead of increasing. But so what, I have work to do, and if it is fool's work, I am not absolutely sure of that, and I am willing to go ahead with the work, and I am even prepared to find out at the end of it that I have been a fool again. I was a live fool, I was there, I visited the Public Library, I bought 14 discarded magnificent books for one dollar, only one dollar, think of it, and on my way out less than half an hour ago I said to the sweet little girl at the check-out desk, "How is the little girl?" and she smiled and replied, "*He*'s just fine." And this is how that happened: last November when she was very pregnant I said, "Don't let this be troublesome, but I believe you are going to have a boy, do you and your husband want a boy?" And she said, "No, we both want a girl." And I said, "Well, you shall have a girl, then."

(Just to be polite, but it was a big up-high pregnancy and for that reason and for no reason at all I was sure it was going to be a boy, due in two weeks. Then I didn't see her for two months and when I was back at the Public Library I said, "How is your little daughter?" And she said, "My little son." I congratulated her, but ever since when I see her I think she is the new young pretty mother of a little girl. Ah, well, the weather all day has been fool's weather, and when my mother's kid sister Verkine's boy Harry Bagdasarian came by in his fine big 1972 car, I said, "Shall we drive to talk, walk the Mall, pick up 14 books for a dollar at the Public Library, and come back?" And he said, "Hell yes," so that's what we did, and so now I am back, and it is time to proceed with the work—and reader let's not be too sure that this seemingly stupid digression, this apparent irrelevance, is not just as right as anything else in this book, or ever likely to be in this book, for there are 14 more days to go. Why does a writer ramble? Why does he make himself into some kind of Muscat Rambler? Why doesn't he stay put and work within those limits which will get him a fortune? I don't know why any other writer doesn't, but the reason I don't is very simple: I both don't know how, and I don't want to. I want to write, by now, the way I write, the way I must, and if nobody approves, I haven't forgotten that when somebody does approve, it doesn't make all that much difference—my books for forty years have just barely earned my living, but they have done that, and I am grateful that they have, because that had never been the thing I was after, at all. I don't know how Eddie Dowling died, but I understand that he was in what is known as a Rest Home not far from where he was born, in Providence, Rhode Island, or somewhere like that, and that he had been there for some time, having apparently given up any notion of actually founding a new Holy Land in Florida—it has a silly ring to it no matter how you look at it. But the next name on the list after Leif Eid (had it been Ericson I might have remembered Frances Farmer, for that Leif had been her husband when she and he had been in favor of having my very first play produced by The Group Theatre—*My Heart's in the Highlands*—and I don't tend to forget things like that), but this Leif, Eid, is a totally unknown quantity to me: and so is Harold Erichs who comes immediately after Leif Eid and immediately before

Morris L. Ernst, somebody I do know, somebody I spoke with at least half a dozen times in New York, somebody I had almost always known had a rather large reputation as a lawyer and a liberal, and it may very well be that it was he who won the landmark case of *Ulysses vs. the United States,* permitting James Joyce at last to become publishable in the United States, and to provide him with a little income from his publisher Random House—but not much, for publishers, like all other big businesses, feel no qualms at all about taking far more than their just and appropriate share of profits from a book, no matter who the author is—and they are even so shameless as to take pride in giving a writer, like William Faulkner, for instance, a pittance in the way of an advance, knowing all too well that what he needs, just to survive, is ten times the total of the pittance, and that what his books are likely to earn over the years is a hundred times as much. Random House is (was) Bennett Cerf, of course, the eternal college boy, even in death, for he did die a multi-millionaire six or seven years ago, bereaving a television program called *What's My Line,* and virtually destroying its constancy: but then Dorothy Kilgallen had died before him by four or five years, and the blight of death had begun to destroy the popular if really silly program—its jolliness was pompous, and there is no worse kind than that. Morris L. Ernst also represented the opposition in a legal situation that was a pain in the ass to me, because it involved two little kids and their cheating mother, and Mr. Ernst's client. I had an idea my goose was cooked, all around, and it was, and continued to be for the next twenty years or more, but the whole thing is so boring I don't want to even begin to get hot about it all over again. Mr. Ernst's client was a prick, but Mr. Ernst took his side without any trouble at all, and no misgivings whatsoever. But of course the poor man had the support of the little woman, and that made it quite a nice time for everybody. I paid 7¢ for one of Mr. Ernst's books, a diary: it was bogus patriotic Americana, idiotic, and totally stupid.

Dame Edith Evans also died last year, and I don't remember having seen her on the stage, but I am quite sure I saw her in two or three movies: she played most effectively ladies not unlike herself, I suspect, but how can we be sure? Play-acting is play-acting, and pretending has no limits, not even of setting or costume appropriateness, as on Huckleberry Finn's raft, sailing slowly down the Mississippi almost 200 years ago, with the two con artists claiming to be the Dauphin and the King, respectively or irrespectively of royalty possibly of France, or of England, or anywhere. Being impressed and believing is easy for boys and men like Huck and Jim, and all the rest of us, but for quite a few years lately I draw the line when the little hustlers put the bite on me, even if they seem to be genuine poets or story-writers or novelists or playwrights, sometimes very famous, too. There is nothing at all I can say, or want to say, about begging among the rich, or even among the financially embarrassed, or writers, or anybody at all: I don't like people to be put to begging, although I am not opposed to the custom of people asking God, for instance, for grace, or intelligence, or the ability to discover that they have everything even when it seems they don't, or certainly don't have very much money. God or the world or nature or the ancestors, or anything else: and luck, as well, or perhaps luck before grace, even, asking God and his partners for a change of luck in everything, from poor to good, and then straight along now and then to excellent, or sensational, such as the time I was walking the beach at San Francisco with my cousins John Saroyan and Archie Minasian, father's side, mother's side, and both of them saw me stand waiting for a wave to come to my feet bearing a five-dollar piece of U.S. currency, and not even wet. Even I was unable to figure out an explanation for that event, and they knew that I had not had any connection with it, at all, that I had not done a small piece of magic, somehow. I am still puzzled by that, but everything about it pleases me, for that very next morning I was flying out of San Francisco to New York, and on to Europe, and so on and so forth, and this preposterous miracle happened as if to let me know that God and nature and everything were with me and that grace and harmony would attend all of my comings and goings and doings, for why had not one of the other two walkers on the beach seen the piece of government paper on the curling wave and waited casually for the delivery of it to his very hand? Why had it been me, if not in answer to a prayer started long ago and never stopped, pretty much? We didn't know, but I was damned pleased, and even proud in a kind of puzzled and humbled way. I still don't know precisely what had happened, and how it had happened: the piece of currency is safe in the archives, so to put it, and someday perhaps a research student will study it, and come to some acceptable conclusion as to how it came to me. Answered Prayers—I may as well notice that Mr. Truman Capote is suing his sometime acquaintance and friend Mr. Tennessee Williams for five million dollars because Mr. Williams has publicly declared that Mr. Capote did not write the work bearing that name and appearing in three large installments in *Esquire,* starting before the death of the founder Arnold Gingrich. This legal action is never really likely to reach court, or to be settled for any real sum of money or anything else out of court: it is simply part of the sort of thing that certain kinds of talented people find it necessary to do—and the publicity is just what is useful on both sides. The playwright a number of years ago got national newspaper attention through a brother who declared that the playwright had been threatened by gangsters and might be killed at any time. Well, that might very well have been so, of course, but then another time came when the playwright himself announced that he was quite sure he would soon be dead, and he was putting his affairs in order, and that is certainly not wanting in sincerity, for he could very well have believed, and have been justified in believing that he was scheduled soon to die. Ernest Hemingway wrote *Across the River and Into the Trees* a good fifteen or twenty years before he died, and did that writing in the conviction that it was to be his last, that he was near death. Well, we all rejoice, even now, that he was mistaken, but we wonder why he had to make his little encounter with the inevitable in any case something not only public but public in a way not likely to do sales or sympathy any harm. As for this sort of behavior among all people, all hustlers, we take it for granted, and I am not at all let down about his poems by the knowledge that Robert Forst (the way my friend the Armenian poet in Erivan last October pronounced his name, Vahan Davidian, but spelled and pronounced in the softer Russian-Armenian manner as Vahagn Tvitian) spent a lot of his time trying to get friends to arrange for honors to come to him, and didn't totally fail, either. Percy Faith also died in 1976, and I know he was in music, he had a big band, he composed, he made arrangements, both for stage plays and for big expensive musical movies, and may even have had some connection with Radio City, the place where Erno Rappe (if I may) did his magic wand-waving. I can't, however, be specific at all about Percy Faith, but he was no Percy Grainger, by a long shot, who did introduce Grieg's piano concerto to the whole world. An Australian, but if you can find an lp or tape of Grainger's version of that famous concerto, alas, you will be disappointed by it—almost everybody has done better, but none better than a virtually unknown pianist of 70 years ago, Paul deGreef, of Holland, I believe.

Hamilton Wright Mabie was the author of some of the literature, or text, in the book from which about two dozen boys and girls at Fresno Technical High School about 55 years ago were finding out how to type, to use a typewriter, without needing to search for the letters on the keys. I've mentioned him not because he died in 1976, or indeed in 1906, or in any year, but because he was a writer, or was supposed to be a writer, and was so named, Hamilton Wright Mabie, at the end of an exercise in the typing textbook, and the thing I remember is the rather rollicking confident rhythm of the name, the music of Hamilton, the rightness of right, followed then by the humanizing qualification of maybe, which might have been of course Wellington Wrong Shurr, for instance. The typewriter was not all that old in those days of the early 1920s, but it was not all that new, either. The big changes had pretty much come to pass: Oliver's inventions had been improved by Underwood, and that was the most universally accepted machine of the time, although the Remington was also highly regarded, as well as the Royal, and not unlike a popular black singer of these days, in name at any rate, the L.C. Smith who certainly deserves a special song as much as C.C. Rider. The machines on which that typing class learned touch typing, as it was called, were not Underwoods, for the rather sharp upright design of that machine would have been remembered, and it may very well be that they were Remingtons, but also possibly Royals. These days there are good machines manufactured by European companies, especially German and Italian, and of course there is the IBM electrical machine, with changeable type designs —very simple supposedly: the metal sphere that is electrically activated as the typist types is easily replaced by another ball, or pica type by elite, the two most popular styles: there is also a kind of type that seeks to approximate some kind of script, but this doesn't make for easy reading. And that is the desired thing in all writing, by hand or by machine. And of course writing that has been done by machine is the most likely to be easiest to read, at least in the long run, for we know that there are styles of handwriting that are even more pleasing to the eye than any order of print, which of course typing is. And that is the reason I transferred from Longfellow Junior High to Technical High: so that I could learn to type with ease and accuracy, and in comparative comfort, and without eye strain, or hectic usage of one finger of each hand, which was supposed to be the way newspapermen did their typing. At the age of twelve, or at the most thirteen, I made that transfer, and not without a certain amount of stubbornness, getting by a good strong beaurubur bure buro (I've got to let that stand, I swear to Christ it is absolutely necessary, I can't even spell the bloody word—bureaucratic? is that it?) opposition: I made that transfer because I had decided that writing was to be my life and I wanted to make the physical part of that life to be the least demanding on my mind and spirit and indeed upon my body and nervous system. I wanted good clear writing to appear in a straight line on a piece of paper almost automatically insofar as the physical action was concerned. I wanted my spirit to be free and comfortable at all times, and never inhibited or even slowed down by the physical action of transferring thought and word and sentence to print and paper. That's all. The typing course was there, it had come into existence as one of several trade courses—for the learning of a trade by which to get a job and earn a living. Well, that would do no harm, either, for while I was serving my apprenticeship as a writer I could be earning money at work in an office, most likely in San Francisco, which I remembered from childhood, long ago, but actually only six or seven years before: and possibly even in New York, for I knew several things about these two magical cities: New York was first and foremost the first city my father (and indeed all immigrants from Europe) visited in America, and that alone drew me in thought to its streets and wonder, but it was also something more: the real capital of the country, and in a sense of the world. And I wanted to get there, and I had an idea that becoming the writer I believed I would become would get me there. And in order to become that writer without undue delay I was sure that I had better learn to type swiftly and accurately, and I did—the best thing I ever got from the public school system of California. Who else had his name at the end of a typing exercise? Well, I could invent a name or two, but I am afraid I would rather not: there may have been something by a writer we are given to thinking of as excellent, but I don't remember any such name: all I remember is Hamilton Wright Mabie, and it would seem that he is no writer at all, and what's worse, nothing else, such as an inventor, a not uncommon trade and profession in the early days and years of what has come to be called the industrial revolution. He just had that fine name and his words and sentences in the typing exercise book were dull, man, they were dull, and I loved them because his name at the end of them identified a writer, established the respect and even honor placed upon any man who happened to write something, even if it really wasn't any good.

Someday (and I have had this in mind for half a century) I am going to look up the man and find out who he was and what he did, but if I don't, the only loss will be that once again a longtime trivial curiosity has gone unsatisfied.

Robert M. Fay is the next name on the *Variety* list, and nobody I know, I am very sorry to say. Frank Fay on the other hand, at the curtain of a play in New York, announced that I was in the audience and asked me to please stand and take a bow. This is the sort of thing I believe I can absolutely honestly say I deeply dislike, but I have also got to say that I did indeed stand and turn to let the audience see my face, and quickly sat down and tried to guess who had told him that I was in the audience. We had never met, there was no reason for him to call attention to my presence—I had an idea that if somehow he had found out that I was in the audience he would not have announced it, and so I knew he had been asked to do so. The play was *Harvey*, about a child-like, harmlessly alcoholic gent whose best friend was a very big bunny rabbit, so to call it, named Harvey, by a lady from Denver, I believe, named Mary Ellen Chase, or at any rate something similar to that. I had enjoyed the play, and it may be that Frank Fay had asked backstage who was in the audience laughing so happily (noisily?) and pretty much leading the audience along, as the goat leads the sheep. This was a fact I was unable not to notice whenever I went to the theatre. I tended virtually to control an audience, and always favorably, both to play and to performers. I knew what they were up to, I very nearly anticipated everything they were doing, all of the little achievements of wisdom, comedy, character, and all-around humanity. Christ Almighty, perhaps you are thinking, Christ Almighty, when is this egomaniac going to stop telling me all about how wonderful he is? Well, you have a right to be annoyed, if you are, and I have no excuse, at all. Unless it may be that in telling as fully as possible selected and haphazard details out of my experience I am actually telling your own, or what might have been your own, or might become your own, or might at this very moment be your own. At any rate, that is how I look at the matter, for while there is probably some element of unfortunate vanity in my version (rather than God's) of my written life, as against my fuller and even unwritable life, I really don't believe there is one jot more of it than there is in the written life of anybody else, whether he himself wrote it, or hired experts to do it for him, or turned the matter over to the people at large, or his friends, or to legend or lore. I am unlearned, and by now I am willing to notice that I am probably unteachable, but I know, and apparently have always known, this rather contradictory truth: that I am very unique but precisely the same as everybody else, now or ever, tied tight and neat into the one body of the humankind. If I have vanity, I come by it from nature itself, as you do, also. Frank Fay was quite a good actor, and when he worked with Bert Wheeler in a rather famous vaudeville act, they brought real laughter to a great many people, but I didn't know him, and I heard gossip at Sardi's in New York that he was the enemy of unions, and of course that was not only reactionary, it was suicidal. And of course when Frank Fay died he was listed in the Necrology of *Variety* for that year-end, although I don't know what year it was, and some people were not at all unhappy about his passing, which is among some people the preferred way of dealing with individual death. It's a passage. I was more surprised than saddened when I learned of his death, and the reason was that he had announced my presence at the performance of *Harvey*, even though at the time, and even now, if I may, I wish to Christ he hadn't done it. I don't need to take a bow. I am an actor of course, but not in that theatre. I go to that theatre, or at least I used to, to be amused by the infinite variety of my own absurdity in the plays of anybody, in the performances of everybody, including the cast of hundreds in the audience. Maurice Feldman is also somebody I don't seem to know, while Charles K. Feldman, agent and founder of Famous Players (but this doesn't seem quite right) and producer of movies, I did know, and believe I may mention, for in 1951 I tried to be of use to him with some screenplays he owned and was trying to peddle for a big profit: one was some trash by my friend John Steinbeck entitled *The Wayward Bus*, a kind of California insipid trick that succeeds so well it is sickening. I took this employment to see about making my second marriage to the same little lady something like a reasonable success, on behalf of the small boy and smaller girl, and any others that might come along. It was unholy work, and Charles K. Feldman was essentially intolerable, at least for failing to conceal the real purpose of his artistic deviousness and his business determination, which was to take from everybody that which would bring him an enormous and totally unjustified and unearned financial profit. He died very very rich, not long after we met by chance at the George V Hotel in Paris when I was on my way to the Aviation Club for bacarat and caviar and vodka, and he was on his way to a play, not for itself of course, but because somebody had suggested that he could buy it for peanuts and turn it into a blockbuster of a movie. What's wrong with that? I think it's unnecessary, and isn't that the thing that really offends us about behavior in somebody we would rather didn't bore us quite so continuously? Charlie, as he liked to be called, was also all right, as Sir Harry Launder used to say to his audiences at curtain time, but although he gathered interesting groups of contrasting people at his dinner parties, alas it was always really because he had further expectations from each and every one of them, as the saying is. Agents are contemptible, they're both pimps and whores—that's what it comes to, and the world insists on having them—and abundantly.

Paul Ford was an actor who at the height of his career played bumbling people like the Colonel in the very funny television series entitled *Sergeant Bilko,* who was played by Phil Silvers, and with absolute authority, as the saying is. The usages of the peacetime and wartime army of the United States have been fulsome, funny, and totally fraudulent: Bilko the peacetime hustling Sergeant exploited the chickenshit of the Army's brass in a manner that was beyond fantasy, even. Not that the brass is not stupid—the highest and most respected and even beloved brass of the army, not excluding, let's say, the great George C. Marshall—is hopelessly held within the steel limitations of stupidity, because if you are part of an army, you are part of a stupidity, period: for you are obliged to use metal, machinery, explosives, transportation, shelter, clothing, food, drink, rest, recreation, health, medicine, surgery, psychiatry, and everything else of the peaceful world in a program of inflicting wounds and deaths one by one upon not only your opposite number identified as the enemy, but upon the people of the enemy as well as your own people. Consequently, there is no way you can avoid being a party to stupid criminality. On a scale so large that it is difficult to imagine how any man finds it possible to continue in his role as a member of the organization. Another preposterous, but frequently also funny, piece of fraud brought into the American dream by means of television is *Hogan's Heroes,* and all that needs to be said about it is that the enemy, the Germans alone, never the Italians, Russians, English, French, or Americans, is consistently, conveniently, and absurdly restricted to a human range of identity moving from almost innocent vanity blended with witlessness to vast pomposity blended with personal ambition about money and girls. Paul Ford was a delight to see and hear, especially when he was being belittled by Phil Silvers on television in *Sergeant Bilko.* Are we to be thankful for even these terrible miscarriages of responsibility and truth on behalf of laughter? Yes, alas, we are, for comedy has got to be cherished, regardless of how it comes into being, and from whence. The dead of the army, and of the wars, and the living who are maimed or inwardly scarred, are surely glad to laugh at how it never was. Norman Foster is a name I seem to know, but somehow I can't be sure who he is, although I believe he is not a writer, as my first notion upon seeing his name on the *Variety* list seemed to suggest. I know a Norman somebody who is a writer, and a good one, and it is that which perhaps gave me the notion. He was an actor, most likely, but no longer, of course, although if he appeared in films, as all actors do sooner or later, we shall all notice him in movies put in garbled versions on television. George Stevens sued to prevent such garbling of *An American Tragedy*, and won, I believe, but later lost. You can sue and sue, but in the end where the getting of more and more money by fewer and fewer large outfits and smart individuals is concerned, you have got to lose, for even after you have won, the opposition can move the case to a higher court, and in the meantime either show the product in their own language, as they please, or deprive the man with intense integrity, for instance, of income, satisfaction, or something else. What is satisfaction? It is folly, of course. Nobody is going to have the satisfaction of seeing the machinery of greed slow down a little, let alone stop, but George Stevens gave it a go, and so did several other directors who worked hard to achieve something like art. Should I say, "Forget it, boys"? No, I should say, if anything "Remember it, boys, harder than ever, especially after each of you has become rich from your good work." Norman Foster, if he was an actor in movies, will be seen again by those who knew him and liked him or hated him, and he will be alive in the flickerings of the story being told in any given movie, as Humphrey Bogart, called fondly Bogey by fans all over the world, is seen again and again in *Casablanca*, and Paul Muni in *Louis Pasteur*, for instance, and dozens of dead men and women flickering and flickering in the memories of millions of strangers who are somehow also friends, or even beloved friends. The revolution of industry is real enough, or more than real enough, and so is the transportation revolution, but perhaps the most magnificent and yet somehow tawdry revolution has been that of moving pictures. Will the human race throw out the thing? No, but it may be deprived of it some day by governments of various kinds. William Red Fox is another unknown among the dead of 1976. Redd Foxx on the other hand is at the height of his fame, playing the part of a black, or almost black, junk dealer somewhere in Los Angeles, by the name of Fred Sanford, and it was interesting to hear Redd Foxx on a talk show make known that his real name *is* Sanford, although I don't remember what he said his first name is, if he did say, as I would imagine he would have to. I don't know David Friedkin, either, but the reader may not especially mind if I remark that I knew David Burns, the actor and comedian who was in the army when I was and sometimes after the first formation of the day would walk with me away from the post at Astoria to a coffee shop where I preferred to pay for breakfast and the privacy if not independence of a civilian captured by the draft and the olive drab of the fucking army. Even in the dark of an early winter morning Davey Burns could make me roar with laughter by telling another of his London cockney stories, and I hope to Christ he put some on tape, so that they can be heard again, or like forever, as the halfwit children of the rich like to say, you know, you know? A language imposed by drugs and pot.

Emil Friedlander is another man I don't believe I ever met, but I have an idea that if I had met him I would have liked him, or I would have asked how he came to be given the name Emil, and we would have talked about Emil Jannings in *The Blue Angel*, starring Marlene Dietrich, a leggy young achievement, and Joseph von Sternberg, himself from Brooklyn, and according to Jim Tully, who used to consider himself an expert at such stuff, not entitled to either the von or the berg: he was Joe Stern, that's all, and so when Jim Tully told me I had to say, "But why would anybody with a great name like Joe Stern want to change it to Joseph von Sternberg?" to which if memory serves Jim Tully replied, "Because he's a fraud and he lives in the town where even beggars are frauds and believe they were only waiting to become stars." I went on the set of *The Shanghai Gesture* and saw Joe Stern or Joseph von Sternberg at work, but not with Emil Jannings, and not with Marlene Dietrich, but with a girl I was crazy about, because of her mouth, her teeth, the shape her smile took, and the strange and irresistible way she spoke English: Phyllis Brooks, a neglected jewel in the crown of American film, as the saying might be, especially in gangster or poor-boy-making-his-way movies. I believe she had even been under contract to Warner Brothers, the home of so many movies of that kind, and all I can say is she brought every stupid movie she appeared in straight to real life, real art, real wonder. It was that incredible mouth shaping words and that delicious slightly husky voice singing forth into the clatter of the voices of the high-priced stars. Joe Stern was the man who started the career of Marlene Dietrich, but in his autobiography he found it necessary to almost regret having done so, and in conversation he didn't hesitate to speak of what he did and how he did it. If you go back in time and remember *The Blue Angel*, you have no trouble remembering that both he and the new actress did their work quite well, and there is really no need for anything like a quarrel about who did the most or the best. She sang in a voice that was lowlife but everlastingly innocent, she was fragile but essentially gross, crude, and conniving. But nobody bothered to give Phyllis Brooks a truly appropriate part in any movie and so she has to be fished out of three or four dozen old movies and studied and honored and remembered as a very rare and special American actress, girl, woman, lady, and person. I loved her, both in the flickers and in person: I could never get enough of seeing her and of hearing her speak—and laugh. Emil Friedlander very probably was not an actor, for if he had been his very handsome name would have been changed to John Wayne, for instance, or Budd Mother, or Tex Tambourine. Budd Mother? Is that possible? No longer maybe, but let's not forget people who are named Father, Brother, Sister, Nephew, Niece, Uncle. You say you can't think of people with such names. Think harder, sir, and lady, just think harder, you'll come to them. Emil Friedlander was probably in production, that is the kind of appropriate name for a producer, and when he died lots of directors and players remembered that he had been the nicest guy of all on the set—but firm, firm as steel, boys, girls, have fun, but you're costing too much. And so on. Then, the name is Jean Gabin, and while that also is probably a name imposed upon his real name, it is also a name that came to stand in the minds of millions of people for a kind of Gallic macho stolidity and forbearance and durability, for in *The Grand Illusion* (and just dwell on the daring that is in that name for a movie from 40 or more years ago: anybody in Hollywood with an ounce of experience could have told the great painter's son who directed the thing, Jean Renoir, that if he wanted the picture to make money he had better call it *German Dogs and French Men*, or something like that, but no, he had to have it *The Grand Illusion*, in which a good dozen or more players did perhaps the best work of their cinematic careers, so to put it. And why? Well, first, because the story was what it was, and second because the director was who he was, and third because the players were who they were. One day in Hollywood, long after the movie, I was introduced at a small party to a man who seemed very like a tailor of long ago, in Russia somewhere, in a story by Gogol or Chekhov, and after awhile people began to chat with him about *The Grand Illusion*, and so it came out that he had played the part of the Jew who broke down tramping through snow and cursed Jean Gabin and became hysterical, because they had all been held prisoner in Germany for so long, and escape through the snow was so difficult, so painful, so really impossible, with a lunkhead companion like Jean Gabin, and with Eric von Stroheim back at the camp sure to track them down and shoot them both dead, with a great deal of Teutonic deliberateness, time-taking, and pleasure. He was looking for work in Hollywood, but if he ever got work, or what his name is, I don't know. Then comes Guy M. Gadbois, and even though I have no idea who he was up to the day of his death in 1976, I like his name, and wish I knew what the M. is for: perhaps Maupassant, since the bois part of his family name is French, and for all I know also the Gad part. James M. Gaines on the other hand has M. for his middle initial, too, but surely for some name other than Maupassant, probably something like Michael, but what he did in showbiz I don't know. Surely something, for is it possible to imagine that anybody who dies has not in that very act itself been a star?—and a big one—in showbiz and any other kind of biz anybody could ever hope to hear about, or to avoid, not excluding churchbiz, governmentbiz, crimebiz.

80

There is a school of thought in the world but especially in America, that puts forward the theory that the well-being of the human race, or at any rate of the economic system, again especially of America, will be healthy, wholesome, and prosper only if there is continuous waste, or turnover as it is called: planned obsolescence, and so forth. The theory is designed solely for a place, a system, and a people who cannot avoid continuous abundance, and excess, but it suddenly comes up short when it comes up against people and places and even systems which have no excess at all, no abundance, and indeed not enough to go around in very small portions. So what's this all about suddenly? This: I hate waste. That's all. I consider the automobile manufacturers and all their advertising agents deadly frauds for discarding classically right and sensible and comely models solely in order to shame their owners into selling or junking them and buying the new models. That's just one example of the kind of waste I hate. And in any case I am obliged to consider anybody bullied by the advertisers into giving up a perfectly fine automobile, for instance, because very few others seem to be driving them any longer, is a fool—so who needs to be concerned about him? Well, there is this ahead a little bit: is death nevertheless planned obsolescence? That it is, that it is, as the comedian's swift reply to the pretty, naive young lady goes. Built-in turnover is basic, and indeed the glory of the human experience. Without it there would be no system at all, there would be nothing at all, there would be no beginning, there would be no end. What happened to the middle, that famous invention of Hollywood movie producers of fifty years ago: Give me a great story with a beginning, a middle, and an end, the old boys used to say, and they weren't mistaken at all: it was just that they didn't know it was impossible for anything human, or imagined as being animal, mineral, ethereal, angelic, devilish, or anything else, not to be with a beginning, a middle, and an end—because that is built into us, into the proceedings of all that we are a part of, and is the basic system of any conceivable and unknown, undiscovered, order of matter in action. We have no choice: it is there in that way, it comes and goes in that way, we are a part of it willywilly willynilly willysilly or watch it and still you will not see it—we are both helplessly and gloriously a part of the only game in town, the only religion, philosophy, science, economy, and all of the other things we have come upon out of necessity or longing, each of them only a small part of the original and everlasting procedure of coming out, going about, going back in, or Life—seed, egg, birth, hatching, chance, moving, putting forth seed, egg, giving birth, bringing forth, and going back in. So where does the waste of any of this come in? How could anything be said to be a waste? Well, in a sense there is no such thing, but we don't understand that sense too well, the human being having been confounded in the head by the obviously necessary but also destructive invention of money. The billionaire with a deteriorated sense of life, for instance, moving steadily to a very pathetic and ugly death, like Howard Hughes, and we had all of us for so long imagined that he was a kind of new Lord, above the Herd, and impossible to intimidate by the government. But although he died in 1976, and is listed in *Variety*, I am not going to jump the gun and talk about him or his meaning here. It is not his turn. The point is that there is probably no waste of any kind possible—in nature, at any rate. There seems to be a great deal of waste in human conglomerates, or nations, or groupings around economic systems, and civil or religious cultures, and there is no way that (in terms of wealth represented by money) we can imagine that the major governments do not piss away billions every year to support their very likely justified anxieties about what their contemporaries are doing—but how can this be? Aren't they all human? Forget it, brother, that way madness lies, or childish absurdity, a child crying it out: "Cut it out, Papa, you son of a bitch—stop choking Mama just because she is a liar." If waste is natural, what business have I got to be so opposed to it? Why do I abhor waste? Why do I work patiently in my own life and world to make do, to use up everything I have, to throw out nothing—clothing, food, papers, shoes, ah well, there is no system to this list, but everything is connected to the self, and that is surely the thing not to be wasted: life, breath, feeling, sensibility, hearing, seeing, eating, drinking, sleeping, intelligence, creativity, everything collective that contributes something to the reasonably meaningful continuance of life, in this instance the life of this self, this immeasurable enormity, this incalculable triviality, this silly jester, this loving comforter, and so on and so forth. I suppose the best answer is not known to me, and I must be obliged to say I don't know why I abhor waste. Even the anthropologists and archaeologists have rushed to the City Dumps, so to put it, of ancient tribes, to understand how they lived. The daily garbage of Americans alone weighs surely more than the total grandeur of Babylon and buries the Tower of Babel every day ten times over. Shall we therefore at least think about finding out something more about the spending of billions on weapons solely because we believe that if somebody else has better weapons we will be forced to change—but we want to change anyhow, don't we, and we never do, do we? Ah well, let us move along, we are living, we are dying, we are not yet on *Variety*'s Necrology list.

The next name on the list is Tim Gale, and alas again, I never heard of him, as the saying is. Tim Pfluegger I did hear of, and did indeed meet quite a few times in San Francisco in the 1930s, all through the 1930s, and I am not going to get busy and say what great times those were: of course they were, they had to be: I was 22 in 1930, I was 32 in 1939, one of the enormous years of my life (but terrible too), and I once thought of writing a big summing up of that year, an enormous work, straight out of my own experiences but involving the whole Western World, and very much including the Invasion of Poland by Germany (not by Hitler, although he shoved Germany into it: the Invasion of Poland was by Germany—the people permitted it, but Christ Almighty, who's kidding who? The people permit everything, they always have, for the simple reason that "the people" is a myth, there are only individuals, and individuals just can't move anything or anybody other than their own furniture and themselves... but isn't Hitler, for instance, an individual? No, he is not: he gave that up when he failed in his desire to be a writer, and he became Germany—good God Almighty, he became Germany itself, and nobody in the rest of the world, nobody in France, in England, in Russia, or in the United States knew how to humor him into being Germany, in being mad, in a way that would not seek to destroy, and nearly succeed, the whole Western World, and murder millions of Jews, Catholics, Socialists, gypsies, or Germans who refused to go along in any way at all with Germany's madness, not excluding trying to get away. The year 1939 was a mother, as we say. If the years of our calendar were put into the hours of our days, I wanted the answer to be the title of that book: and Frank Morley had it figured out and told me the answer, but alas I have not said it right, and if the writer doesn't say it, how shall the reader read it? All the same I began to see Tim Pfluegger in San Francisco after the publication of my first book, in October of 1934, when I began to see more and more people because that's what happens, and a man finds himself being invited to houses and events and nothing is really more educational for a newly-arrived writer. Tim Pfluegger was a building, a genius, and he had connections with the building of the great San Francisco Bay Bridge, upon which I walked on a steel beam at the top of one of the supports and was photographed by Ralph Stackpole's son Peter, working for the newly-founded *Life*, for Henry Luce, but of course the photograph was a souvenir for me, and did not appear in Life or anywhere else. I might have fallen, but I did walk from the center of the beam to the edge, and back. Foolishness? Not at all. I knew I wouldn't fall, because I knew I wouldn't fall, if you like, but I never knew Tim Gale. Tim Pfluegger died but I never even read about it, and have not marked the time or place—in San Francisco, I presume, at the age of 66 or so, I am willing to guess. A big man, a hearty man, an engineer, a good companion in a San Francisco saloon like Izzy's, but I don't remember him there, I remember him at rather fine dinner parties at the homes of the rich. The name following Jim Gale is Paul Gallico, and if I never met him I certainly knew about him—as pretty much anybody past the age of forty may be presumed to have known: for years he had been a syndicated sportswriter, for the Hearst papers, I believe, and then he began to write short stories, and then novels, and for all I know a book of memoirs now and then, as well. He has a fine name in itself: Paul and Gallico are not readily surpassed as two names brought together and placed upon the brow of any man. If he didn't write *Miracle on 34th Street*, he did write novels that were not very much unlike it. I myself long before him, but not before Charles Dickens, wrote Christmas fables and stories and prayers and poems, because early along in time we are all of us caught up in the tyranny of a birth coinciding with the approach of the end of an old year and the arrival of a new, and the longing in everybody for love, and the eagerness of everybody to forgive everybody and to give everybody something. It's a sticky time, and not really fraudulent at all, but easily eased, eased, eased slowly and steadily by the hours of approachment, to use a special Gallic word in English, the hours of the waited-for day, into the fraudulent. I avoid writing Christmas stuff and indeed I stopped more than a quarter of a century ago, just as I stopped writing parts for kids in plays. It won't do, it's not right, but the childish longing of the heart for so many ineffables gathered into the lore of snow and fir tree and color and toys and mother and father and family and candy—good God, it hurts even to think about it. Paul Gallico moved to Lichtenstein and as far as I know after ten or more years of happy living there, died there. William Geer Sr. is also nobody I know, but I am delighted by the Sr., or Senior, added to his name. One doesn't often see that. The son is expected to differentiate himself from the father, but the father being the first has no need to differentiate himself from the son. All the same there have been Juniors whose fathers were so nearly totally unknown as to be as good as dead before the boy was born—a proper and decent story told to children born out of wedlock: placing upon the child the privilege or opportunity to safely imagine the father to have been a good man, and to ever after see him as young and handsome, which he might very well have been, in any case, even if he had been one of the cheaters of the world—a pimp, a thief, a liar, a humbug, or an all-around son of a bitch.

82

Arnold Gingrich. He was a founder in the early 1930s of *Esquire* magazine, with the financial support of a clothing manufacturer who might have borne the name Smart. The magazine was large and fat, and what Arnold Gingrich wanted was something along the lines of that thing that came to be identified or summed-up by the Mexican slang of macho, and machismo: a kind of masculine magazine pure and simple, or whatever. The idea caught on, and he ran *The Crack-Up* by F. Scott Fitzgerald, and he may even have brought that confession into being by asking the rattled writer to earn some of the money that Gingrich had advanced to him for short stories, to earn it by writing anything, anything at all, man, and probably desperately and even possibly very reluctantly the writer told himself, his wife Zelda, his girlfriend the gossip columnist Sheila Graham, his literary friends like Ernest Hemingway and Edmund Wilson, to name only two, the editor of *Esquire*, the readers of *Esquire*, and the world at large, how he had fallen or had been brought down. Like all of his writing, it is good, but it is also sorrowful and a kind of pain. You can straighten yourself out, man, you can lay off the sauce, fellow, you can stop feeling sorry for yourself, boy, you can become alot less pompous about who you are and what you have done, sir, you can take it slow and easy and straighten out and either happily give up writing completely, or happily return to it better than ever. I had an agent in the first years of my career: Ann Watkins. She did quite nicely by me, as I believe the language puts it, for a fee of 10% of the gross. In her office somewhere on 5th or Park Avenue I believe there were two employees: William Duggan, who changed his name to Pat Duggan, and Harold Matson. In 1936 they wired me that they had left Ann Watkins to start a literary agency of their own and wouldn't I wish them well and perhaps even let them represent my writing. For a while they did, and I should have broken my leg as the saying is, and not have permitted them to. When I discovered that they had written themselves into income from my play *The Time of Your Life*, Pat Duggan had left the partnership to work for Sam Goldwyn as the story editor, or some such, and so I confronted Harold Matson with what I had found out and said I wanted him to conclude his connection with that play, and with a number of other works, or properties, as the trade puts it, and he replied, Well, we have contracts, and they are perfectly legal. I pointed out that he had always known that I never read contracts, and that I presumed he would not take advantage of that trust, but since I had made a mistake, I would like him to conclude his connection with my works, and he again said that our agreements were legal and that he saw no reason to conclude his connection. Well, then, I said, how much do you want—I'll pay you. A million dollars cash, he replied, because over the years I figure my share of income from the various properties will be far more than a million dollars. I went away with a properly low opinion of the man. I was nagged over the years by various people about being untrusting, and so in the early 1960s, after having avoided any connection with the man insofar as new works were concerned, I read, in my place in Paris, a letter from him telling me that if I would write an autobiography—all of this is not in sequence, or even accurate, but it is the true essence of what happened—he could earn me so much money that I could pay off the Tax Collector, who had been hounding me since the time of my three years as a drafted private in the U.S. Army, and with enough left over to provide me with enough to feel rich. I wrote the book, he made a deal with a subsidiary of Simon & Schuster (Trident Press), and to show my good faith when it was time to sign the agreement I went to the Ice Rink in Rockefeller Center at the end of the work day to drink martinis and to eat caviar with Harold Matson and a vice-president of Trident Press, by name Herbert Alexander. I said, "I am not going to read this agreement, even though I am drinking martinis, and don't know what's in it, and you have drawn it up, I am only going to sign it, because I have heard that I don't trust people, especially in the business world." So they did not insist that either I must read the agreement or a lawyer must, and they watched me sign it, and I went on drinking and believing that I would soon have the Tax Collector paid off, and be rich. The book was published, first in hardback and then in paperback, and did quite poorly—*Here Comes There Goes You Know Who.* When no money began to arrive long after I presumed the book in both editions had earned back the advance of $25,000, I fished out the contract and studied it carefully and discovered that I had been cheated again, this time by both the agent and his pal the publisher. Well, what has that got to do with Arnold Gingrich? This. Harold Matson was offered by Arnold Gingrich $200 in 1936 for a story called "The Summer of the Beautiful White Horse." I informed Harold Matson that $200 was too little, the magazine was fat and full of big profitable advertisements, and I would accept $500. Harold Matson wrote from New York to me at 348 Carl Street in San Francisco that *Esquire* magazine had already set up the story for appearance in its next issue and that Arnold Gingrich could not possibly remove it, except at a great expense. Furthermore, $200 was the top price he paid for short stories; $75 was the usual price. And the agent asked me to please do him a favor and accept the $200, because Arnold Gingrich was an important editor and the agent didn't want to alienate him and not be able to sell stories by other writers. I said okay, but let him understand that I will never send him another story. He didn't understand, but I never sent him another story. He was worse than cheap.

83

After Arnold Gingrich comes Harry Gittleson, somebody I don't know, although sitting on a train drawing out of Union Station (or whatever its name is) in Los Angeles on my way to New York sometime in 1952 or 1953 or 1954 I saw Harry Carey the famous silent film actor, especially in Westerns, standing with a small group after having put somebody on the train, and as the window at which I sat slowly approached the actor he looked back at me precisely as I was looking at him, with a slightly uncertain belief that I knew him from somewhere, and then knew that I did, but that it was from movies for many years but I had never met him, and he in turn smiled, and compelled me to smile, and nodded, and I nodded, and I knew that he had either guessed my identity or that he was a very sensitive and kind man and acknowledged my concern about his identity with the same kind of concern about mine. Later on I did meet him and his wife and his son and some of their friends, and even though we had good opportunities several times to bring up the train episode, we didn't. Why should he know who I am, even though I pretty much look like my photographs that appear on my books or in advertisements or in magazines, and he had come upon them and had put the face at the train window accurately upon his memory of the photographs. Now, this matter of the photographs is amusing: many writers keep using photographs taken when they were young: certainly for years John Steinbeck and Ernest Hemingway, and there can be no question about many new photographs having been taken, but they or their agents or their publishers just didn't want to spoil the achievement in the dimension of lore brought about by the early photograph. And then suddenly Ernest Hemingway began to have the Yussuf (?) Karsh photograph out in the world of publicity: a very earnest, poetic, and even pained face above an almost monk-like or even ecclesiastical collar made by a turtleneck sweater and sad, sad, patient eyes, not unlike the eyes of a very patient harnessed work horse, ox, or buffalo. Karsh, being Armenian, might be thought to have been the right man to discover and capture that quality in the eyes of the world-famous American writer, but it might be a lot simpler than that: that is to say, if you know your work and you have enough time taking pictures of almost anybody you can very probably get to something like a side of him that most of the time he prefers to keep concealed. Ernest Hemingway in that famous photograph is not the boyo of his fable, he is the man who for so long, and even too long, thought he really had to be the boyo of the fable, or die, as of course he did die, finally. As for John Steinbeck, my acquaintance, and California contemporary, he wasn't photographed by Karsh and so pretty much all the way straight to the grave his public photograph was of a very young man. Harry Gittleson might very well have been not really in showbusiness, but a lawyer whose clients were in that fine if fishy business, the same as Arnold Krakauer who was once the husband of the woman who wrote *Forever Amber* and was earlier married to the clarinet-player and novelist whose name is Artie Shaw. I find it very annoying and slightly sad that I can't think of her name, even though I met her several times while she was married to the clarinet-player, and once visited the apartment at the Sherry-Netherland that she shared with her latest, and perhaps fourth husband, the former U.S. Marine officer and the present representative in matters of legal procedures for many people including a variety of showbiz souls, Arnold Gingrich. He was in the enemy camp in the second divorce proceeding, in which the little woman after having wreaked havoc all around her and the two children, and having all but driven me mad with her dishonest but clever mind, was demanding back child-support payments (I refused to have the word alimony employed, even though had I used it the enormous sums paid the little lady would have been deductible from my annual taxes) which both she and her lawyer knew I could not possibly pay since I was flat broke and no money was coming in. And of course she and her mother never stopped for the 20 years I knew the daughter, putting forward to gossip columnists that she was a rich heiress. There are lawyers up the nose of people in all professions, so of course there are a lot of them tied into the activities of showbiz people. Harry Gittleson might have been one, but I don't know, he also might have been only a showbiz dentist, accountant, personal manager of a singer, or restaurant-owner, for *Variety* lists them all when they die, and a good thing, too. Nobody should be deprived of at least a little fame for having lived: it is heroic, no matter who's looking or how he's looking. Next comes Frances Howard Goldwyn and if she is Sam Goldwyn's wife I know I met her. Twice. Once at a big party at Rouben Mamoulian's house when he was casting Goldwyn's movie, *Porgy & Bess,* which in the end he didn't direct, and Otto Preminger did—a man I had seen many times long ago in New York, who had the ability to sustain anybody's compulsion to find him a large gaseous condition in the bowels, seeking to escape and almost never quite making it. He had a high-volume voice, speech clarity in an accent that was thick and unncessarily prolonged, and a willingness not to be misunderstood about a compulsion to be ruthless in all of his activities. He was ruthless. But I hardly believe it was necessary or that it made a difference. And I am glad that I saw him in action many times. I met Mrs. Goldwyn again at a birthday party for her husband given by the Ira Gershwins: on August 31st, 1958 it may have been, which was my 50th birthday, which I kept to myself.

Reader, are you making any sense of any of this? If not, don't worry about it too much. I may ask the publisher to put into the book an album of photographs, and you can look at them, something I find very appealing to me about any book. I may ask the publisher to run a photograph of every person in the *Variety* list, and the publisher in turn may ask me to go have my head examined. Running such an album costs a lot of money. Publishing a book costs a lot of money. Whoever the publisher may be that is willing to publish this book, he may first find out if there can be any profit for him from doing so, from any kind of book club, from any kind of magazine condensation, after publication, from a shared movie sale, as they put it, or even only from sales themselves. Of the hardback, that is. If the publisher can make a deal with a big outfit (owned by Gulf Oil or somebody) for a paperback edition with a first printing of half a million copies, then of course the publisher will not only be happy to publish the book, he may even find it sensible and profitable to run the gallery of photographs. But let's you and me, reader, forget it, and let me just suspect that no publisher is going to publish this book, and that I am not going to publish it, and that my standing and working every day early in the fine and fantastic year of 1977 has been solely for itself: I have stood faithfully and produced a whole book because I have wanted to. What would I be doing if I were not writing, right this minute? I'll tell you what. I would be riding a wheel all the way to town, to the Public Library, or I would be riding north instead of south, for a visit to Fig Garden Village, or I would be in the backyard of this house and the backyard of the house next door, on the corner, which is also mine, and I would be noticing that the almond boughs of four trees have got buds that have opened into blossoms, and I would be smelling the blossoms for the very fine but faint scent, which had I not given up smoking cigarettes almost ten years ago I would not be able to experience at all—it would be a blank, and that would be a very big loss. On Thursday, February 17th, this day, I am sure to find at least a dozen more buds open than I found yesterday afternoon (about eight in all). Do you know almond blossoms? They are fragile, and they are first. So in standing here from mid-January through all of February, and into the first day of March, I am doing precisely what I want to do, without pain, anguish, or suffering of any order. I have an easy plot of course: the *Variety* Necrology list for 1976, as I am sure you are sick of hearing, but if you are, reader, don't be, I beg of you, it isn't worth it, just relax, cool it, this won't do you any harm at all: you are alive, you are still alive, and that's the thing that counts, and what this is about is for me to know I am alive in writing this, and for you to know you are alive in reading it—or even in not reading it, if I can provoke you into dropping the thing or throwing it across the room and out the window, well, man, what's wrong with that? You've got *that,* haven't you? The only sense you really need to make of this is the only sense you really need to make of anything else (and of everything else): that you are at the center of it all, you are still there, still the hero of the world, which was the name of one of my plays in the early 1940s, still the brave man or woman or child of the age, still famous for your breathing uninterruptedly (I hope you like that stupid word), still anonymous, still unknown, still secret, except to your own hosts, and to your own god, and to the whole earth and all members of the animal family upon it. Fret not, this is your story, enjoy it, read it, don't read it, cherish it, or throw it out: it is for you, it is yours, it belongs to the living who shall soon enough become the dead so that others may go on safely being the living, and may not be unaware that they will soon enough become the dead. Get that from this, and wouldn't you say you have got quite a lot? I would. Paul M. Gonsky I do not know either, but I must confess I like the name Gonsky, however much it may be abbreviated from something else, which I am sure I would have enjoyed even more than the short form. Lloyd Griffin ditto, so to put it, without disrespect, but he might be the brother or cousin of Merv Griffin, and I have met Merv Griffin both on his talk show when it was in New York long ago, and at his home at dinner the same night. Bobby Hackett I have the notion I do know, I must know, but it is not so: I can't place a Bobby Hackett at all, for he is crowded out of the picture, living or dead, by Buddy Hackett, the philosopher, who may be overweight but is certainly still among the living. As for Hap Hadly, stiff again: I don't know him. There have been many Haps but the only one that I know is Hap Farmanian, and I know him from the years 1917 and 1918 in Fresno, when we sold *The Evening Herald.* Hap got his name from his remarkable laugh, which was indeed as different and special as an object of some kind, made let's say of wood, stone, glass, or metal. It was great but it was and continues to be indescribable. He laughed and the sound of his laughter made you feel good—as I trust that the sound of the laughter in this book is going to make you feel good. And then he would speak and the words he spoke made you feel good, and then he laughed again, and spit, for he was a moist boy, a moist man, laughing, speaking, and spitting as he went about his business of selling papers. His corner, the Rowell Building, at Van Ness and Tulare Streets was always wet, not from rain, but from Hap's spitting. His proper name was Harry, from Haroutiune, I believe.

Billy Halop was one of the Dead End Kids, and The Dead End was a place in New York where slum kids both gathered for meetings and swam in the East River—the fashionable river of Manhattan, or slightly more fashionable than the Hudson, though by the time it reached the Dead End the river was pretty far gone to be considered anything better than wet, even in those days of not so long ago but still long long ago. I never met Billy Halop or any of the other Dead End Kids, who somehow also came to be the property and perhaps even the pride of Warner Brothers, who seemed to have a knack for providing the country with new legends that might not be altogether fantastic, for there are always stupid and brainless wiseguys determined to become bigshots with big money in all big cities, and these became the American gangsters, and there are always slum kids, underprivileged kids, worldly kids in a sense, a jump ahead of the cops and society and Warner Brothers. And Warner Brothers. That is to say, somebody made of equal parts of gangsters and slum kids cashing in on the national connection with the game of Law vs. Longing. There were four or five Dead End Kids in Sidney Kingsley's play in New York, and when the play became a movie at Warners (or wherever it may have been, it doesn't matter at all if the picture happened to be done, let's say, at R.K.O. Radio, as I believe it was called for quite a long time—and let's dwell on that name a moment as we go: R.K.O. Radio, and suddenly it comes to me I've got the thing wrong, I must have it wrong, for the R. of R.K.O. is for Radio, the K. for Keith, and the O. for Orpheum, so what's Radio doing at the end of the noise of the alphabetic display? Forget it, for that doesn't matter, either, except to demonstrate perhaps how magical cabala names even fade and disappear.) And when the play became a movie at Warners, or R.I.O. Hamburger (for instance), again the number of kids was five, and some of them, if indeed not all of them, had gone to the movie from the play, from Broadway, and like as not from the slums not far from the original Dead End, as recalled by the playwright Sidney Kingsley. Billy Halop was probably one of them, and it may also be that he himself had been a slum kid, but sometimes it doesn't work out that way. Humphrey Bogart, for instance, was from Main Line Philadelphia Society, so to put it, but eschewed (I hope you like that) the family tradition of acceptable lifetime work in favor of acting, first in plays and finally and for the rest of his life in movies. And saw no reason to regret it, one may suspect, although his closest of kin may always have looked upon his friends in the industry with a certain courteous distrust. They are so really sure and loud, aren't they? and so on. The Dead End Kids had the bodies and faces of the poor, or rather of the kids of the harassed poor, the people whose bones and muscles were given excessive burdens, whose minds and souls were hemmed in on all sides by narrow spaces with few exits—and it was just one such narrow space in a garment sweatshop early in the century with no easy or abundant exits which tragically cost hundreds of parents and children their lives in a literal hell of swift fire and unbreathable air—poisonous air. One such that brought into being the trade unions, or the Garment Workers Union, at any rate. Well, you see, you come to America and you were put to work at very low wages under very bad conditions and it got you started, it did at least that much, got you into some kind of flat on the lower east side, not far from Hester Street, and it got you clothing and shoes and food and a chance to catch your breath and get to night school and to the Yiddish Theatre once in awhile to dream the story of your soul, but after you had got started, and you were all there and working and working—well, it just wouldn't do, the wages were too little, the conditions were really worse than the conditions in Poland (many a Jew said so, and many wished they might go back and die where the synagogue was at least still a rock in the dispersion.) Sidney Kingsley got the Pulitzer Prize for another of his plays—perhaps it was *Men in White*—and, reader, if he didn't write *Dead End*, again, please accept my apology, he is still Sidney Kingsley, and Billy Halop is still Billy Halop, and what I'm saying is as valid as it might ever have been considered to be. No wonder Marxism, Leninism, Trotskyism (so to put it), communism, socialism, trade unionism, the I.W.W. (Industrial Workers of the World), pushed out into the narrow spaces allotted to the immigrants from Europe—something had to help them, and it couldn't possibly be Hare Krishna or any of its Sun Moon or Manson variations, which captivated so many of their great grandchildren, and astonished the rich and pleased parents of those great grandchildren. A revolution was needed to take away from the rich their stolen wealth—until you were one of the rich yourself. And no wonder that then your really spoiled and silly kids scoffed at schooling and took to evasion, escape, and the speaking and writing of gibberish through drugs of all kinds, and of course fretful homosexuality defiantly marching as if for the liberation of the working class from the deadly iron claws of the military/industrial cartels slowly but surely profiting from the unavoidable destruction of the human race itself—and so on and so forth. The revolution may not be lost, but it has become the thing that is to be the cause of another revolution, possibly for a going back to the equivalent of the synagogue (or church, reader) and the values of an earnest group at home in a family trying for truth and dignity.

About forty years ago, sometime in the middle 1930s, a very erudite publication named *Names* was founded at the University of California at Berkeley, and for some reason I have forgotten or never knew, I was invited to write a paper, as it was put, on any aspect of the matter of names as I might prefer, so I sent in a piece somewhat along the lines of the importance of names in writing: in stories, in novels, in plays, and possibly even in poems. I am not ashamed to confess (and not because so many years have gone by) that my piece was no good at all, for it was a million miles from what the subject not only deserves but very nearly compels, but I can say this for how I came to do such a poor job. In those days I wrote on the run, my real joy being getting out to the town and having fun—eating, drinking, gambling, being with the pretty girls who might be at one or another of the favorite places, or spas, if you don't mind, and getting them one at a time to bed somewhere, and like as not I wrote a special piece haphazardly, without research, and in a big hurry, so I could get back to the fun. All right, so what? But before I reply to that excellent question I must comment on speech in which there is a vocal punctuation which consists of the question "O.K." or "okay?". And this speech is the present property of the minorities of various kinds which are seeking some kind of liberation. The speakers are invariably seized by a grand emotionality, a terrible intensity, and are so nearly unread, so nearly indeed illiterate, that it is impossible for them to put into words what they want to say, with the result that they keep asking "okay?" And keep answering that okay with another okay. "Okay? Okay." I don't like spelling O.K. as okay, but the fact is that O.K. is slightly more troublesome for writers because of the two capitals and the two periods. R.S.V.P. may be considered a word. Also: C.O.D., and S.O.S., and several others, but Bergen Evans and other experts will have to tell us what we know they are likely to tell us: anything is a word that is used and understood. Something like that. Minorities of any kind need articulate and calm speakers or their cause is likely to be considered an excuse for the lonely to edge into the limelight, so to put it. O.K.? O.K. In the piece I wrote for the new magazine, a quarterly, entitled *Names,* I talked about the deep significance of names in works of literature, sacred or profane, although I did not refer to St. Francis of Assisi, or Tarzan of the Apes. I referred to Oliver Twist, to Huckleberry Finn, and perhaps to several other great names of literature, but probably not to Penrod, or Penrod and Sam, for the reason that these very special and likable heroes of Mr. Booth Tarkington of Indiana somehow had never entered into my reading. Why? I even now wonder. Very likely because of their names, I suspect, but there are surely other and better reasons, not the least of which is that it was all accidental. What I read, what I came to go on reading, what I didn't read, and what I began to read and dropped. I also didn't mention, most likely, that I made a point of giving the central character—as we in the profession put it—small unnecessary joke, reader—of the first of my popular books, an Armenian name, and what is more a very difficult one: to this day readers mispronounce Aram, which is pronounced correctly precisely as we sound the words "arm" or "army" or "Armenia." And they make a shambles of Garoghlanian, which is quite simple, really, except possibly for Anglo-Saxon pronunciation of the "ogh" syllable. My reason for giving the central character of a big immigrant family that name is simple: I wanted to. As an example for so many sons and daughters of immigrant Armenians who were ashamed of both their given and family names, and as a reply to the absurd people who had made these children afraid to bear their names and eager to change them to something readily pronouncable by trivial, inferior, and frequently vicious people. Lo, I am a writer, and my given name is William, and my family name is Saroyan, and I have given myself in these stories out of my life in Fresno the even more difficult family name of Garoghlanian, and a totally Armenian first name, making that character Aram Garoghlanian, and sir and lady, go fuck yourselves if you don't like it. But of course that last part was only faintly suspected by anybody. The name Aram both belongs to the Armenians and to the Saroyans. We have it and want it and like it and my son bears it, and once at Catholic School in Beverly Hills, sick of being mocked about it by boys named Walter, Robert, James, or Oscar, he told me he wanted to change it to Bill, and I told him to wait a while, and after a year he told me he was glad he had waited: he wouldn't change his name for any other in the world. And rightly. It had become himself, and that's all there is. My mother's mother was a daughter of the Garoghlanian tribe, and so I wanted her name to be noticed in my writing, because she was a rare and great woman, and the strongest force in my family. A woman stronger than a man in a family? You better believe it, as the saying is. After the death of her husband, Minas Saroyan, partly from alcohol, partly from snowed-in annual Bitlis Highlands depression, partly from the genetic force of his tribe, and partly from a disease unnamed in 1901 (possibly cancer), Lucy Garoghlanian did everything necessary to lift them up out of where they had been for centuries, and move them twelve thousand miles or more to America. How could I possibly not celebrate her name, since it so intimately related to my birth in Fresno, California, this very city where I now stand and write? And while my piece in *Names* was essentially trash, it was not because I really didn't understand the meaning of names: it was only that I was rushing to life.

87

Let us consider then the next name on *Variety*'s list, for it is the name that made me remember the magazine *Names*, which was sent to me for its first two or three years, and continued for a great many more, and may still be published, although I would not be at all surprised to hear that it was discontinued long ago, probably at the death of the two men who were its founders, and experts in the science of names (and it is a science: first you name things, and then you charge them with energy by means of verbs, when you establish a language, or even a literary style, although in that event you invent far less than you exercise individual usage, which soon enough becomes your style, if I may. Do you remember? Style is the man. What else could it possibly be? You saw that the minute you saw your contemporaries alive with yourself in the world: Fat, Sharky, Tussy, Alleyboy, Happy, Cookie, and so on and so forth, and so named and so known, some willingly, some with annoyance, but all with at least a fair element of appropriateness. Joseph Henabery is the name, that is to say, and I do not know him, although I have a play called *The Paris Comedy*, in which the gangling Texan run-away from home and family to Paris takes up with the beautiful daughter of a family of highclass whores, or courtesans, and all of these women continue young-seeming and very professional: great-grandmother, grandmother, mother, and daughter. The girl Henna-berry from Texas, rich of course, takes up with, to the astonishment of his first-born son, and to the amusement of his second-born, and to the admiration of his third-born, but in the end he lets her go, with the gift of a magnificent house south of Paris, a glorious sum of money, and something like a moment of full and real love on both sides, in spite of the girl's traditional character and profession, and the man's basic intelligence and skill at finding the spurious in any situation, including his own. Why would I want to write a play like that? Well, I was in Paris, I was broke, I needed to be working, I was like the man himself, in my 51st year, and I believed it might make a million dollars for me. It didn't. It had its world premiere in Vienna at the time of the annual Opera Ball, and I went to the event, and enjoyed it, even though I don't understand German. Once, it might have earned $25,000 for me at Columbia Broadcasting System, but the lady in charge suddenly came forward with the rule that it was immovable policy that plays at CBS had to be unproduced, and although the production had been in Vienna, in the German language, the rule could not be changed. (Don't you believe it, reader, just don't you ever believe it. Then, why was the play which was so admired by the lady producer not produced? For reasons unknown to me, that's why, and I'll be damned if I will permit that little piece of funny business to put my vulnerability for paranoia into action.) The next name may very well be the best or most unique name of the whole list. Please get ready for it: E.A.R. (Kip) Herren. Well, it is well known that in James Joyce's *Finnegans Wake*, the initials of the central character, Joyce, or the Irish race, or the human race, or yourself, stand for Here Comes Everybody—wrong again, and I'm not going to stop to find out how or why, let it go. What E.A.R. stands for is also really nothing I want to work at. Kip could very probably have been spoken once or twice in his fairly long lifetime to Rudyard Kipling, but I doubt it, for we know that he was a finicky man and didn't like having liberties taken: especially we know from stories about his prolonged visit to the U.S., around Boston. Disputes, legalities, court action, absurdities and on and on. Clifton Fadiman once said on a talk show that the interlocutor called him Kip: it was his name. From childhood, one suspects, younger brother William, for instance, not quite equal to Clifton. As for Herren, in German it stands for "gentlemen," or so I am willing to say. Don't know him, wish I did, and especially wish I knew why he wanted Ear in three separate whole letters of the alphabet to be the first part of his name. Earwick? Wasn't that also one of the big names in *Finnegans Wake*? And then comes Arthur Hornblow, Jr., and I know him, and I know that his father, not referred to as Sr., as I remember his name in print in the great and gone and forgotten *Theatre Arts Magazine*, was thereby a rather significant person if not personality in the American Theatre, which aspired to excellence, for *Theatre Arts* concerned itself with the best in all aspects of theatre without regard for commercial or Broadway success. I used to study every issue of *Theatre Arts* at the Fresno Public Library on Broadway after the age of thirteen when I became a summertime full-day messenger at Postal Telegraph, and an after-school 8-hour messenger in the wintertime—and it was better than going to college, that's all it was. Both having that job, and keeping up with the stuff in *Theatre Arts*. I now and then chanced upon Arthur Hornblow Jr., and while we may be said to have been on a first-name basis, we could not possibly be said to have been friends. But of course if that implies that we were enemies, that would be entirely wrong, too. He was a producer at Metro-Goldwyn-Mayer when I was working with L.B. Mayer in a futile effort to both produce and direct my story *The Human Comedy*. And we now and then also met at 21 in New York, or at the Cub Room in the Stork Club, where he would be with his dark bride who was known as Bubbles Schinasi—out of Egypt, I heard, which also for years manufactured great cigarettes like *Melachrino's*. She wrote her memoirs and they were good to read, but I don't believe her husband wrote his.

88

Next is James Wong Howe, who married the American writer from the midwest somewhere, Sanora Babb, and I know him, because his wife introduced me to him in Hollywood, and he was a very American fellow born to Chinese parents either in Seattle or somewhere in China, and very early in life set down in Seattle, so that he was brought up there. How he got to Hollywood I don't happen to know, but he worked for Cecil B. DeMille in some capacity or another, and then became an assistant to him, and then he took still pictures of the stars, and a woman was so taken with his still pictures of her that she insisted that he become her cameraman—something like that. At any rate he soon enjoyed a reputation as one of the most resourceful and imaginative and expert cinematographers in the business, as Hollywood liked to put it. He liked to remember how vain almost every star was, and he told anecdotes, about Leo Carillo for instance, who was fat but insisted on coming out slim, and suffered terribly getting into a very very tight corset for certain scenes, and then, half sick from labored breathing, he quickly got out of the corset, in privacy, and breathed easily until the next scene of that kind. He had a great eye for all faces and figures and if it would help the film or story he brought out what was desired—allure for the girls, manliness for the boys, many of them not just sissies but effeminate homosexuals: but in those days the studios kept all that sort of thing strictly private, as indeed both they and the parties involved do today. The gossip and indeed the knowledge of the truth is known pretty much not only by everybody in the business but in the country at large. Great big manly western stars virtually married to equally great big eastern stars, so to put it, or to television has-beens or lately only now-and-thens. James Wong Howe opened a Chinese restaurant out in what used to be called The Valley, and on a visit to Hollywood one time in the late 1930s or early 1940s I went there and partook, as they say, of winter melon soup, and other expensive and excellent authentic haute cuisine dishes of Canton or somewhere. Once or twice he took me to a sumptuous meal in Chinatown, New York, and I remember that he had also asked Dong Kingman, the great painter from Hong Kong and San Francisco, although I had never met him in San Francisco when we had both been there for years, and about whose work I wrote an introduction or something of that kind that appeared once in a book. James Wong Howe spoke colloquial American English, but Dong Kingman spoke a kind of personal Chinese-sounding San Francisco English, with all manner of very quiet witticisms, some of which were detected later on. They were good acquaintances, and the cameraman, along with his contemporary Leon Shamroy, are the only two first-rate cinematographers I know, if we except Mr. Charles Chaplin himself. At the Chinese restaurant on Mott Street in Lower Manhattan Dong Kingman and James Wong Howe were both superb hosts to about a dozen guests and remarkable entertainers. It may have been a kind of failure to appreciate the exquisite culinary achievements of their friends in the kitchen, to laugh and shout so continuously during that long meal, but the two wits provoked the laughter, and the guests, but especially myself, had to find a way to both eat and drink and roar with laughter, and to even take part in the running human California-New York-American-Chinese movie comedy. James Wong Howe put on roller skates and held an eyemo camera firmly to his shoulder in order to photograph John Garfield in a movie about a kid from the slums who became a prize-fighter and the adored hero of tramps and pretty women, and the thing about the roller skates was that nobody had ever before done that, and everybody believed the eyemo would pass along all manner of defective photography, but it turned out that the very blurs constituted an accurate accounting of what was happening in the ring to one or the other of the fighters involved, and that the up and down and left and right movements of the camera were also precisely right for the action. The next name is Howard Hughes, and it has become clear since his death that he was not really anything other than mad for the last ten or twelve years of his life. He was certainly not at all what I had come to imagine he must be. I misinterpreted completely his refusal to honor subpoenas to appear in court in connection with legal actions brought against him involving tens of millions of dollars. I thought it was the pride of a rare individual. It was instead simple sickness. And it cost him (which is silly), and it cost his corporations (which is also silly), millions of dollars. In the early days of his fame, especially when he went to Hollywood and bought R.K.O. Radio (or whatever it was or is), he was famous as a one-night lover, or more concretely, *non*-lover, permitting the choicest pieces, as they must have seemed to him, to love or service him, if that does not offend the reader. When one of these girls insisted that he must marry her because she had had expensive luggage made with engravings in gold on every piece with the letters *H.H.*, as everybody knows, the story goes that he would say, "Marry Huntington Hartford." But the story is probably no more true than the other things so many people imagined about him, especially out of his surviving after a very bad crash at the end of a test flight. He finally became grotesque and the specialists will look into that case for a long time, as more and more details become known. There was an element of suicide in his conduct, but that's not much help—for years he didn't shave, clip his fingernails or toenails, eat, go out, have girls, or in any other real way continue as a living human being, and yet he somehow managed to keep his organization from total collapse, although it was really there all the time.

Freida Inescourt also died in 1976, and although I never met her, and don't remember ever having seen her on the stage, in films, in vaudeville, on television, or in any other form of performance, I know that she was famous as a comedienne, perhaps as famous as Irene Borodni, Ida Lupino, or Ina Claire, and I am suddenly aware of something about their very names that seems to suggest the significance of having a right sound to the name of an actress, or a comedienne: Sarah Bernhardt, Eleanora Duse, Trixie Friganza, Clara Kimball Young, throw them around, mix them together, one thing stands out clearly: each is each and whether from the fame each acquired, each seems to have vitality, and only one seems deeply enmeshed in sorrow—Clara Kimball Young—but I won't stop or even hesitate to say why: it just does. Duse, I have read in reviews published in books long long after the event, appeared in London in either a great Ibsen play, or in another play calling for a largeness of art in the performance of a very difficult character, and she was so superior to the performance by Bernhardt in that same part only a couple of weeks earlier, that the reviewer was obliged to suspect that there was something like profound fraud in the reputation that had come to the Divine Sarah, as she was called. The reviewer was George Bernard Shaw, and his age at the time was quite young (for him): he was somewhere in his early forties, and as we know lived to be more than 90, bravo saintly whiskerino. I fell in love with Irene Bordoni from a photograph in *Vanity Fair* when I was fourteen years old, and from her very special voice on a 78rpm record entitled "So This is Love," possibly partly composed by her husband, some kind of entrepreneur in the American theatre, after a beginning somewhere in Europe. I visited Ina Claire at her very chic apartment in San Francisco sometime in the early 1940s, along with three or four other young men, all in journalism or photography or writing, and I remember that she had had us all be let in by her maid to wait for her arrival after a shopping spree, so that when she finally arrived, rather breathless with excitement about the neatly wrapped bundles in her arms, and about being late, and about life, and about the theatre, and about San Francisco, and especially and properly about herself, it was as if the event were not taking place in the world but in a light play by either (God willing) Oscar Wilde or (if that was out) Noel Coward or (if that also was out) S.N. Behrman, or somebody. She was charming of course, and quite handsome, but it was quite clear to me that all this, this lighting of a waiting fire with a three-foot match, and the fixing of martinis by the black girl who was fresh and pretty and alive, alive, and being married to a rich San Francisco Lawyer, was not it, no sir, this was while she was refusing to appear in the awful plays her agent was sending her and was waiting for the proper play. I was not able to volunteer that I would write such a play next week, for I didn't believe it would do anybody or anything any real good, although I was positive I could write a play that would be both very entertaining and very earnest and deeply moving. It just didn't seem to be something to throw the entirety of whatever I had into, at a time when the Western World was about to blow up and become a shambles of entangled debris in all of the cherished areas of faith. In Hollywood I met Ida Lupino on several occasions and liked her profoundly, straight through, for she had both very great talent and very great integrity and authenticity. And of course I marvelled about the whole tribe in England bearing the name Lupino. Freida Inescort I just can't remember at all. Richard F. Irvine is also somebody I do not know and also know nothing about. Again I would suspect he is somebody in the fringes of showbiz, a lawyer, a tax expert, an agent, but I won't go on with the trades and professions in the fringes. Pimps might in a sense cover the lot of them, except that it is necessary to suspect, and even to know, that among actual pimps there are pimps, and pimps, and that the bartender-pimp in Eugene O'Neill's play, *The Iceman Cometh,* in that he has two girls bringing him their earnings while he in turn is giving them what pimps have always given their faithful girls—clothes, shelter, friendship, and a sense of security. Now and then even a taste of sex, but that part of their relationship is the least of it, or the pimp would not be a pimp, he would be a customer, so to put it. Sidney James might be a writer, perhaps of western stories of some quality, but I can't be sure. It is more likely that he was a Hollywood haberdasher or barber, although he could very well also be somebody very big in the actual business of getting out movies, I just don't know, and I do apologize to him. G.W. (Johnny) Johnstone also leaves me totally in the dark. I don't know him, or anything about him, and I am sorry, for it is better to know, although it is really not necessary, as Isaac Babel in Odessa 80 years or so ago was told by his grandmother: "You must know everything." Maternal or paternal grandmother? I wonder. You must know what you must know, which is usually what you really have no way of not knowing. It comes to you, both from inside, unaccountably, and from outside, from the world, fairly accountably, but in the end, since usage of it is involved, also unaccountable. It is more appropriate for grandmamas to tell little boys, and little girls, "You must do everything," and then to add, "but in the weird departments of behavior, orgies of sex and drugs and debasement, you must do these things only by acknowledging that they are done, and not infrequently, by people who must be considered finally worthwhile."

How are we to use our time, not in our prime, as the saying is, even though every day is a day in our prime or it is no day at all if you are willing to go along with that sort of thing—and don't be, don't take the writer, the book, the text, as gospel, ready, ready, ready reader, don't always be ready, reader, be steady perhaps, be ready to become ready perhaps, but don't always be ready.... How are we to use our time when we are one day old, one year old, ten years old, twenty, forty, fifty, sixty, seventy, eighty, but especially when we are a hundred years old? Well, of course we really want to celebrate, as the saying is, and if we are honest in our hearts about it our whole lives, long or short, are celebrations, for do we not every day drink water and eat bread? And do we not whenever we wish empty the bladder and the bowel, and are not these acts of celebration? If they are not, then we have not accurately understood either the acts or the idea of celebration. We probably also mean that in going out and celebrating what we really want to do is go out and get drunk in the figurative sense at the very least, or go out and be ourselves, or stop being ourselves, whichever is or seems to be the truth. We want to stop being intensely concerned about getting something done. But of course there is more to the matter of celebration than that, and I have no intention of fooling with it at this time: it isn't necessary to do so. Showbusiness people are always honoring themselves, handing out trophies with cute names like *Oscar*, and the people to whom these souvenirs are given have already been paid in coin of the realm far beyond order, far beyond appropriateness: they are all loaded, rich, stinking, spoiled, and bejeweled and beclothed and shod, really shod, and they themselves have chosen among themselves who among them shall be honored and made even more rich, and the event is gala, and the setting is resplendent, and television is open to them, and rehearsals have taken place, and it is a celebration—it is a party for assholes, there is no other way of putting it—and they gather together in pompous commonness and artful casualness, and they make the atmosphere seem momentous, so to put it, and what is it that they have done? They have made a movie about some nice people incarcerated in a modern bedlam, a lunatic asylum, a psychiatric ward, a hospital. The story had been bought for a song, the film had been made for a fair sum, its earnings had been in the speedy speedy millions, and it took all of the trophies in the nicest kind of asshole celebration in many years, but the writer of the novel was not there and he had to sue and then settled out of court for a small portion of the swag. Well, who got the big portion of the swag? The celebrators of course, the winners of the trophies, and they earned it, let nobody take that away from them for one teeny weeny instant: they more than earned it. It takes doing to do a movie and to have one or the other of the two sharp ladies at *The New Yorker* review it and love it or hate it in a way that is even more useful than love, and to have all the other writers of reviews of movies, all properly erudite souls for the past twenty years, and for the machinery of exhibiting the movies to be oiled so that they will be exhibited, and no writer is capable of even beginning to conduct that kind of a big orchestra: he feels lucky if he can get his book written without breaking into the procedure and going out and getting bombed out of his travail and unwilling and incapable thereafter of going back to it. The writer is another order of fish, unless he is a writer who is not really a writer but some kind of mechanic, and the hell with that, too. How are we to use our time is the main thing we are concerned about pretty much all of the time, and surely every man, every woman, every kid, comes close to a decision just about every day but never quite makes it, is never quite satisfied with the way of it, not even when the way is nothing but fun, doing only the things that he really wants to do—either the people who use their time that way are mentally retarded or they are desperately sick and clearly suicidal. Either they are incapable of being fools as the human race is given to being foolish (as a break from excessively, terribly demanding work, for relief—Christ for a little relief from the tension and strain of trying) or they really want to hide the truth about themselves: which is something along the lines of well, yes, I have lots of money, as the saying is, and I am free to be and do anything I like, but I really am nothing, absolutely nothing. They call themselves the Jet Set and the Beautiful People, of course, and off-duty rich workers fly to them, to get in on the fun, but their use of time is boring, that's all, just boring, and they are bores, millionaires, billionaires, one and all. We are to use our time celebrating, but only on behalf of the refusal of the millions of mothers all over the world living year after year after decade after decade on less than a little something or other and bringing forth more mothers and demonstrating that while the procedure is still not clear it is this tough resilience of the back of the human race that shall very likely salvage the best that is at the top of the back, at the top of the spine, in the brain and in the nervous system and in the spirit and in the soul of the human race—in thought, in grace, in life, in art, in durability, and in full awareness of the short time before the end as well as of the long time before the beginning:

everybody's going to die but never before everybody is also living and right there at the time, noticing, and going to the funeral celebration, or not. That's what we are to do. That's how we are to use our time.

Rant, rant, rant and rave, and make a fool of yourself again: surely you don't expect anybody to know what you are talking about, or to accept your rudeness, calling nice people assholes. There is dying in the world, dying, dying, all over the place, all kinds of people: statesmen, architects, writers of best-sellers, big men in the Central Intelligence Agency taking secrets about Cuba, Panama, Chile, Iran, Jordan, and everywhere else safely, safely with their own secrets into the grave—how dare you call any of these dying and dead dirty names: assholes, mother-fuckers, cunts, cunt-lickers, cock-suckers, buggers, buggerers—that's not nice: every one of those souls was born and in *that* every one of them is God's, nature's own, and the human family's own darling: take back those dirty names, writer, or live to regret it. I take them back, I'm sorry I said them, I don't know what came over me, something surely inferior, probably jealousy about the big money earned by Henry Ford—the original that is (there is no need to consider the heirs at all). Old lanky Henry Ford gave the runaways rubber wheels—big deal, big deal, although it certainly gave the nation, and indeed the civilized or idiotically civilized world its super-highways and its paved roads everywhere and every which way. I am jealous of Henry Ford's earning all that money, but do I really believe he ought not to have given the runaways their rubber wheels? Good God no, he did right, so let me get along to my place in the funeral march to the graveyard down the road a piece. Philosophize and you make a fool of yourself, laugh and the world turns away in horror. Merle S. Jones is the next name on *Variety*'s Necrology list, and I don't know Merle S. Jones, although in my day I have met at least a hundred nice people who had that famous name. Is it keeping up with the Jones, or keeping up with the Joneses, or keeping up with the Smiths, or keeping up with the Smythes, or what? Well, whatever it is let us have no part of it, although we probably ought to speculate about how so many families of the Christian world were born into the various branches of that tribe: what does Jones mean, that is? A Smith is a smith, for instance, but if we say a Jones is a jones, then what is a jones? A smith is a craftsman who, starting from the mending of pots and pans moves right on up into silver, gold, diamonds, and very probably brains, as in surgery or the instruments needed for the conducting of such surgery, but what is the trade or craft of a jones? Well, I am sure there is a meaning to the name, from the word the family put upon itself for purposes of identification and advertising, but I just don't know what it is, so I have got to let it go, or I might be here forever trying to guess the meaning of the word and the probable reason for so many people having the word as their family name. Among the Smiths there are hundreds of eminent souls, even only among the Americans: including the famous bearded Bros. of black cough drop fame—Christ, we were coughing for years, weren't we?—and let's not forget the Smithsonian thing in Washington, for the root of that name, the source, is again Smith. But I can't think of very many Joneses who are big. Alan or Allen Jones was a singer, and his son Jack Jones is a singer, and they are both singers, and nothing is really nicer than to be a singer, amateur or professional, operatic or popular, but who else? Let the Jones people appoint a committee to conduct a campaign of public relations, including a huge book telling their story—I would like that, wouldn't you, fellow? Female? Girl? Well, whatever, then, wouldn't you? *All About the Joneses,* perhaps it might be called. Bernard Kantor also died in 1976, and again it does not seem that he is somebody I ever met, although at Lindy's Restaurant on Broadway one night I was in a booth bullshitting with Jimmy Cannon when Leonard Lyons came along with Eddie Cantor, who after ordering a piece of cheese cake began to let me know in a very decent way how highly he regarded the old-fashioned ways of the poor people of the world, of all races and religions, speaking like a Presbyterian preacher, or an orthodox rabbi, or a very erudite Moslem. And I liked Eddie Cantor and forever after watched him on television or in movies or on the stage with a different eye. He was a believer. They are not always the best, but there are few among the best who are not believers. His wife's name was Ida, I believe, and she gave him six daughters, and he spoke about that a great deal whenever he was on stage, on camera, or in a television spot, or at a benefit—and everybody loved him for it, everybody roared with laughter because Eddie Cantor after six tries didn't get one son from his beloved bride Ida. He could adopt, I once heard a lady say to another. Let him adopt, if it's a boy he must have, let him adopt, there are plenty of nice boys dying for a nice father. He sat in the booth at Lindy's, and Damon Runyon came over from his booth, and they talked about old times on Broadway, and Leonard Lyons jotted down in his little notebook little things they said that appeared in his next day's column, so here's all these years later Bernard Kantor dying and dead in *Variety*, and I wish I knew him, and had talked to him about his family, how they came to have the name which means Singer in the Synagogue, and to ask Bernard Kantor to please sing a little of the singing he heard as a child at home, from his father or his grandfather, so I could learn from it, as I learn from all singing, and the nearer it is to sorrow, including the joyous sorrow of so many Mediterranean people, the more I learn.

Irving Kaufman died in 1976, and if he is the singer Irving Kaufman, then I have something to say about him, for he was a great singer, although not nearly as famous as he deserved to be. At Bacigalupi's on Eddy Street in San Francisco I used to fish for nickel phonograph records in the very late 1920s and very early 1930s and one of the treasures I found was a 12-inch Victor Blue Label (or was it Brunswick?) record of the middle part of Grieg's *Concerto in A Minor*, played by Paul de Greef, and for the same price, another time, a 10-inch record of a song called "What Does It Matter?" by Irving Berlin, sung by Irving Kaufman. Why did I blow a nickel for that record when I had so many 12-inch classical records to fish through? Well, the answer is that among the 12-inch stuff there just hadn't been anything I felt sure I really wanted. Now, of course, you must understand that I had been to New York by bus and back by train, going late in August of 1928, and returning early in January of 1929, a failure, and I shared a flat at 2378 Sutter Street with the rest of the family, and then a less expensive flat across the street at 1707 Divisadero Street, and finally a rather good flat a good two or three miles away at 348 Carl Street, and that one of my treasures was a wind-up Victor phonograph that I had bought brand new in Fresno at the age of 13 for $10 at Nishkian's Music Store on Broadway. I had to have music, that is to say, and I was interested in all kinds of it. The music of the blacks in those days was called "race music," and the whites hadn't yet discovered it. I had listened to gospel, and slave, and sorrow, and jubilation music sung and played by blacks, because it was also my music, as of course so was Paul de Greef's playing of Edvard Grieg's *Concerto*, which became my morning music—shaving, having black coffee, and going out by the nickel streetcar ride either to a job or to look for a job. It was a young time, it was a joyous time, it was a sorrowful time, it was a great time, this sort of thing didn't begin with Charles Dickens in *A Tale of Two Cities*: everybody has experienced it and put it into spoken or written words, but most of all it was a muscular time, a time of holding out for the best, a time of believing for instance that the one (and only) right girl would be found by me, and she in turn would be looking for me, and we would know it simultaneously, and there we would be. All of this was in all of the music I listened to, but it really showed up very meaningfully in the song "What Does It Matter?" sung by Irving Kaufman, and I played it so much that everybody in my family, and everybody visiting the various flats where we lived, also came to know the music, if not the words, and to hum the music. The music is blue—not black, not white, not the blues of the blacks, nor the blues of the whites, but the blue of youth, and of something that has come to be identified as romanticism when it appears in writing. When Irving Berlin wrote the song he hadn't even met Ellen Mackay, the daughter of Clarence, the owner of the telegraph company for whom I worked three years as a messenger and six as a clerk and manager of a branch office (the youngest such manager in the nation). After he met her there was family opposition to the connection from the Mackay family, and it was in the papers every day, but in the end Ellen became the bride of Irving, and one has seldom known of a more enduring and apparently happy marriage, with children, with fulfillment for both man and wife—for Irving went straight ahead with the writing of great songs, and Ellen wrote quite a few rather good novels, and perhaps also a memoir. The song is not among the most famous of Irving Berlin's, perhaps because it was not in a show, as "There's No Business Like Show Business" was, and as "White Christmas" was in a movie, and the first was belted out by Ethel Merman and the second rather chanted (as if he might be Eddie Cantor's grandfather) by Bing Crosby. In fact, one no longer hears the song at all, but I hear it all the time. The record is among my 78rpm records (about a thousand of them at least, in San Francisco), but I haven't played it in perhaps thirty years, and yet it comes back to memory frequently and I sing it out loud, alone or in company, earnestly and for laughs: "What does it matter, if the sun don't shine?"—I like that. It is larger, there is flawed grammar, and it is the beginning of something plaintive, as of course the entire song is, and just right for Irving Kaufman—or the second whatever his name was, for I do remember that another Irving Kaufman was a public relations expert for a very limited clientele for the reason that he worked in a way that did not permit anybody to know that he was any kind of a publicity agent, an order of promoter that some people just didn't want. This Irving Kaufman was nearly blind and made excellent caricatures, and every night before going to bed he took two or three tablespoons of honey, because (he told me) in Beverly Hills his mother had always told him to do that, and if possible he also had a cup of hot lemonade sweetened with honey. The singer I never met, but one day in the King Cole Room at the St. Regis, before it became a part of the

Sheraton chain, along came Irving Kaufman the undercover publicity agent (of among others, Irving Berlin himself), and he took me to a booth where he had Irving Berlin on the line, so the great songwriter and I could exchange greetings and chat for awhile—and then back to my drink at the booth where Michael Arlen used to dutch treat his friends daily for many years. "As long as you are mine, what does it matter? Life is never one sweet song, things are liable to go wrong. What does it matter?"—blue man, blue blue blue blue young blue blue and beautiful that's all.

Leo Kerz was in the theatre, and some of the time he was a designer of sets and costumes, and some of the time a producer, and we met at least half a dozen times in New York accidentally, and three or four times on purpose, because he wanted to produce any play I would care to let him produce, and he had written me several times, but *really* written, like six full pages of single-spaced typing, but done neatly by a secretary, not by himself, as I do my letters. He was a lively and friendly man who may or may not have had the composer of the music for the sensational *Pins & Needles* review as a partner in his program. I forget the composer's name, although I knew him as well as I knew Leo Kerz. Sooner or later just about anybody in New York gets the feeling that he had better take a crack at the theatre, and of course there is a whole assortment of rich people who need tax write-offs, who put money into plays and try to get the good big producers to permit them to do so, because then they get back enormous profits, but that isn't anything I am interested in at this moment. First, I myself produced and directed my own plays on Broadway until the Draft stopped me. It is hard work, and while neither *The Beautiful People* nor *Across the Board on Tomorrow Morning* were hits, they were far from having been flops, either. On the contrary, they are remembered by the people who saw them until they died—such as Tallulah Bankhead, who saw *The Beautiful People,* paying her way in, at that, at least half a dozen times. The theatre has got to be a collective activity, and that is not easy for me, without experts to support what I want to do. Making movies is even more collective and must have the support of kinds of people I tend not to cherish and kinds of behavior of which I am incapable. All kinds of dissembling, lying, cheating, double-dealing—not only with unions and backers, but with members of the cast. And if you want to produce a movie you have got to get to the bankers and I hate the sons of bitches. I mean, I refuse to have them near anything I want to do. Consequently, after the brief foray of play-producing, I left Broadway, and after the crooked shenanigans in Hollywood in connection with the making of a film of *The Human Comedy,* I left any idea of having any connection with movie-producing. And I am mindful, as the saying is, that one of the finest things George Bernard Shaw told me when I visited him at Ayot St. Lawrence near London in early 1944 was that if he were a young man he would write only for movies. Well, he may have imagined that he would, but I'm not so sure. Under the terms and conditions in operation when I tried (and the conditions have not changed in any real way) such work is just naturally impossible for me, and would be for Mr. Shaw, even with somebody like Gabriel Pascal fronting for him, as Pascal had fronted for him once or twice, and had put forth at least *Major Barbara,* as I remember it. And so it never came to me as a surprise that certain kinds of writers and readers flourished as contributors to the moving picture library or archives; it also never came as a surprise that any real writer refused to fool with the terms involved, or the weird and unacceptable people, rendered weird and unacceptable by having submitted so long ago to the necessary. Leo Kerz did produce a play or two, I believe, but I can't remember anything about that, at all. Whoever the composer was, and I feel sad about this on two accounts, he was murdered on a holiday to Jamaica or somewhere, and the police came up with no explanation, or killer, or suspect. *The Cradle Will Rock* was another of his good works. Jess Kirkpatrick also died in 1976, but I never met him and I know nothing about him, although I was fascinated thirty or more years ago when I read something to the effect that having the name Kirk at the beginning of another name indicated that the person was born out of wedlock, or in literal language, a bastard, and furthermore that the people who inaugurated that procedure and established that distinction tended to be kings and other members of royal families, but only males (I believe but am not sure). Furthermore, there was no sense of awkwardness of any real kind in anybody who had Kirk affixed to his family name, and indeed there was frequently a feeling of pride—the line had begun with one of the bastards of King Henry VIII, what more could any man ask for? What more indeed, considering the prevalence of bastards in uncountable numbers from nobodies the 8th or 2nd or whatever. And in any case what is the difference between a bastard and a blessed babe? Only that both parents are known, at least theoretically, although the jokes are worldwide about deceived fathers who find it all the same very easy to accept as a son a man who looks like everybody else in the world and not at all like the loving doting father. And how right that is, too. Fuzzy Knight also died, and I remember him as one of three dozen character actors who were used in films solely for comic relief. He was the friend and stooge of tough guys in fantasy films about greed, malice, and murder. Marc Blitzstein is the name of the composer, and I thank God and time for restoring his name to memory. Fuzzy Knight had a kind of fuzziness to his speech, and that may have compelled his nickname. He didn't lisp, but there was a kind of slush and inaccuracy to his enunciation of words. If you haven't got a comic accent like Henry Armetta, one of the three dozen character actors much used in films, it's a good thing that you have got an impediment of one sort or another—or if you speak in a way that scares the shit out of everybody, as Jack Benny's overbearing snob ticket-seller or haberdashery salesman did, invariably making Jack Benny cringe as if he were W.C. Fields himself trying not to hear the loud "good morning" of his 8-year old ugly daughter.

Fritz Lang is gone. I never knew him. And I'm not even sure if he was a producer, a director, or a writer, or an actor.* He may have been all, but I incline toward the belief that he was an actor, and that I saw him in a variety of parts, although he himself was always the same man, not as Clark Gable was always the same man in each of his parts (for he really wasn't, if the truth is told), but he was always the same man when the parts he played were very different one from another. But I am not sure, that's all. He seemed in the inaccuracy of my memory of him to have been always slim, sharp-faced, and Teutonic. And there was never any impulse on the part of anybody connected with any movie he was in for him to become large in any humanitarian sense: he was conniving, alert, worldly, and could play a sharp archbishop, for instance, full of crass personal ambition, but fobbing it off as the duty to respect canon and serve both the pope and Jesus. Catholicism being a large and sustained government, it is always near the corruption of all other governments, and it is understandable that from the lowest ranks to the highest intrigue and plotting and revolution and even assassination are continuously likely. The Moslems, who number more than the Christians all over the world, never mind the Catholic Christians, don't have any exemption from intrigue in high and low places of the faith, but it is nothing at all beside that of the Catholics. Which religion, which faith, has done the human race the most good? None of your business. All you've got to do is do yourself the best possible good with what you've got to work with, and God knows you have more than enough, and just about really nothing at all, certainly in comparison with some. The movies from the beginning straight through to this point in time (I love that phrase that the Nixon associates, lawyers one and all, hit upon as they improvised new lies as needed) have presented surely a million souls, including extras, background people, and bit players, and while Fritz Lang in comparison with them is a star, and a star of the first magnitude, in comparison with Lon Chaney, for instance, he is not a star of the fourth magnitude. And Lon Chaney, compared with somebody else, might only be said to have been given parts that were impossible not to do well, for they were unforgettable: when you are the Hunchback of Notre Dame, for instance, you are not ever to be forgotten by anybody who happened to see you lurking in the shadows. Lon Chaney never did Harry Houdini of course, they were contemporaries, but one thinks of the two as being somehow related: both accepted and even relished terrible and frightful odds being put up against their temporal truth and prospects for survival, up against their very breathing, and in tight terror of suffocation, in the iron box locked and dropped into the frozen river, in crooked flight from swords and guns, each of them slipped through to sanctuary, sanctuary, and to air and light and breath and freedom, and fame and fortune. Houdini was mad, of course, but then only in that rather than be engulfed by being nobody he chose being somebody challenging the odds to the point of the supreme danger of disgrace that is death—or at any rate so it seemed, although experts tell us that his most difficult tricks were really quite easy. Bullshit: even if by the time the chained iron box was dropped through the broken ice upon the river, even if by that time he was out of the box, and had gone to where he was to swim underwater and to emerge unseen but wet from the river—even that is not easy, and of course nobody needs to tell me he had no trick like that. Lon Chaney was only an actor. He did his weird parts very nicely. *The Unholy Three* may or may not be one of his movies, but I saw it, and can remember nothing about it at all, not even who the other two were: was one a dwarf (that's always nice, as the saying is), and the other Peter Lorre, or somebody like that? It all overlaps, reader, don't let it throw you: every bit of the magnificent show of the great magician, and of the great performer of monstrous parts, and the reality of your own life and of life in birds and worms and endangered species everywhere, they all overlap, and if I don't get any of it precisely straight, that is another side of the overlapping, let it go, and move along. Frances Lastfogel also died, and if she was the wife of Abe Lastfogel who was the top man at the William Morris

Agency, I met her several times, through Abe, and I am quite saddened by her passing, for she was a very sweet slim lady, and very thoughtful and kind, and to her husband a devoted wife, which is something out of date, I suppose, but in those days was not, and was indeed quietly admired by most people. William Morris himself, who at this moment would be perhaps two or three years older than myself, or about 71, I knew and liked, but his wife, from whom he was separated and by whom he may have been divorced eventually, I loved, for she seemed to me in the late 1930s the most beautiful woman in the world, and I can't even remember her first name. The first time I met her she was with a woman who wrote songs and had a name something like Ayer, but that's not it. I think of Mrs. William Morris frequently, and it doesn't matter that all of that, all all all of that love of that beauty is almost laughable, for I never came to know her at all, and that even just feeling that I loved her is also long gone, long long gone in all the years gone, and yet it makes no difference, I go right on being in love with her, as if it made sense of some kind. Why did William Morris leave the agency? Who knows. Why did his wife leave him? Who knows. Jack Lavin also died in 1976, but I know absolutely nothing about him. Jack Dempsey, however, is still with us.

**Fritz Lang was a world-famous director, first in Germany, where he made the classic* M; *then in the United States, where he directed* Rancho Notorious, Scarlet Street, The Big Heat, *and numerous other films.*

I am the Collier Brothers, both of them, but you don't know who they are, and this is about you, so the hell with the Collier Brothers, and I don't mean P.F. Collier (if those were his initials), the founder of the great publishing dynasty, or his sons or brothers, or relatives: I mean the eccentrics of New York who twenty or thirty years ago either died or were evicted from their brownstone house somewhere, which was full from top to bottom with stuff they had refused to put in the garbage, give to the Salvation Army, take to the dump, or otherwise get out of the house. Why did they do that? We all wondered. We needn't have. But we did. The reasons are simple. They hadn't married. If they had, they would have had the family filling the house. Without families, the two of them in one house filled it with trash. Well, I have two houses side by side and each is filled with trash. The difference here is surely insignificant, so the hell with it. I keep stuff, I look at all printed matter not once but again later on some time, and sometimes forty years later on, and by that time it is hilarious and fantastic and stupid but right there in a newspaper or a magazine or a book that was once considered (by the critics, not by me) a great work. What is keeping? It is not dying, that's what it is. And that's why when you fill a house with a family—correction, as they say on radio and television. And that's what filling a house with a family is, too, of course. You work out a procedure of keeping, of not dying, with whatever is there, or whatever has got to come to you anyhow. It goes back to childhood. It goes back to adulthood. It goes back to old age. It goes back to Father and Mother. It goes back to voices and utensils for water and clothes and shoes and glances and counting and papers and coins and stuff to be cooked and stuff on tables and beds and bedding and blankets and visitors and voices and words and words and decisions and changes in the decisions and fights and tears and hollering and let me tell you something, reader, whoever you are, you have had your share of it all, but for God's sake don't imagine that any of it has been anything really really really different, not even if some of it was measurably the worst. There are people who have come home and found the Father and the Mother bloody and dead from murder and suicide, and worse, and worse, so even if it was the very worst that you knew, don't let it throw you, and don't let it give you a lifelong excuse not to be your stupid self just the same, or your brilliant self or your magnificent self, or whatever it is you most believe your self to be, or to be entitled to be. The human race is *that* race, and a little of all of it is in every member of it, from the most saintly easy right to the most deadly dirty wrong, and you have got to be the one who chooses and uses: it can't be me, it can't even be you in a sense, it can only be yourself after you have come to see that you are more the other person than you are yourself, you are more the whole human race than only one member of it, you are everybody from the beginning, and you will soon enough notice that that does not exclude those persons or personages which were lizards on great stones in sunlight. Forget it if you will or be alert to it and largeness will be permitted to reveal itself in you, and you will know it has always been there and has been tightened out of the way by all of the little naggings of hanging on, which also are necessary. This is more on the same subject of course, which is dying and death, which is living and death, which is work and life and health and money, oh boy more and more money, how delicious is money, and how it buys off the undertaker, that most comic of all comedians but never officially, never on stage or on camera or in a television special or series. This is about how we do, as the old family saying is, a bit of Armenian put over into immigrant English not quite a hundred years ago by the first Saroyan to arrive in Fresno: Garabet, my mother's father's handsome kid brother, who arrived pretty much just as the century turned from the 19th to the 20th, having got into scandals involving pretty Turkish girls and dancers and whores in Constantinople, and having been hustled by bribes out of the great city, and the courts and jail and worse, by his big brother Minas, by that time lost in alcohol, his fortune as good as shot, and so Garabet arrived with the new century in Fresno and was soon saying in English, "This is how we do," and ever since all the rest of us have been saying it too. I knew him well after I first met him when I was eight years old and just down from five years in Oakland to Fresno, and I turned out to have first his high forehead, and then his face, including his large white moustache: that's how it is in families, as you know. This little old chapter, this whole book, little and old, is about that and that alone, as we say: how we do, and this is how. We do what is there demanding to be done at the time, and little by little things fall in place all around us, including sons, daughters, and their sons and daughters, and death is born into each of them with the beauty of flowers and flashings of light from the sun upon drops of water and deep into rock pools with anemones and fish and things inside pretty shells, and where is there anything, man, anything at all that may for an instant be said to be anything but beautiful and everlasting? That is how we do. We do we do we do we do, so let's make a popular song of it, as much for the old people as for the new gathering together to cry and go trip trip trip trip trip tripping through their tulips roses lilies geraniums violets violence violins.

96

Charles Lederer died in 1976, and I suppose in Hollywood, which of course includes Beverly Hills, West Los Angeles, Brentwood, Santa Monica, and Malibu, although he may have gone to New York to die. He was a writer of movies, who had spent pretty much all of his time as an adult at that kind of life and work. And he was a nephew, unless I have got it all wrong, of Marion Davies, who was the darling of strange-strange-fellow, gangly William Randolph Hearst, with his mortician's mug and his grand skill at making national mischief. But he hired Ambrose Bierce, and didn't fire that other strange-strange-fellow when Bierce ridiculed Hearst—and certainly that speaks well of him, although other things speak even better of him: such as his remark to blackmailers who claimed they had photographs of his bedroom behavior of just a few days previous involving not Marion Davies but possibly some other, at a time when such matters could ruin the career of somebody, especially somebody destined to be President (as Hearst was not, no matter what he may have believed far at the back of his mind): "Oh, I think those photographs that you have ought to be seen by the American people, so you go right ahead and print them anywhere you possibly can." But of course I've got it all wrong, and why shouldn't I? The story is folklore, and variations of it have been told about just about anybody who ever got hot and rich. Maybe I can tell the story Charles Chaplin told about a visit to San Simeon, Hearst's Castle in Hearst's Kingdom on the southern California coast. Marion Davies, drunk, to Mary Pickford, drunk, about let's say either William Randolph Hearst himself, or one of his guests, such as Rudolph Valentino: "I wouldn't piss on him." Mary Pickford, then, very sweetly: "Oh, wouldn't you?" Doesn't mean a thing, but Charles Lederer was apparently born into that world and those very special people, and he had quite a nice reputation as both a competent scenario writer and a wit or even jokester, although I have no memory of anything he ever wrote or said or any prank he played on anybody—but he did, he did, it is established that he did. I met him half a dozen times but never came to really so much as talk with him past civilities, Hollywood style. His aunt rather loved him, I seem to remember having read, and he was liked by just about everybody in the movie business and in the high society of its people. He belonged to that society and was never embarrassed, apparently, about it: he rather liked the authenticity or the fraudulence of it, whichever he believed was accurate, which he doesn't seem to have published, if indeed he published anything. And we must remember that there are surely a hundred times as many writers, people who earn money, and sometimes big money, doing what is called writing, who never published anything: they have always been swift and agile and acrobatic for advertising agencies, for radio, for television, for films, for politicians, writing their speeches, for virtually illiterate people in business who must give a talk and must have something organized and appropriate to say. These are all writers, and if anything they write ever sees print, it is not known who wrote it, and that not infrequently includes books, but only very infrequently a fair book or an interesting one. Mainly, Charlie Lederer, as he was invariably referred to, was something like a pleasant character of the town, and at the time when a variety of interesting writers had taken little set-ups at the hotel-apartment on Hollywood Boulevard, up at the top, named "The Garden of Allah," he also had an apartment there, or was a continuous visitor: Robert Benchley, Dashiell Hammett, Donald Ogden Stewart, I forget the names. And after the place had enjoyed its fame and was fading I once stopped there for a week, and for two reasons: I wanted to see where the writers had had their big-money fun, and because it was convenient to be within walking distance of the places where I wanted to go. The set-ups as set-ups weren't bad, the garden wasn't bad, the pool wasn't bad, the morning sun coming into the second floor room I had—that being as high as the place went: first floor, second floor, long before motels became big business all over the country and tended at first to limit themselves in that manner—the morning sun coming into the room just about the time when I was getting into real sleep wasn't bad—but it wasn't good, either, under the circumstances. Charlie Lederer knew Wilson Mizener and the other Mizener, and he knew Ben Hecht, and he traded jokes and witticisms with all of the jokesters and wits of the town, but he never quite made it into the dimension of being a legend. Lotte Lehmann is the next name on the list, and I believe I heard her sing, but only on radio. I don't believe I ever saw her, but if she is the large German lady who during the 1939-1945 War spoke about having lost a son in the German army, and another son in the American army, then I did see her on television or somewhere, and I was moved by her unrehearsed words and speech, heavy with the sighs of great sorrow. She was a singer of Wagner who was during the War diminished as a composer because Hitler not only admired his music but lived and argued by it. Richard Leibert also died, but I know nothing about him whatsoever. When Margaret Leighton on the other hand was at the height of her fame and somehow married to Lawrence of Lithuania (because I can't remember his proper and chosen name), I once drank with her and her husband and Leonard Lyons and Billy Reed at Billy Reed's Little Club: she was both pretty and shy and talented, and was soon separated from the actor, who then got himself involved with Harry Cohn's widow, and was badly treated in *Time* for his homosexuality, but he kept right on working, and then died of cancer.

It has been my experience and it continues to be my experience that whenever I am at work on a new piece of writing involving a good number of consecutive days I have a strong feeling that what I am producing, that the writing I am doing, just can't compete with the writing other living writers have done and have published, and as for the writing the older writers have done, the writing I am doing is out of it, man, it is far, far, out of it, and why don't I quit? Why don't I drop the thing and go out in fine cars and in fine easy spirits and holler and jump and have fun like anybody sensible ought to do? Why don't I acknowledge to myself that I can't write, that I am some kind of real weird zombie, a stupid egomaniac who can't write about anybody except himself and can't even do that effectively: an incompetent, a slambang and haphazard gambling writer, a fool, so what right have I got to write, and what right have I to have my stuff printed, and to expect you, reader, to read what I write? Why don't I wise up and at least become reasonably courteous to God and the human race, and to you? Why do I insist as if I were one of those dismal and pathetic souls who go through sixty or seventy dreary years of life believing that oh ho one of these days, oh boy one of these days, wait and see, ladies and gentlemen, one of these days who I really am is going to be known, and I am going to be who I am, and then won't everybody know I am the greatest? Why do I write if I really feel so strongly that what I am writing is no good? Well, one of the reasons is this: what should I do? What's the alternative If it's to read, I am always reading, so that won't do at all. If it's to loaf, I am always loafing, too. If it's to celebrate, to spend all of my time and energy on indulgence, eating, drinking, and working joyously to truly magnificent orgasms with crazy large ripe women and fantastically gorgeous young little girls, well, good God, I can't say that I am always doing that, too, anyway, because that would be lying like a pathetic son of a bitch. I've done it all, I still do it, but with nothing like the regularity of long ago, long long ago. Who's going to kid who, and why should he? I don't stop writing, mainly, though, because if I had stopped at the beginning I would not have ever been published at all, and the fact stands right there and looks us all in the face that I have been a published writer for 44 years and that I have about that number of books published—real books, that is, hardbound, and furthermore that I have in manuscript, many of them long forgotten, surely 44 more unpublished books, and plays, and autobiographical works, and essays—and if the truth is told, it may very well be that I am the writer who demonstrated to a whole new and very bright group of writers that the essay is a living form, it is not at all dead, and some of these good writers have never fooled with the work of trying to write a short story or a novel or a play: they stick to the essay, and in the essay are expected to be themselves all the way through—they are expected to be speaking out of what they saw and heard and felt and thought. Way back in 1933 I began to publish my kind of essay-story, and instantly this writing seemed acceptable as well as significant: "Seventy Thousand Assyrians," "Myself Upon the Earth," "Fight Your Own War," "The Big Tree Coming," "Sleep in Unheavenly Peace," and so on and so forth. Well, had I quit while I was writing those early stories, I would have not had anything for any publisher to publish—those cheap thieves, and fuck them one and all pretty much, how they bamboozled the babies who keep them in business and make millionaires and bogus bigshots of them—and I could not now be continuing in my profession: I could only be thought of as some kind of pathetic fool, instead of being the honored old man riding his bike licketysplit all over Fresno, being greeted by high school kids who have had my stuff in their English courses, calling out to me by name, and asking, "Are you writing any more books?" And I am always able to answer honestly, "Yes, I am, thank you," but there just isn't time to then ask, "Are you reading any?"—not of mine, but of anybody's. And most of them are not of course. If it were not that all writers have always apparently been unable to think well of their work in progress, then it must be that this is an occupational thing, and furthermore, that it would be impossible for any truly earnest writer, trying for everything, including even newness, not to have doubts about this last new job—the writer would have to feel ah no, no, this time it is no good at all, it is hopeless, why am I working so hard? The only writer I can imagine as not being too concerned about the quality, size, style, meaning, usefulness, beauty, simplicity, rightness, and all-around comedy of a work in progress is the plot-writer, the good hack, who like as not in our day can, and according to what I hear actually does hire hacks to fill out the stuff for him, and then puts his own stamp of style upon it, which is usually the using of the plain words for cock, cunt, tit, hair, sweat, fuck, suck, muck, duck, buck, luck, puck, tuck, and so on boring Jesus and delighting a whole world full of nice people who really find such writing helpful to their libidos, and all. Those writers, factory writers, really don't need to feel any anxiety at all about what they are writing, because they know very clearly what it is, and even before writing they have sold paperback rights for one million, movie rights for two, and translation rights for three—just a little joke, reader, because translations don't earn big money even for fuckup writers. Sure I feel my new stuff can't compete with the old stuff of all the great writers, but so what, I'm not leaving for Hawaii in the morning.

98

Leo Lerner died in 1976, and I knew him, a little. I may be mistaken, as always, as usually, but very infrequently (at that)—but it seems to me that he was connected with the Broadway theatre for quite a good spell, and then somehow became a critic of plays, a reviewer, for one weekly or another, or one daily or another, and then took over the editorship of the program magazine, or paper, which is handed out free of charge to people at a play on Broadway. I believe it is officially known as the *Playgoer*, but again I can't be absolutely sure. If Leo Lerner is that man, there is this small anecdote to be told. About three years before Leonard Lyons had a stroke or something and his column was for a time got out by both his wife Sylvia and one or two of his four sons, after a party at his house one night walking to the corner with the famous movie producer from Boston, Joseph E. Levine, I said, "Do you happen to feel as I do that Leonard isn't well?" And Joseph E. Levine said, "Yes, I do, and I don't know what to do about it." He and his wife Rose or Rosa or Rosalyn or Rosabelle got into their limousine, I declined and thanked them for their invitation to ride with them to my hotel, because I like to walk, especially in New York, especially after a lot of eating and drinking. A month later at another party we continued our talk, because now there was no question about it, our friend Leonard Lyons had noticeably changed since the last party. At the Lincoln Center walking home again I came upon a program, the *Playgoer*, and picked it off a railing where somebody had dropped it, and when I got home I studied it, something I tend to do. Anything published interests me. Well, the thing had rather interesting articles, besides the program for a particular play, and these articles were part of a week's supply to all theatres of their programs, in the *Playgoer*, and so I wrote a piece about Leonard Lyons and I sent it to the *Playgoer*. About two weeks later I ran into Leo Lerner who said something along the lines of thanks for sending the piece, the trouble is we are doing a whole issue about Leonard Lyons on the occasion of his 70th birthday, or his 40th year as a columnist, and the stuff in your piece repeats what we've got in our pieces, so we can't use it, but please don't let Leonard Lyons know about any of this. So I didn't, and when my piece came back in the mail I put it aside, to wait for the *Playgoer*'s special issue, but soon I was back in Paris, and when I was in New York again I asked around and no, there hadn't been a special issue of the *Playgoer* for Leonard Lyons. I asked Al Hirschfeld, for instance, because there was one of his grand drawings in almost every issue of the *Playgoer*. Well, Leo Lerner, if indeed it had been he (as one of Ring Lardner's characters trying to cover illiteracy with fancy grammar might say), just hadn't liked my piece about Leonard Lyons, and just hadn't wanted to return the thing on the basis of a flat-out circumstance of undesirability, which was really silly, and reminds me of Phil Balletta the messenger at the

Postal Telegraph Office at 120 Chambers Street in lower Manhattan in 1928 when I was the assistant manager to Ben Amato's manager. Phil and his brother Dominic were difficult slum boys who had had a lot of trouble with a lot of people like schools and police and department stores, and one morning around nine when he came back from delivering a telegram to the coffee wholesaler just across the street, he said, "The elevator guy put me out of the can, so I told him, so all right, I'll save it, I've shit in much better toilets than in this crummy place." And of course I had had stories and essays and writings of other kinds rejected by far better magazines than the *Playgoer*, so the editor really hadn't needed to be so delicate about not wanting what I had written for Leonard Lyons, which I had really believed would please Leonard Lyons and perhaps give him a lift when he needed or possibly wanted one. And of course if there was to be some nominal payment for the piece, as I am sure there would have had to be, that would have been welcome, too, for in those days (as in these) I can always use an extra buck or two, hotel singles being well along into the general vicinity of one hundred dollars a night, think of it—all it really means is that the American dollar is bankrupt. Leo Lerner died, and I didn't even know it, but had I known it, and had I been in New York, I don't believe I would have gone to the funeral, although a lot of people went to John Steinbeck's in New York, including John O'Hara, who either read a kind of eulogy or was quoted by somebody about his high regard for John Steinbeck. I knew them both quite well, and I don't want to knock either of them, but I am sorry, lads, brothers, pals, friends, I have got to say that I don't believe the one thing that each of them should have had, as world writers, either possessed: in O'Hara's case it was largeness, yes largeness, real largeness of heart, mind, soul, and connection; and in Steinbeck's case it was something like an awareness of the comedy in everything and in everybody. Am I implying that I have these things, that they are in my work? Worse, I am saying so straight out. I have largeness, I have comedy, make of my saying so what you will, it is the truth. Will this help? Yes, and of course help won't help at all, but that's none of my business. Edgar Leslie died, and I know nothing about him at all, alas, I wish I did. Rosina Lhevinne died, and all I am able to suspect is that either she was the sister, daughter, or wife of Josef Lhevinne, the violinist (or was he a pianist?), but I can't be sure. Irving Lieberman, Robert L. Lippert and Peter Lisagor died, but I do not know them, and know only that Peter Lisagor had been an admired radio and TV news speaker, or commentator, according to Eric Sevareid.

99

In writing, art is said to come out of tension, and there seems to be a very real probability that that is so, or at the very least that some kinds of art must come out of tension—but whose tension? Well, of course to begin with it has to be the tension of the maker of the art, the writer, and then it has to be inside the art itself, between the characters in a story or a play, or possibly even between the ideas of the story, (and let ideas signify all of the things that people believe they live by: religion, culture, tradition, and so on). When he wrote his plays it is not possible to believe William Shakespeare did so in serenity, without having his very soul in his body shaken up, and if that is accepted by us we have no trouble believing that his own tension heightened the tension in the play *Hamlet,* for instance—but God help us I find that it is really a failure of mind and soul to be forever referring to Shakespeare and to *Hamlet,* and I ought to lay off. Still, still, there is this matter of struggle, and there is its connection to that which is the everlasting source of art: yourself, life in yourself, the world, time, weight, vast weight gathered together in the world and in the human race and especially in yourself, and your struggle with this weight, which is part also of an accumulation of system and procedure and demand, incessant constant demand to go on, to breathe, to live, which is in the minutest units by the billions which constitute the preposterous whole, yourself, with your eyes, nose, mouth, teeth, ears, and the system working, and moving you on and on by unknown and unknowable needs. All right, it starts and it stops, and when it stops if you have had some connection with the world in which William Shakespeare was a kind of star, your name is listed in the annual year-end issue of *Variety*, which is actually given the date of the first Wednesday of the new year: and there you are. Dead. And famous. And clearly a damned fool. (For dying, of course, for not finding a way to go on fighting, for losing the fight, for giving up the body and spirit's use of muscle in tension and opposition.) Or you are an object of pity—you died too soon, you died in a stupid accident, you were shot in the head by a jealous husband, or a jealous wife, or a jealous son, or a jealous daughter, or a jealous stranger, or a jealous Avon Lady in a fit of disbelief about falling so low as to be peddling cosmetics to dismal people not in showbusiness, or in a terrible displeasure that her singing of the *You, you* hymn is restricted to front doors and not part of grand opera. Or if you are not an object of pity, you are something worse that courtesy almost compels a writer not to mention—indifference: you are an object of indifference. You have died, your name is in *Variety*'s list, and nobody gives a shit. All your tension, all your muscle in putting over the campaigns you put over have been apparently in vain. All right again, nobody needs to argue about it: art comes out of tension, or most art does, so the next question is this: since art comes out of nature, does nature also come out of tension: is the universe, in short, a product of tension? Yes, and explosive tension, at that, as we have heard so many times in so many beautiful explanations by so many beautiful experts with patient beautiful minds—charitable about the rest of us who just hang around with the big mouth open because we don't know, we just don't seem to be able to decide how the universe started, and why it is big beyond even the idea of size—it is beyond size, it is past measure, it is everything everywhere everlastingly and who are you to say so or not to say so? Well, it has been my experience from the very beginning of writing, and I mean from the first days of putting words slowly and neatly on lined paper at school, that there is tension in writing nothing more than my name, my place, and the date, and the name of my paper—"The Rich and the Poor," for instance. And then when I went into the thing with everything I had, the tension increased so much that it seemed to efface time, place, and person, myself, and the thing to be made, by writing, became pretty much the only thing, the thing lost inside the unknown of the beginning of things, of systems, the universe and its track, so to put it, its circling and circling, or its moving in a straight line forever everywhere, and straight into you, and after your flash of being, straight out of you, leaving you a name in *Variety*. Reader, sometimes long before I was twenty years old, after I had worked for as little as three hours on a work of art in the form of writing, as little as one hour, as little as half an hour, obliterating self, time, and place, and I came to, came out of it, what do you think I saw in my own face as I stood and pissed and glanced in the bathroom mirror? I saw somebody else, myself but somebody else, not myself alone, as it was when I hadn't concentrated on the production of art with so much intensity: it was all of my own people, all unknown to me, it was the human race itself, it was all of the animals especially, each with its own face, serene and unknowing, like my own face at that moment, and I would be less than candid (as the crooks of politics are forever saying) if I did not say that what I saw was handsome, impersonal, totally without vulnerability, without vanity, without ego, and with the same handsomeness that is in the animals, fish, birds, insects, trees, vines, plants, leaves, flowers, fruit, and the same that is in grass, in blades of grass of all kinds, all the handsome green and green of grass.

100

This, then: I really never got around to thanking one of the sons of one of the wealthiest familes of America for gently letting me know that in 1936, with two books published, I was no longer obliged to let everybody know in everything I wrote, and indeed in everything I said in person, that I was one of the great ones. "It is in the writing itself, anyway," he said. "And it is in yourself." Well, of course he was instructing me in manners, and while I do intend not to understand when I am being admonished, rebuked, or even insulted, I also invariably sense that something of the sort is taking place, and this gives me pause, and sometimes makes me defensive. The man was an editor, and we were at work on a kind of selection of stories from my first two books for a paperback, long before they came into real being, and then became big business. But he was not impelled into his kindly advice by reason of a piece of bragging writing I wanted included in the collection, or by anything I had said as we discussed the collection: it was out of the blue, so to put it: it came as if from observations he had made and considerations he had given long ago, which he had suddenly just remembered by accident, as it were. And it may have also been out of something so unrelated seemingly to the issue as my glance at his shapely young secretary as she left his private office, and I both adored her and lusted after her, as I believe the Old Testament puts it. I don't have any of it absolutely accurate, and that is the reason I am giving several sides of the probable truth or reality of the event, and his quiet recitation of it, in passing, and half-not-even-worthy of discussing. But I heard him the first time, I knew what he was saying, I did not dispute the validity of it, I rather agreed with his volunteered counsel—I do not believe I have ever (and I mean ever) gone to anybody to appeal for help about anything, and if that sounds like madness, let it be so, for if it is not absolutely totally literally true, it is the purest order of truth human beings may experience, and it may be the reason I have only been able to discipline myself into believing that the custom of all sorts of people running to parent, teacher, pal, preacher, boss, doctor, or psychiatrist is probably a good thing for them, at least in that it is what they like to do—but it also suggests to me that this custom belittles them and prevents or postpones the achievement of character, for there is such a thing as that, you yourself being the whole business, the whole race, with the support and love and possibly even admiration of God and the ancient tribe still thriving within yourself, and the casual watchfulness of both nature and the universe, somewhat after the manner of the lion mother with one of its two or three cubs, a seeming awareness without ever a direct look at the newcomer. The point, though, is this: that after all these years, and after variations of the same advice from others, I go right on bragging, which impels me to acknowledge with a great deal of fascination, if nothing else, that I must be awfully insecure about the whole thing. Not to put too fine a point upon it, then, I begin by agreeing that I am. And then I ask myself, and yourself, how it could ever be possible for me not to be insecure, or for you not to be, or for anybody not to be. We are made out of insecurity and a continuing decision every morning, all day, all night, on into sleep and dream, to do something about it. That is surely how we changed and became the preposterous variation of an animal form of life that the millions of years have seen us become. So I heard the son of a distinguished and wealthy family, and I accepted the probable validity of his observation, and his suggestion, and I felt grateful to him, and yet after all these years, precisely fifty, I believe, a full half-century, I have both never thanked him in person, or in writing, and I have failed to heed his wise and proper counsel. I still brag, and there must be a reason other than only that I am insecure about who I am and what I have done, and what I am doing. You brag to avoid dying, don't you? And sometimes you brag to avoid dying of boredom, too, as I have done many times. I don't want to play it safe, I don't want to be invulnerable, I don't want to protect myself, and to carefully guard my possessions, my hoardings if you like, my achievements. If God is God he has got to kid himself, God has got to make known that he is aware of the probability of fraudulence in the condition of being God. And the great boys of the religions have got to have made known that they were never for a moment unaware of the lugubriousness of being who each of them said he was—since it diminished and humiliated everybody else to the point of being contemptible and unworthy of all that righteousness and love and grace and passion and everlasting gladness, and immortality right here and now as well as forever. And of course I also find it slightly annoying that I keep going back to the great mischief-makers who are the makers of lines differentiating one religion and one people from another, because I have neither scorn nor admiration for them, I have only amazement that the people, the multitudes, the masses, as the communists put it, could be so desperately intense about the really silly and meaningless lines. If you want to get all muscular tense, brother, a couple of thousand years ago, let it be only about the awesome failure of your brain to connect with your body, and never mind how everybody else is lost and doomed to death by reason of not believing what you believe, or think you do.

Roger Livesay died in 1976, and I am sorry to say I don't seem to know anything about him at all, and I don't even seem to know his name, although it is impossible that I shouldn't have seen it in print a thousand times during all the years of my reading. It is a name that has appeared in newspapers and magazines, so why don't I know anything about either the name or the man it belongs to? I could answer, "Just lucky," I guess, but the hell with that kind of flippancy. The man is dead, he deserves the respect of any man who has died, and the respect that is given by all of us, even to dirty sons of bitches of all kinds, because we do seem to believe that we must not offend death, we must honor death, no matter to whom it happens. That is probably part of our wish not to speak poorly of anybody who has died, although we all rejoice and even burst into laughter whenever one of us comes right out and says something, "I always hated the son of a bitch, I'm glad he's died, I wish to Christ he hadn't taken so long." I have now got to mention that I was absolutely entertained by one of the television talk show boys who had gone down south somewhere to take part in another foolish money-raising program on behalf of one or another of the diseases that are there, that are in the seed, that blight birth, that insult body and mind, and then become the occasion for people to feel very human and big and stuff by public declaration of sympathy—Mongol children are innocent, let us all give money, time, and talent to the study of why Mongol children are born to Anglo-Saxons sometimes. So this rich boy had condescended to fly south and help raise money for Rabbit children, let's say, and on his own show he is the star and at the start of the show he is announced loudly and clearly as if his name is known to ancient rocks still lying on the surface of the earth in the deserts of the whole fucking world. All of the local southerners, however, didn't seem to even know, or suspect, who he was. They were busy exercising their fine southern accents in the saying of fine southern absurdities of thought and tradition, and the talk show man, who apparently had imagined for years that he was well known to everybody everywhere, by face, by figure, by voice, by speech way, by having done his show a good one thousand and one times, carried by fifty or sixty stations, and each show seen by at least four million people, sometimes many more than four million. Well, he was upset, of course, and it was lonely, and he was on camera, on television, and surely everybody watching knew who he was: why didn't this strange southern Chairman of the Committee? At last he decided to do something about it, and pushed himself directly upon the Chairman, and said that he was Dave Doozey, for instance, and of course he expected the Chairman to immediately apologize for failing to recognize him, and to make up for it by making a big fuss about him, but the Chairman, God bless his soul, just didn't happen to know who Dave Doozey was, he just didn't happen to have ever watched Dave Doozey's talk show, he just hadn't ever believed that having given a thousand and one of the shows that Dave Doozey must therefore be somebody, he didn't really look like somebody, not really like anybody important, and he might even be a crasher, there was something furtive and really confusing about him, and the only thing that happened was that the Chairman appealed to somebody to get rid of Dave Doozey who was holding up the nice proceedings on behalf of Robot Children. Well, the thing that was demonstrated was that it is easy for anybody to imagine that he is known to everybody. He isn't. Nobody is. It is not necessary for anybody to be known if the truth is told to anybody beyond the realm of his reality, and even then it is not necessary (or even possible) for the knowing to be anything better than superficial. Scott Fitzgerald trying to tell people on an airplane that he was Scott Fitzgerald and finding them absolutely willing to accept that fact but not to accept any theory that that was something that needed to stop them from being precisely who each of them was or to stop doing precisely what each was doing. The only person anybody needs to be known to is himself, and the returns are not in fully even on that—it may turn out to be as much unnecessary as necessary, for all practical purposes. Who or what needs to know who or what each of us is, and is to be while we live or after we die, or both, or what? Well, it is all only whatever whoever it happens to be who is asking wants to say—everything and everybody knows each of us as another anonymous very small part of a very large and unstoppable part, of course, but that knowing is pure and involves nothing like our inventions about identity, comparison, achievement, recognition, size, weight, contribution—I'm the man, somebody says swiftly and pathetically, who donated the case of strawberry soda pop to the picnic. Good God, cool it, human beings everywhere, especially in the penitentiary world, in the uncaptured crime world, in the art world, in the world of science, just cool it, folks, nobody knows you were born, nobody knows you are alive, nobody is going to know when you die, so don't give yourself a hard time insisting, just now it's all right, it's just fine, it's a blessing really that no matter how well-known you are you are really totally fully and finally unknown and nobody is going to come up to you and say, Can I have your autograph Mr. Cockroach, even though your name is Mr. Termite, Mr. Flabby Termite, how could anybody think you could possibly be somebody so unlike yourself as Mr. Cockroach. Cool it, you're somebody who is nobody, so be glad about it.

Tilly Losch was a large, beautifully-assembled, beautifully-endowed dancer who worked first in Budapest or somewhere, and then on the stage in New York, and then went out to Hollywood in the middle 1930s and appeared in quite a few films and so now here she is on *Variety*'s list. Big stuttering B. P. Schulberg asked me one afternoon during the six weeks I was employed by him to write stuff for his movies to borrow a tuxedo from Paramount wardrobe and to go that night to the Los Angeles opening of a play called *Tovarich* (which in Russian means Comrade, in the Communist sense), and so he and I, each of us with a broad all rigged out in the traditional manner, sat in the orchestra, and along came beautiful Tilly Losch down our aisle to reach her seat, and in passing said, Hello, Bill. To me, that is. Well, I was delighted, but I really had no way of guessing why she did that. I hadn't met her, as far as I could remember. I decided that there was nothing to it other than a routine kind of accidental overflow of warmth on an occasion of excitement, the opening of a play, already more than famous in France, where it may have originated, and certainly in New York, where it had enjoyed a long run, and where for all I know it was still running, even while this opening in Los Angeles was taking place. If you were in Hollywood, in films, at a play opening, you said hello to anybody possible, I suspected. All the same I always had a warm feeling about Tilly Losch because she did greet me by name. We don't need much to make us feel really good. I wish I had known her, though, because years later I did come to know a woman from Budapest with the same kind of figure, the same kind of bone structure, long of leg, broad of shoulder, with a very pleasant manner and a real attractive and unavoidable accent, and this woman, both in San Francisco and in New York, was a joy to tumble with, so to put it, although the watching of her Great Dane one Sunday afternoon in New York made it necessary for me to burst out laughing, because the animal's eyes seemed to be asking all sorts of questions for which there just weren't any answers. My laughter impelled the sweet lady to say, You're hurting his feelings. I urged her to get him the hell out of the bedroom, then. She replied that he would cry. I let it go, let the Great Dane ask his silly questions, but let her, at her leisure, try to answer them. John Lounsbery also died, but I don't know him, and indeed don't believe I have ever stopped to study the name Lounsbery in print anywhere. It's misspelled, I seem to find it possible to say, somewhat after the manner of the actor rehearsing a play who said of a name, Why plural? The name was Brahms of course, but as far as the actor was concerned—ah well, sometimes I seem to want to explain stuff needing nothing further at all. It's fun. Brahm is enough. One man, one name, singular. (Do I wish I knew grammar, to permit me to make it first person pronoun singular? No sir, I do not.) Judith Lowry died, and I don't know her, although it suddenly occurs to me that she might very well be the woman who married Robert Lowry of Cincinnati, but divorced him, and was introduced to me in New York by her friend the English writer Gerald Kersh. Did that woman die? Well, somebody named Judith Lowry did, and that's as far as I can go, I'm afraid. Leonard Lyons is next on the list, and we met long ago in New York, so that pretty much every time I was in town I would hear from him and we would meet and I would accompany him on his rounds of the famous places where he gathered the anecdotes for his next day's column: 21 Club, The Stork, Sardi's, Billy Reed's Little Club, Leon & Eddy's, Toots Shorrs, El Morocco, and many others. He came to dinner at my house in San Francisco once, and Takoohi Saroyan gave him a nice spread of real Armenian Bitlis Saroyan cooking, which he loved. She liked his very warm and really kind nature, his sharp hawk-like face, his restlessness, his loud laughter, and the next day gave a full and accurate recreation of his speech, song and dance, so to put it. She had that skill, which many Saroyans have. Herbert Machiz died, and seeing his name on the list makes me remember a keyed-up kid who came to my office when I was trying to get L. B. Mayer to let me produce and direct *The Human Comedy*, and he said he wanted to be a producer, how could he do that? Well, we talked and smoked cigarettes, and I asked him questions and he made answers, and he went back to being a messenger on the lot. Fade in about ten years later, he has produced a play on Broadway and the critics have not been unhappy about it, and he is being interviewed by feature story writers, and in one of them he says something along the lines of how I didn't help him when he came and told me he wanted to be a producer— or something like that, although I may have the whole thing all right, it may have been a producer named Jacobs who had been the messenger, but went on to become the producer of the movie in which there is a llama with a neck and head at both ends, and in which there is a song about talking to the animals—*Dr. Doolittle,* is that the name of the movie, or is it the name only of the writer of a series of books for kids? Anyway, Jacobs died, and I know definitely that I knew Machiz and once on a visit to the *New York Times* to see somebody or other, possibly Brooks Atkinson, Machiz and I had a chat, and I advised him on how he might stop being an office boy and become a director or a producer of plays or anything else he might care to be. I mean, I knew him, but I believe I can't go much farther than that about him. So he became a producer.

103

After the name Herbert Machiz comes the name Ted Mack, and immediately I remember Major Bowes, that pompous ass who affixed his name to a popular show called *Major Bowes' Amateur Hour.* He used to say something like, "Around and around the wheel of fortune turns and where it stops nobody knows." Something idiotic like that, spoken like Omar Khayyam 100 proof ancient Persian wisdom, but altogether inappropriate to the nice if slightly sad and very depressing, not comic, people who presented first a vast radio audience with their talents, vocally, and then on television both visually and vocally. Well, it was very nearly impossible that among the hundreds of ambitious people there would be a few who would go on and become famous and rich, but after I think of Art Carney I can think of nobody else. Eventually Major Bowes retired or died, and the show stopped, at least for a while, or a new man was brought in to be the presenter of the people who wanted to get to the big time, even if only to be sent out on the road in one of the touring companies of the *Amateur Hour,* of which now and then over the years there were half a dozen in circulation. Got to be famous. Got to sing. Got to dance. Got to do magic. Got to do imitations. Got to do acrobatics. Ten thousand little girls tap danced in studios all over the country believing they might become good enough to go on the *Amateur Hour.* Twenty thousand twirled batons. A million cheered in school assemblies and at football games. It was all part of the show business of being an American girl. There was a snickering condescension about Major Bowes which he cleverly followed with a probably authentic sobriety made out of sincere pity for the really terrible and untalented people who made him rich by appearing on his stupid show. But it was less stupid than dozens of other shows which belittled people, all somewhat like the others, beginning with *People Are Funny.* A fellow I used to know named Jackson Stanley wrote the material for *People Are Funny* for good money for many years but hated the work, or said he did, deeply, and Jack Stanley one year published a novel entitled *The Florentine Ring* and his publisher sent me a copy and I read it and thought it was very good, although as I wrote from Paris to Jack in Malibu I couldn't quite understand why it hadn't been a novel about himself, *People Are Funny,* Art Linkletter, and the whole television business which he knew so well. I shouldn't have asked such a question, I suppose, because I should have known he was sick of all that stuff and wrote a kind of tour de force set in Florence precisely in order to get away from the fraudulent program he himself had helped to sustain for so long. Ted Mack wasn't as bad as Major Bowes. But he did share the Major's subtle pomposity—there is really no need for the little souls who do for the Network owners the nervous work that makes them rich to feel, however shyly, that they are God, but I have never seen any of them not do that. Maybe it just can't be helped, maybe they are in touch with more people at one crack than God ever was. André Malraux died and it is generally felt that he was both a great writer and a great man. I wouldn't know about either, but I did read his big autobiographical work which he called something like *Anti-Memoirs,* and it was phony, and the unintended exposure of a hustling publicity seeker—he dedicated the book to the widow of the boy President John F. Kennedy, and such a dedication could not possibly be remotely in order, on its own. Señor Mardo is next and that would seem to be the professional name of either a magician or a ventriloquist—or possibly an acrobat, Señor making the name in English Mr. Mardo, that's all. I don't know him, or his act, and I wish I did: also his name. Nino Martini on the other hand was a popular singer who is said to have been introduced to Tallaluh Bankhead at a party and a half hour later she introduced him to somebody as Mr. Olive—well, she knew his name had some connection with a very popular and welcome drink at the end of the work day, usually with an olive on a toothpick dunked into it. And the name was used in comedy routines and in *New Yorker* cartoons—"Bartender, give me a Martini, and I don't mean Nino." And so on. (It's not fair, one can suspect the singer saying from the graveyard—and if it happens to be the one in Genoa, which I haven't yet visited, it is supposed to be one of the best in the world. Ararat in Fresno, the Armenian cemetery, is for me maybe not so great but certainly most deeply satisfying as a place for a summer afternoon visit.

Before anything else, this: what is it that may be said to be the sure sign of life, especially in man? It is waking. When waking ceases, in any sense, after any kind of interval, we have the sure sign of the cessation of life, the absence of life, the sure sign of death. But of course there are wakings and wakings. It is not unheard of that somebody shall sleep longer than 24 hours, even, and without any kind of narcotic or drug or trauma there have been sleepers who have slept a week or even longer, but have not been in a coma, or apparently have not been. Thus, we are put into the arena of that side of the matter: we sleep, we waken, we sleep, we waken, and the pattern is simple: out of every twenty-four hours we tend to sleep under ten hours, sometimes under eight, and with some souls sometimes well under six. This goes on and on the whole lifetime of the person, so that the other side of the line is vital to this side of the line, we are never out of touch with it for much longer than under extreme emergency three or four days, but even then we are clearly in touch with it another way, in dreams of non-sleep, in hallucinnations, in tricks or deceptions of memory and sensibility: we know we are awake, but we believe we are awake in a dream, or more likely in a nightmare, for the tiredness which has taken place in our fragile apparatus. But eventually, after something that seems to us like a terrible ordeal, we are permitted to sleep properly, and after enough of it to restore us to our traditional connection with this side of the line, we awaken, and we are alive, but this time not in a dream, not in a nightmare, but in a serene reality—if we are lucky, if that is what our daily reality is by reason of luck or labor, anticipation, preparation, thrift, money, practicality, and other things, including of course something strange called health. But waking is waking, and so it has come to bebe put into several forms of our lore that the dead are to waken, that the beauty asleep is to waken, that somebody deeply beloved shall come again, as in the famous Second Coming of Christ. To awaken is to be still among the living. Not to awaken is to have gone over to the dead, but we have taken it into our heads and into our souls, in longing, in faith, in competitive religion, in pure science, to believe, to disbelieve, and to be open-minded about awakening from death, in one sense or another. As the man on television said who had won a refrigerator instead of a trip to Paris, "I don't want it." One could readily believe this refusal of such a gift, just as anybody with any real awareness of the nature of things and of living and variable truth in things would reject the notion of living in this world, in this life, in the form of a human being for an indefinite amount of time, such as a hundred years, a hundred and fifty, two hundred, five hundred. The thought of himself, and only himself, being prolonged so long is in itself painful, and heavy with that which we call boredom. For each of us is only himself, and our tolerance of that truth is restricted to apparently a maximum of sixty years, which is prolongable to a hundred in many cases, and a few years longer in a few cases, but by then there has taken place something so like real death that it needn't be considered real life. But it is of course as real as any life is, for the person breathes and awakens. What may be said to be the thing that permits us to know that we are truly alive, in the sense of living as we understand it, not excluding sex, procreation, the engagement of emotions appropriate to what is called love, passion, fatherhood, motherhood, and care of the young: it is of course movement, or dance. And we are all of us dancers dancing. After waking we begin to dance: out of bed, into the shower, out of the shower, into the exercises of the day, very light but very intelligent, into clothing, into shoes, out to the house, out of the house, dancing as we go, into the transportation to work, into the place of work, and for us in show business, and for us only on the edges of show business, it is rehearsals and rehearsing, one and all, on and on, try it again, dear, just once more, buddy boy, give it one more go, and we do, and for what? Applause. We want that applause. We can't breathe without it, we can't sleep without it, we can't awaken without it. So what is it that brings the final curtain to people in showbiz? The failure of applause, the cessation of hands clapping and voices murmuring, and a few shouting exclamations of several kinds in several languages—hired people or members of the family, a bullied bride, a mother threatened with murder, a demented but darling daughter, clapping and standing and shouting things. Cut those things off from the showbiz soul and the soul shrivels. The tap dance stops. The waking stops. A stiff is found in bed, bereft of sleep and dream, and God knows where the person has gone, some say to heaven, some say to hell, some say only to the graveyard, some say back to nature, and some leave instructions to burn the body and to sprinkle the ashes upon the gently flowing waters of the River of Day, or Life, while others say dump the whole urn of ashes right into the Ocean of Night, or Death. I don't believe in such silly stuff as going to heaven to sit on the right hand of somebody fictitious and damned foolish, or going to hell to be roasted by somebody else even more fantastic and silly—just dump my beloved ashes (along with the ashes of the expensive coffin in which the funeral services compelled me to lie, like a window dummy) into the raging ocean, which as you know, as you surely remember, was the character of my soul, and the style of my eight minutes of dances, songs, and witty sayings, Sun Time.

105

Christ, man, it's fun, it's fun, having the sun, having the seasons, having the whole damned thing all around and in depth, just as in depth as a study of cycles in weather patterns, having it all, all, all of it going on all the time, what could possibly be more fun than that? Surely it could not be not having it? Having is better than not having, and I don't mean just money, which is also fun to have, but the real fun is having that sticky stuff from men reach the sticky stuff from women in deep dark sticky places and becoming some thing in the animal family steady steady steady until it is somebody, and once and only once you, yourself, man, that is fun, so don't forget it, for it is forgotten by hundreds and thousands every day all over the world in showbiz, and one of them who forgot it last year, sometime in 1976 was, alas, Waldo Mayo, and I don't believe we can imagine that he was one of the brothers, perhaps a very younger brother, a rebel, a refuser, a smart fellow, a sharp-dresser who said to all of the Mayos, Look, you're you, I'm me, O.K.? O.K. You want to do brain surgery, I want to make people laugh, O.K.? O.K. You want to fool around with all kinds of stuff in sick bastards, I want to entertain healthy sons of bitches, O.K.? O.K. And off he went into showbiz, beginning with a one-ring circus and working his way up steadily to stardom of some kind. Well he died and I never met him, never saw his act, and wish him well, forever and a day. But let no one say he should not have repudiated the family tradition of medicine, surgery, and healing in favor of song and dance. It is not nice to do that after a man has put in a whole lifetime of strong ambition and frequently very little talent, although this unknown man, this unknown dead of showbiz is not of that order at all, he was not even in the department of it that was behind footlights, for all I know. I only applaud him for having been in any department at all, that was enough, and if the truth is told and he had worked forty years for Woolworth's as a clerk and a floorwalker I would have applauded him, for let us try not to exclude Woolworth's from showbiz and walking the floor from the great turns, not for ten or eleven minutes, but for eight hours a day. That's real dedication, brother, and you know it. I take off my hat to every man who ever put in a good long run at Woolworth's and took his applause with grace and a grain of salt and finally awakened not to himself in his own private personal body but to something else, not somebody else's body, but something else in some kind of dimension I know nothing about. I also take off my shoes to such a person, hat is not enough. And let no man think in his heart, or through his head, that anything here is to be construed or misconstrued as mockery, think of it, a scoffing at death, a laughing at the one thing the whole human race has always been agreed upon: that the end of life in anybody is the occasion for dignity. Is that so? Then, what about the beginning of life, or the interruption of it by the Draft during some kind of fraudulent war? Is getting born the occasion for kidding around, as it seems to be. Is getting drafted into the stupidest aggregation of mothers in the world the occasion for levity? No sir, these are the appropriate occasions for dignity, for we do not know who has been born, there were not three wise men to tell us, and we also do not know how long the conscript is going to be able to take the chicken—before shooting members of his Draft Board, the officers of his outfit, or his brains out. That calls for being dignified. That kind of ignorance demands strict sobriety, no going around dead drunk but still on the feet and mumbling messages to madnesses in everybody everywhere.

Another person who died was Mary Margaret McBride, and I know the name, I know it, but I don't really see Mary, I can't quite bring her to the interior optical miracle of visual memory, she was there and I saw her on television, I believe, but now Mary is gone, and we are all less for it, although I don't quite know how or why. I loved Mary Margaret McBride because English is my native language, so to put it, and alliteration is one of the joys of the English language. When somebody's names run three letters of the alphabet together at the top of three words we all love it, it is like M, M, M, or yum, yum, yum, and it both sounds and feels good. In a sense Mary Margaret McBride was in her very name a kind of candy, and don't let anybody kid you, brother, sister, we all love candy, but did you know that the sugar in candy is not unlike the alcohol in schnaps or booze? I didn't, either, until a very stupid cousin told me so, and I am willing to learn from anybody. Ruth McDevitt also died and is also in showbiz, and in *Variety*'s famous list for 1976, which in its day listed the very founders and editors of *Variety*: Sime Silverman, Abel Green, and a number of writers, just so they were not insignificant in their connection with the famous trade paper. Joseph L. McEveety—yes sir that's the name, precisely as it appears in *Variety*: McEveety, and I have never before seen such a name, and have never heard it pronounced, and have never seen the owner of it, called Joe, most likely, for short, God rest his soul, and also Mary Margaret McBride's, and Ruth McDevitt's and when you die, reader, your soul, may God not fail in that routine little piece of showbiz courtesy, and when I die, too, let God remember to rest my soul, and let the whole human race understand that I was there, I was who I was all the way, I was big, I was right, I was nervous, I was over-stimulated, I was the most courteous writer of my age, and always put in a good word for the real minorities, like the excessively rich and their honorable problems.

Reader, take my advice, don't die, just don't die, that's all, it doesn't pay, people aren't that sincere, you know, they will pretend to be sorry but really they don't care, they think it is perfectly all right that you died, and it isn't, so don't do it, don't die, figure out how, and stay put, there is plenty of time, let it go for this summer and next winter, and give the matter your best thought, even as you go about on your feet in your shoes and clothes and enjoy the business of looking and moving, it is right that you should not die, so don't do it, don't do what Charles R. Meeker did last year, I don't know why he did it, but he did do it, but don't you do it, sir, and lady, Oh lady, lady, don't you do it, either, you just take your good time about it, and if your husband had to rush away so you could get the insurance and all of his estate, don't you do what he did, and as for you younger men and women, and you adolescent boys and girls, and you teenagers, listen: suicide is no solution, just as drugs are no solution, and if you feel that nothing is a solution, don't be sure of that, that may very well not be so at all, it may be the consequence of something you can't even know about—bad weather, in a cycle, a cold winter of the soul, freezing, so hang in, hang on, hang over, hang under, and wait, and while you're waiting go for something, go fetch somebody something he thinks he needs—fresh bread is good straight from the bakery unsliced, go buy a loaf and take it to somebody and get a good sharp knife and take the round crusty loaf of sourdough bread made by the Basques of Fresno and very smartly slice the bread straight down the middle and smell the sourdough baked bread, man, it is good, at 80¢ a loaf it isn't half bad, the loaf has a weight of 24 ounces, a pound and a half, and you can make a meal out of some of the bread, breaking bread as the saying is with the man or woman or the both of them who sent you to fetch the bread, take a quarter of a pound of good sweet butter or good sweet margarine and smear the slice of sourdough with that stuff and smell it real full and well and bite it and chew it slowly and swallow it, and live, that's living, and if you really want to make it a kind of celebration of living, friend, young or old, brew a pot of plain tea, Lipton's, and pour, and without sugar or milk or anything sip a little of the piping hot tea and let it flow and wash upon the sourdough Basque bread and the butter or margarine, and yum yum yum, remember Mary Margaret McBride, swallow and know you are alive and doing nobody any harm, doing nothing any harm at all. Another man who somehow or other fell into that trap and died is William Melniker, but again he is not somebody I know at all, and about whom I also know nothing, how he rated the mention in the *Variety* list or anything else, although I like the name Melniker and wish I knew what it means, in Yiddish perhaps, or in Polish, or in German, or in another language brought to the New World by one of William Melniker's good ancestors long ago, but not all that long ago, just recently long ago. And then Johnny Mercer died, and I know him, I knew Johnny Mercer, I saw him sometimes at parties in Hollywood, and sometimes at Stanley Rose's bookstore, and sometimes at various other places. He wrote the lyrics, the words, to many great songs, but he also sang those songs, and he sang them well. He made good money, but his father died broke and in debt, somewhere in the South, possibly in Atlanta, and quietly Johnny Mercer went to work and paid every one of his father's debts, even though legally he was in no way obliged to do so, it was a simple matter of pride, of a son not wanting his father to have left anybody holding the bag, and once at a party I told him that I thought he was one of the great writers of words for songs, one of the really good singers of songs, but I had lately heard about what he had done for his father, and that was the thing I now admired about him above all other things, and I was glad that he had not been able to suppress the news of his devotion to his father, and to his own sense of family, as he had wanted to do, for it is necessary for all of us to hear about such news, and Johnny Mercer in his shy way smiled and thanked me, and we talked about the stuff people always talk about at parties, especially Hollywood parties, and that stuff is never without its comedy, that is the best thing about all talk at all parties, perhaps on account of the booze, and the fact that everybody is free again for a little while, and it is permissible and in order to talk about the funny stuff in the world, what somebody said to somebody else at a time when something else was expected of him traditionally har har har har har har. Christ, reader, take my advice, don't die, Johnny Mercer died, but don't you, and don't get the kind of headaches that made Johnny Mercer agree to go to the highest branch of the medical profession for the latest kind of examination and then don't be told yes, yes sir, yes Johnny Mercer, we've found it, you have a brain tumor, it has to come out, because it may be benign but also may not be, and in any case, it appears to be the thing that is hurting your soul by way of pain in your head, so Johnny Mercer agreed and they did their good work, and he died, a great artist, a great man, a great son, a great living member of the human race died, and he is gone, and don't you do it, and don't think you may have a brain tumor, too, because thinking about it may start a little one growing in your head, watch out for giving the mystery of cells any hint of fear, because those cells may be like dogs and if they sense you're afraid of them, they'll go to work and start multiplying in a kind of disorganized way and hurt you so badly you will risk dying on the operating table, and then lose your bet, and die. Don't do it.

107

Jo Mielziner is another of the showbiz losers of 1976, and he was somebody I both know, and know about: a great artist in the arena of the theatre, in the branch known as scene design: he was a great one, and his sets helped many a play come through in a fine way, especially Mr. Arthur Miller's *Death of a Salesman*—death, death, death, reader, all over the place, bad for you, painful, if it can grab Jo Mielziner, be careful, it can grab you, too, and that's what's bad for you, that grabbing, death is always grabbing, taking a man away from his work, there were great scenes for Jo Mielziner still to design, but he was stopped cold. I was shaking-up Broadway with my own idea of what a play ought to be, and with my high spirits, and kidding around, and breaking of rules, and carrying on for laughs, yelling at everybody that I was the one, and all the rest of it, when I met Jo Mielziner who seemed to be a very sober sensible man, ten or eleven years my senior, and the author of a book about his branch of showbiz. I said, But the imagination is the best designer of scenes, why prevent it from having its own easy way with where any play is taking place, why not let it be in the scene which is the beholder's own past and truth, and stuff like that, kidding around some more of course, and Jo Mielziner said, Well, of course that is true and for centuries great plays have been done without scenery and nobody has felt they needed scenery to really enjoy the play or be moved by its tragedy and delighted by its comedy: it is really impossible in a modern theatre to put on a play without scenery, however, because if you work on a bare stage, that in itself is scenery—all I do is try to help certain kinds of plays a little, especially when scenery is part of the drama. He was a friend of all of the other scene designers of course, and of most of the good painters and sculptors of New York, and with some of the good architects, for all of these things are related, and elements of them are demanded by the craft and art of scene designing—you have got to know about them, and he did, and so did, and so does Boris Aronson, a great artist in or away from the theatre, and Sam Leve who did the fine set for *The Beautiful People*, and so was Watson Barrett who did the really perfect set for *The Time of Your Life*, and these artists are people who think and think all the time about places and shapes and light and shadow and densities and literature and life and how bodies in action in a play, with breath moving through lungs upon mouths and tongues and voice boxes making a kind of orchestral work of speech, how all of these things intermingle and make a kind of something that rewards people for sitting side by side like cells side by side in a beehive, for instance, each occupant of a seat something like an embryo of something to come though fully formed as a bee of some sort or another: worker, gatherer of honey, dancer, or whatever one or another of the several bee categories are. I used to love getting to my own individual seat in a theatre, any theatre, any play, because this permitted me to study life the way the scientist studies stuff under the heightened vision of a microscope, and I sat there in that private seat and watched the stuff on the stage, mostly vaudeville at the Hippodrome Theatre, and it was great, it was so great that years later I wrote a fine story called "The World and the Theatre", and one of these days I am going to read it again because in it is the stuff I put in it so that I would know how it was after the failure of memory, which is right now—but I did it, I held it all fast in that story and I know how and why I found my private seat in a great auditorium, after sneaking in, as a matter of fact, and always preferred sitting in a theatre that was almost empty, the whole place becoming almost my own property. But these days, and for years, I don't do that any more, it isn't age, it is selectivity, I don't feel like going in like an abstract morsel of some strange form of life to behold something I know from having seen it a dozen times and also from having myself put it into the play form. Jo Mielziner was a good workman in the scenery department of the American Theatre. But Sal Mineo—there is a young man whose murder by stabbing is still painful to think about. I suggested to Robert Saudek that *Omnibus*, a Sunday afternoon cultural TV show sponsored or underwritten by the Ford Foundation, should invite interesting old men of America to simply sit and recall their earliest years, and so a number of people decorated the variety program by doing that, and that Robert Saudek invited me to do it, but I said no, I would put it in a play, *A Few Adventures in the California Boyhood of William Saroyan*, or something to that effect, and Robert Saudek hired Sal Mineo to play William Saroyan, and when I saw the boy I swore he was myself, that is how it really was, reader, and he did the part absolutely flawlessly, and I was amazed: his brother Tom was also in the play, and I enjoyed chatting with both of them between my own chores on camera, before tapes, live, really live, and these chores were simple: I told about what happened, and then Sal Mineo performed it: I also hired a Greek who played the mandolin and walked up Van Ness Avenue in Fresno during World War I and played "There's a Long Long Trail Awinding Into the Land of My Dreams," and it was magic, that's all. So last year walking from his car in its proper place in the basement parking space of his apartment in Hollywood young Sal Mineo was stabbed by somebody who ran away, and Sal Mineo died, crying out in terrible protest, and the dirty killer, Death Itself, was never apprehended. I'll never forget him, he was great. Walter Schulze-Mittendorf also died last year, but I don't know him, and I wish I did.

108

I have been called a sentimental writer, and this has annoyed me, but it may be that I haven't understood the meaning of sentiment, or of sentimental. That is not something unusual—for me, for you, for anybody. The fact is it is usual. We almost never know accurately anything at all. Language is supposed to protect us from inaccuracy but it may very well be that it compels more of it. All the same I have taken the written statement in book reviews that my writing is sentimental as a lie, an insult, and a deliberate attempt to belittle me. Does this reaction constitute something like paranoia? Bet your ass it does, and proudly. Name the least sentimental of writers—of men—and he is far more sentimental than I am. That becomes my reply. Shakespeare? (Poor Shakespeare, his name is dragged into every dispute of every kind everywhere.) But name him just the same, I say his writing is more sentimental than mine, and even while I say this, I think, Have you flipped your wig again, sir? Shakespeare has nothing to do with any of this. Nothing to do with this world, or its literature, or American writing, or California writing, or Armenian-American writing, or Armenian California Christian writing, or Saroyan-this-that-the-other writing, or sentiment, or literary criticism, or anything at all, you are just throwing a name around, and it would be far more sensible to make the name something really irrelevant, like Gaston Lafitte, or somebody. Gaston Lafitte was believed to be the least sentimental of men but he was far less sentimental than you, sir, so don't get hot, just don't get hot, that's all, so some jerk writing a stupid review has said you are sentimental, so be like Ernest Gallo or somebody and go about your business with your natural aloofness, who cares what the jerk reviewer says? We don't really ever know fully what we mean when we use certain words, even words as simple and as clear as good and bad. This is good, this is bad. We can say it, but we can't know what we mean unless it is grapes for instance, because a bunch of grapes can be seen and can be tasted and chewed and swallowed, and we can know what we have, and we can be absolutely certain that these grapes are good. Take muscats, for instance, which long ago became especially pleasant for me to take from vines and dust and eat, for all grapes have what is called a bloom, a mixture of actual soil dust and something that belongs to the nature of grapes themselves, of their slow ripening, or swift ripening. The muscat grapes on the muscat vines that I pruned when I was kicked out of Fresno High School and decided that I wouldn't even think of trying to get back, as I had been forced to do a number of times, in the dead of winter, little bunches overlooked by the grape-pickers and left on the vines, hidden sometimes low on the vine and under dry crisp leaves, these grapes came as a delightful gift as I worked and I loved eating them. Let that stand. Let almost fifty years go by. I have bought a flat in an old building in old Paris, the original Paris, and from the fruit and vegetable carts and shops I have bought stuff and eaten it, and one day I paid about a dollar for about a pound of grapes—everything is expensive everywhere, but I wanted these grapes because the sign said muscats—and the first thing I noticed was that they had a touch of purple in the skin, whereas the color in the California muscats was what is technically called white but is more transparent with a touch of green and yellow or golden, but just a touch. The second thing I noticed was that the untouched bunch of grapes was slightly scented, and touched, broken by accident for instance, the scent became strong and was most pleasing, and when broken by the teeth and tasted the Paris muscat grapes were absolutely new and special, and I thought better than the California muscat grapes.

Look, I wouldn't think of being a man of power, a man of power over other men, power of life and death and money, like the leaders and politicians and all such, for they are the sentimental souls of the human race, of the human world, of the human time and life, and their sentiment is stupid and limited to the self, to themselves, each of them, although they invariably put the self out into something abstract like the name of the people themselves, totally unreal of course, or the region, or the religion, or the philosophy: they claim they are everybody, in short, it is an awful crime of sentiment and dirty dishonesty. There is clean dishonesty, as when a decent man doesn't happen to know but does believe in the opposite of what is the truth, and does so with passion and innocence. What I'm saying is, let's just get things inaccurately as we have always done, and let's have the clutter grow beyond all limits, and let's every one of us know his own little portion of the inaccuracy in his own way, to suit his own participation in the dance, the labor, the play, the fun, the anguish, the joy, the pain of being, of having connection, place, property, clothing, memorabilia, letters, stamps, coins, shoes, souvenirs, bottles, china or at any rate dishes, silver or at any rate stainless steel (including little sets from airline meals), napkins of both cloth and paper, and let us not demand that what we have and know is all there is, all there is, take it or leave it. Don't tell me I'm sentimental, you sons of bitches. You are contemptible, your dishonesty is contemptible, your careful plodding with words, to keep them safely captured inside your silly little theories are contemptible, but I don't hate you because each of you is a sad little pompous son of a bitch, with a chair at a university, and you are fighting bravely to seem to be somebody.

Talk about incoherence and nobody will believe you are incoherent, but talk sense and people will look at one another as if asking, What did he say? Do you understand him? Well, listen here, friend, you're not dead yet, you're reading this, and it's not too late for you to do just a little more about that fact, your good luck—yes, your astonishing and beautiful good luck—and this is what you can do, besides all the other things that are to be done: you can honor the dead, honor the dying, honor the living, honor the unborn, and love them, love them, but truly love them by first hating them pitifully, with something like charity, but without sorrow. You have got to do that, because that's all we have, that's who we are, I've said it once, I've said it twice, love all the daughters and sons of bitches, and legally married and socially respected daughters and sons, love them separately one at a time in the built-in largeness of the cells of the ancient brain in your head, and collectively all together love them with all of the fire built-in over the millions of years into your soul, and by loving them permit yourself, your unself, your allself, your soulself, your timeself, your lifeself, your deathself, your pettyself, your greatself, your unknowableself, your allself, everself, bornself, unbornself, beyondbirthself, beyonddeathself, constantself, Godself, and unGodlyself to hate them all with the cool serenity of ice, and to love them with the cooler serenity of fire, and to go about your business of peeling an onion, breaking a loaf of crusty bread—bread, friend, bread bread, you know what bread is—eating of the onion and the bread, and while eating, while chewing, knowing, friend, knowing with all your selfself, un and non and all and all, that there is that, and the thing that comes from growing in the earth is called onion, and the made thing is from wheat also from the earth and mixed with salt and water and yeast and baked in some kind of oven, or fire, and is called bread, and washing it down with water, water, cool water, precisely as sung by the sons of the pioneers from the beginning of sons and of pioneers and places, know that friend, know that you are there, for soon enough it will be somebody else knowing that you had been there but are there no longer, pray it is somebody out of yourself partly, mingled with the daughter of strangers, a strange daughter of strangers, and these others out of that participation of procedure, pray they are good kids and good kids of kids, and you know how we have got to be easy about what we mean by good, our easiest meaning is that they are not flawed beyond the flaw of being human itself, for there is that, a being human, and it is all we have, and we don't need to feel we are fools to be glad about it, or annoyed if our folly is put down as sentiment. High road, low road, somebody will be in Scotland before you, and it may be me, not far behind Jasper MacGregor, or Kaspar der Krikor, it comes to the same thing, you know, and highlands are highlands, whether in Scotland or Armenia, whether traversed by Robert Burns in actual singing strides, or by myself in shouting laughing strides of spirit both in Scotland and in Armenia thousands of miles from the streets of Fresno. I want you to live, and while you live I want you to make the most of it, but I want you to understand, to find out from what I am saying, that the best possible way to do that, to live, is to keep it very simple, not to get yourself all exercycled out of all shape by the clutter of more and more and more, and therefore less and less and less until there is none at all, which is death, as by now you surely know. Write your will but keep yourself dead center of the only enormity and abundance you can possibly really enjoy and by which you can move along serenely in simple actuality and enormous unknown truth—dead center of self, the self which is everything and everybody walking the highways and the highlands and seeing. If you didn't have a self, if you didn't have that self, the self of all, you would not have been born, as a billion billion times as many were not born as were born, remember that, you were chosen, and if you cry out in the voice of an idiot adolescent, I didn't ask to be born, just remember that you also failed to ask not to be born, just remember that and take what you have in that, in that event, your own private and privileged birth, take all of it and live out of it, and in it, and wend your way through time like another of the sons or daughters of the pioneers chanting water, water, cool water, and with the onion take all of that family of things and enjoy them one at a time, always one at a time, and raw, direct, and with the bread, take all of that family, which is language, literature, story, legend, gossip, news, eulogy, baptism, speech, speech, and much listening, and with the water take all of that family, which is music and singing and dancing and walking and running and tumbling and painting and sculpture and politeness and laughter and whispering and impregnating and permitting the flowing out of the great pools of life of another water baby laughing and crying at the same time from the billion-year postponement of that joy of arrival. Look, reader, if birth is sentimental, death is sentimental, and getting born is sentimental, and not dying is sentimental, and all of this is really none of my business, none of your business, if you ask a corpse why do you have a head, you're dead, he can't possibly reply, saying the truth, which is something like, I had it while I was alive, for years and years, and I still didn't use it.

110

I am sorry that John L. Murphy died in 1976, but I am glad Dudley Murphy didn't, because I knew Dudley Murphy, and had a cup of coffee with him at the Automat on 57th Street near 6th Avenue, and just down a bit from the narrow entrance and long hall to the front desk at the Great Northern Hotel, which was brought down and is gone forever, shall we cry out alas? Yes, let's do that. I believe I was writing the *Time of Your Life* in six days, Monday through Saturday, at that time and had gone to the Automat for a coffee break, and along came gangly Dudley Murphy to introduce himself as the producer of something called *One Third of the Nation*, and to ask if I might give him a play to produce. Well, I might, but I might not, too, and as it turned out I didn't, for a variety of reasons, not the least of which is that he left New York and the business of producing plays. Later, when I lived in a small house on the beach at Malibu, he opened a restaurant on the highway sort of northwest from my house, and I sometimes went there with friends to drink and eat, and he frequently joined us to chat, and sometimes he brought along his wife, or his new wife, and once or twice I was introduced to a daughter, and to her husband, a boy from China, or somewhere. People we knew long ago stay with us, like it or not, and I almost invariably like it, not excluding people I disliked long ago but no longer want to be bothered with one way or the other any more, or find I want to rather cherish even them, because they were part of the past, and part of what I somehow have remembered, knowing all the while that there were surely dozens of other people far less unappealing or acceptable to me which nevertheless I have somehow forgotten. Memory makes friends of enemies, so to put it. The past transforms but does not lie. We simply choose not to make too much of the truth. It doesn't matter that much any longer. For instance, there was in New York when I was producing *The Beautiful People* at the Belasco Theatre an especially offensive man about my own age who deliberately interrupted me at my work, coming backstage, or knocking at the door of the office in which I considered both how to stage the play and to revise parts of it, and add to it, and he was so obviously a sneak and a simple son of a bitch that I ordered him to get out and stay out—and how right I was, for when I received from Washington the Federal Bureau of Investigation's file on me to which I became legally entitled some years ago, but which the F.B.I. somehow managed to legally have the right to withhold various peoples, among the papers I did glance at, here was the name of this boob, having assumed the role of patriotic informer, stating that I was clearly a Trotskyite, something I could never possibly have cared to consider, even: and I remembered the silly son of a bitch, and tried to guess why he had done that and concluded that it was to avoid being drafted, and as far as I know he was not drafted, but precisely how he avoided that I cannot be sure. The point is that after I had done three years in the Army, both in California, New York City, Dayton, London, and

Paris, and had been permitted to return to myself, yes precisely that, and to my proper work, I ran into this sneak again in a group at some kind of party or celebration and although at that time I remembered only that he had been a contemptible little sneak and did not know that he had sent a message to the F.B.I. with the false information that I was a Trotskyite, I did not find it necessary to feel contempt for him, openly as I had long ago, or inwardly out of civility, and I did not resent that during the war and after he had gone along into a small business that had not failed and permitted him to feel a part of the scene. In fact, I was helpless not to feel that because he had been around when I was putting on my own plays at the Belasco Theatre, he was somebody I cherished. Do you follow me? The death of Mary Nash in 1976 also sorrows me, but I don't believe I ever met her, and while I have known a great many women named Mary the woman who somehow now comes to mind is May McGarry, but as we know May is frequently actually the name Mary. May McGarry was the very efficient clerk at U Office at 405 Brannon Street in San Francisco early in 1928 when I was made the manager of that office. She was Irish and married but for some reason either used her maiden name—or I've forgotten. She spoke about the Troubles, and the Black and Tans, and the 1916 days, and I liked May McGarry, that's all. I am also sorry that Charlie Naughton died in 1976, and although I don't know him I am able to suspect that he was not in the American theatre, he was in the British theatre, and that with a partner he did good vaudeville or music hall turns, and I saw him around Christmastime in 1944 in a Pantomime, as they are called, but had seen him earlier in other turns, but he may not be the man I am thinking of at all—Naughton and Somebody, like Nervo and Knox, another time, Flannagan and Allen, and so on: greatest of the wartime comics was the favorite of the American troops, and pretty much everybody else: Sid Field, who after the War was sent out to Hollywood and appeared in a film or two and then went home and took sick and died—prematurely, and a terrible loss to comedy. He was the funniest man I had ever seen on a stage, in a way, and I have been lucky enough to have seen two or three dozen very funny men. Sid Field had it—and I mean genius. I have his biography, but alas, it doesn't do him justice, and until somebody like Bert Lahr's brilliant son John, for instance, does Sid Field's full life and story, he won't really be remembered with anywhere near enough of the hilarious truth about his genius.

111

I am also deeply saddened to find in *Variety*'s list the name of Barbara Nichols, for (as I have said) we met and spent some time together, both in New York, and in Hollywood, and by time I don't want to be misunderstood, I mean very superficial time. She was an ambitious girl and I was glad to see her succeeding. But why did she die, that is the question. There may have been something killing in her that gave her body a kind of strangeness which I have noticed in a number of other girls or women but especially in the body of Jayne Whatever the Last Name Was, with the thick chest but somehow small breasts—who was tragically killed in an automobile accident, and was the leading lady of a play called *Will Success Spoil Rock Hunter?* by a playwright who was almost as clever as Neil Simon, by name Axel something, of whom Bennett Cerf who only happened to be his publisher said that he was one of the great playwrights of America. Axelrod, also wrote *The Seven Year Itch*, I believe, which was also clever but a better work than the other. The bodies of some women are off-center, so to put it, and that seemed to be true of Barbara Nichols and of Jayne not Meadows—ah ha, got it, Jayne—well, I had it—not Matthews, Mansfield, is that right, Jayne Mansfield, the same as the husband of the novelist, Irving? Big upper body, that is, standing upon comparatively skinny legs, Something wrong. Allardyce Nicoll is not anybody I know, and neither is Phil Ochs, but I am sorry they died. I hope the reader, I hope you, sir, and you, lady, or woman, or girl, will understand that insofar as it is possible for any of us to be sorry about the deaths of people we do not know, that I am sorry, no matter what I say, or how anything said strikes you—I really can't care or be expected to really care about the dead all over the place, it just isn't possible, necessary, or desirable, but I can say without any feeling of insincerity that insofar as anybody surviving those who died were saddened, I am, also. The joke about the beautiful young wife refusing to leave the fresh grave of her young husband is well-known. She was gently drawn away by a friend who said, Yes, but please remember that time will heal this loss, and you will even someday fall into the arms of another man with even more passion than with your husband. And the mourning wife replied, Yes, but what about tonight? Phil Mollica (rather than Phil Ochs) is the name of one of the clerks at the Postal Telegraph office on Warren Street in 1928. Another was Phil Reiser, yes, two Phils in one office. But Ochs is the name that I need to think about a moment, for it is the name of the family that moved from Cincinnati or somewhere to take over a paper dying and for sale cheap in New York, none other than the *Times*, which along with the London paper with the same name, is one of the truly great papers of the world. There aren't many left, however. But even if there were still as many as when New York alone had a dozen dailies, give or take, the *New York Times* would continue to be the greatest, most likely. But descendants of the family have some of them taken to spelling the name Oaks, more Anglo-Saxon in implication than German in fact, which in the original Ochs of the *Times* was proudly Yiddish. Names change, and should, as everything changes, and should. I long ago told both of my kids that they need never hesitate to drop my name in favor of a name that they believed was more appropriate to them, but so far they have continued as Aram Saroyan and Lucy Saroyan. That's all right, too, but that doesn't mean they might not have hit upon far more useful or usable names by studying both the matter of names and themselves. Writers are known to bestow pen names upon themselves, and early in my time I gave the matter quite a bit of thought, and sent out a variety of stories to pulp paper magazines and to such slick paper magazines as *The Boulevardier* of Detroit, and *Inland Topics* of Chicago, or near there, under such names (as I remember it) as Will Sahara, for instance, or something else equally dismal, desperate, and silly—and I know that not all of the stories came back, even though I sent stamped addressed envelopes, in accordance with the rules. If somebody could find the stories, they would find trash, but it would very probably be interesting trash. Floyd B. Odlum died, and he is altogether a stranger to me, although the name Odlum interests me. I believe it is in the Social Register of New York or Boston or Philadelphia, among other things that might conceivably make it interesting to me, or to anybody else. Rich people. Lorgnettes for the ladies, spats and sticks for the men. (Bullshit, too.) Rex O'Malley is another stranger, in life as in death, but Rex Beach is a name I sometimes think about, idly, for he was a writer and he lived out West and it may even be that it was he who for a while became a kind of eccentric in the boondocks not far from Fresno fifty or sixty years ago. It was certainly somebody of that kind, and while he was out there he continued to publish books, but I don't have the facts. *The Spoilers*, I believe, was the name of one of the more famous of the books by Rex Beach, though. I knew some people rather intimately for a while that I consider worse even than spoilers, I thought of them as defecators on life. I just somehow got that feeling about them. It was far past only belittlement of life, I mean. Harry G. Ommerle died, and I have nothing to say about that, and so it is also about Santos Ortega, but I do earnestly pray that they rest in peace, or continue their showbiz work wherever they may be for as long as they may happen to wish—and if they are nowhere I hope they and their work will not be soon forgotten.

It goes around and around that to look back is a bad thing, and to live in the past is the worst thing, it is death. Well, of course anything that goes around, anything that becomes lore, anything that people believe has merit, has truth to it, but this truth is invariably only some of the truth, not all of the truth, and it is some of the truth only to some of the people—all that someing and truthing which we are supposed to have got into the American variation of the English language by way of Abraham Lincoln makes for a jingling kind of fun, but it may also be a few other things as well, one of them being something in the dimension of confusion, or further confusion. But what we are talking about—always, always, remember that, reader—is the connection between life and death, living and dying, being and not being, and this large connection connects with many other, lesser, connections, but especially to the connection between words used in living languages and the people who live and use the language, and indeed live by them, so that when the lore gets around, by way of a grand old baseball player, for instance, like Satchell Paige, that it is not a good idea to look back (because you may see something catching up on you), there is really no reason for us to dispute the lore. The fact remains just the same that it is a good idea to look back, and to keep looking back, pretty much as long as you live, every day, literally by turning and looking and figuratively by making a point of remembering, if you need to make a point of it, and most us tend to remember without trying or even without especially wanting to. The thing that may be something to think about, to be concerned about in this connection between popular sayings and popular beliefs, and the refuting of them, or of part of them is not so much what the lore says is probably wrong but why it is done, at all. Do you follow, reader? You don't, well that certainly suggests the wisdom of dropping the matter and moving along, for we just haven't got forever, have we, any longer, although up until my fiftieth year I seemed to believe I not only had forever, I would always have forever. But before it's dropped, let me say that all we are really ever concerned about is the improving of the quality that is in everything we know and experience, and to move nearer to excellence and away from less than it. In other words, make a point of looking back so that you may more fully notice and appreciate where you are, and the time it has taken to get there, but if I were now to follow through with this indicated pattern and say don't look back to enjoy the fun you think you had twenty years ago or twenty days ago, or to be astonished at the trouble you were in but got through, or to feel again the joy and sorrow you felt simultaneously because you were involved in an affair, if I were to follow through and say don't do that because it is silly and indulgent and at its core destructive and even deadly, that would be just as inaccurate as the other. And at best a demonstration that anything can be done with words, with language, with print, with writer, with reader, but especially with voice, speaker, and listener, for we know all too well what the great speakers have done, and how near madness so much of their doing has been. Language, words, speech, voice, style, ranting, raving, and something like orchestration of achieved emotional changes in the listeners did it. Prolix is the word for what is going on right here, right now, and also for what I am talking about. But there is no use at all commanding ourselves to shut up, it can't be done, however grand it would be if there were to be as little as 24 hours of shutting up all over the world, what a profound change that would bring to all of us, and if we might also have another day, not the same day, during which everything was stopped—nobody did anything, possibly not even eat, and just be there, everybody in his own gift of hide and hair, foot at the bottom, head at the top, arms at the side—this might be the beginning of the arrival of full and real humanity to the human race. But it might not, too, that is what I am getting at. And full and real humanity might not help, and is for all practical purposes what we have and have always had in any case, only we have been astonished or annoyed that it has been so flawed, that out of it could come so much that is inhuman and indeed insane and criminal and monstrous, and totally, totally without the innocence which not one animal has so far in any tribe of animals lost, even the man-eating tiger has not lost his innocence, he tracks down that order of game because the tiger is too old and slow to track down any other order. Prolix, too many words for what is being said, and I mean right here and right now, but listen here, sir, and lady, man, and woman, boy, and girl, this prolixity is nothing at all to the prolixity of nature before we ever came into possession of words and language and began to see about working things out so that having what we had would be fun and life and not pain and death. Besides, I can't be bothered about avoiding any of the theories about the most effective use of language. This is the most effective—for me. And I would be willing to at least suspect that it might be the most effective for you, too. And let the other writers write their writing and the other readers read their reading and let the aged and feeble tigers stalk old men and have them, shall we imagine that any tiger can really enjoy the liver and lights of a tired old man, that must taste really flat to a tiger, but it is a meal, and it demonstrates that the tiger hasn't looked back, at any rate.

Daily bread, daily work, daily life, daily laughter, daily sorrow, daily this, daily that, because we do have sun arrival and sun departure, or when the season prohibits a noticeable daily arrival and daily departure, we know it is happening just the same, and even if the lights of London, for instance, must be turned on at high noon, or earlier, because the whole city is in nighttime darkness, we all know it is day, and we must go to our daily work, and without too much despair, for soon enough there will be the grand break called lunch. Going to lunch is some kind of thing in London, New York, San Francisco, and Los Angeles, to name only four places, but perhaps it is nowhere the special thing that it is in Paris, continuing for as many as four hours, and the hell with it, it bores me, I swear to Christ the whole rigamarole of lunch bores the bajesus out of me, and yet if you are in a rotten situation of daily work, as being in the stupid Army first in America and then in Europe, man, lunch can be something like your best chance not to flip your goon at last, for sure, postponed as that probability has been for the whole two years you have been the captive of the people and machines of cleverness and corruption in the Army. Who is it that goes to lunch and carries on and on and on, enchanted and enchanting? Actors and actresses, that's who, even when they are at work, rehearsing, performing, or waiting for costumes and makeup, or whatever the hell it might be. And are they perhaps our best connection to both life and reality, to full and varied life and to mapped reality and totally uncharted reality? Yes, it would seem to be so. Are they, really? No, they are not. Well, are they or aren't they ourselves, that's our question, do they connect with ourselves far from any but the only stage—the floor of civilization, the ice, rock, and soil of nature? They are, they are, or so many of us wouldn't have bothered to write plays and parts for them year after year, cultural period after period, one social, religious, or economic revolution after another, and whambang man there on cue out they come to let us behold ourselves on stage, just back of the footlights and the lights from overhead and from all over the auditorium. And then on they go and go with their chants of humanity, of struggle, of dispute, of anxiety, of peace, of love, of suspicion, of falsity, of treachery, of faith, of deception, of everything, man, just naturally everything—and in the background an old wily Norwegian by the name of Ibsen for instance contrives with friends to have larger honors and profits brought to him for having done the work that he would have done had they threatened to imprison or even hang him for doing. And he went to lunch, or had people in to lunch, and so did Strindberg in Sweden, and so did Goethe in Weimar, and so did Pirandello in Sicily, for instance, and so did Moliere in Paris, and so did Chekhov in Moscow, and so did a hundred others in each of those places, each of them in some way connected with the theatre, the drama of life, the play of truth, the battle of the soul with the body, the quarrel of the fools and frauds, male and female, the classic and the romantic, the disciplined and the free, the deprived and the privileged, the brilliant and the stupid, the comic and the tragic contrasting of the opposites in all areas of possibility, on and on and on, and at the fine table for lunch with the enormous menu the actors and actresses study what they might choose while the fine waiter in spotless uniform waits patiently and jots down their wishes and fetches a drink to enlarge and sharpen the appetite and then begins to bring the food—man, that's living, that's not dying, that's being actor and actress together at the table on the stage of life, talking talking talking, and wondering, Is God listening? Wasn't that really bright, reallllly reallly briiiiight, what I just said, how did it go, just what was the alignment of the words? My dear, you have an excellent memory, but rather overlarge breasts. Did I say, Sometimes these days I'm not sure I didn't die long ago and just happened to forget it and am now actually on into the after-life we have heard so much about—is this, then, the after-life, having this glorious table in this famous restaurant on this grand street in this famous city, and all we have to do is just sit and eat and drink and know that if we choose, my dear, if we choose, after we have had our fill we need only have one another for dessert. Is that what I said that I am trying now to keep for God and posterity, or am I indeed dead and am dreaming it all? Who are you, you gorgeous creature? Daily bread, but in China, not far from the Forbidden City, the good people by the millions really have their daily bread and sit and take it—in the form of rice, but it comes to the same thing, and they are so healthy each of them, and so strong and simple, and there are so many of them that Russia is quaking in its boots, and far away America is watching and wondering—they go to lunch the same as we do, but they are stronger in every dimension of reality than we are, they are simpler, they really like themselves, and their land and sky, and we have got to carry on all over the place just to find ourselves tolerable for a short time longer—going out in our cars to escape from the failure of everything, and eating and drinking and drinking and drinking—do you call this living? What are we going to do about China and the Chinese? If Russia doesn't drop the bomb on them, if we don't drop the bomb on them, they are going to get us, that's all. And that's going to knock the bottom out of our going to lunch, and we are not going to sit and order and eat and drink and talk and talk and not die.

Noticing who has died lately, being concerned about the dead, remembering all the dead on a list in one way or another insofar as that is possible, those known to me by actual encounter, those known only by reputation, those not known at all, is probably neither a morbid nor a mysterious activity—it is something I find in all truth that I have done pretty much since the beginning of awareness. People died all around me, and I wanted to consider the probable reality of that very private event to themselves, as well as to me. I never lingered long with anybody who had died, and I still don't. Knowing that the person was dead pretty much called attention and restricted speculation. If the person had long been dead as far as I was concerned because the person had not been seen for years, I was able to remember the person from the days when the person was known to me—person rather than he or her, or him or her, not so much to support the tension of American Women about being treated badly by society and by men, but also not without support, but rather because person is who each of the dead is, in body, casket, memory, graveyard, hospital, heaven, or hell, as the old black song goes: I mean, among my collection of nickel records from Bacigalupi's on Eddy Street in San Francisco there is a record with that name, "Hospital, Heaven, or Hell," one of the surely half a million songs written, composed, and performed by a great many artists of one kind or another. On talk shows one frequently hears the interlocutor enquire of a guest, How many songs have you written? And then one hears a rather interesting but essentially dull and even stupid man reply, Well, I actually had to have the matter looked into by a biographer who is writing my life, and he has them listed by title, and there are eight hundred and twenty-two so far—there are still others that he will come upon among my papers. Well, it can happen, but the songs tend to be along the lines of people and activities, abstractions and misconceptions, that I would rather not hear about, in the words, and the music tends to be even less than banal. There are so many pieces of music by great composers that can receive words of many kinds that one really finds it difficult to take seriously the people who in twenty or thirty years compose more than eight hundred of them. But the hell with that—there is this matter of death to the archbishop or the altar boy or the secret bride of the sexton, and how finding out about a death affects us, as we go along with ourselves steadily and heedlessly to our own last moments and last sayings: Get out of the light. Is this all there is? I forgot to write. I've got to go now. And so on and so forth. I like last sayings, even though I must consider most of them spurious, inventions of the survivors, members of the family, exploiters of truth and falsity alike. What were his last words? Nobody has replied, He didn't have any? Or, He made a sound, a noise. I'm not sure it wasn't vulgar, but surely unintentionally, and I was looking away so I can't be sure how he made it. Or, he only breathed in a way that was slightly different, and then exhaled and stopped. And so on. Ben Iden Payne died in 1976 and I don't know him, but his name instantly brought to mind Idi Amin Baba, the big black man who usurped power in Uganda and has been a world-wide clown-criminal ever since, and has lately taken to individual killings by revolver, followed by statements that suggest he has learned dictatorship well: a couple of Christian missionaries that he is reported by witnesses to have cursed and shot, he has insisted died in automobile accidents. Where have we heard that before? He will also have others he dislikes fall from high windows, but if he has no high windows he will have them fall off cliffs or out of trees. The astonishing Entebbe rescue by Israel of hostages found him strangely half-an-admirer of the brilliant achievement, but then he had been trained by Israelis who had indeed contributed significantly to training and management of the Army which keeps him in power. And he even kept telephoning an Israeli general or politician whom he regarded as a friend. Is this mysterious? No, not really. What it does suggest, though, is something I have believed is inevitable eventually and the sooner or better: the Middle East will relax about Israel and will welcome the skills and tradition of achievement of the Israelis. Nobody is going to push the Israelis out of Israel and into the Mediterranean. That may be the beginning of a settling down to another order of intensification of identity by both the Jews and the Arabs. Mary Petty also died in 1976, and although I never met her I loved her stately drawings of nice old ladies, and others, which appeared in the *New Yorker* for at least a quarter of a century. Gregor Piatigorshy I met at Leonid Kinsky's backyard barbecue in Beverly Hills many years ago, and while drinking vodka, since it was a Russian party, and nibbling little pieces of toast covered with caviar, I had a good time chatting with the great musician, who was by nature given to wit and comedy. Kinsky was a fine character actor, and a friend of Rouben Mamoulian, who had him in several pictures, and an active member of the Russian professionals of Hollywood. Fyodor Challiapin's son may have been at that party, too. Lily Pons also died in 1976 and I only remember having liked both her sweet voice and her small pretty head at the top of her small pretty body, costumed as Carmen. And I remember actually feeling sad that she and her husband separated after many years: Andre Kostelanitz, but I don't know him, either, alive or dead. Martin Rackin is another I do not know, but I remember having seen the name among the credits of a movie, perhaps he was a producer, but I don't believe he was a director.

115

Stanislas Radziwill died in 1976 and is on the *Variety* Necrology list, but was surely not in any sense in showbusiness. He was a Pole, from a family that was titled, and he married one of the two Bouvier daughters, by name Lee, who bore him several children, but soon either left him (but not the title) or agreed that he would live his special life, and she would live hers. It is nobody's business of course, except that it is, just as her more famous sister's life is nobody's business, except that she does the sort of things that oblige photographers to pursue her for pictures that can fetch them good money, and so on and so forth. The two sisters appear to be soft, or at any rate soft-spoken, and sweet-smiling, and one accepts these facts without question until reports in the media about their activities are put forward. I have met a good variety of titled gents and ladies, and the wives of the gents, many of them Americans, and while it is something nobody need make too much of, the holding fast to titles by right of inheritance or marriage is at best a little pathetic and at worst very boring. I once knew one of the Mdvani brothers, who were supposed to be, and probably were, Georgian princes. They married rich American women, as if that were their work, and perhaps it was work. The Mdvani I knew superficially was (alas, truth compels it) a bore, and if unsuperficially he might have been something more, there was no hint of it in any part of his character that I saw. He had married a rich woman, she was not happy about him, but they were a family, and probably had kids. That is the best that can be said about the Mdvani brothers—from some of their rich wives they may have got something other than money, houses, investments, comforts, easy living: kids, half-Georgian, half-American, and having that Georgian strain in the American river of strains seems a rather interesting thing. Or doesn't it? The Georgians, just north of the Armenians, are famous for their handsome women, not men, and for their love of good living, easy living, good food and drink and lots of dancing and singing. Stalin, or Josef Djugashivili, does not seem to be all that much of a celebrating Georgian, for if he had been it is not likely that he would have muscled Trotsky out of his way and then seen to it that nobody else crowded him, even a little, even Beria, who is said to have danced for joy because Stalin had been felled by a stroke, and Beria imagined that he would take over, and didn't have the sense enough to realize that even while seemingly in a coma, Stalin was aware of his joy and lust for succession, and immediately upon sufficient recovery and restoration of animation he had the poor assassin of hundreds of thousands—himself—neatly assassinated. What a surprise that must have been. But Josef, Josef, I'm innocent, I'm your devoted friend, also from Georgia. And so on. Greta Rauch died in 1976, and is in *Variety*'s list, but I never heard of her. The derivation of the name Greta is also unknown to me, but it does seem to be a popular name in the Scandinavian countries, and possibly also in Russia and Poland. It is certainly not entirely avoided in the United States, but less these days than when Greta Garbo was the elegant lady of the silver screen. William Redfield died, and I have no idea who he is, or was, or why he is brought among the people of showbusiness. Sir Carol Reed on the other hand I did meet in London during 1944 and with whom I had a number of conversations about usages of moving pictures in both the winning of the war and the establishment of a durable peace, as the saying is. He was a shy man who listened carefully and was able to conceal the truth that he knew far more than I did—but did he? Perhaps he didn't? I said any usage we might make of films is just fine, just right, but that it would neither win the war nor assure a durable peace, it would give employment to some of us, and it would bring fame and importance to some of us, but in waging the war (although absolutely beyond avoidance by the time 1938 had come around) we had assured the Western World that any kind of real peace was at the very least unlikely, and very probably impossible. We hadn't goofed in taking up arms, but we had in not being smart enough to neutralize the madness of Hitler by means in our possession abundantly—and not by his assassination, either. There really is not much use in the kinds of things I brought up in chatting in London with a man who at that time was not yet into his full fame but was definitely established as an excellent maker of films, just as in the American ranks were such bright and experienced talents as John Ford, John Huston, and a good dozen other famous names. They all volunteered, and consequently they were bigshots, far bigger even than the generals who theoretically gave them orders and permission of various kinds. I make no bones about it that I considered all such activity as dismal, absurd, worse than useless, a perpetuation of big scale governmental folly filtering down to the helpless multitudes, and that I continue to do so. L. B. Mayer said that if I would sign a seven-year contract with him he would get on the phone and see that I would not be drafted and furthermore that by the time the war ended I would be both very rich and very important in the most important art and propaganda medium of all time. I told him no thanks, and paid the price. I hate a man who can call a President and get the big man in Washington cracking. Laurence M. Reid also died, but I don't know him. Laurence Harvey however is the name of the actor I couldn't remember, and he was a good actor, carried from his birthplace in Lithuania as a small boy to London where he did Shakespeare on the stage before moving along to the big money of movies. He was married to Margaret Leighton.

116

Don't be discouraged, folks, don't let the going get you down, dream your little dreams, live your large lives, go, come, go again, and take a book, so if there is a moment to spare you can use the time improving your mind. And of course the only way to do that is by reading books, or so we would be asked to believe, but believe me, folks, just believe me, it is not by reading books alone that we improve our minds or anything else. Exercise, that's the smart thing to do, but don't overdo it, because if you overdo it, things happen that nobody who believes in exercise had so much as suggested might happen. An acquaintance almost twenty years ago had a heart attack but it was mild and the worst that may be said of it is that it scared him, so that he began to be thoughtful and even philosophic about the whole business of life, of getting born, of getting unborn so to put it, and he took up exercise, and was soon addicted to it—calisthenics right there after the shower in the morning, a couple of hours of work, he was a writer and could make his own hours, and then he went on to tennis, and back to work, and then a little swim in the pool, and then some civilized loafing, and lots of happy moments with his three sons and infant daughter, and with their mother, but little by little—and here comes the sad part, the consequence of overdoing exercise—this acquaintance who had been scared by a mild heart attack into building his body began to be aware that his wife was getting sloppy, and so he urged her to shape up the way he had, but she just liked to be sloppy, and she began drinking martinis earlier and earlier in the day so that even before a light, almost a token, lunch with one or another of the other mothers who visited her she would have at least one martini and soon enough two, and finally three, and like as not barely touch the lunch, however token and tiny it might be, and the man looked at his wife one evening after the kids had gone upstairs to look at TV and he used a phrase on his wife that he never believed he would ever use, and he used it seriously, compelling his wife to look at him as if he had to be kidding, and she was quite bored by him and his big fat ego about his slim muscular fine body and his beautiful health and his success as a TV writer: Shape up or ship out, he said. And his wife shipped herself back to the bar and mixed another double martini and after about a week she replied, I don't want to, and his first impulse was to insist that she must see a psychiatrist because there had to be some reason why she refused to keep up with him, to be bursting with health, and to be in possession of his wits at all times, but he decided to keep quiet, and this went on until he decided he must leave her, that's all, so he did, and here's where things may be said to have gone wrong. He began to enjoy life more fully, or he thought he did, at any rate, because his sloppy unmuscular wife wasn't in his hair all the time, and he met a new woman and she moved in with him, and they had a lot of fun keeping their bodies in good shape, and not shipping out, and then at the height of his fame and in possession of big money, he was on the tennis court ready to serve to his new woman when it came again, and even with mouth to mouth resuscitation attempts by the woman, who had seen how it was done on television several times, he died. So what? So don't be discouraged, don't let the going get you down, come and go and come and go and take a book and if you have a moment or two to spare look into it. Man does not live by anything alone—bread, books, bed, beauty, brains, business, belief, or even health, even perfect health, for if anybody could be said to have been in perfect health not only of body but of mind, it was that acquaintance, and his doctor who had given him a full checkup only a week before his fatal heart attack and had told him that he had the health of a man of twenty, and at that time the man was in his late forties. As for the abandoned wife who refused to shape up, and then laughed at his military command to shape up or ship out, she is still sloppy, still loves martinis, her grown kids are devoted to her, and she inherited everything, under California law, or under his old will which he may or may not have meant to revise some day, perhaps forty years later. This is the thing, folks. The Lord giveth, and the Lord taketh away. But don't let that discourage you, either. Or the silly story of the acquaintance. Or the continuing diminishment of the meaning of doctors and their reports—they are business men, and the wisest of them seek out amateurs and ask them for guidance in maintaining their own health, so that they can enjoy their wealth. Doctors and the conduct of their profession have become mechanical and except for emergencies like a broken leg, doctors should be avoided, and their drugs kept out of reach of both children and adults. The idea, folks, is to have fun while the having is good, if that's the way the expression goes, and leave the timing of both life and death to chance, God, Jesus, or most probably to your good (and bad) ancestors. That'll get it every time. You won't kick the bucket until your name is on it, as I'm sure you've heard, so just don't get discouraged, just know that there are boys and girls on talk shows who have read a book in which scientific evidence has been assembled which clearly proves that death is not death, it is a moving on to another form of life, and so even if you happen to die just when you are about to have the pleasure of more and more fun in the sun on a California tennis court, don't be discouraged, you are very probably going straight into another dimension of the indestructible reality of your tribe. You can't lose—and I mean ever. Our ignorance doesn't permit us to lose.

I am sorry to see the name Elisabeth Rethberg on *Variety's* list of dead, for I believe she was a singer, and I happen to like song and singing almost more than any other activity that is our own, is the property of humankind, and while most singers are terrible bores away from the songs they sing, or out of their parts in operas or oratorios, once they are back singing, they are the opposite of bores. As for the non-singers who quickly become millionaires and multi-millionaires, they cannot really be considered singers at all, for they are listened to only by young people who are becoming slowly reconciled to the probability that there is a shortage of something basic in their natures, under the rules of legend and reality, they have a shortage of gray matter, and they have pride in never having strained to achieve anything, and they go in groups of tens of thousands to a great open field and stand or lie on the ground and smoke pot while the multimillionaires do the appropriate—to make the weed and its effects coincide with the ugly and dirty noises of the singers, fishy-looking men with girls names, and fishy-looking women with great intensity about the preserving of whales (from the dirty money-mad people who kill them, and would much rather sing at Woodstock or San Leandro and be paid ten times more than they are for the beautiful whales). That's another territory entirely, and I am not sure that anybody has the wit to carefully identify what has happened to song, to singing, and to listening to song, and the music it is set to, as these things relate to basic changes in the desires of youth and in their pleasures. What I like best though about the weird singers is that they invariably wear the clothes of people who have no money, and they sing about the heroics of being deprived of money by the whale-killers or their equivalent. All right, all well and good, they cry their eyes out, they hate, they complain, they smoke pot and shoot coke and mess with LSD and uppers and downers and find people who don't, square and contemptible, and they infect themselves and die of hepatitis, and they come up with the clap and with syphilis, and the girls have babies and the men have beards and here's the thing never never to forget—the kids are the human race, American branch, and they are beautiful. That's really lovely, and insofar as the millionaire non-singers with their electric guitars were connected with it, it is desirable to rather respect them, and even to admire them, and to be grateful for them, but it isn't easy. When they stop to talk, as on a television interview, one is not permitted to overlook that they are just plain stupid egomaniacs, and humble withal, very much with the little people who make them rich, not snobs about the Rolls Royces they own, and the airplanes, the Lear Jets, and the great ranches hidden away. What did it? Agents, agents, for God's sake, the same smart boys who have pimped down the ages. Package makers, deal makers, bookers, arrangers of happenings, publicity experts, and a time is bound to come when even the young shall see through the whole manufactured absurdity and stay away—to read a book, or just be alone. But if Elisabeth Rethberg is not a singer, let that be so, and let the singers sing on, the great, the good, the ordinary, the fair, the poor, the bad, and the rotten. If you yourself don't sing, reader, you really owe it to yourself to give it a try, and to limit yourself at first to only songs out of yourself, and they don't have to rhyme or make sense or be anything more than what any song is—an overflowing, which can be of gladness or sadness or neither, and is sometimes an overflowing impossible to classify. On the other hand another person who died in 1976 has a name I seem to know, Hans Richter, but after seeming to know it, I am lost: did he write, or was he a scientist, and if so, what is he doing on *Variety*'s list? Isn't there, wasn't there a Hans Richter who very patiently studied life in nature and photographed all sorts of activity never before seen in such detail and profusion by human eyes, thank heaven, as we say, for photography in all of its magnificent branches. We have certainly on film for permanent reference the mating of pretty much all creatures, including elephants, and other large and heavy animals, and I believe there was once exhibited all over the world such a movie, all kinds of procreative behavior, not excluding that of various tribes of the human family. But I can't be sure who Hans Richter was. Maybe he rode a unicycle, or did magic, or walked wire, or worked with the big cats, or did publicity for Gertrude the Boy and for Adolphus the Girl. Paul Robeson was a singer, unmistakably, and the first black man to perform *Othello* in America with a white Desdemona, Uta Hagen, I believe, and I saw one of the first performances in New York, with Jose Ferrer doing a great job as Iago. But Zarifian at the White Theatre in Fresno when I saw him in 1919 or thereabouts, when I was eleven, did Othello with the greatest and most believable vulnerability, doubt, jealousy, insecurity, astonishment, hatred, and all-around madness, which is required of the actor who presumes to do Othello. Robeson was not that great, but in his own life he was one of the greatest men of our age. My father's kid brother Mihran became one of Paul Robeson's devoted friends, after the great man had come to Fresno in concert. And I have always been proud of Mihran Saroyan for that. Dick Roman I don't know at all, but the name has something. Moxie Rosenbloom on the other hand I saw several times in his nightclub act in Hollywood, on the same program with the great Ben Blue—who might have been, should have been, the kid brother of Charlie Chaplin's little tramp.

Maxie Rosenbloom was one of hundreds, possibly thousands, of fighters who saw the ring as their best chance to escape from the slums, or worse. The one exception that is well-known was Gene Tunney, man of education, culture, and science, all of which were skillfully employed when he took the title from the folk hero Jack Dempsey. I used to go to the Biltmore Hotel steam baths in New York in the late 1930s and the idea was to both get over excess of all kinds—especially drinking—and Gene Tunney was also frequently there. The baths presented pictures that Goya and

Daumier (and many other fine makers of drawings and lithographs) would have liked, because of the strange variations on the theme of the male human body. There were old men whose bodies were really fantastic, almost deformed, and yet the bodies at the beginning had been altogether regular, or normal, but time and excess had rendered them all disproportionate and really goofy and weird. Almost everybody was well under the age of sixty, I would imagine, and yet to me the old men were really very old men, so to put it, and the reason this was so was that their naked bodies were shot, that's all, their asses had all shriveled to virtually nothing, their torsos had thickened, their backs were bent or hunched, and their legs had become spindly. But when they got into their expensive clothes they appeared to be rather distinguished-looking, most of them, and of course all of them were indeed men of importance and wealth. They are the only kind who go to steam baths and have their bodies worked over by experts at restoring to the inner man a sense of location, of being at home in a body still moving along, if nothing else much. In under an hour, including a short nap after the steam and spray and salt massage, a nap I never chose to take, I became healed of a bad hangover, and hurried along to my day's work. Tunney at the Biltmore Baths was still a man in possession of an athlete's body, but it was softening. One of his children became a senator from California, who finally lost to the Language Specialist Hayakawa who also acquired a measure of notoriety as the breaker of mischief-making gangs at San Francisco State College, and as the wearer of a fine Scotch tamoshanter. He is said to receive quite a lot of mail intended for the famous silent film actor of the same name, Sessue first name, who came into notice again as an important actor in *The Bridge Over the River Quai.* I remember the actor in silent pictures at the Liberty Theatre on Van Ness Avenue near Tulare Street, so named because it was opened in 1918 before the end of the War, and Hayakawa Sessue was one of the first villains who was also a hero, and the secretly adored of housewives and other ladies with erotic fantasies. Maxie Rosenbloom was not a first-rate heavyweight, but being any kind of fighter at all did very likely deliver him safely and once and for all from the environment that he couldn't possibly be expected not to despise. In all divisions, at all weights, other boys and young men made similar forays out into the world of excitement, lights, audiences, money, and now and then something like fame. The minorities in their ghettoes kept the fight promoters and managers well supplied with the raw material from which they derived both their meaning and their money, sometimes very big money. The blacks, the Jews, the Italians, the Irish, the Mexicans, the Filipinos, the Poles, and just plain white Anglo-Saxons from the hills and shoeless poverty. You had to have an aptitude for the calling, you had to have been a tough kid in the neighborhood, a street fighter, and after that you had to train, and train very hard, although there were great fighters who trained a whole week before a big fight on pretty women, good food, lots of booze, and nothing but fun all the time, and then went into the ring and demolished the opponent in something like two minutes. How could that be? I say it was the training, and that had the fight not ended so swiftly, the winner would soon enough be the loser—and disgraced. Consequently his own instinctive strategy was to explode and destroy the enemy and go to the showers laughing and famous and rich, and ready for more girls and high living and fun. One or two of these boys were finally shot by angry inferior idiot husbands of crazy women—but it was worth it, most likely, even with that ending. Maxie Rosenbloom was not in that class, if indeed he was in any particular class: like a number of other fighters he held his crotch suddenly and bent over and grimaced and groaned and claimed that he had been fouled, only to rest a little while the referee considered the probable truth of the matter and then ordered him back to the contest. After the ring as a way out of poverty and insignificance came comedy, and it is understandable that most of the best stand-up comics also came from the minorities and the slums but just weren't right to try the ring. You could fail as a comic, but at least you weren't likely to be killed. And of course quite a few fights ended with the death of one of the boys. But even after Maxie Rosenbloom switched from the ring to the nightclub floor he remained ordinary, although always rather pleasant to see and hear. And it is right that he should have also used the third most popular avenue of escape for the poor and belittled: acting. He appeared in a dozen or more movies, and one or two of them were not too bad, and his performing was at least appropriate to the story, and believable enough. He usually played a thick has-been who in his best days as a heavyweight had suddenly clutched at his crotch and cried foul. But then who can say he hadn't been fouled—somewhere along the losing line?

119

Another name on the list that I don't know is Danny Ross. Well, I know the name, for there it is, what I don't know is who he was, who he is, who this particular Danny Ross was, or is, for there are surely a dozen or more of them in any big city. And then the next name is Lenny Ross, and again I don't know the man. Jack Benny may or may not have had a singer with a good tenor voice named Lanny, not Lenny, Ross, but that's beside the point, entirely—as I suspect the reader has noticed so many things are, not in this study alone, but in the reader's life itself. Sing, Lanny, Jack Benny used to say, and the man would open up on "When Irish Eyes Are Smiling," for instance. Whoever it is that I am thinking of, I know he is among the living, and well among them, and that he has a family of by now I expect a dozen kids. I like that. He performed the part of a dumb innocent on the Jack Benny comedy hour, both on radio and television, and his high-pitched speaking voice was just right for a sincere, simple, good fellow who either knows nothing at all or misunderstands everything. That particular Lanny Ross, if that indeed is his name, enjoyed a lot of fame on that show, along with Rochester, as he was called, and Mel Blanc who could give sound even to inanimate things, or meaningful voice to such things as virtually defunct automobiles like Jack Benny's Maxwell, or the horse that ninnied with an English accent. And of course there was also Benny Rubin who laughed or giggled to the tune of the first two bars of the national anthem. Benny Rubin was well-known in

San Francisco when I was breaking away from the business world and into the literary world, pretty much from 1926 on, and in his youth Benny Rubin was a very funny man. I suppose there were two dozen or more good character actors brought into the Jack Benny radio or television program over the many years of its national fame. The writers made these people very effective, along with Jack Benny's meticulous directing, and his flawless sense of timing. Even Alistair Cooke visited the rehearsal set of several of the Jack Benny shows so that he could report about the great comic for readers of the *Manchester Guardian*, which finally dropped the Manchester part and possibly moved from there to London, entirely. Danny Boy, Lanny Ross, the national anthem as nervous giggle, the old horse with the English accent, they all worked together to amuse the nation, and pretty much to transform every viewer into Jack Benny himself—that is, the astonished witness, er who watched everybody, and listened to them, including the race track tout who whispered hey, buddy, and pretty nearly terrified the nation with his smarmy confidence and muscle about the winner in the next race—an actor out of an orphanage somewhere in the East, as we put it, who went on and became a very successful and wealthy producer of television shows, including I believe one of the most pioneering and daring of all: the one that put a black man with a white man, as pals doing spy work all over the world. I can't remember the name of the white man, but I can of the black, Bill Cosby. There are a great many graduates of orphanages, so to put it, who have moved along into the glaring world of showbusiness, and quite a few who have chosen that branch which gathers together in penitentiaries all over the country—for if anything is really showbusiness it is unquestionably crime—of all kinds. I believe I read somewhere that one of the bigtime writers of trash novels is from an orphanage, and so is the hey buddy actor who became a big producer. He said so on television, possibly even on *Person to Person*, that show cooked up by Ed Murrow, smoking his cigarette nervously. When he invited me to appear on that show, I said sure, how much would he pay me, and again he was astonished, as so many people in similar positions are, that I would expect to be paid. He was well paid. The network (CBS) earned enormous profits. But I was expected to welcome in the cameras and the crews and from San Francisco chat with Ed Murrow in New York, as if by telephone, free of charge. What horseshit, but how the big operators—television, newspaper, magazine—have exploited the willingness of just about anybody to be a source of enormous profit for them, at none to himself at all, on the theory that the publicity is his reward. I asked Henry R. Luce for payment and was refused, and therefore I refused to be interviewed, which in turn may or may not have resulted in my never again having a book reviewed by *Time*, and fuck *Time* and Henry R. Luce both, dead or alive. Rouvan is also on the list, but without any other name, first or last. What could he have been, or might the name be a woman's? I mean, at first glance I imagined it was a man's, how or why did that happen? Is Rouvan masculine, especially? Mike Roy also died, and I don't know him, either. And Rosalind Russell—well, she was one of the American actresses at the fashionable Paris Hotel Orill-on on Place Concorde just across the narrow street from the American Embassy during the last months of the War, and I was asked to a party there by George Stevens or somebody, and Rosalind Russell was very beautiful and warm to everybody, not excluding me, a total stranger. If not there, though, I saw her two or three times at affairs of one sort or another both in New York and in Hollywood. There were many kinds of ambitious girls who identified themselves as Rosalind Russell types—this meant something everybody instantly understood, and usually rejected, but nobody really cared about, for the reason that it is not really desirable for any new actress to be like any established or famous actress. Rosalind Russell herself had largeness and great warmth both as actress and lady.

There is a whole new school of thought about death, and it's about time, even if the reason for its emergence is the prolonged hanging on of old men and old women who at their prime were producers and tax-payers and now are nothing but community responsibilities, the victims of muggers and the problem of social workers. But there are other and better reasons for looking a little less foolishly into the whole business of death. People who have "died" for short periods of time have been returned to the vale of light or tears, and their reports have been invariably favorable, or better than favorable—serenity and joy seem to be the thing that comes over them the instant they are "dead," and in all probability would have continued to be dead had not somebody come along and worked one or another of the miracles that drive off early death and restore old life. Boy, I sure didn't think death would be like that, they say, or, Man, it's beautiful. On T-shirts there must be messages like Death Is Beautiful. Everything else had declared itself in that way. And so something in every person listens to all the propaganda and asks or half-asks silently, Yes, Death is beautiful, but is it Hollywood? Is it New York? Is it San Francisco? Give me the names of the cities of Death, so I can make comparisons and decisions for myself, and instead of hanging around until I am 99, man, I may be willing to say I've had enough by the time I'm only 96. We've got to want to know about everything, of course. We've got to *want* to, at any rate, and we've got to try to find out, but it would appear to be most probable that we must wait, although immediately we find that we can't quite accept that idea, either, for if we wait until we have been extinguished and put out like a fire, totally, and sentience of any order, and memory and thought and everything that constitutes mortality are gone, and we are dense, and divorced from light and air entirely, we will not even know that we have waited, and that there is no more. That is the death that seems to be pretty much what everybody expects, because it seems to be logical, if nothing else, and if not quite everybody does indeed expect such a death, a part of everybody does, not excluding good people who believe one or another of the programs of continuance, even everlastingly, which means either a lot of time spread far out into the future or a different conception of time in any portion. We don't know. We aren't sure. But nobody does not die in the flesh. That established by billions of instances and not one exception is that death during human life is always possible at any time, and that eventually it happens to every person in possession of life. What about Jesus? Well, I leave that to the experts, the theologians, as I believe they are called, and to you yourself, reader. If he didn't die, he isn't here, at any rate. Adrian Samish died and is listed in *Variety*. He may or may not be the man somewhat well-known in San Francisco years ago as Artie Samish, but if he is Artie Samish, I don't know him, but I did know a variety of people who did know him. He seems to have been a professional lobbyist for various interests, and he seems to have taken on new clients as he and they agreed on terms. A lobbyist is a legal seeker of desired consequences through favor or persuasion, threat or enticement, or whatever. Consequences, advantages, results, you choose your word. Artie Samish is said to have been a man of large bulk, and not without a certain kind of pleasant acceptability. And yet there was always hanging over him a hint of wrong not far from crime, not excluding crimes that attend the organizing of girls, gambling, drugs, theft, murder, blackmail, intimidation, and any other setting up of a government, essentially secret, which exists solely to bring in a steady stream of big untaxable money. A government which the elected government of the United States has not been able to overthrow, eradicate, or in any other way to neutralize. On the contrary the secret government has steadily invaded the elected government and brought it into secret partnership: all the way up to the President, who of course might not even know that he has become a partner, but does acquire income that he believes is both legal and something he is entitled to—because his lawyers say so. The lawyers are of course knowingly most of the time go-betweens, and frequently pimps between the two sides of highly organized systems. Somewhere along the line Artie Samish was indicted and prosecuted and sent to jail, but after doing his time, with good behavior, he was sent back to himself as a free man—but who's free? How can anybody consider himself to be free who must hustle state legislators and other small fry? Or anybody at all. If you must hustle, you aren't free, you are imprisoned far more deeply than you might be at San Quentin or any other state or Federal Penitentiary, such as Alcatraz in the old days, the most nicely located jail in the world, most likely. So in the end big bulky capable smiling Artie Samish died, and is now dead. But let's just not forget that the minute he was gone, somebody like him, or two or three who were like him, edged each other to take his place. So what's wrong with that? Well, the fact is you might as well ask what's wrong with anybody or anything else? Asking is both easy and meaningless. The interesting thing is that whatever it may be, whoever it may be, that thing is real, and he is alive. Some of the boys in gambling who used to tell me about Artie Samish in San Francisco lived rather full lives for a while, but they are all dead, along with the man they spoke of with so much admiration and warmth, Artie Samish, the very sound of it soft, fat, and yet somehow powerful and legendary.

The unnamed dead are the fascinating dead, and so are the dead, generally in fields of far-away combat, members of various branches of the military, by the thousands right now, in late February of 1977, presumed dead, but where or how or when not known. The survivors believe the man they knew is dead, but they would like to have a few details if possible—and the remains, for Christian burial, for family sorrow, or whatever. But the Unknown Soldier is something else again, for he might belong to the enemy, as other victims of other governments, mismanaged, manipulated, mutilated, and finally murdered are named and identified—as long as they are alive, and therefore theoretically some kind of danger. The minute anybody in a war is dead, but unidentified, he becomes automatically another Unknown Soldier. The jokes about the Unknown Civilian have never been very funny, but there are always more of him than of the other, and no great shock or sorrow attends his passing, his murder or his suicide, for there are psychiatrists who will find the language by means of which to demonstrate that anybody who dies under any circumstance at all has not only been willing to die but has elected to do so, which is suicide. Let it go, everything cannot be discussed at great length. But is is impossible to study the obituary page of any newspaper in the world and really know who it is who is listed. I have always loved the obituary page of the *New York Times*, and I mean that earnestly and with a full awareness of the possible implications of the remark: yes, I actually enjoy reading short biographies of the recent dead. Death concludes every man's story and permits it to be summed up. Everybody who dies is instantly fascinating. He did it, she did it, they did it, by God, and this is what happened on their way to the doing of it. While they were alive, if they themselves began to tell us what they had done we might not have really wanted to hear the story, although speaking only for myself I have an idea that I would—provided the story were told as if the teller knew he was scheduled to die, which the obituary writers don't need to concern themselves about, since it is a fact that the subject of the obituary is indeed dead, and certified so. The famous remark by Samuel L. Clemens about a premature consignment of his self and bones to the obituary-writer's corner is amusing, especially if you don't happen to have heard it, but what did he say when his self and his bones and everything else in which he was situated for so long was the subject of the undertaker's craft and the obituary-writer's skill, not to mention the art of surviving contemporaries who both knew him and were also writers? He said nothing, although (perhaps in anticipation of some such speculation on the part of somebody or other) he did write, or dictate, a book of autobiographical fragments upon which he made a point of placing a title that said he was speaking from the grave. And in that book it was his understanding of himself and his society that his statements on many subjects would be shocking, for their simple honesty, or deliverance from any social compunction on behalf of courtesy, charity, or even love. But when I examined the book for the first time twenty or thirty years ago I wasn't especially disappointed that it was really more of the same, for what is it possible for anybody to say from the grave that he hadn't already said from before the grave? Unless it is something weird and really boring by one or another of the brethren of deviation, so to put it, there is almost nothing. And one suspects that the good fellow was nothing more, ever, than a very decent and proper man, never mind how given he was to the utterances of swear words, if I may put it that way deliberately, the telling of jokes, some of them possibly in the category of dirty, the addiction to the smoking of cigars, which is a gentle and childish continuation of sucking on nipple or thumb, as the specialists go on and on telling us, the taking of a glass of spirits at appropriate times and in appropriate company, and a hearty look at a well-turned leg in a handsome red silk stocking under a short summery dress, the shooting of pool or billiards, and the shuffling of cards and the dealing of them in stud poker. So go back to the male and female deviants, with their overlapping borrowed ways, and at worst what may be said to be their menace, and at their best what may be said to be their marvel. Well, small boys have sometimes been murdered for the orgasmic pleasure of some dull dismal arty fraud in Texas, but the small boys had either willingly gone into his realm for various reasons, or had found life in that realm not all that unappealing after they had gotten over having been forced, or raped, into it. And now and then rather brilliant male partners have taken to the hammer upon the head in terrible jealousy, and fear of loss of prestige, or whatever, as in the celebrated case of the brilliant playwright of England, Joe Orton. Americans over there, so to put it, tend to hint at *wanting* to be murdered and eaten in some kind of sexual way, but they manage to appear in public reasonably ordinary and uneaten, and busy with their careers and profits. It is the named dead, not the unnamed, that one comes upon so abundantly on obituary pages who fascinate us: Mann L. Scharf, for instance, although we all know that to many he is very well known. And L. J. Schlaifer, next on *Variety*'s Necrology of 1976, who is he? And Taft B. Schreiber, although I seem to suspect that I know something about him. Wasn't he some kind of agent, and a big one, successful, lots of clients, lots of profits, lots of real estate, credit cards, and extra telephones on his desk. Well, we don't know, do we? He died.

122

Do we mock the dead by staying alive, by reading their names in lists, by remembering them in the world, by speculating about those we never knew? Do we perhaps take pleasure from our own survival, and even from their sad or joyous failure to do so? Bet your life we do. And don't let us hang our silly living heads in shame, making our ugly faces even uglier by a sense of guilt. What is true of us may very well be helplessly true of us, and more connected with laws we do not know too well, and with natural conditions that at least slightly exempt us from any need to be ashamed or astonished. There is probably no son who hasn't in part of his identity, part of his soul, been deeply pleased because his father has died, at last, but just bear this in mind, reader: without demolishing or spoiling or belittling any of his equally real sorrow and sense of loss. And I have known men in my own family who at the death of a mother have felt inconsolable and have never ceased to speak with profound admiration for her until they have also died. But the death of every mother, even, is also partly a welcome change in many dimensions of capture, connection, responsibility, to any son, or any daughter, again without diminishing or changing real sorrow and real awareness of real loss. That is how it is with human beings, or so it would seem for at least a couple of centuries, so it would seem since the time of advances in knowledge about the body, mind, spirit, soul, and all of these things gathered together in one entity, with a name. Fred Segal is a name I do not remember ever having seen before, so I am sure I don't know him, and so I am neither pleased nor displeased, glad nor sad, that he has died, but his kids, if he had any, would find themselves caught up in a variety of simultaneous and contradictory struggles involving emotion and intelligence about this event. It is very easy not to be a hypocrite, but it is even easier to be a hypocrite about anybody or anything. Very few people want to reveal precisely how they feel about anybody's death, and apparently almost everybody who is confronted with an unexpected death for a moment or two wants to sing out a sorrow that is probably not unreal, but is surely at least slightly unnecessary and probably hysterical: what poems were written when John F. Kennedy was killed. What telephone calls were made by people to share the terrible news. Might it be said that everybody enjoyed feeling rotten and astonished about this death? I think it might. And might it further be said than many in the midst of actual vocal crying were really indulging in a form of exquisite pleasure, so to put it? And what about when revelations began to be made about certain similar notions the President had entertained about at least one other resident of a country, or Dictator, or whatever we might choose to call him? How did we feel then about having been so saddened by our President's death? If the revelation that he had through appropriate intermediaries sought out the proper people of the American underworld, to put an end to Fidel Castro—to put a contract on him, as every American small boy and girl knows from television crime stories, to arrange to assassinate him, bump him off, take him for a ride—if that revelation happened to be true, how would we feel about the death of our President, whether it was connected in any real way with a counter-plot and program from Cuba, or not? Would that do? Might working with professional criminals to kill a leader, and thereby to overthrow a government, be acceptable as an American way to achieve peace and harmony with a neighbor? Could that procedure be considered admirable? If a man in his heart is an assassin, and he is assasinated, how are strangers likely to feel about it? Well, he got his, didn't he? Killers or potential killers have got to be either extremely vigilant at all times, or they have got to be surrounded by protection, as Idi Amin Dada of Uganda believes he is, in his Army, as Haile Selassie was for a good long time, in his Army, but the truth is that there is no protection for anybody in the human family, and indeed in any animal family—from death, that is. It is there from the first breath, it will arrive when the time comes, and the time is for human beings scarcely ever more than a hundred years, or one century, and of course we know what a paltry tick of time ten thousand years really are in the story of things, actions, meanings, and meaninglessnesses, if you will allow that word—and you'd better, brother, or I'll have you killed, you see. What I am doing is for God, you see, and you had better never, never forget that, because it is written that God is wrathful and if provoked will snuff you out. In not giving over to any order of terrible sorrow about the death of anybody at all we neither mock nor take pleasure, although we might easily be said to be near mockery and pleasure. We have no choice. Pallbearers smiling that they are holding the box containing Old Joe himself, smiling inwardly, and really not displeased that he is finally out of the way, the son of a bitch, Stalin liquidated at least ten million human beings, the theory goes, the pallbearers themselves at his funeral smiling and rejoicing inwardly, while outwardly they continue to be faithful members of the Party, the continuation of the Tyrrany, the Dictatorship, the terrible failure of a theoretically noble but actually ignoble system from which each of them is unable to escape, short of dying, such pallbearers are not any safer from the inevitable because Old Joe is gone than they ever were, and possibly even less safe, for the rivalry between them to take his bloody place.

123

I was thinking a moment ago about fathers and mothers, and did not include in that thinking my own, for never really having known my father, and very probably for never having known, or wanted to know my mother—and that may be taken in any way anybody wishes: sexually, for instance, the sense during late boyhood and early manhood I felt that unknowingly of course she wanted me as a man did indeed infuriate me, for I didn't want her that way or in any other way, so why was she stopped deliberately right in front of me when I was in a hurry and smiled at me as women do who are saying, Here it is, boy, come and get it, or possibly, Do you dare, are you man enough? And so on. But after that, after acknowledging the actuality of such episodes, I am obliged to recall that she was always faithful to herself, her own character, which was aloof, austere, intelligent, and a good variety of other things that were not in any sense evil, as I have heard so many mothers of so many writers have been: when Edmund Wilson revealed that the mother of Turgenev was really a very vicious woman, and when Ernest Hemingway himself remarked that his contempt for his mother was justified, was accurate, because she was a mean and hateful person, and seemed to both hate her son and to hate his very great achievement as a writer, I must confess I was amazed, even though by that time I was a grown man, and more than grown, I was a father, I had witnessed the arrival and early growth of a male and a female member of the human race, and noticed that while I was helplessly enchanted by each of them I was also let down by each of them, because I really could not honestly believe there was anything anywhere near remarkable enough in them to compel not admiration, but awe itself. I loved them helplessly of course, who really ever doesn't? And how easy it is to love any order of creature intimately connected with yourself? Takoohi Saroyan saw people so clearly that she could mimic them in all exteriors after one meeting, however brief, and this ability I enjoyed fully. But I must also remark that I am one of those who is addicted to full appreciation of any kind of performing by anybody, however inept it might be. I am audience, so to put it. I am the audience. Performance pleases me, the fact that somebody must perform pleases me. And noticing from my earliest years that I was such an audience my mother did perform almost daily, bringing home from plain hard work at Guggenheim's Fig Packing House, or from a cannery in Armona, or from the fresh fruit packing house of her kid brother, Aram, in Fairview, or from charitable work at the church, or from looking after a relative by marriage dying after childbirth, she told the news of her day, and became each of the new people who had appeared in that world. And there I was helpless with happy astonishment, wonder, awe, and admiration—excepting when she did not perform at all, and served supper to all four of her kids in total silence, permitting me to know that the beautiful young woman married to Takoohi's husband's brother Missak had died. But it works both ways, and something in my character both astonished and troubled her: You work hard, nobody works harder than you, she sometimes said. Why do you throw away the rewards of your hard work? This was after I had become a published writer, and into money, and gave to everybody and gambled, and got rid of every dollar and went back to work again. Dostoyevsky at Baden Baden hocked his new bride's jewels and fur coat to gamble some more, and lose, so that he would be compelled to go back to work. Was that how it was with me? I don't know, but even if it was so, there were other things that were also so: having money made me nervous, and I enjoyed throwing it around, and other things of that order. And I did indeed avoid really working until the money that had come to me was gone. If cousins and friends crowded me when I had money and I doled out portions and took them all out to enjoy the world, she might suddenly say very softly, They are not like you, do you know that? If they had money and you didn't, do you think they would treat you as you treat them? Your own unawareness, which is a kind of innocence, you place upon all others, but you are mistaken, they are not guileless, it is only yourself. And you drink and smoke until you stink. And you shout for hours and laugh like a crazy man. Well, you've earned it, you've earned it, but what is the good of gathering with a teaspoon and dispersing with a pitcher? Quite true, quiet true, and the good is that I can do it, I know I can make almost all the money I might ever care to have, and there is no end to this, or certainly none that is in sight. Jean Servais died and is listed in *Variety*, but I have no idea who he is, or was. And so it is with Sam Shain, Robert

Sherman, and Geoffrey Shurlock. But when we come to Ethel Shutta, pronounced Shuttay, and heard for years on the radio, I know she was a rather good singer, and made a couple of popular songs part of American history, possibly "Ten Cents a Dance," among others. And I believe she appeared in a number of fairly good movies of the kind that are memorable not for excellence of any kind but for the gauche (Armenians pronounce their word for it gohscht, is there a connection?) totality of the thing: a contribution to that branch of American reality that edged over into the dimension of fantasy, dream, and the ambition to make big money by giving multitudes of Americans what they really wanted. This sort of thing has that use, at the very least: and it is all over the place in television. Americans want excitement, brother, sister, the hard cock, the wet cunt, danger, violence, blood, murder, death, and orgasm. Do you believe that? Well, I can't say I do, but the boys who run that show insist on it.

Let me tell you how I live. I live like this. I get up in the morning after all the sleep I think I want. I put fresh water into a kettle and turn the electricity on that is rated from 0 to 10. I let it work at 4, so that by the time I am done with the morning routine the water will just be coming to a boil, and be ready. The ablutions are as follows: brush the teeth, shave, shower, do light exercises, get into the appropriate clothes for the day, and I mean in accordance with the weather which has been pretty cold this winter, even in California, in the rest of the country it was the worst winter in a century or more, the winter of 1977, that is. But all this is not how I live at all, and this is, this now is how I live: I live in the spirit, in thought, in exercise of the spirit, in work, in writing, in reading, in riding a bicycle every day, and in visiting the gardens to observe the growing things once a day. I bought two tract houses and had a young Japanese gardener set out trees in the front and back yards of the two houses: many varieties of trees, and half a dozen or more vines, not excluding a Concord grape vine which is really no good at all for Fresno, or for me, but I let it continue just the same, for I have not the heart nor the will to stop anything that is alive. Well, almost anything. The soil of the gardens is very rich because I have watered and I have permitted fallen leaves and grass to become mulch and to enrich the soil, which almost from the beginning began to be full of worms, and when worms thrive soil is rich—that is not a principle of some kind, but it is something I seem to know. My work is writing, but my real work is being. That's not kidding around, that's the truth. I like being and I am concerned about its continuance for me, myself, and I—once in a while I remember that phrase of boyhood in Fresno sixty years ago, and I enjoy using the phrase, as silly as it is to do so. I breathe, and I enjoy breathing. I used to smoke cigarettes very heavily, from about the age of 18 to about the age of 60, when I quit, cold, and the reason I did was that the business was no pleasure for me at all, on the contrary, it was a pain first thing in the morning and all day and half the night. It was sickening. Before I had taken four puffs, inhaling to the bottom of my feet, and to the depths of my mind and spirit and soul, I was sick of it. My spirit didn't leap like a trout in a lake, it sank like rock, but not a fine clean smooth rock, it sank like a rotten rock. That went on for many months, and then I began to feel exhausted after I had been up only an hour into a new day, and I knew it was from the poisoning of the smoke. So I gave it up, and that slowly cleaned out the lungs and the blood and the mind and heart and soul and spirit, and ever since I have enjoyed breathing. I can smell the faintest scent of new almond blossoms, and that is a very fragile scent, and worth going after. I like to eat, too, of course, but plain stuff pretty much, which I can fix or set out for myself, as when what I eat is no more than something you need only put on a table: walnuts from my own two trees, enormous seedless raisins made by my cousin Louis Saroyan of Sanger, dried peaches from my cousin Harry Bagdasarian of Selma, cousins from paternal and maternal sides, respectively, and like as not cold water from the tap. And that's living, and something I insist upon, water from the tap, everywhere I go, for if the people are having it, I ought to have it, too. But surely there is more to living than that, and there is, and don't we know it, though, but we are here and now concerned about pretty much an outline of my way of getting through one day to another and thus through the years, which might be worth comparing with your way. I ask for a clear head, and that means that I don't drink, I don't take popular drugs like pot, or any other kind, I don't take medicine, not even for pain, like aspirin, and if I find I have got something that is loosely referred to as a cold, I give the whole man more rest and recreation than ever, and I take to hot lemonade with honey, as desired, and I spend time in bed reading trash (but glorious) books. I do not read systematically, for the acquiring of information. I find that my wisdom is sharpened and deepened by haphazard reading of all kinds, and that is the kind of reading that gets me over any cold, and the kind that either banishes discontent, depression, impatience, annoyance, anger, despair, and all of the other negative states which are continuously real, and likely to be very troublesome to a man, at home or abroad, with wife or without, surrounded by people or in the midst of solitude. How do I live? Well, very simply, and very gladly, and very much in a daily fight with death, believe me, old reader, young friend, with despair, with discontent—who? Me? Yes, me, myself, and I, so old pal just remember that one of the really joyous sons of bitches in the world, and everywhere else, for that matter, one of the perpetual songsters of the human race, one of the laughers, has to fight every day not to be undone by the damned sorrow that is in things themselves, it would seem, in matter itself, and in spirit, and in procedure, and in energy, and in action, of any kind. But Christ, what would I do if I didn't have the fight to fight? I don't think I would know, or begin to know what to do with myself. Just to avoid dying every day is the joy of my very dream of myself and my truth and my meaning. Do you think anybody would have done anything at all except for that daily fight? I feel sorry for people who for some reason do not seem to know, even, that they are in any such fight. They have got to be bereft of the best that is man's alone.

What is it that we have got to do in order to live well? In order not to give ourselves an awful time when there is reason to believe that doing that is absurd, not necessary, and of no real use to ourselves one at a time or to anybody else? Are we to do charity? Are we to go around doing good? Are we to become Dr. Schweitzers? God help me, I'm sure I've spelt the name wrong, but let it stand, a name is a name, and somewhere in Africa he set up a hospital for the natives and did good works. But did he? Did he? If you can ask that question, you've got your answer, and it is that he did, but very probably he really didn't, at all. For there is no doing of good works. It is something like wanting to improve the lot of those creatures in the ecological chain which must serve as the food of other creatures. But that is part of the charm, if you will, of man. It would very probably be enough for each of us to work out his own way of going to the grave, and a good start is not to permit that travel and that destination to seem terrible at all, but rather both to seem and to be just fine. Where else might we go, and to what end might it take us that in any way could be different from the one end which is our destination, insofar as we know? To live well is not to die, and then to have prepared the coming of the next day so effectively that its arrival is not a pain but on the contrary is if not a joy, at least a kick, as the saying is. It is a kind of joke of course to be a human being in a human body. The least we can ask of the joke is that it permits us to enjoy it. Well, who else is enjoying it, or what else? Well, I don't know. I could say well it seems to be God, but we've said all that sort of thing, and it continues to be at the very least more than slightly inaccurate. But each of us ought to find out how to get a kick out of his own comic improbability. In order to live well, though, each of us has got to have a few basic things, and as matters stand we don't have them. I do, most likely, and so do you, most likely, but most people don't, and that's where the doing of charity comes in. Well, there is something to be said for it, but I won't say it, let the people who raise millions of dollars every year begging money for charity say it, they have the facts and figures. And since it has been going on for at least two centuries can we say a change is noticeable in the life of man on earth, in the world, under the sun? Maybe we can, at that, but I don't see how. The name of the game is life and death, I suppose we may say. Human beings are in the game by being born, out of it by being suddenly dead, for death while a long time coming always turns out to be sudden, as if had somebody done a little something or other right then and there it might have been avoided a little longer, and it turns out that this is not entirely untrue, although the practitioners of this part of the game, the brethren of the medical profession, do really absurd things, just in the nick of time, and then fight desperately even in the courts not to be prohibited from continuing the absurd play in a game long lost by that particular player. I am referring of course to the business of keeping somebody in a coma for a long long time, because the doctors insist that the body is not yet dead—but only because the brethren are preventing it from reaching its end, and they are doing this by all manner of absurd preventive measures that are meaningless. I used to like doctors. I used to know doctors who deserved to be liked. These days I find them inferior men who have acquired routine skills which they use very nearly meaninglessly and thereby in a year or two become rich. But as matters stand nobody may be expected to get through the game without now and then being attended by them, and since that is so one can only hope that the son of a bitch won't do so much good so brilliantly and with so much expert assistance that one does not find his way out of the game to the end, he is driven out, he is murdered. What? Murdered? By the American Medical profession? Heresy, blasphemy, animosity, childish fear and hatred of the one profession that does good all the time for everybody, rich and poor alike. True, true, true, so to put it, but the fact remains that there are probably ten times more people carried to death in hospitals than die more or less decently at home where they belong and where they have meaning, and their own private smells. Ah, but this won't do at all, you are thinking, and again you are not mistaken at all. That's the kind of situation living and dying has become. The two are inseparable, we have got to be agreed on that, at least, but the simple fact remains that there is no doing of good for any of us that is not from ourselves straight through the whole game, and when we seek that good, we make the playing of the game (good God, what an unfortunate turn of language) more and more inept, and we make the end of it more and more dismal and really deeply wrong for us. Good God, give birth at home, right where the act of procreation usually takes place, and die at home—or go to a hotel or a motel and enjoy room service, and I mean food, drink, flowers, books, call girls, if even only for conversation, and either die there, or make it to morning, and then to another morning, and another, and accepting your own good for your own truth, check out and go back to the game, if that's how it turns out to be. The fucking doctors and nurses with their charts and statistics are bound to get things wrong every inch of the way to the supreme error which is the end of life in yourself, which is also written down in their stupid inaccurate and meaningless records: he died of himself, but it was really of us that the poor bastard died. He believed in us.

126

About twenty years ago, shortly before I left my house on sticks in the sand at Malibu, and moved to Paris, my cousin Sipon Rostom Bagdasarian, called fondly Bagdad by Julie Haydon and George Jean Nathan in 1939, began to tell me to take it easy because I was beginning to have a reputation as somebody nobody in Hollywood could talk to, and this prevented studios ready to do business with me from even trying to reach me. I told him that he was very kind to let me know about something like that, but I had known it long ago, and there was really neither any reason for me to take it easy, or to adjust to the peculiarities of people in business, nor any reason for me to feel that this situation could ever possibly be detrimental to me, in any way, since my work is writing and not peddling in any of its forms. "Ah, shit, man," he said, "but don't you see that there isn't a writer in America with ten cents worth of talent who hasn't become rich, while you go right on just making a living and paying stupid child support?" My reply was that that was all right, too, and in any case I was fully aware of the success of my contemporaries, some of whom I knew, and not one of whom I found especially guilty of anything other than a natural wish to get along and get rich. From the beginning my passion was to get right and that meant that getting along was not all that easy, or even possible, and consequently I gradually concluded that I needn't bother about getting along at all. With whom? To begin with, somebody else knocking his brains out to get along, and to get rich, but actually only sending himself farther and farther away from himself and from any expectation of arrival, or of anything like a reasonable meaning. How much money does a man need, after he pays for his mistakes, pays the child support to the mother who had the children for her own support, and after he settles his account with his impulses entangled in gambling? Not very much money, actually, and if the worst comes to the worst kids become adults in not very many years, and so it came to pass. My cousin became a millionaire and was on his way to becoming a multimillionaire when he got up one morning and told his wife he wasn't feeling well, went downstairs in the mansion he had bought in Beverly Hills and an hour later was found in an overstuffed chair, dead. Apparently of a heart attack, something unknown among the members of his father's family, and for that matter even more unknown among the members of his mother's family, our connection as cousins, my mother being his mother's big sister. I couldn't believe he had died, for nobody enjoyed the rewards of success more than he did, and he bought one Rolls Royce and then another, and had shoes made of alligator leather when nobody else could either afford them or wanted them, and he bought a vast vineyard and went into partnership in the outright ownership of a very big winery, and raced around night and day, as his brother Harry kept telling him not to do. Ross, he would say, you don't have to run this way forever, you've won the race, relax, but Ross would say, Harry, I can't, the way it is if I don't keep running things could all collapse. But it wasn't my cousin alone who told me I wasn't getting along with the world, it was pretty much anybody I had ever had very much to do with. My own close family, that is to say, my mother's mother Lucy Garoghlanian, said of me before I was much more than fourteen, even, Our Willie is in one place, the world is in another. I knew it, though, before she said it, and I also was entirely willing to believe that this was folly, and even downright stupid and even destructive. All the same, nothing changed. I do indeed mistrust the world, the human race as it puts itself into affairs, all systems, religious, social, economic, and pretty much everything alienated from, or forgetful of, the universe, the solar and time systems, the earth, the unknown, and nature. So what? So let anybody who remembers that I suddenly surprised them by apparently unexpected and unaccountable shutting off of myself from them that I found it altogether necessary to do so. I am working on my own absurdity and vulnerability and fraudulence, I can't work on anybody else's, and so I sooner or later have got to stop—and that doesn't exclude relatives like a son and a daughter. It says here that Alistair Sim died and although I never met him, I know and remember him from his patient presence in movies, always courteous and thoughtful. As for H. Allen Smith, who is also on the list, I knew him and one time in Hollywood he bored the bejesus out of me by his stupid telephone calls saying he must see me right away and could we meet and then telephoning that he had got lost but he would be right over to the Knickerbocker Hotel in Hollywood and then an hour later phoned again and said could I take a taxi to the Edgerly Arms on La Cienega because somehow he was there with a writer who had a room there, and I said no, bring the friend, but another hour later he telephoned and said where was I, again? His passing along of information on the telephone through every call had been indecisive and really absurd—I had never met the man, I had read some of his short pieces, which had a touch of amusement in them but nothing great, at all. When I finally did meet him, in New York, at the office of his agent, Mr. Harold Matson himself, the three of us had a drink or two right there, bullshitting as boys do in offices, writers or hustlers of writers, and then we went on to a bar, and the boredom was so profound in my soul that I finally went away without comment or explanation. He had a watchful nature, as if he was figuring out somebody's real character, so to put it, and he said things that permitted him to somewhat chuckle, and his writing made a lot of money, both for himself and his agent.

127

Perhaps you are saying, or feeling, Yes, but the man died, you son of a bitch, he died, you could at least either shut up about him or remember something good about him. O.K., something good, then. One day when I ran into him and was obliged to be with him for five minutes, not once during that time was he cute—but of course in his own unique, underplayed way. Now, being cute is a very patriotic American custom: we have very few people who are not so enchanted with themselves as to find it unnecessary and undesirable to be cute: Franklin Delano Roosevelt was one of the cutest public characters ever to appear on the scene, and take if from there into all of the big events of his time, a cute kid virtually running the world, it doesn't stagger the mind or imagination, but it does something to the soul in the whole human race. Would it have been better had he been like Hitler? Like the ally Stalin whom he met several times, and who took him for a real rollercoaster ride every time. Ah, well, don't forget that this book is also history, and the cuteness of big and famous and powerful Americans has never got to be looked upon as anything short of dire and disastrous. Overlook the boobs in public entertainment, perhaps it is understandable that they must be cute—except that if you will remember the greatest of the entertainers you will notice that they are never cute. Bert Lahr, for instance. He lived his whole life and conducted his whole art with doubts about both himself and his art—he was never cute, and he was always funny, and great, because he sensed the nearness to himself and everybody else of tragic failure. Robert Solomon is next on the list, and all I can say about him is that I have always cherished his family name. Next comes Harold S. Stern, and I don't know him. Furthermore, I don't know Ira S. Stevens, or Donald Stralem, although I find the name Stralem extraordinarily charged with some kind of special reality, just by itself. Don't forget to Stralem, so to put it, and the tribe took it as their name? They were the people who straled. And of course to strale, for all we know, was to make them feel right. Hudson Strode is a writer, but that's all I know about him, and while the name Strode is also a word of the English language, a variation of stride, it is probably actually an adjustment into English of another name in another language, possibly German. I have looked into a book or two by Hudson Strode, and one of them I believe was some kind of anthology that concerned itself with life in New England, but I can't be sure. I really don't know the writing of the man, and I certainly never met him. There are writers and writers, and this may or may not surprise the reader, I would rather pick up a book by any writer at all, however rotten or crooked or inept or dirty or pompous or phony, than a printed report to stockholders about a year of money-making by some stupid outfit, not excluding a publishing house, for that business is not only not different especially from any other, it is dirtier than most, especially in its sneak plays upon writers who tend to be childlike. Imagine a writer like William Faulkner needing to feel grateful to Random House for sending him a $250 advance against a new book. Good God Almighty, Bennett Cerf was a multimillionaire at the time, but forget it, forget it. Frank Sullivan died and he was at least a comic writer, a contemporary of Robert Benchley, a bachelor who lived up around Saratoga, the Spa and Racetrack being nearby, I suppose, and he was the man who wrote the annual doggerel greetings to people in the news, for the *New Yorker*. This piece of verse was atrocious if clever, and it doesn't matter that at least once, and possibly twice, my name appeared in it, rhyming, I suspect, if it was put where a rhyme had to happen, with the word annoying, with the g soft, something I first became aware of in the lyrics to a song that Yip

Harburg passed along to me—quite clever. One evening after the War when I was fighting off the destructive effects of three years of being a convict in the American Army, Frank Sullivan caught up with me by telephone, calling from his home, Saratoga to San Francisco, and he was spirited as a consequence of having had a glass or two of spirits. I tried, cold sober, to join him in his jubilation, but failed dismally, I'm afraid. It was around Christmas, the time he saw his jingle in prominent print in the famous weekly magazine, and while I suffered his jolliness and tried to understand the reason for his call, I couldn't figure it out, at all. Furthermore, the number was unlisted and virtually unknown, and I wanted to find out how he had come into possession of it, but of course I didn't ask. At last it was agreeable for him to conclude his telephone visit, and I am still unable to figure out why the call was made. I mean, he might have helped a little by simply saying, There's no reason for this call, I'm drunk, and I'm making long distance phone calls, that's all. Maggie Teyte is next on the list, and I have always liked the name, and I believe I have seen photographs of her in magazines, but maybe not too, and I have never met her, either. Was she an actress? Or a newspaperwoman, or a writer? As for Sybil Thorndike, like all English actors and actresses, she had learned her craft well, and it was not at all difficult to notice her doing her work expertly, both in films and on the stage. She became a personality with the passing of time, but she never stopped performing parts in plays and movies, not herself—and never cute. Somebody cooked up the false but now real word, cutesy, and it is used by Madison Avenue to put down something actually rotten but probably less rotten than Madison Avenue itself, but that's our story, isn't it, old buddy, out there in Reader Land. (Talk about cute?)

After having acknowledged that the telephone is a marvel, I find it necessary to acknowledge also that I hate it. And I know why. It is an invitation—having a telephone and a number—to intrusion, at any time and by anybody, including good people who have had the bell of your telephone ring in the belief that they were having the bell of somebody else ring. The wrong number souls, and if you use the telephone a greal you yourself are not unlikely to get a wrong number, too. On the other hand, I do not hate the television. I can turn it on or not. It cannot turn itself on. Announcements of any kind are related, so that when the telephone bell rings it is itself an announcement, the larger and more proper announcement of which the ringing of the bell may be considered a kind of prelude or preparation. There is no such situation with television. And the ringing of the bell is unnecessarily dramatic, or loud, or jarring, or insistent, and therefore startling, frightening (as in the middle of the night), and annoying, even if the caller is somebody close, somebody in the family, for instance. Death does not follow a telephoned announcement, but the fact remains that there is something of that sort in the announcement of the announcement, the sharp brisk ring, sometimes in a patter of two fairly prolonged statements, sometimes three slightly shorter statements, and now and then only one very long statement with a slight pause and a repetition of the same statement. How the telephone company arranges for these automatic patterns of ringing is something I can only guess, but however it may actually be, it is simultaneously right in that it is substantially unavoidable and intolerable, because the ring is noise, which if repeated enough, will do several things to those who must respond to the noise: drive the trauma of the ear and nervous system into a state of anesthesia, so that the ear will go on hearing but as if it isn't hearing; or put the entire person on edge waiting for the next ring, so that being on edge will become chronic; and finally the exposed soul will be made sick, or even suddenly killed, as if by a sharp blade swiftly upon a vulnerable and vital part of the connection between the person and the world, and life, and the continuance of living things, especially of that specific form of it. The telephone is killing everybody, in short, even though there are good people who use the telephone as a life-saving device, which of course it is, up to a point. The telephone screams urgency, and urgency accelerates wear and tear and accident, and finally death. Most of the people on *Variety*'s Death List were expert users of the telephone, but I love the souls who had somebody fix their phones so that the telephone company would have no way of knowing about their calls, and permitting them to call anybody anywhere in the world free of charge. A blue box is in some instances involved as I understand it and quite a few showbiz folk, so to put it, have paid some electronic specialist, probably not long ago fired by the phone company, a fair sum of money to have the box installed, and so on and so forth. A maker of free long distance telephone calls may be on *Variety*'s List, but the secret has gone to the grave, although I hope some such hero leaves a document, along with a will, so that his dear ones may know that during let's say the last year of his life he made expensive phone calls that would have ordinarily cost him half a million dollars, for which he did not pay one red cent. A monument would surely go up for that brave soul, I expect. The showbiz characters caught in the act, as it were, by the telephone company, have been advertised as sharpshooters in the newspaper and weekly news magazine stories about that event, but I have never seen a follow-through of such a story: I suppose the blue box is seized, the lawyers of the various parties meet, and an out of court settlement is made. But let's just remember that these boys are actually not seeking to outwit the telephone company, they only believe they are being truly showbiz in character, and they are actually seeking to outwit only the Big Number, so to put it, and that's Death, or as in our time we might find it desirable to put it, Brother Death, or Father Death, or Mother Death, depending upon where we stand in the doling out of identity to various things. Is it Father Russia, for instance, or is it Mother America, or is it Uncle the United States? The answer is that it is all of these, and others. But Father, Mother, Brother, Aunt, Uncle, Cousin, Wife, Husband, Son, Daughter, whatever it is, it is by telephone a variation on Life, and therefore also a variation on Death, and because the connection follows a loud and nerve-wracking noise in the form of an electronic ringing of a bell, it might be sensible to consider the variation to be on Death, and to suspect that there is a rather passionate if unknown and unsuspected love of Death in most people who use the telephone. Next, it is easy to predict: a tie-in between the telephone company and the television companies, so that anybody can dial the television set of anybody else, and it will go straight to a channel, and at the same time the caller will be able to speak over the program, and furthermore that all TV sets like all telephones will be listed in a book, and all usages of them recorded, and be subject to reference by automated electronic machinery, cancelling out any need for polls, for instance, or guess-work about the living of the population in television and on the telephone, and thereby of course also many other chronicles of a statistical order, not excluding the moment of anybody's expiration.

James Tierney is the next name on *Variety*'s alphabetical list of the showbusiness people who died in 1976. I am nothing like sure of this, but if he was not an actor, I have an idea he was a writer, for I seem to remember having seen reviews of his books. At the same time, and without any further delay, I must remark that had I died in 1976 my name would have appeared on the list immediately after the name Adrian Samish and immediately before the name Mann L. Scharf, so that four names either side of my name would render the list like this: Rouvan, Mike Roy, Rosalind Russell, Adrian Samish, William Saroyan, Mann L. Scharf, L. J. Schlaifer, Taft

B. Schrieber, and Fred Segal. So of course I am glad I didn't die. There are other annual alphabetical lists for other pieces of action, achievements, failures, distinctions, and the various forms of the opposite of achievements and distinctions. The F.B.I. has my name on at least one alphabetical list, but, boy, what horse's asses those people are, for if ever this country had a pal, a real friend, it is me, and let's nobody ever forget it, shall we? And I have never had any use at all for any kind of foreign government or system, and was especially amused when all of the supposedly or theoretically good and important writers of America got themselves into a lather believing that by God at last the world was going to be decent to everybody and that the whole human race was going to be given a chance to breathe freely at last and enjoy the fruits of wealth—by means of Marxist, Leninist, Stalinist, Russianist, Bullshitist Social Revolution. Gad, what jolly and mean bastards all those superior punks, male and female were. What poisons they released inside themselves and through the pores of their bodies upon such fools as all who did not join them—and I did not, could not, would not, both because they were full of shit and because they were all sentimental slobs, and all-around assholes. But for a while, during my earliest years as a published writer, I actually believed that something, by God something, could and would make for a more equitable balance among all of the peoples of the world, or in any country, or on any continent. I believed that because I wanted that balance to happen, but after I visited Russia during the first half of 1935 and saw the truth, and the light, and came back to America, I knew I had better put my thinking and longing and believing on another track moving in another direction and likely to reach either something like the same happy destination, or likely to reach the kind of awareness that would make the imbalance at least a little less painful and wrong than it has always been. What would that awareness be? Alas, if any answer at all is possible, it would have to be that every person possessing life, body, place, privilege, disadvantage, or whatever it might be, would have to decide for himself, and that his decision would necessarily have to come about as a consequence of his own truth, the same as it was with myself, and yourself, and everybody else, regardless of who, where, when, how, why, and all the rest of it. In short, being alive is a personal matter, no matter how groupings make it convenient for theorists to work out their ideas. Getting born is private, surviving is simultaneously intensely personal and essentially impersonal in that it is what everybody else is also helplessly doing or trying to do, and finally getting out of the whole thing, whether gladly, willingly, unwillingly, painfully, gracefully, with meaning or without meaning, is the supreme form of private event. To die is a denuding of the clothed body from a lifetime of the meaning of being clothed: concealed, hidden, secret, private, personal, nobody's business, ornamented, given dignity, given identity, given honor (of sorts, at any rate), and given most of all protection, lots and lots of protection, which with a swift gesture is drawn away at death, revealing as birth did, a pathetic red body attached to and accompanied by a lot of throwaway stuff which up to that moment had been vital to the survival of the person: the umbilical cord attached to the universe of magic called the after-birth, which some primitive peoples dined upon, and others used as magic fertilizer for trees, but most people either bury or flush down the sewer. However systematized the management of great numbers of people may be, being born, surviving, and dying, are private, personal, and experienced always only by one person who has no way of not keeping it secret, first because most of it is unknown to himself, and second because he doesn't know how to pass along, even to his kids, for instance, how it was—unless of course he is a writer, but even at that what he puts forward as the story of his life, and his experience, is pretty much a shambles of inaccuracy, disproportion, self-defense pose, and most nearly excusable art, for that is the deepest longing of the soul—for life to have the elements of design that make for beauty, whether in architecture, engineering, poetry, music, drama, story, painting, sculpture, dance, and yes, acting—which is pretty much the specialty of people in showbusiness. But I have long been in the national archives by way of the F.B.I., at any rate, and I tell them all, as I always have, Folks, friends, mothers, fuckups, have fun, that's all, just have lots and lots of fun, it's quite clear you haven't got any brains at all. I am on a lot of lists, most likely, but not on *Variety*'s Necrology of 1976, and that is a simple joy, because I have in mind finding out a few more things that cannot be found out until the finder is eighty, for instance, or ninety, and I want to witness more and more of the change that is straight ahead.

Dan Totheroh died, and he was a playwright, or so I seem to believe, also believing, as I believe that, that Dan Totheroh was a California-born playwright, and that he may very well have lived in the great San Joaquin Valley, the most fertile and productive piece of land in the world, or so the local hustlers in agribusiness seem to say. But I can't remember the name of any play he wrote, as for instance I can remember *They Knew What They Wanted*, a glorious title when I first saw it, and a grand play when I first read it, away back more than fifty years ago, but this play is by Sidney Howard, a name I have been struggling to summon up from the depths of memory. The play is about an Italian vineyardist around Stockton, north of Fresno 150 miles or so, who sends away for a mail order bride who cuckolds him—but does she get pregnant, and does he decide he wants her just the same, along with the little bastard when it is born? These themes go on and on, in every country, every community, in the world. As a name it is not easy to improve on Dan Totheroh, but I can't guess to what people the family name belongs. Would that be German? Well, I am not unaware that the reader might be asking, Why doesn't he look up anything? Well, the point of this book is another thing, and if it is to be achieved at all, it has got to be achieved out of what I am able to make of the names on the list, of the living people on the list, who died last year, as I remember them, or know that I never met them, or know something about them, as I seem to believe I know that Dan Totheroh was a playwright but can't name one title of a play he wrote. The people in the Ozark hills, called hillbillies, are said to be pure Anglo-Saxon English, whose very speech is what English speech was a century and a half or so ago, and yet when it was revealed about thirty years ago that these people did not know the identity of William Shakespeare, I was really not astonished. There are a lot of people right now everywhere in the world, there have been a great many more over the centuries, it is not necessary for people living far from the Globe and Stratford on Avon and London to know the identity of William Shakespeare, and if he can be unknown even to the very people of whom he was one, so to put it, imagine how it has got to be with Dan Totheroh, and everybody else. I have no doubt, either, that there are hundreds of thousands of people in the United States who don't know who Hitler, Stalin, Mussolini, Churchill, Roosevelt, De Gaulle are, and many other people who pushed around so many people for so long. They are born since those days and know other people, singers with electric guitars for the most part. Dalton Trumbo died, and in 1936 after I had been fired by poor bumbling B. P. Schulberg, or at any rate by his Assistant and All Around Manager, a man with a sickly soul whose name was George Auerbach, who had a habit of pointing an index finger at his right temple in a gesture of shooting himself but finally died of sickness in New York, fired by the Stooge on behalf of his Boss for refusing to work on a very stupid scenario written by the Hungarian protege of the Hungarian director Charles Vidor, with whom I had worked on an absurdity called *A Doctor's Diary*, James Geller, working out of the William Morris Agency, almost immediately got me a job at the same wages, $300 a week, at Harry Cohn's Columbia Pictures, working with a producer who was supposed to be literate, Edward Chodorov, who had also just hired Dalton Trumbo. He brought us into his office by appointment and told us the only property he had for us to work on consisted of three stories by Clarence Buddington Kelland which had been published in *The Saturday Evening Post*, which he hoped we could work into one good scenario for a light, easy comedy, and so Dalton Trumbo and I agreed that since neither of us knew how to be a member of a team we would flip a coin to see who would write the scenario, while the other only saw to it that he did not inadvertently disclose that he was loafing all the while, and fortunately I won, and Dalton

Trumbo agreed to do the job. This was fortunate, for I hated the stupid stories, the characters, the American success absurdity running through them, the irrelevance of them, while Dalton Trumbo on the other hand, although just starting out seemed to have a flair for such work and would soon begin to be one of the truly eminent writers of screenplays. Our only discussion of the possible management of the material in the stories was in Edward Chodorov's office, and if the truth is told at that time I had not quite been able to really read the stories, although I had somewhat run through them. I had got the silly idea before I had gone through the first of the three stories. Dalton Trumbo had been born in Colorado, near Denver, he said, and a friend of the family had been William Dempsey, called Jack, who became the first American prizefighter to draw a million-dollar gate, as it was put in those days, promoted by a hustler named Kearns, as far as I can summon up his name at all. That job at Columbia lasted precisely six weeks, the same as the job at Schulberg's unit attached to Paramount Pictures, and housed in the old Pathé Lot across Melrose Avenue, but this time instead of being fired I quit. I had had it, and I wanted to go back to San Francisco. The next time I saw Dalton Trumbo was a year or two before he died, and he was coming out of the Central Park West door of the Plaza Hotel, accompanied by a rather elderly lady, who was his wife, and he said, Bill Saroyan, and I said, Dalton Trumbo, and that was it. He had gone to jail because Bartley Crum's defense of the Hollywood Ten had been technically inept. His only novel, called *Johnny Got His Gun* I found unreadable, and the movie he made of it painfully boring.

Cecil Underwood also died in 1976, but he is unknown to me, although Underwood & Underwood seem to ave been very much involved in the taking of photographs of all kinds which appeared in school books as well as in all kinds of publications, not excluding the magazines and newspapers which enjoyed the greatest circulations—long, long before Henry R. Luce and his *Life Magazine* gave employment and importance to news and all other forms of photography, and thereby helped to impel every possible kind of improvement of cameras, and extensions of the kinds of photography they could do: from microscopic to telescopic, down into the tiniest living action, up and out to the largest action. And of course the first typewriter I bought was an upright Underwood, a standard machine as a matter of fact, because it seemed to be the sturdiest one manufactured, and could hold up under a great deal of usage. Newspaper editorial offices had them, and reporters with hats on their heads and cigarettes dangling from their lips rattled the keys with two fingers only, and got out their stories or editorials or features or essays or columns, everybody aware of the exemplary work of such frauds as Hearst's Arthur Brisbane, O. O. McIntyre, and Grantland Rice. Man, you could both earn a living and not be prohibited from writing literature, but let me remark that I have always found writers associated with newspapers, and news weeklies, especially *Time*, to be laughable, and this is why: they are excitable, and they ask questions in such a way as to control their stories, which in turn compels a change in behavior. If it were not for newspaper, magazine, and television reporters more than half the absurd behavior of mobs, not excluding unions, would settle down into almost nothing, and a lot of the solo criminal behavior of childish eccentrics and psychotics would never take place. Everybody who is sick wants to be the showbiz star of his sick behavior, and this doesn't exclude writers, but I am not going to seem to be suggesting that any of this ought to be changed, prevented, prohibited, stopped: everything that happens has to happen and is part of the very special order of ecology that is human. Let it be, there is meaning to it, and there will follow consequence: it is scheduled to include the dropping of hydrogen bombs with a thousand times the destructive power of Harry Truman's Missouri Mighties dropped upon innocent people in Hiroshima and Nagasaki. Even so, even so, so be it, and let the human ecology pick up the pieces and worry its way back to another start, which is also scheduled to happen, no matter what kind of chain reacting is triggered by the dropping of one such bomb, and no matter how many human beings are destroyed. There will be another start, and from surviving humans, not from animals. William L. Vallee died a total stranger to me, and so did Victor Varconi, although I seem to have heard that name. Bruno Vesota, however, is a name I am hearing apparently for the first time, when it is too late, at least for me. Ethel Keith Vigoroux is beyond my ken entirely, although both her maiden name Keith and her married name Vigoroux are quite pleasing to eye and ear. Luchino Visconti is a movie director of Rome about whom I have heard, but as far as I know I have not seen any of his rather highly-praised movies, including *Death in Venice*, if he did indeed direct that story into a film, a story by the glum and to many people mighty Thomas Mann—not to me, though: his Teutonic build-up of his case may be grand to some people, but I won't have it, everything in my nature resists it, and is indeed opposed to it, although the long short story we are talking about is reasonably acceptable, but not as effective as a similar story by Ivan Bunin, a contemporary, entitled "The Man From San Francisco." A Russian writer is a Russian, a German writer is a German, and it is not any kind of racism that implies a meaning in this, it appears to be quite simply a fact. Russians are arsonists, Germans are builders, and for me fire is more meaningful than piled playing blocks. Slavko Vorkapich worked all kinds of wonders of trickery or even reality in special effects for movies: explosions, earthquakes, tornadoes, tidal waves, collapsing skyscrapers, and possibly an animal belonging to an organ-grinder, enlarged a thousand times and seduced by the white beauty of Fay Wray near the Empire State Building, madly in love with her and terrified of the objection of Hollywood and the whole human race. The writers for the Sonny & Cher TV show hit upon one of the funniest schemes for a good dozen or more chapters involving Cher lying upon the hairy palm of King Kong and chatting with him about his hangups as if he were possibly not only Jewish but a second cousin of Philip Roth's mama-captured Portnoy. Murvyn Vye has a great name, but I never met the man and I know nothing about him, and so it is with the woman Miriam C. Walsh. As for Ned Washington, now also among the dead, I seem to believe he was in popular music, either with a band, or as a singer, but I can't be sure. Linda Watkins I don't know, nor do I know Sanford W. Weiner, or Niles Welch. What it comes to most likely is very simple: you can't win 'em all, you can't know 'em all, but from winning a few, and from knowing a few, you can at least suspect that you have won them all, and that you have known them all, at least insofar as winning means anything, and knowing isn't entirely an illusion and a desperate misconception. I am thinking of August Strindberg's play *The Dance of Death*, and how the old, old couple both hated and loved one another, but after half a century or more were total strangers. What a deadly, dismal, delightful and deranged picture of human life. Over the years of marriage the boy and the girl had become the original male and female of the human race, or at any rate August Strindberg's experience of it—tricky, terrible, and terrific.

It comes as something like a surprise, after all these years, that I am sometimes annoyed by an unkind word about my writing (which means myself), when I ought to be very indifferent to both kind and unkind words. Something sometimes—right there I would have to be critical, so why shouldn't somebody else, making it something sometimes somebody, not right in English, but I let it go, if you can follow, dear reader, and of course it is also this dear reader business that can annoy some reviewers of books, or even some critics who seem to have brains and know how to write. Last night, the last night of February, I read a snide belittling reference to my writing and of course my name was spelled out in full and very neatly, William Saroyan. Something about the most atrocious or spurious rapture of William Saroyan. Think of it. Somebody having the gall to say such a thing about my writing, about me. Dear lady, reader, dear gentleman, leader, that's not right, it isn't right for living folks to put down other living folks, and least of all is it right for any kind of folks whatsoever to put down this writer or his writing. And I'll tell you why, too: it hurts, that's why. It is no fun to start getting hints that your writing isn't the greatest, the most real, the most useful, the most helpful, the most entertaining, the most life-giving, the most death-defying, the most death-delaying writing of this or any other time. But Christ, the competition, have you ever thought of the awful competition, reader, as you sit or lie somewhere eating bonbons and turning the pages of this book, or of any book. The competition is fierce, it is ferocious, and everybody has his own favorite, or favorites, and that means a lot of other writers have got to be left out, or scorned, or belittled. It was the competition that I thought of last night when I read the slur on my name and my writing. Well, there is no other writing anywhere in this living world that is better than mine, and I mean on almost any level, not excluding care about the sound of English being accidentally wrong in an arrangement of words, such as something sometimes somebody—and right there, let me tell you, a lesser writer could leap upon just those three words and work steadily for seven years, being encouraged on the way by his agent, a bright lady or a clever man, and then have a clever publisher (part of an oil company, however, for extra millions of dollars for just about everybody) bring it out like the greatest novel ever, and he means ever. Something Sometimes Somebody—wow. And they have the audacity to be snide and sneering about my beautiful writing, using such slanderous terms as the bullshit rapture of himself. That hurts, folks, I expect better than that from the human race. Any rapture I have ever known, any I have ever put in writing, has been straight, not bullshit. People try to understand why writers commit suicide by jumping off boats or by alcoholism or by being heroic continuously or by rope or gun or drug or knife or water, and I can tell you, and not in the strictest confidence, I can tell you straight out, right outside, right out in company, right out where everybody can hear, it is reading slurring remarks about their writing that drives writers to the grave. Dirty remarks passed by dirty dirty but damned nicely educated and very highly-paid ladies and gentlemen have the effect of killing writers. Yes, that's right. Dirty words on toilet walls or in slick paper magazines read by smart people do kill writers, they do murder writers, they do assassinate writers—and boy let me tell you I am all for it, even when by some miscalculating or misunderstanding the dirty words are directed to me rather than to the party really deserving them. Accidents happen, dear clever reviewer or critic, and let it not be said that William Saroyan is one not to see a situation from the point of view of the other party, yourself, lady, not myself, and the same to you, sir, and I shall be the first to defend your right to be critical and even sarcastic, knowing full well that it is not about me and my writing, although my name is by mistake taken in vain by you. One has heard of the enormity of charity by the original friend of us all: forgive them, they forgot. But go on, go on, do your good clever writing, every one of you, I am home, and you are home, and we are each of us not yet on *Variety*'s Necrology list, so if we can't take it, who can? The dead grow sometimes, but most of the time they don't, and it is a lucky thing for most dead writers that they probably can't be watching their terrible dying after they have died, their steady diminishment from something huge in the living world to something so easily forgotten and thrust aside that it is almost unbelievable. The dying of the man, the breaking-down of the machine that produces the art, especially the art of letters, of writing, is the lesser of the two dyings that are in store for everybody who goes out to compete in the forum, in the agora, in the pantheon, to accept rivals and to run with them in the short races and in the long long races. That dying, man and machine together, for we know that no sustained effort permits anybody not to become also a machine, to go past the graceful limits of humankind, is not the dying that tells the full story, ends it, starts it, brings it back, throws it out, weighs it, measures it, sells it, gives it away, grades it, trades it, revises it, and publishes it in new editions, new translations, with new illustrations, drawings and paintings by the greatest artists, new introductions by the best appreciators of such stuff. There is the dying-dying, the death-death, and it is that thing which tells it all: Rapture, yes. Spurious, yes. Great nevertheless, bet your ass.

This is a book about life, not death, but let's not use language in any such convenient and beautiful and mistaken and misleading way, it is a book about everything and anything and nothing, folks, nothing at all, excepting himself, and yourself: a writer and a reader, and if classrooms take up any of this book then it is himself and the group, on behalf of life, on behalf of death, on behalf of something like the truth, on behalf of laughter, and never not on behalf of all the dark things across the street everywhere. An old writer, an older writer, an adult writer, a child writer, a boy writer, a young writer, a wild writer, a brilliant writer, a stupid writer, a running writer, a running running running writer has got to run, has got to write as he runs, has got to quickly choose a scheme for another book, has got to see the scheme through, and that is how it is here, in this book. There are no excuses, there is always the beautiful comedy of a writer in America on a talk show telling how he did it, and I have loved every moment of such delicatessen on such pushcarts. What I cherish especially is the casual ease and seeming unawareness in a rich writer about the huge thing he has done, working steadily for seven years—everybody works seven years, the idea probably came about from childhood references heard from adults quoting the great chronicles about plagues and pestilences, droughts and upheavals. A writer telling one or another of the beautiful owners of popular talk shows how he did it, how he actually pieced together a great book, that is the thing to cherish—and everybody is so pleased, so deeply delighted by the writer, and the talk show host, as they are called, so pleased about being the host and being rich and having his show exhibited in 48 cities to a daily audience of 48 million people—wow, that's fun, that's life, that's getting it, or nothing is getting it. And thank God that so far no talk show host has made it to *Variety*'s Necrology list, or if any have, it is not known to me, and so it comes to the same thing. And what a parade of great souls they fetched to their chairs for presentation to the nation, and in some cases even to the world. Just thinking of the stars of the talk shows makes a writer glow with patriotic pride. The men, the men, the men, comics, national heroes, statesmen, horsemen, cocksmen, and the women, the women, the women, experts on summing up conditions of mental illness among slumdwelling pregnant unmarried prostitutes with mouth sores, the whispered message about the findings at Johns Hopkins, and the former girls now large and high-scented women telling all about their experiences with their famous husbands and their more athletic and physical lovers, and the jeering fat women who roar with such laughter and song that small men try not to imagine how sex could possibly be managed with them. What a loyal group of American citizens they are, enriching the national soul, and themselves in high finance. But what have talk shows to do with anything? Anything at all? Well, they have a lot to do with everything, because they have become several things quite clearly, one of which is the national graveyard. For the living, that is. Everybody goes to the talk shows as during a funeral and a musical march to the graveyard for death and burial. But surely it is not the talk shows alone of all of the stuff on television that do it, provide the funeral service and the march and the eulogy and the casket and the body and the plot and the burial. No, indeed it is not, but it is the last program and the most effective conclusion to all of the others, it is the show that ties everything together into a corpse. Well, what's wrong with that, since it has got to happen in one way or another, in any case, so why not have it happen on television, on the talk shows? The fact is that not only is nothing wrong with it, almost everything is just right with it, so that when one soul dies in one body, it is invariably after that soul in that body has been sent out into the whole nation, into the whole world, and transformed into a part of the whole national body and soul, and into a part of the whole human body and soul, of reality, of imagination, of intelligence, of folly, of God, of Satan, and folded together into some kind of sweet pudding and put into the oven to rise and become sweet-smelling and in a way rather beautiful. Or a soufflé or something. And television came along just in time for the end of the world, so to put it, although the world will end only when it will, and nature will end only when it will, and there is no evidence of the end of either in the foreseeable future, as the saying is. Death is fun, life is fun, death is unnecessary but only if life is, too, death is educational, it provides all of the things everybody who has never had them has always longed for: travel, fulfilled fantastic sex, orgies, fame, enormity of personal significance, recognition and reverence from everybody including animals everywhere, wealth beyond any order of need, wit, charm, beauty, generosity—does this little nation want its land and sovereignty restored, voila, it is restored, go and be who you are, if you know, or if you think you know (the Americans thought they knew, you know, and suddenly they were not so sure) and beyond generosity a serene and wholesome hatred, a hatred like supreme love, and gentle in its clinical ruthlessness, all things criminal (in the opinion of the dreaming dead one) ended forever with a gesture of sweep it away, Joe and Jenny, death is love and life is hatred, and the two together produce the only beauty, the only reality, the only truth, the only art—what's that mud in my head for? Why am I forgetting something? Why am I leaving out so much?

Is it sad that we die? Only as children, most likely, and only to children is that mystery of the failure of breath in a father or in a mother something outrageous for being so stupid, and I have the memory of the boy on the porch in Oakland raging against the death of father or mother inside the house, himself about my age, five or six or at the most seven, although I think less, and that crying hurt and informed me as nothing else ever has about the impossibility of death to be acceptable to a kid, and in a sense to any of us if we don't want that death, if we don't want somebody we know to die, if we aren't ready for that person to die, and still don't know how to understand that boy's very loud and angry crying, more than sixty years later. A few minutes ago I opened a letter from a reader of my last book and she said she liked to know about a tough old man, and there I stood not really any older than I had been when I heard the crying boy in Oakland in 1914, reminded of him by the woman's statement that her errant son had been placed in that same orphanage, the Fred Finch, ten or eleven years ago because of unavoidable conditions at home—but by that time the Orphanage had become a home for disturbed kids, with funding, as the saying is, from Sacramento, from the state government. A tough old man is the thing that got to me because I have not yet got into anything like the proper dimension of summing up to think of myself in any such term, and yet I know that even to people in their forties I seem to be old, and to people in their thirties I seem to be very old, and to people in their twenties I must seem to be as old as anybody in the human family is ever likely to be permitted to get, but to nobody do I seem to be at death's door as the saying is, perhaps either because I demonstrate by continuing my work, which is writing, or because those who know my name are not quite sure I didn't die long ago, about the time of going into the Army, after the short swift full foray of my plays and myself in theatrical action on Broadway, after the time of *My Heart's in the Highlands*, *The Time of Your Life*, *Love's Old Sweet Song*, *The Beautiful People*, *Across the Board on Tomorrow Morning*, and *Hello Out There*. It does seem that if you get quite a bit of national publicity for two or three years, and then don't get any at all for two or three years people tend to believe you have died, and by people I do mean the majority of people who hear names and know a little something or other inaccurate about them. For instance, there is absolutely no similarity in the name John Steinbeck and my own name, and yet perhaps because he was born in Salinas and I in Fresno many a reader thanks me in person and in letter for my book

Travels With Charley, for instance. And I do seem to remember, or believe I remember that John Steinbeck once told me at a party at his house in Los Gatos when a dozen or more of us including his first wife Carol Henning had a lot of fun eating hearty spaghetti and drinking lots of red wine and telling stories and singing and doing small entertainments that he had now and then been thanked for writing "Locomotive 36," "The Ojibway," or "The Summer of the Beautiful White Horse," stories from my book entitled *My Name Is Aram*. And I wondered, How could that be? Well, people just don't get things right, because they haven't got the time or interest, and there is no real necessity to do so. Furthermore, it goes beyond names to titles of works getting themselves assigned almost anonymously to various incorrectly identified writers, if you will permit that meaningless sentence, and if I will, why shouldn't you. For instance, after I had done three murderous years in the American Army my little bride insisted that I must take her to a movie somewhere in Movieland, Santa Monica perhaps it was, and the movie turned out to have the name *The Best Years of Our Lives*, and it was the most preposterously phoney damned job of expert belittlement of both the truth and people, in the Army, or home waiting for the return of people in the Army. I was so annoyed with the crooked movie that I wanted to leave the theatre, but the little lady begged me to please not leave her alone in the movie. Well, from that day to this, and that was in 1946, or more likely later, people at parties have told me how much they enjoyed my movie *The Best Years of Our Lives*. Well, of course I am not unaware that the confusion has been the consequence of having heard the name of my play The *Time of Your Life* and taking the meaning of both titles and running them together. But I have never corrected anybody, for it is too much of a bore to do so, and in any case it doesn't matter. Well, this sort of thing runs through every bit of the human experience, including the founding of religions and the establishing of systems, the putting forward of literature, of art, of the world itself: so of course we needn't be surprised that such simple and yet mysterious events as birth and death are deep inside misunderstanding, inaccuracy, absurdity, pain, sorrow, anger, rage, hatred, and the kind of disbelief that freezes sorrow into a universe of unendurable ice, darkness, isolation, meaninglessness, and finality—there can never be any sun again, for instance. And yet there always is, and the boy on the Oakland porch goes to sleep upon the universe of ice, and wakes up and remembers the death of the father or the mother, and sees the sun, and forgets it all, and ten or twenty years later doesn't really know the details of his howling of rage and bereavement—but I do remember, and I say no, death is not sad, not at all sad, excepting perhaps to a small survivor who doesn't know what else to do about it except howl.

Linton Wells is the name of the next man on *Variety*'s list, and I don't know him or anything about him, although I find that I am willing for some reason to suspect that he was a newspaperman rather than a more traditional member of the family engaged in show business. But then Jack Chancellor himself speaks on his early evening news broadcast of other features on "the program" which does suggest that the listener is encouraged not to dispute his enjoyment of hearing more world, national, and even local gossip. And of course news is gossip, and gossip is entertaining, and in a sense the staff of life for rivals—for everybody is a rival of everybody else, and good gossip about one person is nourishing food for another. On the program Idi Amin Dada of Uganda will tell us that the American missionaries will not be harmed, he is arranging for tribal dances, music, and entertainment—he will give a big party for them. And so on. Well, what he doesn't know, and nobody else is sure of, of course, is that one branch or another of the United States government, possibly without the approval of the President, Jimmy Carter, as he prefers to be known, is looking at the encouragement of somebody very close to the Big Boy to suddenly murder him, and to change the government away from personal capricious dictatorship to something else. Forget it, but it is going to happen, and nobody in the American government will ever say that he helped arrange for it to happen. Robert G. Wenzel is somebody else I don't know, but Wenzel is a fine name, and one is again reminded of the remarkable variety and richness in names of all kinds. A man who became a friend to me and of my writing was Stephen Vincent Benet who wrote a whole long poem about the names of American places and rivers and lakes and meadows and plains and hills and mountains—each, each, each had its own name. We had lunch once at a good restaurant in New York, and he was a good man to be at a table with, quite slim, softspoken, courteous, the son of a General, the grandson of another, how did the French come to settle somewhere in the South? That's why I must examine all lists of all kinds, and have always loved examining the phone book in a new city, or in my own city whether it is Fresno, as it is at this moment, or San Francisco, or New York, or Paris—all those people, with their names, all, all, all of them, what a beautiful assembly they are. The next name of *Variety*'s list is Princess White, which instantly permits me to put her into a circus, or into a tribe of Indians perhaps, but it is really no use to guess, I don't know her. Joseph G. Wickham is another man I do not know, and the only thing I can say about the next name, Morris L. Wolf, is that it reminded me for some really unworthy or insignificant reason of Morris L. Ernst, the lawyer who near the end of his life appeared on TV talks shows and spoke big rather silly patriotic gibberish, and I always wondered, Why is he doing that? Is approaching death partly responsible? Does he imagine that his absurd and silly words and sentiments will crown a great career and go down in American history, or what? Robert Yeager somehow suggests an executive position, as the saying is, at a big movie factory, but again I can't be sure. Felix Young I don't know, but I do remember that around the Golden Gate Theatre in San Francisco, off Market Street, on Taylor and Golden Gate Avenues there was a slim eccentric whose name was Felix and nothing else. He wore spats and patent leather shoes and striped trousers and a cutaway coat, and he was a joke among the chorus girls who livened up the stage show that supplemented the movie at that theatre. He was always smoking a cigarette in a long holder, and the gossip was that rich relatives, or friends, financed him, which was never all that costly in any case. The band leader of the orchestra at the Golden Gate was a short Irish Catholic man who seemed glum and one day proved it by going out to the beach where he either walked into the surf and drowned or shot himself. I forget his name. At the Warfield Theatre, competition for the Golden Gate, away back in the late 1920s and into the early 1930s, the stage shows were productions of Fanchon and Marco, and big bands were brought to the theatre for runs of a couple of months, so that I saw Paul Ash in action leading his band and announcing the numbers and the boy and girl singers of them. His rendition of "Meditation from Thais," which was like a title, the same as "Bye Bye Pretty Baby," for instance, was a big hit, and a piece of syncopated blue music that I was devoted to, and which was central to one of my earliest short stories, called, I believe, "1, 2, 3, 4, 5, 6, 7, 8," which was the counterpoint rhythm that really got me, as the saying is. Bernard Youngstein, I am sorry to say, is also unknown to me. William Zechendorf I sat with at El Morocco one night in New York drinking and chatting about some of his enormous architectural projects and deals, including his plan to put the biggest building in the world over Grand Central Station, but he went broke, and he never did it. Zorran, another single name character, I don't know, and as for the last name on *Variety*'s Necrology of 1976, it is Adolf Zukor, as I mentioned earlier in this work, and need not mention any further. He was probably not a bore exactly, but somehow his life was, and his best possible meaning was, whereas your meaning, reader, is not a bore, it is fascinating, and while it is perhaps not quite as fascinating and as great as my meaning, it's not half bad, either. That's it, that's the end of the list. I did my best, and let me urge you to do your best, too. Isn't it the least we can do for one another?

William Saroyan was born in 1908. He presently divides his time between Paris, France, and his native Fresno, California.

64

Necrology Of 1976

Seventy-First VARIETY Anniversary

VICTOR ALESSANDRO
ALYCE ALLYN
GEZA ANDA
WARNER ANDERSON
ROBERT HARDY ANDREWS
MICHAEL H. ARENS
RICHARD ARLEN
JAN AUGUST
GINA BACHAUER
ANGELA BADDELEY
ABEL BAER
MARY BAKER
STANLEY BAKER
NED BARRINGER
MERNA BARRY
HARRY BAUM
SIR GERALD C. BEADLE
CYRIL BEAUMONT
HARRY BECKER
WILLIAM BELASCO
JAMES WARNER BELLAH
EARL BENHAM
BUSBY BERKELEY

DAVID FRIEDKIN
EMIL FRIEDLANDER
JEAN GABIN
GUY M. GADBOIS
JAMES M. GAINES
TIM GALE
PAUL GALLICO
WILLIAM GEER SR.
ARNOLD GINGRICH
HARRY GITTLESON
FRANCES HOWARD GOLDWYN
PAUL M. GONSKY
LLOYD GRIFFIN
BOBBY HACKETT
HAP HADLEY
BILLY HALOP
JOSEPH HENABERY
E.A.R. (KIP) HERREN
ARTHUR HORNBLOW JR.
JAMES WONG HOWE
HOWARD HUGHES
FRIEDA INESCORT
RICHARD F. IRVINE

MARTIN RACKIN
STANISLAS RADZIWILL
GRETA RAUCH
WILLIAM REDFIELD
SIR CAROL REED
LAURENCE M. REID
ELISABETH RETHBERG
HANS RICHTER
PAUL ROBESON
DICK ROMAN
MAXIE ROSENBLOOM
DANNY ROSS
LENNY ROSS
ROUVAUN
MIKE ROY
ROSALIND RUSSELL
ADRIAN SAMISH
MANN L. SCHARF
L.J. SCHLAIFER
TAFT B. SCHREIBER
FRED SEGAL
JEAN SERVAIS
SAM SHAIN
ROBERT SHERMAN
GEOFFREY SHURLOCK
ETHEL SHUTTA
ALASTAIR SIM
H. ALLEN SMITH
ROBERT SOLOMON
HAROLD S. STERN
IRA S. STEVENS
DONALD STRALEM
HUDSON STRODE
FRANK SULLIVAN
MAGGIE TEYTE
SYBIL THORNDIKE
JAMES TIERNEY
DAN TOTHEROH
DALTON TRUMBO
CECIL UNDERWOOD
WILLIAM L. VALLEE
VICTOR VARCONI
BRUNO VESOTA
ETHEL KEITH VIGOROUX

Sr. CLAIR BAYFIELD
(Aug. 2, 1875–May 19, 1967)
"His life was gentle and the elements so mixed in him that nature might stand up and say to all the world 'this was a man'"
"Julius Caesar," Shakespeare
Always in my heart, his wife KAY

JOE BIGELOW
MILTON BIOW
DAVID BLAIR
KERMIT BLOOMGARDEN
CONNEE BOSWELL
WARREN BOWER
ALEXANDER BRAILOWSKY
CHARLES BRAVE
ROMNEY BRENT
BENJAMIN BRITTEN
HARRY R. BURKE
MARION BURR
GODFREY CAMBRIDGE
NELSON CASE

SIDNEY JAMES
G.W. (JOHNNY) JOHNSTONE
MERLE S. JONES
BERNARD KANTOR
IRVING KAUFMAN
LEO KERZ
JESS KIRKPATRICK
FUZZY KNIGHT
PAUL KOSSOFF

supervised trade news publicity. She is survived by her husband and parents.

ALBERTE TINELLI

Alberte Tinelli, 54, a singer specializing in operettas, died Nov. 30 in Brussels, after a short illness. Her career spanned many years and she performed as well in France as in Belgium, where she belonged to the company of the Royal Theatre in Liege and Verviers. She was often seen at the Brussels Folies Bergere, a theatre destroyed by fire some years ago. Survived by her husband.

CARL HEUMANN

Carl Heumann, 69, former manager of Warner Bros., MGM and Paramount in Bogota, Caracas and Lima died last November of a heart attack in New York. During the latter years of his life he had operated his own insurance adjuster office in Lima, Peru, but had maintained his contacts with film people around the world.

THOMAS W. TALBOT

Thomas W. Talbot, 57, manager of Niagara Falls, N.Y., radio station WJJL, died Dec. 21, of a heart attack suffered while he was shoveling snow in front of the station. He had been with